Unemployed People
Social and psychological perspectives

Edited by

DAVID FRYER
and
PHILIP ULLAH

Open University Press
Milton Keynes · Philadelphia

Open University Press
12 Cofferidge Close
Stony Stratford
Milton Keynes MK11 1BY, England
and
242 Cherry Street
Philadelphia, PA 19106, USA

First Published 1987

British Library Cataloguing in Publication Data

Unemployed people: social and psychological
    perspectives.
    1. Unemployment
    I. Fryer, David   II. Ullah, Philip
    306'.36   HD5707

    ISBN 0-335-15507-3
    ISBN 0-335-15506-5 (pbk)

Library of Congress Catologing in Publication Data

Unemployed people.
    Bibliography: p.
    Includes index.
    1. Unemployment — Social aspects. 2. Unemployment — psychological aspects.
    3. Unemployed. I. Fryer, David. II. Ullah, Philip.
    HD5708.U57 1987   305'.90694   87-5792

    ISBN 0-335-15507-3
    ISBN 0-335-15506-5 (pbk)

Editorial and Production Services by Fisher Duncan Ltd,
10 Barley Mow Passage, London W44 PH
Text design by Clarke Williams
Phototypeset by Burns & Smith, Derby
Printed in Great Britain by St Edmundsbury Press,
Bury St Edmunds, Suffolk

Dedicated to Norma Shepherd

Contents

Contributors

Kenneth Cooke   Social Policy Research Unit, Department of Social Administration and Social Work, University of York, Heslington, York YO1 5DD.

Stephen T. Evans   MRC/ESRC Social and Applied Psychology Unit, Department of Psychology, University of Sheffield, Sheffield S10 2TN.

Stephen Fineman   Centre for the Study of Organizational Change and Development, University of Bath, Claverton Down, Bath BA2 7AY.

David Fryer   Department of Psychology, University of Stirling, Stirling FK9 4LA.

Peter Halfpenny   Department of Sociology, Faculty of Economic & Social Studies, University of Manchester, Manchester M13 9PL.

John T. Haworth   Department of Psychology, University of Manchester, Manchester M13 9PL.

Felicity Henwood   Science Policy Research Unit, University of Sussex, Mantell Building, Falmer, Brighton BN1 9RF.

Paul R. Jackson   MRC/ESRC Social and Applied Psychology Unit, Department of Psychology, University of Sheffield, Sheffield S10 2TN.

Marie Jahoda   17 The Crescent, Keymer, Hassocks, Sussex BN6 8RB.

Julian Laite   Department of Sociology, Faculty of Economic & Social Studies, University of Manchester, Manchester M13 9PL.

James McEwen   Academic Department of Community Medicine, Kings College School of Medicine and Dentistry, Denmark Hill, London SE5 8RX.

Stephen P. McKenna   2 Finney Drive, Chorlton cum Hardy, Manchester M21 1DS.

Ian Miles   Science Policy Research Unit, University of Sussex, Mantell Building, Falmer, Brighton BN1 9RF.

Susan Walsh   MRC/ESRC Social and Applied Psychology Unit, Department of Psychology, University of Sheffield, Sheffield S10 2TN.

Philip Ullah   Department of Psychology, University of Western Australia, Nedlands, Western Australia 6009.

Editors' introduction

What is in a name? A rose by any name may smell as sweet, but naming a book has repercussions for the expectations with which it is approached. When the book is about people, the issue becomes more important still: for the way in which we refer to people is revealing not only about those doing the referring, giving clues to their underlying model of humanity, but may also have repercussions at the individual, social and policy level, for the referents themselves, that is, unemployed people.

Unpacking the title which we have chosen for this book provides an introduction to our main preoccupations.

Unemployed?

We believe it is important to distinguish employment from work and unemployment from worklessness. Jahoda has usefully defined work as activity for a purpose beyond its own execution. Research, not least her own, suggests that for many people unemployment leads to reduced activity. Yet there is still a need to develop our understanding of purposeful and meaningful activity and how it functions in contexts of employment, unemployment, retirement and leisure. One assumption in this book is that one of the major causes of distress during unemployment is the frustration of personal agency. We still need to know how and how far such agency is facilitated by employment itself and how other social and material factors can affect this facilitation. The theme of purposeful activity, and its relation to special schemes for unemployed people, is one which runs through several chapters in this collection.

Employment as opposed to work is not in itself an activity but an institutionalised social relationship. To be more precise, employment is a voluntary, but institutionally regulated contractual exchange relationship between two parties, one of whom wishes to sell work and the other to buy it. This relationship entails rights and responsibilities, the province of powerful social norms and legislation, on both sides (Fryer and Payne 1986). Yet the complexities of this, and the implications for unemployment and worklessness, have often been overlooked in the rush to understand the latter. Employment now tends to be viewed as the benchmark against which to compare the negative experience of unemployment, and we seem to lose sight of the fact that in another flourishing area of occupational psychology the harmful and alienating effects of employment require the full attention of researchers. If we are to properly understand the experience of unemployment, we need to re-examine the hazards of employment which, in these times of recession, we have tended to forget. For the vast majority of people, unemployment is a time sandwiched between periods of employment. Once again this is a theme which cuts across a number of chapters in this book.

People?

Looking at the titles of major books in the field one is struck by how many fix their focus on adult males. For examples *The Unemployed Man* (Bakke 1933) and *Men Without Work* (Pilgrim Trust 1938) will suffice but there is a plethora of publications with similar titles.

We believe the field to be blinkered by the conviction that unemployment is essentially a man's problem, with the unemployed man the proper focal point for research. The unemployed man is one legitimate research focus given social expectations regarding gender roles and this is reflected in this volume. However, it is also emphasised here that unemployment is a youth, woman's, family, household and community problem.

One also notices that many titles of books and papers in the field refer to 'the unemployed' — for example, *Memoirs of the Unemployed* (Beales and Lambert 1934), *Understanding the Unemployed* (Hayes and Nutman 1981) and *The Unemployed: a social psychological portrait* (Tiffany *et al.* 1970).

It is as though once we know a person is unemployed, this tells us all we need to know about their experience. Yet people are not simply unemployed; they are specific ages, genders, family members, and belong to different social classes and labour markets; they have different life histories — and in each case the experience is different. Moreover, in emphasising that it is people who are the focus of this book, we are also avoiding the tendency to view them as 'respondents'. We would argue that such a tendency is the result of an overemphasis on the large-scale survey as a research technique, where what matters is getting people to 'respond' to the structured instruments included in the standard questionnaire. Whilst acknowledging that useful information can be uncovered in this way, we believe it to be at least as important to discover how *people* interpret, anticipate, and initiate, in line with expectations, values, information and feelings within specific social and material contexts. The studies described in this book, therefore, reflect a range of methodologies where such concerns are allowed to emerge alongside issues of quantification and comparison.

Our approach is based on the assumption that the experience of unemployment is constituted by a conjunction of material circumstances, social institutions and individual variability.

We have reservations concerning individualistic, psychologistic accounts which not only describe the phenomenon at the level of the individual but which also suggest that the explanation of that phenomenon is to be found simply in an examination of the individual characteristics of the person: for example, in terms of motivation to become employed, personality, general hardiness and age.

On the other hand, we accept that these variables, as proxies for more complex social factors, may prove to be keys, following appropriate analysis, to unlock some of the complexities of the experience of unemployment. We also accept that unique aspects of individual agents do have a role to play in explaining the documented variations in experience.

We doubt the extent of the contribution which can be made by research conducted as if unemployment is experienced within a social vacuum. Such experience must not only be located within the wider material, social, cultural and political contexts to be comprehended, it must be seen as constituted by the conjunction of such contexts with the agency of the individual person.

Our collection begins with a study which illustrates and supports many of the points we wish to make. Marie Jahoda in Chapter 1 describes in detail a subsistence production scheme for unemployed Welsh miners. What makes the publication of Jahoda's chapter all the more remarkable is that it was written almost half a century ago, and is concerned with unemployment as it was experienced during the 1930s. Since that time, for personal rather than scientific reasons, she has witheld it from publication. We believe the report ranks alongside her previous work, *Marienthal*, in terms of its detailed description of the many diverse effects unemployment can have upon a whole community and the way the inhabitants attempt to introduce meaning and control into their lives. The eventual failure of the scheme is shown to be explicable in terms of a combination of individual, material and environmental circumstances, and the prevailing ideological and sociohistorical context in which it took place. There are of course limitations to the extent to which some of the findings can inform current approaches to the study of unemployment, yet so much of what Jahoda highlights bears upon the underlying themes of today's experience of unemployment. One of the reasons for placing her contribution at the beginning of this book is that we hope the reader will recognise some of these themes as they reoccur in later chapters concerned with contemporary studies.

In Chapter 2 David Fryer compares and contrasts Jahoda's work in Marienthal and Monmouthshire. The Marienthal investigation is still the most influential empirical work in the field and Jahoda has more recently offered, in addition to this description of *what* the experience of unemployment is, an explanatory account of *why* that experience occurs. The Welsh research, it is suggested in this chapter, is a revealing link in the development of her thought and in the history of ideas in this field.

In Chapter 3 Felicity Henwood and Ian Miles present the results of recent studies which test hypotheses derived from Jahoda's explanation of the psychological effects of unemployment. The authors focus not just on male unemployment but on female unemployment too. In so doing they offer an empirical examination of the employment status category distinctions among women (e.g. full and part-time employed, non-employed, registered unemployed, retired) which are typically left obscure in the scant research which deals with female unemployment.

In Chapter 4 Philip Ullah describes how an ethnographic approach was used to explore the meaning of unemployment for a group of young black people living in a deprived urban area. He argues that their experience of unemployment is to be understood against a background of racism and disadvantage. The study also describes their experiences of youth training schemes, and so provides an intriguing comparison with the description offered by Jahoda of the 1930s scheme. The study also highlights the variations in the experience of unemployment among black youths, who like women, have typically been treated as homogeneous for research purposes.

Unemployment is experienced, by most unemployed people, within a context of severe material hardship. Roughly two-thirds of unemployed people are now dependent on means-tested supplementary benefit, either alone or in addition to unemployment benefit. Yet the role of poverty in determining how unemployment is experienced, though often acknowledged, has been largely unexplored. In Chapter 5 Ken Cooke makes an important contribution to this issue by investigating the impact of increasing durations of unemployment on living standards, and considers whether unemployment contributes to poverty over and above the effects due to low income. Illustrating our point about the dynamic processes involved in job loss and re-employment, the author also considers whether the return to employment carries the unemployed person out of poverty or is merely the continuation of poverty by other means.

Most experiences of unemployment follow a period of employment and Stephen McKenna and Jim McEwen, in Chapter 6, focus on the health and safety aspects of employment. The authors question the accepted wisdom that employment is good for most or all people, and in so doing provide an alternative perspective from that reached by an emphasis on psychologically supportive consequences of employment.

In Chapter 7 Paul Jackson and Susan Walsh present a framework for understanding unemployment as a family experience. The authors argue that the social aspects of unemployment are made intelligible when located within the wider experiences of the family where one member is unemployed. Such a framework is designed to allow a productive research effort to grow, through questioning the assumption that the proper focus of unemployment research is the individual.

This theme is continued in Chapter 8, in which Julian Laite and Peter Halfpenny examine unemployment in the context of the household and its association with the domestic division of labour. The authors compare the experiences of unemployment and employment in two towns in the North-West of England, and show how the relationship between labour market participation and the domestic division of labour is mediated by household structure, highlighting the role of women and their own employment. Also considered are the reasons for both the levels of performance of domestic tasks and variations in those levels.

In Chapter 9 John Haworth and Steve Evans examine the role of purposeful activity during unemployment and consider how far this can ameliorate the harmful psychological effects of unemployment. The authors begin with a discussion of the similarities and differences between work, leisure and meaningful activity. By incorporating retirement into their framework they address what has largely been treated as an anomoly, being neither unemployment nor employment but having features in common with both. They then address, through empirical research, a number of questions concerning the psychological significance of activity during unemployment.

Finally, in Chapter 10, Steve Fineman asks whether re-employment is the end of the problem for those previously unemployed and considers the social and psychological legacies which may be left by a period of unemployment. Using longitudinal data stretching over a period of six years, the author follows the life histories of people who have been unemployed and who have remained scarred by their experiences.

References

BAKKE, E. W. (1933). *The Unemployed Man*. London: Nisbet.

BEALES, H.L. and LAMBERT, R.S. (1934/1973). *Memoirs of the Unemployed*. Wakefield, UK: E.P. Publishing.

FRYER, D. and PAYNE, R. (1986). 'Being Unemployed: a review of the literature on the psychological experience of unemployment.' *International Review of Industrial and Occupational Psychology*. Chichester: Wiley.

HAYES, J. and NUTMAN, P. (1981). *Understanding the Unemployed: The Psychological Effects of Unemployment*. London: Tavistock.

PILGRIM TRUST (1938). *Men Without Work*. Cambridge: Cambridge University Press.

TIFFANY, D.W., COWAN, J.R. and TIFFANY, P.M. (1970). *The Unemployed: A Social Psychological Portrait*. Englewood Cliffs, N. J: Prentice-Hall.

Marie Jahoda

Unemployed men at work *

The Subsistence Production Society

The central feature of the Subsistence Production Society (SPS) was the co-operation of a number of unemployed men in producing goods to be used for their own subsistence and not for sale in the open market. The men got no wages; they purchased the products of their work, paying prices calculated on the basis of the cost of the raw materials plus 20% for overhead costs. They continued to receive their normal unemployment allowance. The economic advantage of the Society for its members was that the money they spent on its products had a higher purchasing power than normally. Besides, the quality of SPS goods was often much higher than non-members of the scheme could afford, or could be bought locally.

The principles and ideas of the SPS

The basic ideas on which the SPS rested were those of an Order of friends and of its leader Mr Peter Scott, and much in the organisation refers directly to those ideas. The immediate and central object of the SPS was to overcome the disastrous economic and human consequences of unemployment. These consequences were described as follows:

---

* In March 1935 an 'Order of friends' established at Cwmavon a Subsistence Production Society (SPS) for the benefit of unemployed miners. Henry Ecroyd has recently described the history of this Quaker idea, its administration and financial arrangements (Ecroyd 1983). From the autumn of 1937 to the spring of 1938 I lived in the area in order to study the impact of the SPS on its participants. The following pages present the results in the manner in which they were formulated without the critique I could add today.

Continued on p.2

'... Under such circumstances the father of the family realises sooner or later, that he is no longer needed; he grows slack and spiritless, lies late abed to save cost of fuel or food, drifting finally to the street corners and all they stand for. His wife and home suffer accordingly and the children are brought up in an atmosphere of unhappiness and unrest made worse by malnutrition. The rot that follows — economic, social, political, and moral — is deep rooted and is accompanied by an apathy more deadly than the spread of an extremist political doctrine .... Enforced idleness is not leisure; a man who is unemployed has no true leisure; nor are his problems to be solved by the occupations and interests associated with the proper use of leisure. Spiritual factors, at least as vital as the material ones, are at stake.' (Order of friends 1930).

The convictions thus expressed led directly to the conclusion that the remedy lay in work that gave opportunities for the production of real goods (real in the sense that unemployed men and others could experience benefit from them) and from the association with others in work which was, for those then unemployed, a life-long habit.

A further objective, less explicitly expressed but certainly present in the SPS, was to overcome the 'disastrous consequence' of employment, under the conditions that had prevailed in the Eastern Valley. These consequences will be described below. The foundation of the Society was plainly looked upon as an opportunity to set an example of a new type of social and economic organisation in which the effects of the old type should be avoided and through which the workers should have an opportunity of recovering not only what they had lost through *un*employment but of gaining what a life of industrial employment had never yet given to them.

This Subsistence Production Society in the Eastern Valley of Monmouthshire was founded by an Order of friends. This particular Order, led by Mr Peter Scott, was a group of men and women which began to form in the year 1926 and came to South Wales for the first time in 1928. Originally concerned only to bring a spiritual message based on the ideas of the Society of friends, they felt compelled by what they found in South Wales to do something practical. At Brynmawr they first

---

The publication in 1987 of a study completed in the summer of 1938 requires explanation.

In 1937 I came as a stateless refugee from Austria to England at the invitation of Alexander Farquharson, general secretary of the Institute of Sociology. He had been instrumental in my release from prison and was unceasingly concerned in helping me and other refugees to find work. He suggested to the originator of the SPS, Peter Scott, and the Cwmavon area organiser, Lord Forrester, that I should conduct a study there; they and I happily agreed.

During the field work period Hitler marched into Austria where my Jewish family still lived. Lord Forrester understood what that meant for them and me. On the spot he decided to go to Vienna and visit my family. He arranged a code in which to correspond and brought them hope and support at a time when fear and despair ruled their lives. A few months later he read my report which showed the gap between the idealistic conception of the SPS and the reality of its functioning. He said the report destroyed his life's work. I decided not to publish.

Continued on p.3

developed relief work and later on many other constructive activities. This experience led them to see the need and possibility of a larger-scale scheme for the unemployed; and this in turn led to the foundation of an experimental Subsistence Production Society, the Upholland Scheme, near Wigan in Lancashire, and a little later to the founding of the South Wales Society.

The Upholland Scheme started in March 1934 on a very small scale. The pioneer group consisted of only 11 carefully selected unemployed men and two tailoresses. Their success in the first few months encouraged an extension of the experiment, which was rendered possible by a gift from Lord Nuffield. Any one of a large number of places might have been chosen for a further subsistence production experiment; in fact, the choice fell to the Eastern Valley in Monmouthshire.

Employment in the Eastern Valley of Monmouthshire

The Eastern Valley lies in the western part of the country; it is, however, in the extreme east of the South Wales coalfield. The Afon Llwyd, which runs through the valley, follows a north to south course, rising in the mountains above Blaenavon and joining the Usk near Newport. From Blaenavon through Cwmavon to Pontypool the valley is narrow, with steep ridges on each side, broken here and there by gentler slopes. In the west these ridges reach their highest point (about 1900 feet); the eastern ridge is somewhat lower. South of Pontypool the valley of the Afon Llwyd becomes broader and the hills lower until below Cwmbran the river reaches the widening plain north of Newport.

No one visiting the valley in 1938 could fail to be impressed by the contrast between the western and the eastern ridge. In the upper part of the valley, houses and signs of industry on the western ridge contrasted with the mainly agricultural impression the eastern ridge provided. This was in no way accidental; the western ridge from Blaenavon to Pontypool formed part of the South Wales coalfield. Colliery tips were scattered through this area and were the most obvious signs of human effort in the

Lord Forrester died all too young, soon after the war, his life's work prematurely ended. There then followed a remarkable period of two decades in which unemployment was not an issue. Now this has changed. Once again millions of men and women in the Western industrialised world find themselves without jobs. Many social scientists, now as then, are trying to deepen the understanding of the social and psychological impact of unemployment and of measures to mitigate its worst consequences. Some of them read the SPS study, found it relevant to their present concerns and have urged me to make it more widely available. In doing so I hope that it will be read as a piece of social history, as a demonstration of social psychological field work and as a documentation of the immense difficulties that confront efforts to mitigate the consequences of unemployment, when all that people want is jobs.

I want to thank David Fryer and Philip Ullah, who have gone to great trouble in shortening the original text, improving its organisation and its imperfect English.

landscape. Other clear signs of coal in the valley could be noted; for example, the river ran black and its mud was greatly valued by the unemployed men as fuel, because of its content of coal powder.

The valley contained the Urban Districts of Blaenavon, Pontypool, Cwmbran and Caerleon. The population of the Eastern Valley in the 19th and 20th centuries shared the rapid increase of the South Wales population as a result of immigration; the great expansion of the central portion of the coalfield began in the 1850s. In 1861 the population of the four South Wales counties was 666,000. By 1911 it numbered 1,736,000. The influx of the workers lasted throughout the First World War; it showed the first break in the depression of 1921. The decline of the population by migration from the area started only after 1923.

Taking its total population in relation to its total acreage the 1931 density was not high (2.5 persons to the acre). Included in this total acreage, however, were wide areas of uninhabitable hillside. The inhabited area was comparatively small. Following one of the usual bus-routes or one of the two railway lines — one at the bottom of the valley, the other on a terrace on the western ridge — an observer got the impression of considerable density of population.

From the social and economic point of view however, the valley formed a unit with similar valleys in South Wales; it shared with them periods of boom and decline. This unity was further strengthened by the inclusion of the greater part of the Eastern Valley in the special areas as defined in the Special Areas Act of 1934.

The chief industry in the valley was coal-mining; all other industries were numerically of relatively small importance. While the situation, both before and after 1937, had been altered by the prevailing depression, it was still true when this inquiry was being carried out that coal-mining was by far the most important industry in the area. The dominance was strengthened if the metal industries, which depended on coal and had been closely connected with coal-mining throughout their history, were taken into account.

The population had been used to employment in mining for more than 150 years. In about 1750, there were works at Taibach and coal was obtained at Cwmbychan, a valley branching off from Cwmavon. At the beginning of the 19th century, opening for coal and ironstone by levels began there and a blast furnace was started. In 1838 copper was first made in the district, together with iron and tin at the Cwmavon Works. The tradition was to start work in the coalmine as young as possible. Around 1838 boys of six or seven years old were taken into the mines: they went with their fathers and mothers and soon learned to do their share. The age at which they started work was gradually raised, but for most of the boys the inevitability remained of working there as soon as the law permitted.

In 1938 only a very few people had any personal memory or knowledge of rural life. Yet, being at the boundary of the coalfield, they had some connection with, and knowledge of, the agricultural area beyond the eastern ridge. Generally, in talking about past times and their early memories, they told about working conditions, strikes and accidents; but periodically one or another mentioned a personal experience in connection with the life beyond the hills, revealing a deep longing for participation in this type of life.

Such rare contacts, however, only influenced the wishes and dreams of a very few. It was the industrial tradition, formed and handed down through several generations, that governed the attitude of the great majority. This was predominantly a tradition formed through employment in the mines and the life associated with it.

The main feature of the then current tradition in the Eastern Valley (as in all the coalfields) was a strong antagonism between the mine workers and the mine owners, stronger than the then normal antagonism between workers and employers in most other industries. This specially bitter feeling on the side of the miners was not easy to analyse, but it was probably due to the constant risk to their lives, (a risk which was almost always related to the management and equipment of the mines), and to the size of the contemporary mining unit, which was generally too large to favour a personal relationship between the men and the manager. Further, the miners felt, having no direct contact with the coal consumers, that they were producing for the mine owners only. The difference between their wages and the coal prices on the open market increased their sense of being exploited. On the mine owners' side, the trend from profit to loss during the period from 1929 to 1938 emphasised this antagonism between their interests and those of the men.

The opposition between owner and worker was envisaged by the latter as a conflict between the huge colliery companies on the one side and the steadily increasing power of the trade unions on the other. The trade unions represented and seemed almost to exhaust the collective effort of the workers against the overwhelming power of the coal owners. Through their unions the workers had carried on the struggle for an improvement of their standard of living, on which almost all their embittered feelings and capacity for organisation had been concentrated. This conflict was epitomised by the general strike of 1926; even in 1938 the unemployed men got excited in remembering those weeks of fighting for better conditions.

In spite of this antagonism, and perhaps inevitably because of their interests in the same economic complex, the mine owners and the trade unionists had been compelled to adapt themselves to each other. The owners had realised that they had to accept the trade unions; the trade unions did not aim to change the whole system of big business but in turn had accepted it in practice, and tried to get out of it as much as possible for the workers.

Speculation in the coal industry led to the alternation of boom and slump. In times of boom, the good money earned induced the miners to give themselves to their jobs and endure the constant dangers and hardships in the mines. In times of slump, fear of losing the basis of their existence persuaded them to carry on, even if the amount of money they earned was not sufficient to give them the satisfaction they knew before. There was no room in such periods of anxiety to experience joy in the job or any creative urge in production. Another important element in the then current attitude of the miners was their universal acceptance of the system of measuring a man's worth in terms of the amount of money he could take home every week. In earlier times, earnings had been associated with bodily fitness and special skill but these qualities had gradually faded into the background, with only the pay figures remaining.

Yet there was a certain kind of equality realised in the industrial system and on it were based the miners' ideas of social justice. Every individual was treated and paid according to his capacity in the job. A fixed relation between the amount of work done and the amount of money received was the basis of this equality. This relation was embodied in the piecework system, which appealed to the men as an expression of social justice. When they expressed dissatisfaction with the inequality in the world, they meant that some persons, usually the proprietors and managers, were not included in this system of relating amount of money to amount of labour done. At the same time the men did not envisage the system as applying directly to each individual worker. They were accustomed to working in gangs, which worked together and shared the money received for the common effort according to proportions fixed by themselves. This system produced a sense of a certain amount of freedom in the regulation of their income and of real companionship and common interest in their work.

Membership of a trade union did not imply any definite political outlook. Although a considerable proportion of the men in the Eastern Valley were interested in politics their political attitudes sometimes showed a striking contrast to their trade union attitudes; there was no consistency. Their political behaviour, their knowledge of political facts, their political principles, and their political faith were often on extremely different lines.

The need for a political label — a name under which political ideas and schemes could be readily recognised — was felt as strongly in the Eastern Valley as elsewhere. One man, (formerly a collier) working at the time in a tinplate factory, expressed this perfectly clearly: 'A political view', he said, 'makes the unity of a personality. It helps you to know what you have to think on different occasions.'

Generally speaking the little towns and villages in the area had then a Labour majority on their local Councils. Active members of the Labour Party were, however, few in number; a still smaller group sympathised with Communism. Liberals and Conservatives were rare, especially amongst the male working class population.

Political behaviour was evident in the reading of special newspapers. *The Daily Herald* was by far the most frequently read in the valley, yet almost every large London newspaper had some circulation in the valley; the interest in them was far greater than in the local daily papers. The local weekly papers were, however, the most appreciated. It seemed that there were many different reasons which determined the choice of a newspaper, among them being the fact that newspapers offered benefits of various kinds to their regular readers. The political colour of a paper was often overlooked. In one family where the man was Labour, and the wife Liberal, *The People* was read on Sundays. Asked about its political outlook, the man said: 'it's socialist', the wife: 'it's liberal'.

The relation of their political ideas and principles to then existing political and social groupings and institutions was not easy to define. The idea of fair play in political controversies was remarkable. One Labour man said, with the approval of all those assembled, in a discussion: 'One has to be fair towards the capitalists.' Another added: 'What we want is decent wages. Let the Capitalist have the chief profit; he runs the risk, anyhow.' Whilst they were critical enough in speaking of their local authorities or the British Government, for example, in connection with lack of new houses, the Means Test, the cost of living, or the negotiations with Italy, they generally agreed in the end that 'Britain is in spite of all the finest nation in the world.' On this point, Socialists and Communists were united with Liberals and Conservatives, for 'nobody has to starve in this country and everybody may say what he likes.'

It was, however, true that when politics were being discussed, the unemployed men were generally thinking of themselves as a social class and not as individuals. This 'class consciousness' if it could be so called, made them feel that they had a more or less direct influence on the political machinery without being able, however, to express clearly how this influence worked.

Two distinct faiths had popular appeal in the Eastern Valley. Of these Welsh Nationalism was the weaker and the less general. Nationalist propaganda had been active in recent years but the political aims of the movement were not generally understood and did not make a strong appeal. It was perhaps in the cultural sphere that the influence of Welsh Nationalism was most important.

On the other hand, faith in Socialism was almost universal among the workers. The faith, however, had little to do with contemporaneous political, economic and social measures. It was Utopian and stood in a close and full relation to religious faith. Socialism meant the realisation of the principles of Christianity. To help each other, to love one's neighbour, to be unselfish — this was Christian and this was Socialist. So far apart from their practical political behaviour was this that nobody was surprised to hear a lay preacher speaking in a sermon about Socialism as an expression of Christianity, although everybody present knew that he professed to be 'Conservative to the backbone.' Thus their political ideas were by no means as definite as the economic and social ideas developed in relation to the industrial system represented in the collieries and the trade unions.

Besides these ideas it was religion which formed the most important pillar in the building of the ideological background of the population. For several generations employment in the pits had brought the people of the valley into daily contact with danger and death and had demonstrated to them how, without the possibility of foreknowledge by human beings, questions of life and death were decided. This had made them, on the one hand, anxious to participate in all the pleasures and joys of life while they had the chance and, on the other hand, it had created fatalism, a strong faith in providence and a deep religious devotion. If God knew and decided whose fate it would be next to be killed by an accident in the pit, then there was no need to tremble when going underground. The men sometimes expressed to the observer in a very significant way what religion meant for them. A collier said: 'We have to have trust in our maker. Do we know whether we shall be alive tomorrow?'

A deeply religious attitude, a personal relation to God and a personal idea of God, was noted again and again, even in matters apart from religion. Two events of general importance which occured during the beginning of 1938 illustrate this: The Aurora Borealis in January and the Eden crisis in February. Different as these two events were, they had one thing in common: neither was foreseen. The reaction of the population was similar: in each case thinking turned immediately from the normal rational course to a magical and fatalistic line.

On the evening of the gorgeous spectacle of the northern lights I was sitting with a family round the fire, when suddenly someone outside cried 'fire'. We went to the door and saw the dark and clear night sky covered with red spots on the horizon. Whilst we were discussing which house on the top of the hill might be on fire, the red spots left the horizon and went to the middle of the sky, which became bright and strange. Blue lights appeared here and there with green and orange margins. White rays of light flashed over the sky. It was evident that this was no fire. None of us had ever seen such a phenomenon. All became very quiet. The mother called for the children in a very suppressed voice: 'I don't like the idea of somebody not being at home on a night like this.' The little boy began to cry, maybe because it was rather cold outside but it fitted into the atmosphere of dumb and anxious admiration in the face of something supernatural. 'It is a miracle' someone said. For a long time we stood out in the cold night watching the sky. When the light had gone, we sat again round the fire, depressed and uncertain, speaking about death, and war and plagues, for which this miracle might have been a heavenly sign.

Rational thinking was abandoned again in favour of magical thinking on the morning when Anthony Eden's resignation from the UK premiership was in the newspapers. I started a discussion on this with some SPS Brewery workers. They all seemed puzzled, and before beginning any argument they sent somebody to fetch the year's horoscope. Unfortunately enough for rationalism a 'change in English politics' was forecast. Only then did they feel able to start the discussion again, proving with rational arguments that this was bound to come, but believing this development necessary because it had been in the stars. All the members of this little discussion group were Socialists or Communists.

God and religion were not separated from the rest of life. A strong belief was carried into every action and event in daily life, especially with those who were members of the many small sects and were not only practising but militant adherents of their religious principles. They thought of God as being responsible in a personal way for everything that happened. One woman (a member of the Bible Students) sometimes let her husband do the housework, because she felt like going out with her gramophone and records about the Kingdom of God on Earth. One day she tried to save my soul from eternal death by telling me the 'Truth', describing the unlimited happiness and the heavenly graces for those found worthy to enter the future Kingdom. She did so in kneeling before the fireplace and poking it. 'And everything will be electrical, no fireplaces to be cleaned anymore in God's Kingdom on Earth' she finished.

This anthropromorphic notion of God continued even with those who began to doubt. In a talk with one of the women about the recent events in Spain and China, she said: 'Sometimes I sit down in the middle of my work and wonder if there is a God. All those cruelties are daily in the newspapers, so he is bound to know. Fair play: why doesn't he do a miracle against those scoundrels like in the old days?'

A whole world of naive religious thinking was expressed by this 'he is bound to know because it is in the newspapers', and the application of the notion 'fair play' to God. Yet there were only a few who thought about God in such a critical way; most of them had a strong faith, which came into existence and was steadily strengthened by their former daily experience of their dependence on forces beyond human understanding.

The relation of the Socialist faith held by the great masses of the workers to a vague but deeply felt Christianity has already been mentioned. An example of a case of individual conversion illustrates the same relation from the religious side. A woman of 45 years told that eight years previously she had visited Ireland. She had been brought up in the English Church and had never failed to frequent it. In Ireland she had stood before a Roman Catholic church and had seen how a very distinguished looking gentleman helped a poor woman, dressed in shabby clothing, up the few steps to the entrance of the church. Observing this incident, she had felt deeply moved and had entered the church too. 'I was interested in a church where a gentleman behaved like this.' She had had a talk with one of the priests and soon afterwards she turned Catholic. At the time of our conversation she had induced her daughter to join her and was trying tenaciously to convert her husband and her sons too.

This conversion was evidently the result of a deep and socially unsatisfied longing to be treated as she felt human beings ought to be treated. Suddenly this woman had realised that her social inferiority did not need necessarily to exist in every sphere of life. This had made her embrace Roman Catholicism.

While this vague sense of the unity of religion with social justice for all was widespread, the religious tradition of the Eastern Valley as a whole was Protestant. People migrating into the area from various parts of England, Scotland and Ireland, had brought their religious traditions — in the main Protestant — with them, and had established the many religious centres already mentioned. They thought of themselves as being in an individual relation to God: this was a religious fact of overwhelming importance. Their relation to the little group with which they were associated in Churches and Chapels was socially significant but it only provided the framework of the essentially individual religion. The effect of the existence of many sects was to break up the social life of the local community into various separate non-cooperating units.

Within these limits the Churches and Chapels formed the effective centres of social life in the area. The parties organised by them attracted not only their members but friends and acquaintances from other religious groups. The Sunday Services gave the opportunity for social contact; here one went in one's best clothes and was able to show to oneself and to others the social position held in local life.

Organised education seemed not to be in very close contact with employment which was the centre of life, and therefore organised education was of much less importance. In the elementary schools and the few secondary schools teaching was on the established lines, without special adaptation to the conditions of the area. Its general intellectualism provided the younger generation with a picture of the world and of those desirable things in life which they had only a poor chance of experiencing locally themselves. A result was that those who were genuinely interested tended to take up professional work in England.

Some of the teachers, however, had a deep interest in the special conditions of the area, but the prevailing educational system made it difficult for them to establish a close connection between their ideas and the school routine. In this respect the various organisations for adult education had an easier task.

Family life in the Eastern Valley, as everywhere else, was bound up with the type of family dwelling and its condition. The houses consisted mostly of four or six rooms, with half the rooms downstairs and half upstairs. The windows were small and scarcely opened during the winter months. Fresh air came in by the door. The outward appearance was very simple and without ornament.

The rooms were small and, when there were more than two children in a family, it was practically impossible for all to sit round one table. In many homes, meals were taken in two shifts because of the lack of room. The average size of a family in the Eastern Valley was 4.2 persons at the time. During the winter months generally only one room, the kitchen, which was at the same time the dining and sitting room, was used by the family in order to save fuel. Even during the summer months the tradition of keeping the front room downstairs for visitors and for special occasions normally confined the family to only one room, the 'parlour'. Any visit to a home by a non-member of the family was somewhat rare and if it occurred was generally limited to near relations who were included in the family tie.

This severe limitation of housing space and the constant contact of all members of the family had the effect of building up a strong family unit with no provision for any privacy of any of its members. Everything was discussed in front of the children, who were thus much more conscious of the family situation than they would have been in a middle class family which could afford a separate room for them. The family as a unit kept closely together and was rather suspicious of any interference from the outside.

Those limitations were bad enough if the houses were in good condition but in some parts of the valley the condition of the workers' houses was appalling. There were still in the area a number of inhabited houses which had been built at the beginning of the industrial revolution, many of them were by the time of the study in slum condition or condemned. Only Council houses had been built since the First World War.

Blaenavon in particular had, and deserved, the sad reputation of the worst housing in the valley. Through this little town with its narrow streets much traffic was obliged to pass on the way to Brynmawr and Abergavenny, and the lack of open space in its centre created a most depressing atmosphere. The finances of the Urban District Council had been affected by unemployment, building had been impossible and overcrowding inevitable. I visited one family of two adults and three children in Blaenavon living in two rooms: a sitting room which was at the same time the kitchen and scullery; and a small bedroom. The narrow streets prevented any sunshine from entering the rooms. The traffic in the street made it impossible to send the small children out into the open air. The little girl of three years, in her hunger for air, asked her mother 30 times a day to be taken to the lavatory, because the way to it (about 20 yards long) gave her what she wanted. In the whole valley only a few houses had lavatories indoors; many of the houses were without running water. Only a number of County Council houses had bathrooms. Whilst the average for Monmouthshire gave 0.87 persons per room it was 0.91 for Blaenavon, and 0.88 each for Pontypool and Cwmbran.

Employment in the mines communicated a jazzlike rhythm to life in a miner's family and home. There was no fixed hour for getting up or going to bed nor even for meals, as a consequence of the shift system in the pit. One week the miner had to get up at 4 o'clock in the morning, the next he could lie in bed until 11 o'clock. When there were members of the family working in different shifts, the house was kept under tension almost continuously, day and night. One man came home, wanted his bath, his meal, and went to bed. Another got ready to leave: his working clothes and something to eat during the shift had to be prepared. Children came home from school and wanted their meal. The housework had to be done when there were a few moments for it. This irregularity was the normal way of living. The description of a week-end in a miner's family given in the Appendix at the end of this chapter illustrates this and other features of daily life.

These notes on the peculiarities of the Eastern Valley must be sufficient for present purposes. This account of the religious, political, social and cultural atmosphere of the valley is not complete; it is but an attempt to show the connection between the coming into existence of an ideology and the economic organisation of the area. For the three factors important for the ideology then current in the valley — big industry, trade-unionism, and religion were centered in the pits: there they experienced the power of finance and Capitalism; there they experienced the power of solidarity and trade-unionism; and there they needed and got the support of their faith.

Unemployment in the Eastern Valley

With the decline of the coal industry a large number of men in the Eastern Valley became unemployed; many of them, because of their age and their skill in partly obsolete processes, had no chance of getting employment again. In June 1935 when the SPS started, the official number of unemployed men for the area from which the majority of participants came was 6,868: about 45% of the male working population. In March 1938 the unemployment figure had declined to 4,233, partly due to migration, partly to a slight improvement in the economic situation.

In 1938 unemployment had, for many years, been the most important feature of life in the valley. Although the decline of the area was a gradual one and had occasionally been interrupted by periods of improvement, the threat of unemployment had never disappeared since 1921. After the General Strike in 1926 unemployment was more than a threat: it was for a great number of individuals a reality, aggravated by the hopelessness of a general revival of the industry in the valley. The effects of unemployment on the standard of living and the general attitude of the unemployed men were to be noticed everywhere. It was by no means a disastrous effect in the sense of an acute catastrophe. Nobody had to starve in the valley. The population had become used to its prevailing standard. The local doctor said, that after a figure of 11 suicides had been reached in 1927 this figure dropped down again to the normal level of one or two cases a year. The normal attitude amongst the unemployed was one of resignation. The fact that nothing worse than resignation was found in the Eastern Valley, while in Marienthal despair and complete apathy were discovered, may have been mainly because of the size and permanence of the unemployment allowance in Wales. The resignation manifested itself in an almost complete cessation of any capacity to make an effort. A few miscellaneous observations about the personal and social life of the unemployed illustrate this.

One of the small, miners' villages, Garndiffaith, used to be known as 'Little Moscow', because of its Communist trade union organisation. In 1938 only the remembrance of this attitude remained. The men had not changed their conviction; Garndiffaith and most of the other villages had a strong and undisputed Labour majority. Almost all of the unemployed miners declared themselves to be Socialists, and a few said they were Communists; but apart from their saying so and their voting at election times, there was nothing left in the valley to demonstrate it.

The enforced leisure had brought in its train a general inertia which affected every sphere of life. The continuous attempts of the Employment Exchanges to favour migration projects were met by a slack and uninterested attitude.

Many of the unemployed got rid of their surplus bodily energy by walking for many hours every day on the hills. They limited all their needs in a kind of self-protection, because life would have been too difficult if they had adhered to their former level of expectation. The Employment Exchange, to which they had to go twice a week to sign on in order to receive their allowance, had become the social centre of their otherwise asocial life. For those two-weekly events they prepared themselves carefully, they got up earlier in the morning, dressed better and went off to the Exchange to fetch their money, to have a talk and sometimes a drink with the other chaps. When they got home they took a rest, and the remainder of the day was filled up with talking about this great event, repeating to their wives what one or other of the fellows had said, and thinking about the arguments used. I got the impression that the unemployed man had the feeling of having spent a well occupied day.

A good part of their time, probably more than with employed men, was spent on the elaboration of systems for the football pools. That they were spending a regular and sometimes considerable amount of money participating was not a matter for indignation, but had to be understood as a normal reaction of those who otherwise would have had no hope left. Novelties which did not rise above the standard of the cheapest of shops had a great attraction and certainly fulfilled a similar cultural function.

The lowering of the standard of living meant poorer food and lack of fresh ingredients. Fruit was scarcely ever consumed; even fresh milk was rare and was generally replaced by tinned milk. Tinned food of every kind was common in the households. There had been no possibility during the previous few years to introduce gradual unobtrusive improvements which would have maintained pride in the household and kept it in step with developments in hygiene: tradition in many little things persisted only because there were no means of getting something new. Many of the families with whom I stayed did not use a toothbrush; some of them possessed none, some of them had one for the whole family. In one family it was noticed that washing the children, washing the baby's linen, and stirring the Christmas pudding was done in one and the same bowl. One family invited me heartily to come and stay with them for a week. They praised the nice bed they had for me. The first evening it turned out that the bed was very nice indeed; but I had to share it with three children. This I did for two nights but then I felt it was impossible to carry on research without having a real rest in the night. Not to offend them I pretended to have caught a cold and suggested a change to another family because the cold was too risky for the children. 'Oh, if it is because of this,' the wife said, 'we can put up for you a single bed. We only thought it would be so frightfully unkind to make you sleep quite by yourself.'

To complete the picture of unemployment in the Eastern Valley mention must be made of some attempts from the outside to break the prevailing inertia. There was an educational settlement in Pontypool and several Social Service Clubs were scattered about the area. Good as those may have been for the few unemployed who took part in their activities, they remained on the surface of local life, without altering or influencing the main trends. The situation could have been described as a change in the atmosphere in the valley to which the the traditional way of living had gradually been adjusted. The same lines as before were followed but on a restricted level. On this lower level the old traditions maintained themselves with unchanged strength. A break up of those traditions leading to an alteration in the outlook of the population was probably impossible unless the very basis of their lives had been affected.

This valley, with its long tradition in mining and its economic distress, with its remembrance of periods of high vitality and of the continous physical and mental tension during work in the pits, with its inertia and resignation, well established habits, fatalism and suspicion against any outsiders, was selected by an Order of friends for a Subsistence Production Society experiment following invitations to do so by various local people and by members of the league of service, the group that subsequently formed the Pontypool Educational Settlement, and the Special Areas Committee of the Eastern Valley. In March 1935 the Subsistence Production Society of the Eastern Valley was founded.

The founding of the Subsistence Production Society

The choice of the Eastern Valley was due to several factors. One reason was no doubt the urge to relieve by subsistence production the misery of unemployment where it was most heavily felt. As the Eastern Valley was included in the area of operation of the Special Areas Act it had the advantage of the possibility of getting financial support from the Commissioner of the Special Areas. The Eastern Valley was also one of the few valleys in South Wales where English was almost exclusively spoken. A Welsh speaking valley would have presented greater difficulties in establishing the contacts required, for the organisers of the Society were almost all English speaking.

Important as those factors were, the choice had its disadvantages. The scattering of population along the valley made it difficult to find a single centre within a reasonable distance of the various settlements where the unemployed lived. This difficulty was, however, not realised from the outset. As men of the valley had happily walked many miles daily to and from a job, the organisers thought that they would have just as cheerfully walked to and from the SPS. This was found to be a fallacy. In most cases a walk of more than two miles proved to be too much. To overcome this difficulty a regular transport system had to be established, the cost of which was a very heavy item in the budget of the SPS.

Early in the spring of 1935 the Eastern Valley heard for the first time of the ideas of subsistence production. Meetings were held all over the valley and often led to violent discussion. Opposition arose from different sides. There were the little shopkeepers and the co-operative societies, which feared a serious loss of their customers. There were the trade unions and the Labour Party which feared any connection with the Government and anticipated that some compulsion to work for the unemployment allowance lay behind the Society. The Communists went so far as to threaten to take very active steps against it. Finally, and more important than all the other reasons put together, there was the apathy of the unemployed; their strong and well-established habits of thought and habits of life which had to be altered before they could make up their minds to take part in such an experiment.

The arguments they used against it were chiefly the result of their unwillingness to try something new, for which they had the expressed backing neither of their unions, nor of their political parties, nor of their churches and chapels. A central point was the fear of going back to a time some 50 years before, when their fathers had worked in the collieries and had been compelled to use a large proportion of their wages buying the necessities of life from the 'company's shop': What they had bought there was always said to be of bad quality and at high prices and often a working week had ended for the worker not in the receipt of cash but in the discovery that he was indebted to the 'company's shop'. As the benefit for the SPS members consisted in buying goods at the Society's shop for lower prices than in the open market the analogy was only very superficial. It was sufficient, however, to be a reason for not joining the new venture.

Another argument used by the enemies of the SPS was that working there meant working for nothing or just for the allowance and that this system would influence the whole existing wage system for the worse. Such arguments were at first very effective in preventing the unemployed men from joining the SPS for they made them look ridiculous in the eyes of their fellows: 'I did not want to join because all the other men made fun about it. They laughed at every member when they met them at the Exchange. It was my missus who did not rest until I had joined.' Another member, at that time one of the very best members of the SPS, described what induced him to join: 'I learnt about the scheme by the meetings they arranged all over the valley. I have been at one of these meetings; there were about 50 persons, 40 of whom were present only to be able to express their opposition. We all are workers and we all are Labour and we thought that the Government wished to compel us to work in this scheme. I was not convinced by the meeting but I got interested in the scheme and I joined soon afterwards for mere curiosity, yet still with a certain amount of opposition.'

The first group of pioneers differed from the rest of the members in their attitude towards the SPS. They felt in some way responsible for it, because they had had to stand up for it, defend it, and suffer the sneers of the other unemployed; and also because they had watched it growing and had shared its development from the outset.

What this meant for them might be illustrated by a significant form of expression used by one of the pioneers who had found regular work and had had to leave the SPS. He continued to say 'we' in speaking about the SPS, e.g. 'we are going to have a Christmas party this year', although he could not take part. In speaking of his colleagues in the colliery, he always said: 'the others'.

Gradually the membership increased. In March 1935 there were eight, in January 1936 there were 180, in January 1937 there were 345, and in January 1938 there were 377. As a consequence, to be a member of the

SPS became a less exceptional thing, and opposition decreased. There was no longer any need to defend the Society. Even a number of younger men were attracted by the advantages the SPS offered. The shopkeepers realised that it was not so dangerous for them as they had feared; their opposition became gradually less and less obvious. Leading members of the Labour Party and the trade unions visited the SPS and declared their agreement with its principles and practice.

This cessation of opposition was not altogether an advantage. To be a member ceased to be a matter of personal conviction; men who used to be opposed to it joined the SPS because they realised that their opposition had not succeeded and some of them made up their minds that the best thing to do was to get as much as possible from the SPS and to put in as little as possible.

The advantages of the SPS became gradually greater because the growing membership allowed the inclusion of more kinds of goods in the process of production. Some of those who joined worked in a slack way, buying as much as possible and leaving the Society after a short period with a large unpaid bill. These bad debts became a serious economic and administrative problem. In the attempt to get at least part of the money back, the distribution of goods to some of the men who had left the SPS in debt was continued, with the hope that these debts would be repaid by and by. This meant giving a definite advantage to the debtors, who continued to participate in the benefits of the Society without working in it. This was immediately recognised by the others, especially by the pioneer group. They claimed that they had a special right to receive the benefits of the SPS because they had worked for it at a time when the advantages it offered were far smaller than they had become. Some of the pioneers who had left the Society because they found regular work had left it with no friendly feelings when they were told that the distribution of milk to their households from the SPS had to be discontinued.

When the first eight members joined in March 1935, their first concern was when they would be able to have a coal supply. The organisers had described coal-getting in all their meetings in the valley as one of the activities the SPS would endeavour to start immediately. Yet, this did not prove to be possible. The men explained that most of them had been in the habit of spending two or three days a week — days when they did not sign on — getting their coal from the tips. Some got it free from the washery streams, others paid one shilling for a weekly permit to pick at a good tip, or half that amount for a poorer tip.

Working for a full week for the SPS would have compelled them to pay for their coal; naturally they could not afford to do so. In the hope that within a few months the SPS would get its own coal, and wishing to encourage the pioneers, the organisers decided to buy coal and distribute it to the members at a lower price, sometimes at only 10% of the purchase price. The cheap coal worked as an inducement for joining the Society. Many of those who were members at the time of the study joined chiefly for the sake of getting cheap coal. The financial burden of this arrangement soon became very heavy for the Society, and it could not be continued indefinitely as the membership grew. Between 1936 and the end of 1937 the price of coal for the members was raised by 25%. Protests against this were, of course, frequent and sometimes very bitter, even though the members were still receiving a considerable subsidy from the Society for each ton of coal they bought.

In the circumstances it was natural that the organisers should keep in view the suggestion of producing coal within the activities of the SPS. This suggestion however, which according to reports by the organisers had been welcomed by the pioneer members, was opposed with passion by the members during the time of the investigation. A vital factor in this opposition appeared to be the possibility of accidents. Although facts were produced to show that when the unemployed worked their own coal, as at Rhymney and Brynmawr, they could work with much greater safety and comfort than in commercial mining, the SPS members always returned automatically to the same point.

Less emotional but yet very active was the opposition among the members to any other extension of the activities in a new direction. The majority of the men accepted anything new very reluctantly. For example, everybody agreed in 1938 that the products of the bakery were one of the greatest benefits that the SPS offered, yet the construction of this bakery in 1935 had met with strong opposition from the members. The scheme of constructing a slaughterhouse, in the hope of being able to reduce the price of meat considerably, had again been unwillingly accepted.

In the early spring of 1938 the question of limestone burning arose. In the two preceding seasons limestone had been burnt for use on the cultivated plots and on the farm by special arrangement with an outsider. To reduce the costs of the SPS it was suggested by the organisers in a special meeting that limestone burning ought to be included in the activities of the members. A stranger coming into this meeting would probably have got the impression that he was taking part in a normal industrial gathering where workers were putting forward their wage demands.

The meeting started with a short report given by the Area Organiser, in which he set out the problem and asked for volunteers. The season was already advanced, limestone was urgently needed but the SPS chimney did not smoke.

The first reaction to this speech was a strong but silent opposition. The men stood in a group together, looking at each other and encouraging each other by signs to speak. The Organiser was isolated; not only literally but also by the hostile atmosphere. Finally one member started the discussion by saying: 'What are you prepared to give for it?' There followed an explanation from the Organiser that it would mean an increase in the individual benefit for each member, if limestone were burnt, that special concessions were against the principles of the Scheme, and so on. The answer came: 'But this job is too hard, and includes too much responsibility, to be done for nothing. Clothing and shoes are ruined.' An agreement was reached that working clothes would be provided. In spite of this no volunteers appeared, and the meeting had to be postponed to the next day. Then some members were found although during the whole period of limestone burning, their reluctance to work was difficult to overcome.

This same attitude showed itself in regard to one of the chief activities proposed for the near future: the construction of new houses. The fact that many of the members lived miles away from the Brewery at Cwmavon prevented their full participation and that of their families in the social life of the SPS. The attitudes of those living on the spot and of those living far away showed so great a difference, to the advantage of the first, that, especially if one took into account the appalling state of many houses in the valley, the idea of building new houses near the SPS workplaces seemed fully justified. Again, however, the opposition was great, particularly amongst the group of carpenters who would be among the first called on to work for it.

The events described above belong to the early months of 1938. The organisers, however, stated that such opposition was much more serious in the early stages of the Society and that difficulties in its development showed a tendency to decrease since the meetings of group leaders came into existence. In June 1935 one of the members had suggested that 'men's leading lights should meet administrators at least once a fortnight to compare views etc. in regards of running the scheme till we get a better system.' This idea was taken up with much approval on either side, until the whole Society was organised in some 25 working groups, each with its own job and its own group leader chosen by the group itself. In February 1936 the first group leaders' meeting was held, and after that they took place regularly once a month.

Those group leaders' meetings suffered badly in the beginning from the inefficiency of the first chairman, one of the members, who had been unable to fulfil this function. At the end of 1937 a new chairman was elected with much better results, as his experience in the Labour movement and the trade unions had given him the training and outlook required. It was, however, significant that the Area Organiser continued to play the most important part in these meetings. At first sight this might seem to be due to the fact that the financial situation of the Society was known only to him, and therefore every important matter really depended on his consent. There were signs that some of the group leaders, particularly those who were used to the procedure in political and trade union gatherings, resented this position of the Area Organiser. Indeed one of the last meetings discussed the question whether this Organiser was a 'dictator' or not, and without deciding came to the conclusion that there should be an arrangement which would make it possible for the group leaders and other members of the Society to get an insight into the financial situation. A field worker observing what happened in those meetings would not have doubted that the Organiser maintained his position as much by virtue of the social tradition and outlook that he represented as by any special knowledge that he possessed.

From the beginning of the experiment to the middle of 1936 the Society had traded with its members by a cash/hour system. Account had been kept of the hours spent in the SPS by each member and a certain fixed number of hours entitled the member to the purchase of different goods. Twenty hours of work, for instance, gave the right to buy a load of coal, 40 hours a suit of clothes, five minutes a cabbage, 15 minutes a stone of potatoes, and so on. The Society price for each article had also to be paid.

This system was found to be 'complicated and unsatisfactory for a number of reasons' as the Annual Report for 1936 stated, and was given up in favour of the subsequent system which was certainly less complicated. That system was described by the annual report in the following way: 'Today, goods are costed and charged for in cash alone, and are supplied to the members at a price fixed by the cost of material, fuel, etc. used, plus 20% for overheads. A member who works satisfactorily for the Society for one week, is entitled to obtain from it such goods as he requires for use in his own household the following week', that is, such goods were offered by the Society and for which the member was able and willing to pay the cash price fixed by the Society. The unemployed man received an unemployment allowance in proportion to the size of his household and could therefore purchase goods also in proportion to this size.

The change from the cash/hours system to the subsequent system implied more than a mere question of administration, although this had nowhere clearly been admitted. It meant shifting from one idea of equality — treating everybody in proportion to his efficiency - to another form of equality — treating everybody according to his needs irrespective of his efficiency. As both forms were called 'equality' and as this could be justified by the indefinite meaning of this term, it was only natural that one found a certain confusion in this respect amongst the members.

The activities of the SPS in 1938 included industrial and handicraft groups centred in the Old Brewery in Cwmavon, horticultural groups at the various plots and agricultural ones at Llandegveth.

The Old Brewery had been erected as a Brewery in 1901, and had gone out of action in 1928. In 1935 an Order of friends bought the premises. Besides the main building with its five floors, there were stables, garages and a few small workshops in separate buildings. The following groups, equipped with the necessary machinery, were working there in 1938: blacksmiths and boilerhouse men, handicraftsmen, decorators, electricians, flour-millers, kitchen groups, tailors and weavers.

The largest amount of agricultural work was done at the farm at Llandegveth, which lay between Usk and Newport at a distance of about ten miles from the Brewery. It extended to 300 acres. There was a hostel for about 20 men on the spot, and six cottages, four of which were built by the Society for members and their families. The dairy was equipped with modern machinery, milking being done by machine, and there was provision for cooling milk and sterilising bottles. A new road had been built and an old one repaired, connecting the farm with the main road. The cowsheds accommodated about 60 cattle (cows, one bull, calves, heiffers) horses, pigs and poultry. A large amount of hay was harvested in every season; barley and oats were cultivated.

The plot at Cwmbran covered 31.25 acres, the plot at Pontnewydd 11.25 acres, the plot at Griffithstown 15 acres; at Pontynewl two glasshouses were built for the growing of tomatoes. The plot at Trevethin — 29.25 acres — specialised in fruits (apples, plums and black currants). Beili Glas near the Old Brewery in Cwmavon was 21 acres in area, including the quarry, and provided limestone and other uncultivated land.

The Society possessed two vans for bread and milk transport, one van for general distribution, one lorry for bulk transport and two vans for general purposes.

The activities were directed by a supervisory staff of 24 members, of whom 12 had been found within the South Wales area, four were old members of the SPS and eight were outsiders. The 24 consisted of: one area organiser, one farm bailiff, two cowmen, one wagoner, one horticulturalist, one poultryman, one organiser for transport and distribution, one accountant for the members' accounts, one accountant for all other book-keeping, two secretaries, one workshop organiser, one baker, one handicraft instructor, one cook, two masons, one millwright and joiner, one tailor, one tailoress, one weaver, one wireman and one wood-working machinist.

The production figures of the Society did not alter very much within 1938. Of course development from the beginning showed an enormous change, but by 1938 the standard of production which suited the consumption power of the members seemed to have been reached, at least in several commodities such as bread, cakes, eggs (during the season), and milk. Further progress in production could then therefore only mean either the inclusion of commodities which had not then been produced, or the production by the members themselves of commodities which had until then to be bought from the funds of the Society for re-sale to the members. The inclusion of new commodities was strongly favoured by a number of members who took an active part in the discussion of the working of the Society in 1938.

The extent of production is shown by the following account, giving the production for the four weeks ending January 29th, 1938:

Bakery	10,924 half-quarter loaves of bread
	1,428 lb of self raising flour
	677 slabs of cake
	miscellaneous smalls
Brickmaking	5,000 bricks 9in × 4in × 3in
Boot repairing	147 pairs of shoes and boots repaired
Butchery	7,769 lb meat distributed
	1,128 lb meat products
Dairy	15,349 pints of milk produced
Kitchen	4,337 dinners served
Knitting	81 pairs of socks
Mill	400 cwt wheat milled
Tailoring and	60 outer garments
Weaving	100 sq. yd of blanket
	miscellaneous items

The development of the SPS up to the time of the investigation showed a steady increase of membership and of output. Social, technical, and financial difficulties had grown with the general extension. Future efforts of the organisers were to be directed towards a reduction of these difficulties. This was taken to involve a reduction of the costs of the Society, an increase of its social activities to strengthen the bond that kept the membership together and also fresh technical development.

The members of the SPS

In March 1938 there were 4,233 unemployed men in the Eastern Valley; 377 of whom (8.9%) were members of the SPS. The percentage of men connected with the Society in some way was higher, if one took into account the number of men who had previously joined the Society, but left it after a period. The number of those was about 360, or 8.5% of the men unemployed at that time. Of those, 170 gave reasons for discontinuation of membership: 64% had failed to settle accounts, 24% had left for paid employment, 7% expressed dissatisfaction with the Society, and 5% had died. Thus, about 17% of the unemployed in the valley had first-hand experience of the SPS.

A comparison between the age of the unemployed men in the valley and the age of the Society membership showed, however, that the membership had a higher average age, which is in accordance with the principles of the SPS. A total of 82.8% of the members were aged over 35 years, yet only 62.2% of the unemployed men in the valley as a whole were over 35.

The average age between 1936 and 1938 dropped slightly showing an increasing attraction of the Society for younger people; on the other hand it seemed to be related to the needs of the growing work of the SPS. It was certainly not possible to carry on many of the activities — building and transport for example — without young, strong men; so the age policy of the organisers had to be changed. In 1938 they were in favour of young men joining the Society. However, it did not seem to be easy for men to decide to join the Society. Mainly, those who had long experience of unemployment made up their minds to try it. Whereas 58.8% of unemployed men in the Eastern Valley had been unemployed for less than one year, the corresponding figure for SPS members was just 10.2%. Of the remainder, 35.4% had been unemployed for between one and five years, 41.5% for between five and ten years, and 12.9% had been unemployed for more than ten years.

The average duration of unemployment for SPS members was six years. Although the SPS membership included many old age pensioners who were not included in the unemployment figures for the Eastern Valley, the SPS appealed chiefly to those who had been out of work for a very long period. Hence the Society had chiefly to deal with persons who had lost the habit of working.

Formal organisation of the SPS

The SPS was guided by two main principles:

1. The SPS as an economic organisation was to be based on equality and mutual friendship among all working in it, irrespective of their various functions in the productive processes. 'While there are great variations in ability and capacity there must be a realisation of the equal worth of each personality' (Order of friends 1930).

Production was always and only for use. There was no thought of private profit to any one of the members or the staff. The benefit that the members drew was in no relation to their special skill or productivity. It varied, however, according to the size of the family of each member. The higher the consumption power of a member's family, the higher the benefit he could obtain. Membership in the SPS enabled each of the members to raise the standard of living in his home and that of every member of his family to the same degree.

There was, however, one departure from this principle of equality within the SPS: the members of the staff received salaries which were in some cases very much higher than the unemployment allowance on which the members depended.

The idea of equality was also applied in the relation between the members and the organisers of the SPS. 'The right relationship between human beings is friendship — free, equal, and spontaneous' (Order of friends 1930). They all addressed each other by their Christian names as an expression of the equality of personalities. Members, the supervisory staff, and organisers shared their general midday meal in the canteen and thus tried to establish close social contact with one another.

2. The Society was organised on the basis of the idea that only voluntary work with a complete absence of compulsion would allow the growth of the creative urge so as to give satisfaction and happiness in work. Therefore the rules in the SPS were not upheld by authoritative orders and no serious consequences followed if they were not strictly kept. If somebody came late in the morning and left just after dinner, this did not diminish the benefit he drew from the SPS. In spite of this there had been an attempt to regulate the hours of work, by decreasing the benefit for those members who were in the habit of being late: dinner was given free to anybody who arrived on time in the morning, but those who were late had to pay for it. This regulation existed however only for a short time and was never strictly observed.

Even while they were present there was no compulsion on the members to work, or to work at a particular rate; everybody could do just as much as he liked, or just as little. There were, of course, criticisms from fellow-workers, and the organisers believed that those critisisms ought to have been sufficient to make men work, if pleasure in work had not yet become an incentive for them.

This absolute refusal to apply any form of compulsion was found through the whole of the administration. When the members were consulted on the working of the Society, even the normal democratic system of compelling a minority by the vote of a majority was not used. Instead the Quaker system of getting unanimous consent on every question by discussion without vote was applied. Neither was there a vote in the meetings of the group leaders; the discussion on each topic continued till an agreement between all present was arrived at.

The application of these principles in detail is shown in the rules of the SPS which may be set out here:

The object of the SPS is to enable older unemployed men to raise their standard of living by their own efforts. Every unemployed man in the Eastern Valley is invited to become a member of the Society on a voluntary basis; he may discontinue his membership at any moment. There are a few rules which regulate production and distribution:

Members receive no wages from the Society.

Goods produced are distributed to members at the cost of production.

A member may obtain goods from the Society on the understanding that they are for consumption in his own household exclusively.

Payments for goods obtained from the Society become due on the Friday of the week during which the goods were received.

A member who fails to pay his account in full on that day is suspended from the privilege of membership until his account has been settled or other arrangements arrived at.

A member found guilty of stealing the Society's property or of selling goods obtained from the Society loses his membership at once.

Members are expected to work 30 hours during five days of the week.

Members are protected by insurance against personal injuries or death arising out of an accident sustained whilst occupied in the work of the Society.

The working hours are from 9.30 a.m to 1 p.m then follows the dinner hour; work is resumed at about 2 p.m and finishes at 4.30 p.m. The normal working week in the SPS has 30 working hours from Monday to Friday. Saturday is entirely free except for the supervisory staff and the members occupied with the transport of milk and bread.

The economic benefit of the Society compared with its cost

'There are three ways of getting a benefit from the scheme', one member explained confidentially, 'one legal and two illegal ones'. The 'legal' was to buy all or any of the commodities produced or distributed by it. The illegal ones were a) reselling the goods at higher prices to persons not working in the Society and b) pilfering.

The first will be dealt with in full below. Before that, however, a few words on the other two kinds of benefit may be in place. It was inevitably difficult to get any exact data on the selling of goods, because everybody knew that the penalty for this was expulsion from the Society, and therefore only occasionally a statement by a member, or personal observation, could throw light on it. From such evidence, however, it seemed that selling the goods was a very common procedure among many members. There were two different ways of making those sales: one without making a profit out of them, the other with profit. Even the first way was opposed to the rules of the Society, let alone the second. As, however, there was no private profit connected with the first, many of the members did not see anything wrong with it. Only in a very few cases was the identity of the Society's interest with that of the individual member realised. Normally the Society was looked upon as something apart, not connected with the individual by any effective bond.

One of the mildest cases of sale and purchase of the products of the Society in this 'illegal' fashion was the following:

A woman whose husband had left the SPS and returned to employment but who wanted to continue participation in the milk distribution, said: 'I could easily ask one of the other women to order more milk and let me have it, as many do; but I think it is our right to get it further, and therefore I shall first try to speak to one of the organisers.' Her request was refused but it seemed almost certain that she continued to get the Society milk.

Another rather striking case may be mentioned. It showed the discrepancy between general norms and actual behaviour, and the obvious difficulty of adapting oneself to one's own standard. In a discussion on the Society between three persons (one of the members, a working miner and the investigator), the member said: 'The scheme would be alright only some of the men are playing dirty tricks to the scheme, selling the goods and so on.' The discussion turned to another subject, the miner saying how badly he wanted a good and cheap table and asking if he could not get it with the Society. 'Alright', the member later said, 'I'll say I need it for myself.' The discussion went on and the member said: 'The honest fellows have to pay for those who try to get out of the scheme every sort of benefit no matter for whom.' Again and again, indirect allusions as to the selling of goods were made. One member, for example, complained that since he joined the Society he was boycotted by a number of persons, and went on: 'They all run the scheme down, but when it comes to buying a bit of bread or milk from there, they find their way to us.'

It seems, however, that whilst now and again nearly everybody was inclined to sell something, there were only a few who did this regularly. The figures of the regular sales to the members suggested that resale of bread, milk, eggs and other provisions was not very important since, on average, the amount of money spent with the Society increased with the members' size of family.

It was more difficult to get an idea about the amount of 'pinching'. Only two men admitted it to the investigator without the slightest sign of bad conscience. The others only told about pilfering going on; and now and again one had the opportunity to see it happening or to notice that something (e.g. a tool) had disappeared. Nothing dependable could be said about the amount of stealing. The frequent comments of members about it and the observations of the organisers as well as of the investigator, left no doubt that it happened frequently.

Both selling and stealing were revealing of the attitude of some of the members towards the SPS; each, however, revealing a different element in this attitude.

Selling, for example to a neighbour, without making profit by it, was an expression of the existence of traditional social bonds which were evidently stronger than the shorter lived bond established with the SPS. Selling with profit showed that the individual neither felt that he belonged to the traditional neighbourhood community, nor to the social unit the SPS represented; he had adopted an individualist position.

Stealing goods from the Society seemed to prove the individual regarded the SPS in the way any other large industrial undertakings were very often regarded by working men; namely as something on 'the other side of the fence', where moral norms ceased to exist. For those men, the SPS was not envisaged as a new experiment, different from other industrial undertakings because it belonged in effect to the men working there, but as just an ordinary industrial undertaking that was not entitled to expect a co-operative attitude on the side of the men.

There were some objections to any attempt to calculate the 'legal' benefit in terms of money, because all such calculations could not really do justice to the economic benefit received by being members of the Society. It has to be kept in mind that, if not members, the unemployed would certainly not have paid more money than they spent in the Society for similar products on the open market, but they would not have been able to afford the same quantity and quality of goods. Asked to express the benefit of the Society in monetary value many of the members actually refused to do so. 'We don't save money. I have no more in my pocket, but I have a better table and something to occupy my mind' one of the men answered. However, of those who did offer an estimate, most showed the tendency to underestimate the Society's benefit, often to a very high degree. This confirmed the statement made above, that they would not in fact buy the same amount or quality of goods in the open market. For example, in January 1938 a total of over £615 was spent by the membership in the SPS to buy goods which would have cost more than £1,213 on the open market. In addition to this saving there was the benefit of subsidised coal and a free midday meal (consisting of meat, vegetables, and potatoes, tea and occasionally a sweet). This midday meal was far larger than that usually consumed in the homes of the unemployed where, in the majority of cases, there was no hot dinner except on Sundays. For many of the bachelors especially, this meal was one of the chief attractions of the Society.

The figures did not allow for the quality of the goods obtained through the Society. Certainly the quality was higher than that available in local shops. One of the most important items from the point of view of nutrition was milk. In all of the families of unemployed men not in the Society who were visited to form a control group, tinned milk was used, either always or, at least, half and half with fresh milk. In none of the families of the members was tinned milk found in use.

This illustrates clearly that membership of the Society was certainly a help for the unemployed, and raised their standard of living in a remarkable way. It is, however, necessary to mention the view held by some members, namely that they derived no economic benefit whatsoever from the Society, if they took into account the hours they spent there, calculated what they would have earned on the basis of an average wage, and compared this with their estimate of the cash value of the actual benefit received. For example a man who worked 30 hours a week in the SPS and estimated the benefit received at ten shillings, said that he had been working for a third of a shilling per hour. To this something should have been added in respect of the free daily meal. Obviously, however, the productivity of the Society was low; the reasons for this are dealt with later.

The data quoted above give a picture of the significance of the Society for the household budget and the standard of living. The benefit was, however, still greater, if account was taken of the pleasanter atmosphere in which the work was done, the better standard of health, and the intellectual and emotional effects of membership in the SPS. This also was not measurable in monetary value and will be dealt with in a different connection. Here only one statement of a former member who had recently returned to work in the pits may be quoted: 'I wish I could go back to the scheme. The work kills me. And I don't get out so much more that it compensates the expenditure for bus fares, tools, clothes, and what I need more in food.'

To clarify this statement it may be added that the wages he was earning were about £2.10 shillings a week, which was less than a father of a large family got in unemployment allowance.

The economic benefit that the Society conferred on its members should also be considered in relation to the cost of establishing and maintaining the Society. For example, it was calculated that in the year ending March 1936, the average financial benefit per member for that year had been £26.10 shillings. On the other hand, the combination of capital charges, current and recurrent expenditure amounted to £135 per family. It might therefore have been said that it would have been cheaper to distribute £26.10 shillings in cash to each of the members than to set up the administration of the Society.

Such distribution of money, however, would not have had the same effects as the Society; it might not have meant that the quality and quantity of food was continuously improved, it might have meant nothing from the point of view of health, it would not have brought with it any of the mental and emotional advantages of regular work. But whatever the value set upon these effects, and last but not least the experimental value of the project, the economic situation of the Society could only have begun to be found if the unfavourable difference between benefit received by the members and expenditure required to produce this benefit had disappeared. A further step would have been the achievement of a benefit greater than the expenditure, for only then would the work put in by all the members have found a place in the account.

From the point of view of the organisation, the 1938 result had to be called unsatisfactory. The members themselves realised sometimes that the economic situation was not as sound as it ought to have been, as the following quotations indicate: 'The scheme is all right as a supplementary benefit for the home; but this benefit is in no relation with what has been put into the scheme. Perhaps you don't know it, but it is £120,000. If they only would have distributed this money amongst us'; 'It is impossible to make this scheme economically good. In its present form it is absolutely senseless. One man with two paid hands can produce twice as much as 20 members. It is impossible to carry this scheme on. They put money in it without getting anything out';

Many of the men said again and again: 'Make it self-supporting. Let's sell the stuff on the open market. Then it will be all right.' Production for the market instead of production for use appealed to those men (whose traditions were so deeply rooted in the industrial system) as the only way out of the economic difficulties of the experiment.

One of the items which weighed heavy on the Society was the waste of material belonging to the Society by the members; SPS property was, they thought, nobody's property, instead of thinking of it as the property of them all. For example, 400 milk bottles worth about £6 were not returned during one week in December 1937. Waste of material was not accompanied by any bad consequences for the individuals responsible. They were not compelled to replace the waste.

The carelessness of one member one day brought about the loss of about 20 lb of malt; he had forgotten to close a pipe, and only remembered it when it was too late. The personal influence of the instructor of this group, who was a craftsman in the best sense of the word, made the man realise that something had happened which ought not to occur again. On this occasion however, it was notable that the members of the group called their instructor 'boss'; not because he received a salary but because he felt responsible for the property of the Society and thus made them realise that there was a difference in their outlook, which they tried to express by calling him 'boss'. Another man wasted quite a large amount of flour in breadmaking by not taking the exact weight for the dough. He did not take any trouble to rearrange things, though this would have been possible. He was only concerned to hide what he had done from the instructor.

Another very serious, connected problem was the cost of transport. Transport of men and material during the six months ending September 1937 cost the Society over £706 quite apart from the depreciation of the vehicles. In an ordinary week the total mileage covered by the Society transport was 1,767 miles and 171 gallons of petrol were used. The two milk vans covered 626 miles in one week, using £4.25 worth of petrol and oil. The value of bread and milk delivered by the vans was £47.

Besides this, the vans seemed to have an irresistable attraction to those concerned with the transport. All the drivers had a passion for driving, transporting the milk seven days a week without getting tired of it. Unfortunately, this passion did not make them understand the motors thoroughly so that a good deal of waste of material and cost for repairs may have been due to them. It did, however, make them keen on driving outside normal driving hours. They had invented many tricks by which they were able to take the vans out of the garage without anybody noticing. One of them who had been a member of the Society for three years, hardly ever missing a day, stated that he was — as a Communist — whole-heartedly against the Society. 'It is fundamentally wrong.' 'Then why are you working in the scheme?' he was asked. 'Well, because I am fond of driving.' Another of the drivers said: 'There are three things I love in life: My lorry, my missus, and my boy.' (Note that the lorry came first.) This man offered once to take the investigator with the van to a village some 15 miles away, pretending that he had something to do there for the Society. This offer was accepted, but shortly afterwards it was found out that this was only a pretext for driving his beloved lorry in the evening. The thought of waste of SPS property obviously did not occur to him.

A number of similar examples of waste of material and disregard of the economic interests of the Society could be given. This attitude was partly due, as already suggested, to the industrial tradition in which the men were steeped. Another factor was the lack of ideology — a reasoned view of the SPS and of its place in their life and in the community. A third factor was the lack of a production plan which might have fulfilled two functions, an economic and a social one. This point will be dealt with later.

The individual in the SPS

The SPS was directed, as was pointed out in a previous section, at overcoming the disastrous effects of unemployment and of employment under the then current industrial conditions. Those effects have already been described in general terms; they will now be discussed in psychological terms.

The established tradition of industry and the adjustment to a condition of regular unemployment had both affected the normal pattern of individual development. The concept of a 'normal' pattern of development was well established in the then current thought and had found frequent expression in literature and art. Of course there were, and are, scientific and philosophical difficulties involved in the use of this concept. Any such pattern of development would have been the result of a long historical process over the course of centuries. It would, therefore, not have been quite correct to speak of a 'normal' pattern as if unchanged 'inborn' laws determined the course of human life irrespective of the dynamic processes which constantly altered and influenced people. This, however, did not exclude the idea of a wider application of this concept. The pattern I considered normal at the time of the study consisted of the passage by the individual in the course of life through various stages which had been defined psychologically by Charlotte Bühler, professor at the Psychological Institute of the University of Vienna.

Charlotte Bühler, in studying a large number of life stories and biographical material, had discovered a psychological curve roughly parallel to the biological. Her material included cases occuring in all social classes and was spread over the period of the previous 200 years.

Her fundamental idea was that corresponding to the biological expansion, maturation and restriction of each individual there was a normal psychic development which might be represented by a curve of parallel shape.

For the description of this curve Charlotte Bühler introduced the concept on 'functions' of life, by which she understood each separate activity or series of experiences, such as work, friendship, love, marriage, religious and political activities, and so on.

The functional content of each stage was given by an exhaustive psychological analysis of cases; the turning points (or better, the turning periods) were described in their various forms. Charlotte Bühler explained that to decide about the beginning and ending of a stage, three aspects of the given material had to be considered and analysed.

The first aspect was the analysis of the behaviour, the second was the analysis of the experience, and the third was the analysis of the achievements. Their relation to each other and their sequence in time is fully described in her book on the subject (Bühler 1933).

In relation to the development of an individual then, the first stage considered was the stage of childhood and adolescence, during which the individual was economically and socially included in, and dependent on, the family unit. The second stage considered was a period of transition, of trial and error, a time of preparatory action leading to the third stage in which life took on a definite, settled character. This third stage was taken generally to coincide with the period of full vitality. In personal relations, and in the sphere of employment, men were taken to settle down or to experience at least a strong urge to do so. The fourth stage was taken to coincide with a decline of vitality; emotional factors began to lose the importance they had had up to that time, and employment dominated almost all the other spheres of life. The fifth stage was hypothesised to bring further restrictions in vitality and work. Old age, and often illness, then became a problem and the approach of death had to be faced.

Before long-term unemployment had become an important factor in the Eastern Valley these stages were passed through by each worker under the specific conditions and limitations imposed by industrialism.

An example of a miner's life story, typical for the area, may help to describe these modifications: This man was born in Talywain in 1870 as the second son of a blast furnace worker. From the age of six to eleven years he went to an elementary school. He was not very keen on learning and always envied his elder brother who already worked in the pits and earned his own money. At 11 years old, he too started to work underground. His father did not care for trade unions, but the son became a member and had never since discontinued his membership. He had a good time, came to earn decent wages, had a number of friends with whom he spent his time after work, and many a love affair. At 24 he happened to meet in the street a girl whom he did not know very well. He was in the company of some friends, and only as a boast said: 'This is my girl.' The others did not believe this, and so he set out to prove it; one year later he married her. They rented a house in Garndiffaith, and had one child after another. It was a difficult time and the house was too small for the growing family. They had 12 children in 20 years; nine of them were still alive at the time of study. When working conditions became difficult he went to London and worked there in a metal factory for about a year. He sent the greater part of his money home. He soon became 'fed up' with his life, which was neither the life of a bachelor nor that of a married man, and went back into the pit: 1921 was a very bad year for him. There was a serious strike and his wife had a nervous breakdown and had to go to the mental asylum for one year. The children left him one after the other. In 1926 the great strike came. After that he had employment for three months then he was dismissed and never got work again. In 1927 the daughter whom he had liked best died. He took her little son into his house. They got a County Council house and he became interested in allotments. In 1938 he had three allotments near the house, did all the work himself and was very proud of it. At 65 he had started to get his old age pension of 10 shillings a week.

The commencement of earning life with 11 years marks the transition from the first to the second stage; at the same time new interests and contacts began, (trade-unionism, friends, love affairs). The third stage set in with marriage; the renting of a house shows clearly a wish to settle down. After 25 years this stage drew to a close; the fourth stage was marked by the illness of his wife and the fact that the house became empty again because the children grew up and left the parents. The fifth phase began with the definite loss of employment. Thus industrialism interfered three times in a marked form with this individual's course of life; first, by closing the first stage prematurely at the age of 11. The significance of this first period was that the individual guarded by, and included in, a family unit which looked after the economic aspects of existence, had time and liberty to learn and to develop. In 1938, this period lasted normally for 14 years among working class people; in the middle class and upper middle class from 18–25 years.

The second stage in this life course was deprived by industrialism of one of its most important features; it did not provide the possibility of experiencing trial and error in choice of employment. Middle class people during this time changed their interests at secondary schools or universities, they saw other countries; there was a chance for them to shift from one type of job to another as they gradually acquired knowledge about the world and themselves. The worker's son in a mining district had no choice nor did he think of any; he started his life's employment in the pit at 11 years of age.

The third interference of industrialism in the normal course of life occurred in the fourth stage, which was suddenly and prematurely ended by the strike of 1926 and its consequences: some weeks of employment followed the unsuccessfully ended strike and then final unemployment ensued. Thus the fourth stage was artificially shortened. Industrialism did not provide for the worker the possibility of experiencing the main psychological feature of this period, i.e. a changed outlook towards employment, an inner drive to complete the life's work, to specialise and to achieve a final result. The interference of the social event of unemployment with the normal development of the individual was sudden and brutal. Those miners who became unemployed during their fourth stage of life were generally forced to complete the step into the fifth stage earlier than their own development required. When a man of 45 said: 'Since I have been unemployed, I feel like 65': or another 'Men should die after 40, there is no room for them in this world' they expressed the conflict they felt between the social forces compelling them to move into the fifth stage of life and their own outlook and attitude which was still anchored in the fourth. They felt 'fed up with the useless life we live' as one of them said. Ten years later they certainly would have not felt like this but would have taken their enforced leisure as the natural privilege of old age. Thus for them unemployment set a premature end to the fourth stage of life and led at once to the fifth.

However, not all of those who were affected by long-term unemployment were in the fourth stage of life. A rough survey of the unemployed in November 1937 showed that 12.6% were in the second stage (up to 24 years old), 45% were in the third stage (24–44 years old), and 34.2% were in the fourth stage (45–59 years old). Thus the greatest proportion of unemployed men were probably in their third stage; it was in this stage that the individual was most seriously affected by unemployment, for this period was normally characterised by steady and continuous employment and by well established social contacts which, in a worker's life, generally had their centre in their work place. Loss of work meant loss of social contacts and activities; it meant restriction by the loss of the many opportunities which involved expense beyond the means of an unemployed man. The inner experience corresponded to this restriction (which had no justification in the development of the individual) and was expressed by a man of 39 years who said: 'The best years of my life are lost here.' Thus unemployed men in the third stage experienced a conflict because the chief features of their way of life were more appropriate to the fourth stage but without the advances, normal in that period, in specialised skills and command over their jobs.

For men in the second stage of life, unemployment meant a prolongation of this period of instability, and the continuous threat that they would have no chance to complete the step to the next period. They could not develop in the ways indicated by their normal desires; they did not experience the period of trial and error because there was no opportunity to try and to err. Their restlessness, their surplus of energy found no normal outlet. One young man of 25 years in Cwmavon agreed to take employment at wages and under conditions which he had to justify before his older trade union friends, who would have preferred him not to do so. He said: 'I am young and I feel as fit as a horse for work. I can't go on like this.' No other age group felt as dissatisfied with life as the unemployed men belonging to the second stage and for no other group did it mean a more serious danger for their future.

One objection to this analysis of the effects of unemployment on the normal course of life might be raised by those who have daily experience of the behaviour of unemployed men: did every individual in the same stage of life feel and behave towards unemployment in the same way? The answer is: certainly not; personal differences were evident but these were in a field apart from the pattern here in question and may be explained by what could be called the 'level of life', that is the difference between a 'full' and a 'poor' life in regard to the number and character of functions exercised.

To illustrate this, two examples of unemployed miners in the Eastern Valley may be presented in terms of functions. Both were in the third stage and married. The first had one child and his sole interest lay in his weekly visit to church. The second had four children, was a member of several clubs, attended political and social meetings, engaged in sports, and had interests in reading, listening to the wireless and visiting the cinema. Both these men felt somehow degraded by unemployment. They spoke of themselves as of old men for whom no hope was left. Both were in danger of a premature transition to the fourth stage, they were looking backwards to the zenith of their life which lay behind them. In both cases the decisive function of employment was lacking; in the case of the second man the higher level of life was reflected by his much wider and more varied interests.

The conflict explained above — dissatisfaction with not being able to live as one wished, or resignation in being made to feel older than one was — was the common experience of those unemployed men who joined the SPS.

The basic idea of the SPS showed indeed a deeper intuition and understanding of their needs than other charitable efforts for unemployed men in that it provided something to replace the chief loss due to unemployment, that of purposeful activity. Work provided outside employment by the SPS had in many respects, although not in all, the same function and significance for an individual as work within employment had in the normal industrial field. It certainly had the function of enabling him to establish social contacts with other men coming from various parts of the valley, and also with many other persons whose different outlook and traditions widened his horizon and may even have induced him to acquire new interests. Among these were the instructors from different parts of England or from abroad.

These persons sat with the men at the dinner table, talked to them and told them of their work and experience. What this could mean in some cases is illustrated by a statement by one of the members who said: 'I don't want to say anything against the scheme, because old as I am, I have never known before what socialism really is. Two years ago two visitors came to the Brewery from Palestine. They gave us a talk on the settlements and I had a private talk afterwards with one of them. Only then I suddenly understood: this is socialism.' Since that time he had always looked for news about Palestine in the newpaper; he was evidently worried about the continuous troubles there, Palestine meant for him a new line of thought and interest.

Apart from this social life which widened the outlook of each individual, work in a so far untried and new trade added a new sphere of interest to the individual's life.

Thus the man in the fifth stage of life got from the SPS something that normal life never would have given him; new functions, something to occupy his mind, social contacts which helped to make this period richer for him than he could have normally expected. No wonder that one found the old men happy and satisfied as members of the SPS.

The man in the fourth stage found that he could gain experience in accordance with his special needs at this period: he had the opportunity of specialising on some job, of carrying it on and completing it. The bitter hopelessness of the years of unemployment with the feeling of a premature, prolonged, and useless old age was taken away. These men tended to become SPS 'patriots'.

The result was, however, different for those in the third stage and second stage of life. In the third stage the vital 'urges' or impulses were strong and therefore the conflict between them and the social order which prevented the normal development and experience in this stage, was active and deeply felt.

The opportunities provided by the SPS did not seem to be sufficient to resolve this conflict. Many of the Society members in this stage thought and said that they were losing their best years in the Society instead of getting along with normal employment in the normal course of life. They did not want an experiment, they wanted industrial reality. That the SPS was not quite real for them was due to two factors: first, the economic benefit was not large enough to permit them to live a normal life; secondly their habits of thought did not permit them to envisage any development that did not imply enjoying normal wages and working conditions in the prime of their lives.

Men in the second stage of life were also not satisfied with the Society. They objected to its lack of prospects for the future and to its 'humdrum' character. For example, a comparison between those aged 45 or less and those aged 46 or more showed that although both age groups attended irregularly, the younger attended less regularly than the older and were more likely to express negative attitudes towards the Society.

This was again a confirmation that the younger men were less likely to become convinced members of the SPS than the older ones. On the other hand a certain number of jobs in the Society could not be done by old men; for example, the transport jobs. Although there was a considerable number of younger men in the SPS, my impression was that the turnover of younger men was greater than that of older men. This brought about a constant change in the membership which was good neither for technical efficiency nor for the social atmosphere of the Society. There seemed to be one possible solution: namely, to have organised the SPS so that it could have given the younger men what they were entitled to demand from life. That this could have been done at least to a certain degree, was proved in 1936, when a group of younger members of the SPS had been sent to Manchester for some weeks to learn how to handle knitting machines. In speaking of that time two years later all those who participated became quite enthusiastic. For them it combined learning, a prospect for the future, and a change of the social atmosphere; besides it was a sort of adventure. Stressing the learning aspect of the work would certainly have been one way of helping to overcome the difficulties of the younger men in the SPS.

The following conclusion may therefore be drawn: the power of the SPS to overcome the effects of unemployment depended chiefly on the stage of life of the individual member. His attitude towards the Society was fixed by the degree to which it succeeded in this task. He was, of course, not consciously aware of this relation; according to his character, temperament, and intelligence he developed a rationalisation of his attitude towards the Society and formulated his comments and criticisms in a general way, without any relation to his personal situation. Nevertheless those rationalised arguments provided clearly marked symptoms of the personal situations involved. How did the members put such arguments?

The positive attitude of practically all the members was expressed in the fact of their membership; they generally did not think it necessary to express it further by words. This attitude of general acceptance of the Society and willingness to co-operate in it, was not for the members inconsistent with a tendency to find reasons for grumbling or criticising.

Any figures of verbal expression of negative attitudes should not be given undue weight. Therefore it is perhaps better to judge attitudes by classifying members into three groups in accordance with all observations of, and statements by, each individual.

The first group found enough to complain about in criticising a meal in the canteen or some unimportant regulation. To satisfy them it was generally sufficient to wait for the next meal or to give a short explanation of the rule criticised. In contrast to their words their behaviour proved often that they enjoyed the SPS as a welcome pastime. They must be called the indifferent type.

For the second group the success or failure of the SPS was a personal concern. They thought about its ideas and principles and tried to put in their best to make it successful; but they again grumbled; they complained that the SPS did not realise what it had, or what they thought it had, promised to realise. They objected to special concessions to individuals, to any sign of inequality, to the limited amount of cultural activities. Their criticism was aimed at making the SPS better than it was at the time.

The third group were in the SPS, as they more or less frankly admitted, to get as much as possible out of it. They were not content, because they did not get out enough. They combined this economic criticism with individual methods of increasing their benefit; pilfering and selling of goods was freqently found among them. They sneered at the idealism of the organisers who, they said, strove for the impossible by introducing a new type of social relationship. Thus one found amongst them those who longed for more discipline and authority.

The records were sufficient in the cases of 98 members to allow their classification into these three groups. These showed that the first group accounted for about one-third, the second group accounted for slightly less than one-third, and the third group slightly more than one-third. The age distribution showed again the unfavourable attitude of the younger men towards the SPS. With increasing age the indifferent type became predominant.

Thus the SPS met the wishes and needs of individuals in the advanced stages of life, but did not do so with those in the earlier stages. If the organisers of the Society were to develop a new type of community life they needed the support of the younger generation, which they could only get by providing adequate opportunities for the development appropriate to its needs.

A conflict of ideas

The overwhelming influence of the industrial tradition of the Eastern Valley on every sphere of life has been described above. Employment, social life, and ideas formed a comprehensive system, even though constant tensions existed within the system between some activities and ideas such as those associated with trade-unionism. Political ideas — far less influential in this area than syndicalist ones — did not form a new system of thought independent of industrialism. The thought system then current was rooted in the tradition of mining.

Since the basis of the whole structure, i.e. employment in the mine, had been withdrawn, the whole system had lost its balance. There were still habits of thought well established in the minds of the working men, which did not fit to the new social reality, and yet were not abandoned at once. The power of habit which is — as Karl Marx said — stronger than the power of arms, ruled at least to the same degree in the sphere of ideas as in that of outward behaviour. Thought projected towards the future has its roots in, and is determined by, experience of the past. Hence the great difficulty in conceiving something new.

If, however, a new concept is developed, there remains the difficulty of applying it in the existing social situation. Traditional features as expressed, for example, in social conventions, hinder the application of a new concept. This difficulty is widely experienced and leads to more or less conscious conflicts. Those whose ideas and whose formal power of thought is highly developed exhibit this lacuna between ideas and behaviour just as well as individuals who live an almost entirely practical life.

This type of conflict — although the individual was quite unconscious of its character — showed itself in a dramatic way in one of the miners in the Eastern Valley. The view that lying is one of the fundamental evils of misery on Earth, was set forth one afternoon in a long and vivid discussion by a working miner. The discussion started on race problems, went over to the principles of Christianity, included a short recital of the Sermon on the Mount and resulted finally in condemning lies as the source of all misery in the world. The miner, who was also a lay preacher, professed to have vowed his life to the fight for these principles. It was then about 7 p.m. and I had to stop the discussion because of a promise to take care of some small children whose parents wanted to go to the cinema. 'Oh no', said the miner, 'you must not go just in the middle of a conversation. You'll tell them that I suddenly fell ill and being at home quite by myself, you could not leave me.' Although there was not more than an interval of two minutes between the discussion on lies and this suggestion, it did not occur to the speaker that he himself in real life did not stick to his principles.

Times of social instability and economic change tend to increase conflict of this type; its frequent occurence in the Eastern Valley might therefore have been expected. Three different economic systems existed there at the same place and the same time: the then current employment system, sanctioned by tradition and therefore most effective; the system (if it may be so called) of long-term unemployment, and the system of the SPS. Each of these influenced the outlook of the men in the valley in a special and different way. The conflict which thus arose will be dealt with here under a few headings only.

First, the conflict was between behaviour and ideas. An illustration of this was the fact that many of the SPS members who claimed to be Socialists and to be against the privileges acquired by birth felt an inhibition in addressing the organisers by their first names, as they wished to be addressed. One of the men said: 'The scheme can't work if an organiser allows everybody to address him as "Jim". Somebody must have the authority. If they all would say "Mr. F.", the whole scheme would be better.'

Eventually a new form of behaviour finds justification through a new development in thought, so that the conflict becomes a conflict of ideas. Equality was the slogan on which the trade unions and the political parties had fixed their minds. It has already been mentioned that the members' ideas of equality were determined by the industrial experience of their work in the pit. Ideas, thus determined, influenced their outlook on, and their expectation level of, the future.

'What the whole world needs to make equality possible and general is more unselfishness'; this was the essence of many conversations about the world situation. Asked to express in a more concrete way what the result of 'more unselfishness' would have been, they said: 'Everybody who works will get the same.' By the 'same' they did not mean the same amount of money, but the same sort of treatment in relation to their capacities. This was explained and proved by their belief in a sliding wage scale as the expression of equality.

All this was turned upside down by the practice of the SPS. Equality here was something totally different. The basis on which the individual received from the Society was not the amount of work put in by him but his needs. This system of taking into account the size of the family was also applied by the Unemployment Assistance Board. Pilgrim Trust (1938) drew public attention to the fact that this sometimes involved the paradoxical situation that unemployed men with large families were better off 'on the dole' than when employed. This arose because the UAB paid according to the individual's needs, in contrast to the normal wage system, which paid everybody according to their output irrespective of needs. There was, however, a difference in applying this system of equality to an allowance scheme and to a working process, because the first provided the minimum of existence not expecting any equivalent from the individual, whilst the latter involved an amount of work to be put in voluntarily.

No wonder, then, that this sudden change from one idea of equality to another represented itself in the eyes of the members as 'inequality'. One man (62 years old) said: 'We are not all treated alike. X who has a big family gets out a real benefit from the scheme. I am alone with my missus and so we have not very much. Is it just?' Of course, it was just, if the new idea of equality based on production for use was acknowledged. This idea had never been explained to the members of the SPS and therefore no consent to it had been given; had this been attempted, however, there would probably have arisen much opposition to it. One of the blacksmith group expressed this opposition quite unequivocally and definitely: 'I want to get the money which corresponds to my earning power and do with it what I like. We are brought up in this system and this is what we want.' The industrial idea of equality naturally took into account the special capacity of a man because the profit made out of human labour depended on his capacity. But the workers had realised that some capacities were due to higher level of education, which they could not reach because of the social standing of their parents. Therefore they had always resented the fact that types of work which demanded a special education should be better paid than types of work in which the individual could show his capacity independently of the socially determined factor of his education, Not what a man *knew* but what he *did* ought to have been the basis for the amount of money he was able to make. Resentment against the better wages of office workers was a result of this attitude. This found its expression in the frequent remarks of the manual workers in the SPS against the workers in the office group. A man (48 years old) working in the quarry said: 'I believe in sliding wage scales. That's the only way of equality I can think of. It is not fair that I am getting only the same benefit as a member working in the office, where they are doing practically nothing.' This man apparently thought that it was unequal to have the same standard for manual and non-manual workers. He wanted the manual workers to have a privileged position over the others. It was interesting to notice that those who stressed the point of sliding wage scales, or of special concessions for doing more work than others, were always able bodied and in possession of their full strength. None of the old men was in favour of such a system in the SPS.

The dissatisfaction with the form of equality or inequality in the SPS had frequently found expression and had compelled the organisers to make some compromise with the ideas of the members. The compromise was embodied in the system of giving special concessions either to individuals or to a whole work group. There was another influence which made it almost impossible to avoid this compromise; namely the tradition of special concessions in normal industrial life. Every bakery in the world realises that it would be against human nature to make bakers buy at the normal price the loaves of bread they have produced. To attempt this would only encourage pilfering; and a kind of pilfering which is not only difficult to control but would be easily justified. Therefore bakers generally receive what they need for themselves gratuitously or for a reduced amount. Those unwritten and never discussed traditional rights of special groups of workers were as already indicated, a main source of the special concessions granted in the SPS. These had not been limited to working groups, but had also been given to individuals, and had naturally created a new source of dissatisfaction amongst those who, for one reason or the other, did not participate in such privileges.

The following were some of the concessions and compensations in the SPS. Carpenters were allowed to use fragments of timber for their own purposes; bakers had for a long period received a free loaf of bread daily; now and again an individual got working clothes, or a member had been allowed to pay his bill later than the others; specially long working hours before Christmas had been rewarded by additional supplies of food, and so on. A member strongly opposed to this system of granting concessions said: 'If others get special concessions, one is inclined to get them too. I tell you frankly, that's what I am trying all the time. But it is wrong, it ought not to be.' Very often the opposition against special concessions was the result of not sharing those privileges. This was very clearly expressed by one of the blacksmiths, who said: 'Special compensations ought to be stopped. They get extra food in the kitchen and in the stores. I can't eat my iron.' His criterion of equality was work done; he was against special concessions, which were not given because of the particular amount of work a man put in. But this view was, as his way of expression showed, the direct consequence of not having been able to 'eat his iron'. There is no doubt that he would have been in favour of concessions if he had been a member of the kitchen group. The discussion on limestone burning has already been mentioned. Here they all agreed that special concessions would be in place. 'It is not fair to expect me to do the limestone burning without putting me on the standard of an earning man. There are differences in work, there must be differences in benefit.' Another man, who in private discussions two days before a general meeting had emphatically argued for more unselfishness among the members, was asked at this meeting to take over a new type of work: 'What sort of compensations do you offer for this?' was the first reaction. Another man said: 'I am a Socialist and I agree with the principle of equality. But first I am a realist. And so I want to get out of the scheme as much as I can.'

A few of the men generalised their demands for special concessions without reference to their personal advantage. This procedure showed how general ideas were developed through consciousness of individual needs. One man said: 'I would suggest giving a special benefit for those who put more work in than the others, because you have to encourage people.'

It seems to be necessary to distinguish two types of equality: the first may be called 'functional equality', meaning that equality is a function of the need of an individual or of a family. It seems that most of the members preferred work as the basis of equality rather than needs.

The second type may be called 'formal equality', meaning that everyone should be treated alike, in some or every respect. This is the well known point-of-view of many children who justify their actions by saying: 'But John did it too, so why shouldn't I?' knowing very well that what

John did was wrong. In the SPS this attitude was met, for example, in the case of the man, who while opposed to concessions, tried to get as many as possible for himself, because the others did it. This attitude was specially frequent when the question arose as to how much work to put into the SPS. One of the brickmakers objected to the tempo of a fellow worker in the following way: 'Don't work so quick; we are not going to have a better dinner if we do more than the others.' Again and again a member would say: 'Oh, I would put in all my strength, if the others would do the same'; or 'If all would pull the same string, we could produce more. Why should I do more than the others?'

The men who had to fetch their allowance or old age pension in the morning on a particular day each week were officially permitted to start work at 11 a.m. on that day. One of these, who lived next door to the Employment Exchange, got his money at 9 a.m., brought it home at 9.10 and then sat down to have a smoke. An observer could tell by his look that he did not feel comfortable. The fire was not yet warm enough, his wife was moving about cleaning the table and making a noise; indeed this man never seemed to be comfortable in the presence of his wife who was his superior in every way. He stayed at home, however, on this day anxious not to be too early at the Brewery. His explanation was: 'They are all coming at 11 today. It is human nature to want always the same that others have'.

Whatever the truth may be about this view of 'human nature', such demands for formal equality had great force at the time of the investigation. Any experiment which neglected them would have had to fight against tradition, many centuries old.

To alter traditions of thought is a most difficult task. That it could not be carried through without changing the conditions of life seems to be evident; but the ability to change the conditions of life seems to be dependent in some way on having already altered the traditions of thought. This vicious circle lies in the background of all discussions as to whether evolution or revolution is the right means to a better social order. The sociological problem involved was first formulated by Marx and since then has been discussed again and again in the form of violent opposition to his 'materialism' or just as violent affirmation of his basic idea as expressed in the sentence: 'social conditions determine consciousness'. (Das gesellschaftliche Sein bestimmt das Bewusstsein). Is the world changed by ideas or by social conditions and their development? Karl Mannheim in his *Ideology and Utopia* thought that Marx underestimated the function of ideologies in the social process. Marx's view in this matter was generally incompletely reported. Besides the sentence quoted above, Marx put a good part of his life's work into the task of developing in the circle of his friends and collaborators a different ideology in spite of the impossibility of changing their economic basis of life. He certainly was convinced that he could only succeed with a few persons of a particular disposition.

In the SPS were found some facts that illustrated this problem in an interesting way. The SPS represented a new organisation of production which was not accepted by all those who might have taken part in the experiment. Only about 17% of the unemployed men in the valley tried it; the membership in 1938 represented 8.9% of the possible membership. We can therefore infer that the members formed a group which for one reason or the other was more ready to overcome old traditions, at least in so far as they were willing to participate in something new. It has already been demonstrated that not all were able to grasp the ideology of the Society in spite of their altered behaviour. They had to be educated and this was done by their experience in the Society as well as by word of mouth, in discussions in the Society or outside. The many more unemployed men outside the SPS did not seem to be able or willing to alter their traditions so quickly.

Asked why they were not in the Society they either answered that the idea had never occured to them or that they were strictly against it. It is curious that many of these men were in great need of help; it is as if the lower the standard of living, the less were they able to take any steps to improve matters. In one particularly difficult case — a man of 35 years of age, seven years out of work, with three children aged five years, three years and 18 months old, and suffering from poverty aggravated by the housing conditions, when asked 'Why don't you join the scheme?' replied 'Do you think I ought to go? I never thought of that.' Asked why, he said it was not because of trade-unionism; he never cared for trade-unionism nor for politics. He had, however, heard the men at the Employment Exchange talk about the SPS in the sense that they feared the result of the experiment would be compulsory work for the allowance. One man told them that calculations proved that the average hourly wage in the Society equalled a third of a shilling an hour. They did not care to work for this.

These arguments — fear of compulsory work and calculations regarding the benefit in wages, were indeed the chief arguments against the SPS among the non-members. 'Cheap labour' — that was generally their first answer to the question of why they did not join the SPS. That they were doing still cheaper labour in picking coal for many hard and dangerous hours of work did not occur to them, no more than the fact that producing without private profit was something closely connected with their political and socialist principles as well as with the co-operative ideas, of which most of them were fervent adherents.

Many rumours about the SPS were spread by the non-members. One man did not join the SPS because 'if the scheme had not started the Government would have established a new industry in the Brewery.' Another man said: 'I am Labour, but one has to be fair towards the capitalists. And the scheme is not fair to the tradespeople.'

The conflict between ideas and behaviour was widespread. None of those who decried the SPS objected to sharing its benefits by buying

Society goods secretly. In the sphere of behaviour they realised the advantages of lower prices and better quality. In the sphere of ideas they made no link with this.

It was noted again and again that the women had a far simpler and more single minded attitude to the SPS than the men; they seemed less burdened by traditions and habits of thought. This may have been explained by their way of living, which bound them to the house and its interests. In the past they had had no opportunity to acquire fixed habits of thought in regard to trade-unionism and industrialism. They were, of course, not free from tradition; their home and family life was full of it. Yet it was a most important part of their traditions and habits of thought that everything was right that helped them to keep their homes going. From this point of view membership of the SPS fitted in quite naturally with their general outlook. There was no ideology in their minds preventing them from seeing the immediate economic advantage in the SPS.

The influence of habits of life and thought was again clearly seen in the attitude of the members towards the Society, regarding building a village for SPS members. The suggestion that the building of new houses should be one of the activities of the SPS had arisen on various grounds. First of these were the housing conditions in which many of the members lived; new houses would have made a very great change for the better in their living conditions. Second was the advantage of concentrating the members round their work centre; this would have developed a closer social contact within the membership of the Society, and would also have effected a saving both by cutting down transport expenditure at once and also by making selling and pilfering more difficult than it was at the time.

The far-reaching influence of living right by the workplace was illustrated by the behaviour of one man, who joined the SPS two years before the study began, when he lived 6 miles away. He had joined because his wife had made him do so; he himself had been reluctant and full of suspicion. He was late every morning and his work was slow and poor. With the help of the SPS a house had been found for him that reduced the distance between home and workplace from six miles to next to nothing. Subsequently he became one of the best members of the SPS. He had become a group leader, he understood how to make his group work, and — still more important in this connection — he himself worked steadily and with pleasure, even outside the regular hours of work. Being always on the spot had given him so strong a link with his work that he could not have done more for it if it were his private concern. He was wholeheartedly in favour of the village scheme.

The attitude of the members to that scheme was not uniform. In general those living in very inconvenient houses were in favour. One family living in an overcrowded old house said 'we are looking forward very much to the new village.' 'It is like a new Utopia', the wife said.

There were some others to whom the idea of the village appealed because their houses had become too large for them after their children had grown up. They were quite few in number. For some members again there was no ideological problem, the only question for them was the amount of the rent. A fairly large group was opposed to the idea of living in the proposed SPS community for reasons connected with their whole outlook, habits, and attitude towards the Society. One of these declared: 'I never would care to go to the village. I have discussed it with my missus, and we agree that it would mean giving yourself as a whole into the hands of the organisers. I always have loved my independence more than anything else.' Another said: 'I think in such a village there would not be enough variety; especially if there are only older men. You can't start a new life with old men. And younger men could not very well go because they are liable to take a job through the Exchange. It would be only possible by a special arrangement with the Government. And I personally would not care for a Government scheme.'

Many of them were repelled by the exclusiveness of such a village and its long distance from other communities if it were built at Llandegveth. Thus: 'I do not believe in the idea of the village at Llandegveth, nobody would like to live three miles from the bus.'

Frequently they showed signs of a probably unconscious fear of community life and they expressed this attitude in very strong terms indeed: 'I am against this village. It gives me the idea of imprisonment. And besides there certainly will be no end of work. One of three men who are living in the three new houses already built at Llandegveth complained to me, because he had to come and work at the call of the organisers. Even in the evenings and at night.' It should be mentioned that this man added: 'But the scheme is good. I hope it will go on.' He was one of those who needed time to make up their minds. In spite of having been unemployed for four years, having had two children and having got no help from relations, he had joined the Society only during 1937.

One of the Communists in the SPS found an argument against the village scheme that was especially interesting in a Communist, because it showed so clearly a break between the two lines of thought he was trying to follow; one concerned the future, the other the present; one in favour of collectivism, the other quite individualistic. He said: 'I would not like to live together with the other men, neither now on the farm, nor later on in the village. One wants to have something private, something that belongs to you and with which nobody else can interfere.'

Even some of those whose home conditions were bad did not want the village scheme. One of the most active members of the SPS, who lived in a house much too small for his large family, declared that he would never go to the village. 'We would lose contact with the world. And what about the children and their future there? We would hate this uniformity of life. The wife likes to go shopping. We all like to take the bus now and again. In a village as they imagine it, all this would be impossible.'

In conclusion it may be suggested that there was only one way to overcome those conflicts of ideas, and to adjust the thoughts of the members to the new economic situation in which they were working, namely by a general educational process, which would first have enabled them to see the dependence of their old outlook on industrialism and then expounded the new ideas. This process would have encouraged them to discuss these ideas and prove their validity by daily practice in their work. It may be doubted whether such an educational process could have been successful with older unemployed men; and it could only have been accomplished by teachers who reshaped their own outlook completely and without compromise.

It could not be said at the time of the study that all those who held responsible positions in the SPS fulfilled these requirements. For this and other reasons the basic ideas of the Society were never clearly expressed nor were they openly and purposely put into practice. No doubt so far as these basic ideas were actually embodied in the practice of the Society they would eventually have influenced the outlook of those taking part in it; but this would certainly have been a very slow process.

Group organisation in the SPS

The organisation of the membership of the SPS as a collection of working groups developed almost from the beginning of the Society as a consequence of the separation into different departments of the various types of work undertaken. These working groups, however, had at first no recognised social function within the Society. This stage lasted for only a short time, while the members were few in number and every question that arose could be discussed easily with the organisers by the whole body of workers either at the common meal or on various other occasions. The comparative isolation of the more remote plots may have, from the first, produced a greater social cohesion in the groups working there.

With the growth of the membership new problems arose. The daily face-to-face contact of all the members at the Brewery disappeared and the possibility of getting an informal general consent to the proposals and actions of the organisers ceased to exist. How far the working groups had by this time developed any marked social cohesion could not be discovered by the investigator at the time of the field work, nor was it possible to do more than speculate as to the pattern or model that such social cohesion as already existed tended to follow. It may well have been the pattern in the mines known through practice by many of the members of the working groups, a pattern itself possibly derived from older groupings in the days when mining was a small scale handicraft and a mine was worked by five or six men, or less.

It has already been mentioned that the members — or at least a few among them — showed an inclination to obtain some say in the working of the Society — not only by occasional conversation with one or other of the organisers but by achieving official recognition of their right to put forward ideas and criticism. It is probable that the model followed here, consciously or unconsciously, was that of the trade union; from this would naturally have arisen the suggestion of an election of group leaders who were supposed to meet the organisers regularly for discussion. Further, the idea that groups undertaking different types of work should each elect a representative to deal, in the name of the group, with the organisers, seemed to have a good deal in common with that of 'shop' organisation under shop stewards to deal with the owners or managers of a factory.

The proposal for the election of group leaders was accepted. Each group, however, already had an instructor who, though not a member of the Society, had a leading position by virtue of his economic status (being a regularly paid man) and by special skill. As the organisers had been especially careful to put men or women with a sense of social responsibility in these positions, these instructors frequently had the will and the ability to undertake the social functions that might have been performed by a group leader. In appointing them the organisers also had in mind that, where possible, they should be persons who understood, and were in sympathy with, the ideas underlying the SPS. It was, however, not possible to find such persons for all the departments; and it may be suggested that in this respect the organisers were attempting to find an unusual combination of gifts. They saw clearly that the performance of two distinct functions was required to carry out their ideas to the full. Technical knowledge and skill must be available, and also sympathetic knowledge of ideas and power to communicate them. Had their views been carried out systematically, it would have been necessary to separate these functions and place them in the hands of different persons.

Turning now to group life in the SPS, as observed in the course of the field work, it did not show any clearly established pattern. There were groups in which the instructor had never been replaced as social leader by the elected group leader; there were other groups where the instructor played no part at all in the social life of the group. In some of the departments the workers had formed a group, in some of them not. There were great varieties in the degree of social cohesion and group consciousness. The role of the leading personality of the group, and the outstanding features of these personalities, differed from one department to another.

Social cohesion was specially strong among the bakers, the boot repairers, and the old men doing the farm work at Beili Glas; it was specially weak among the flour-mill workers, the tailors, and the kitchen workers.

The group pride of the bakers was enormous. Practically every member of this group took occasion to tell outsiders confidentially that 'the bakers are the best group of the whole lot'. They kept together as a group in the most complete manner. This seemed to be due to various factors; first, they were deeply convinced that they were doing the most important job for all the others by producing the daily bread. They had dinner separately from the others in the bakery, because the change from this very warm room to the colder canteen for half an hour would have been unwholesome. This common meal of the eight bakery workers without any interference from the outside established a specially close contact. Many questions of a personal and general nature were discussed by all during this private dinner time. Further, they had the advantage of having as an instructor a man whom they all respected because of his knowledge of his craft and ability to communicate this knowledge to them. They had also been fortunate in their choice of group leader. He was a man with full understanding of the ideas of the SPS who had a strong sense of social responsibility and was also a capable worker. It was difficult to decide whether the personal influence of these two men, or the love for and sense of the value of their work shown by all the workers, or the exclusive formation of the group, was the more decisive in developing social cohesion. It was certain that the combination of these three factors had created group pride and consciousness to a very high degree, and this was even strong enough to survive the loss of some members of the group and coming in of new men.

The reason for the strength of the group consciousness in the boot repairers group seemed to be different. Their work and the ideas of the SPS played a much smaller part in it. They were formally united by the common purpose of repairing shoes but they had substituted another purpose as their real basis of union. As one of its members the group had a man of outstanding personality, to whom all the others looked up, and whose influence upon the rest of the group was enormous. He was the effective link in the group, an interesting personality with many of the qualities of a real and good leader, although he had others which prevented him from undertaking leadership on a larger scale.

The extremely good atmosphere of comradeship and group feeling developed by the influence of this man brought the members to discuss personal matters as well as principles. So far-reaching was their interest in these discussions that they often interrupted their work to gather round the fire to talk and listen. There was only one man in the group who seemed a little removed from the others. They all objected very much to his going on with his work and thus making a noise, whilst they were speaking about the deepest problems of life.

There was a remarkable difference between them and the bakers' group, where Conservatives and Socialists were in friendly contact with one another. In the boot repair group they declared at the first opportunity: 'Here we are all Socialists and trade unionists'. One might have been justified in speaking of a group ideology, developed under the influence of a leader. It was difficult to speak to one of the members alone, because everybody took part in every dicussion. They shared a common dinner in the canteen but rarely mixed with members of other groups. So close and well established was their social cohesion that they did not object at all to a member of their group not working or being late.   Such discussions as the 'equality discussion' mentioned in a previous section, could never have occurred in this group. Whilst the bakers' group was chiefly a work group, thus keeping its original unifying purpose, the boot repairers were certainly a group of disciples gathered round a leader; a number of less conscious elements which tended to become stronger than the conscious unifying purpose held them together.

A third type of group was represented by the old men working at the farm at Beili Glas. To begin with, they had not always been a group of old men, that is to say a group of men more than 60 in average age. At the time of the study, however, most of the younger men had left the group and the remaining members considered this an advantage. Their attitude towards younger men was prejudiced. 'What is wrong with the scheme', one of them said, 'is the young men there. They are discontented with everything, and they are pilfering.' Another man who was particularly proud to be a member of this group said: 'The younger men did not fit in with us. They did not work. Now they are away and the group is very nice indeed.'

Their age determined their way of working; their tempo was naturally rather moderate, they gave themselves many intervals. They did work, however; work may have meant that they felt younger again, that they were keen on proving to each other and to themselves that they were still able to work. They did not exaggerate this part of their group life; they did what was necessary, taking plenty of time for each job, and yet one could rely on everything being done in the course of time. There was another factor working for social cohesion in this group: their little hut had a hearth in the middle, the teakettle was always boiling and benches stood round the fire. Here they sat when the weather was too bad for work, or whenever nothing particular had to be done. Here they waited in the morning for those who were late — they would have thought it unfair to start without them — smoking their pipes, preparing their tea, speaking about life and work, about their children, about accidents in the pit, and so on. Now and again they discussed the SPS, but only if there was a special reason for this. Their group leader was the youngest of the group, a man of 43, whose outstanding quality was his perfect joy in life, which never seemed to leave him. He laughed, joked, made fun, was liked by everybody and liked everybody, without being a leader in thought — like the boot repairer described above. Their group-pride was well developed, and sometimes even excessive. 'We are a happy lot here'; 'If everybody would work as we old men, the scheme would be better off. But look at the other groups, they don't.' They were enormously pleased when the instructor of the building group told them one day that he would be happy to have them work at the slaughter house which had then been begun but which was making very poor progress. So strong was their group feeling that they all thought it quite natural if one of them took home potatoes or vegetables, in spite of the fact that they often complained about pilfering going on in other departments. This attitude found its indignant expression in what one of them said one day: 'Young X is becoming impudent lately. Just now he saw Y taking a few potatoes. He wanted me to stop it. Now I ask you: what's the harm in an old man's taking some potatoes?' Their group feeling was certainly stronger than any moral rules; they understood each other and were ready to justify anything that one of their group may have done. Norms were only applied to the world outside, beginning with the other groups. It was clear that group building factors here were still less conscious than in the boot repairing group.

Of these three types of group the first — the conscious working group of the bakers — was the best in the Society from the point of view of reliability. The boot repairers' group would have been excellent for the Society if the leader had completely adopted its idea, which was not the case. The third type certainly received more from the SPS than it had to give to it.

There were also departments which had not succeeded in forming a group with noticeable social cohesion. Those working in the flour-mill lacked the regular face-to-face contact with each other, because their work placed them on different floors of the mill, two on each. They had no instructor and their group leader was not much interested in the SPS. Their work was spread over the same number of hours as that of the other groups, but for technical reasons there were long intervals in which there was nothing at all to do; even if they had wished they could not have kept busy without interruption for long periods at a time. They had no experience of a common effort in which all took part at once. It seemed to be this absence of team work that was chiefly responsible for their failure to become conscious of a common purpose and to acquire social cohesion. The lack of the other more or less unconscious group building factors, mentioned above, was also notable.

That regular face-to-face contact does not form a sufficient condition for establishing a group with social cohesion may be shown by a short analysis of two more groups which, in spite of their members working together in one room all the time, did not develop anything comparable to the cohesion of the bakers, the boot repairers, or the farm group.

The kitchen group had a group leader who was chosen because no one else wanted to take the job. This was in itself evidence of lack of group spirit; in some of the other departments the position of group leader was sought after and much jealousy was displayed in connection with it.

Nothing of this kind happened in the kitchen; the group leader very rarely showed himself. The instructor did all the difficult types of work; the ordinary work of the group was cleaning potatoes and vegetables and washing up. One of the members was feeble-minded and was exposed to much teasing and many bad jokes from some of the members of the group. This common activity might have established some group feeling — the common purpose lying in teasing this man — if it had not been that two of the members kept apart from it and even tried to stop it. The instructor of this group always dined at a separate table; this placed a certain distance between the group and the instructor. There was no leading personality among the men, no great interest in their common work, or of any other kind. The members were of all ages. It was interesting to note that a kind of group feeling suddenly developed amongst them on a special occasion; but the occasion was one that must be regarded as unfortunate from the point-of-view of the Society. One day the cooks had eaten several puddings which ought to have been kept for general use. The instructor happened to discover it and showed annoyance. In a moment the attitude of the members became that of a closed group, like a group of schoolboys. They did not justify themselves, they stood and looked at each other understandingly, grinning faintly in remembrance of the common pleasure of eating forbidden fruits.

The building group provided another example of the sudden development of a strong temporary cohesion by the substitution of another purpose for the recognised purpose of the group. One day, when five or six members of the building group came at 11 a.m. instead of at 9.30, they were refused their usual free dinner tickets. The other members who were working at the slaughter house knew nothing of this. Suddenly, however, they saw a small group of men approach, coming forward slowly with their hands in their pockets, in the determined attitude that workers usually assume when they have agreed to go on strike. An uneasiness made itself felt; voices became very low; two or three of the men already at work began to whisper with one another not knowing whether or not they ought to join this 'strike'. The attitude of this group to the five late-comers was one of the strongest expressions of group spirit in the SPS ever noted by the investigator.

The tailors were another group without any social cohesion. The group leader was a man who had made up his mind to undertake this function after all the others had been asked but had refused to do so. He did not care at all for the task and thought he had got rid of the matter by having permitted his election. He did not take part in the group leaders' meetings because 'I am against useless talking'. In his department each member worked at his own machine, independently of the others. The two instructors of the group, a man and a woman, worked very hard themselves; so much so that they had no time to take part in the group life or to influence it, let alone initiating fresh development. The department received a considerable number of 'visitors', that is to say members who left their own group for half an hour or more to go about in the Brewery and talk with the others. They seemed to be especially attracted by the tailors' department, where 18 visitors of this type were counted one morning. This may have been due in part to the pleasant manner of the woman instructor of the group. These visits, however, also helped to prevent the group from developing a common tie; there was less opportunity for this during the constant coming and going of outsiders.

In summary, regular face-to-face contact seemed to establish a disposition towards social cohesion and group feeling but did not inevitably develop it. Even if a group were organised purposely in that way it need not develop real cohesion.

There was one group in the Society — the office group — which showed a strong social cohesion and which at first sight might have been taken for a group having developed similarly to other departments, because of the frequent face-to-face contacts among its members. Closer observation, however, led to the discovery that another factor was responsible for bringing and holding this group together; this factor was the special function of the group in the whole Society. The outward evidence of social cohesion was the following: the group not only sat together as other groups did in the canteen but had managed to secure a separate small table of their own instead of using the large tables. They were all better dressed than the other members because they had no manual work to do, their hands were always clean. If you talked to them you would always hear something like: 'we from the office'. What they were proud of was that they 'know what is going on in the scheme'; they saw the weekly accounts of each member; they knew who paid his bill regularly and who did not, they knew the personal details about each member and could easily find out — if they cared to — if someone consumed more than the needs of his own household. This knowledge gave them a feeling of superiority, which was strengthened by the process of their selection. The organisers selected people for this job who were able to handle figures and make calculations. When somebody was asked to join the office group it was generally stressed in talking with him that his intelligence was highly thought of. Valuation by the organisers probably reinforced valuations already present in the minds of members as a result of early school education with its emphasis on formal intellectual achievement. The 'superiority' of this group was even acknowledged by other members.

The members of the office group therefore enjoyed a general prestige, but they had to pay for this by giving up something else. This was made clear by one very significant event: One day, during the investigator's work in the carpentry group, a member of the office group came into the room. He lingered about taking up each tool and looking with eyes full of envy at the working carpenters. He began to talk: 'This is the finest job in the whole Brewery.' 'Then why don't you work here?' he was asked.

'Well, you see, when I joined the scheme I wanted to become a carpenter, but the organisers told me to join the office group, because I am intelligent enough to do that sort of work.' He was asked: 'But, why don't you change now if you like it so much better?' He answered: 'Now I am used to the office work and the other chaps would perhaps think it was a step backwards if I were to shift now.'

Here the sacrifice made in exchange for social prestige became clear: the abandoned joy in manual work. The little episode illustrated the mutual attitude of manual and non-manual workers; the manual workers generally got more satisfaction out of their work, but they were jealous of the social prestige of the non-manual workers; this produced a kind of feeling of inferiortiy in them. The non-manual workers were full of envy because they missed the satisfaction that manual work could have provided for them. To overcome their feeling of dissatisfaction they overstressed their social position in a way that generally led to a widening of the gap between both types of workers. The obvious solution of this conflict situation would have been to find men who were 'born' clerks, and thus would have gained satisfaction in handling accounts instead of from the accessory advantages of office work. Such men seemed to be rare in the Eastern Valley, especially amongst men who had been miners for many years.

The gap between the office group and the rest of the membership was a small scale example of the problems arising from the growth of a bureaucracy which always tends to become a separate social class owing to its distinct social function. There were also some signs in the Society that the miniature bureauracy aimed to increase its influence and power, which again was a consequence of the growing importance of its functions in relation to the whole Society.

This 'class attitude' of the office group in the SPS was, however, less marked than the class attitude of the organisers and of the instructors, as a group; for these combined with their official positions in the Society definite economic advantages. The instructors — skilled workers, who knew the job — were paid at normal trade union rates and thus lived on an economic basis quite different from that of the membership. They generally enjoyed respect on account of their superior ability and knowledge in the process of production. This attitude of respect was mixed with envy and jealousy, first because they were better off than the members, and second because of their attitude. Although they were selected with an eye to their social qualities, some of them preserved an attitude (which would have been far more outspoken in many men following the same crafts) of craftman's pride, which prevented some of them from communicating their knowledge to the members. This attitude, however, seemed to be less marked than some of the members asserted. Again and again a member would say — confidentially — that the instructor was afraid to lose his job and therefore did not communicate all his knowledge to them. Although this consideration played, at least consciously, only a very small part in the minds of the instructors themselves, the contrast between their economic situation and interests and the position of the ordinary member existed, and served to make the instructors a separate group. This group, however, was not formally organised. Any social cohesion that existed among the instructors was developed through informal meetings and talks amongst them and through consultations between them and the organisers.

Now and again the existence of paid instructors was openly criticised and resented by the members. 'There shouldn't be paid hands, it is against the spirit of the scheme', some of them said repeatedly.

On the other hand, some of the active members had open or secret aspirations towards becoming paid themselves. It was a common reaction among those who failed to see a solution of the problems of their class to wish to escape into a more privileged class — in this case into the group of paid instructors. Another factor which operated here was the impossibility in the SPS of offering an improvement in the standard of living for the future.

No study of the group system within the SPS could have neglected the group of organisers. This group was small in number and was not formally organised. Its social cohesion depended on the close face-to-face contacts of its members, but also on their having much in common in education, tradition, and social outlook. Its place in the Society was, of course, supremely important. With it lay the initiative in new activities and the responsibility and final decision in every important matter. Its members had an economic, educational and cultural level high above that of the membership. These differences in function and standards were felt by the membership to exist and were more or less consciously resented by them.

There was a genuine desire and effort on the part of the organisers to overcome class distinctions between themselves and the unemployed. Yet it would have been foolish to pretend that those distinctions did not continue to exist; indeed there seemed to be small chance of their abolition within the SPS. Although the social atmosphere in the Society was certainly different from the atmosphere in a normal industrial undertaking, habit and outlook due to class distinctions were deeply fixed on both sides. Among the men they found expression in occasional hostile remarks, of which the most frequent one was: 'They do not know us, they are outsiders.'

Thus, analysis of the group structure in the SPS showed two different types; a) groups whose composition was fixed by economic status and social class which, just as in normal life, combined with these features a special central function in the Society; b) groups of workers which were remarkable because of the variety of internal structure that they revealed.

Having no vital economic importance for the life of their members, they presented themselves as groups similar to clubs, voluntary societies, and other leisure time organisations. The special character of each group was to a large degree determined by the leading personality. Whether they tried to maintain a common outlook in accordance with the ideas of the SPS was left more or less to the chance of the leader being sufficiently interested in the Society and influencing the members of his group in a positive sense.

It was no mere chance that these two types were found in the organisation of the Society; they were, in effect, complementary to one another. Power and responsibility rested with the first group, though they had no marked economic control over the lives of the members. If the contrary had been the case, the members would probably have organised for protection against the superior group. As it was, they felt no pressure and their group organisation therefore took the freer 'leisure time' form described.

Incentives to work

In normal industrial life, and specially in areas where one type of industry predominates, employment has a central and basic influence on every aspect of life. This influence, as felt in the Eastern Valley, has been described above. The knowledge that everything — all personal and social affairs, all good and bad experiences — could be referred back to the main occupation, created a complex social atmosphere in which the employment rhythm mastered all others. This atmosphere — penetrated by conscious and unconscious forces — embodied as it were the main incentives to be employed; and so strong was its effects that hardly anyone tried to withdraw from it and find another job environment.

An abstract analysis could, of course, find several isolated incentives to labour in this complex atmosphere. Such isolated incentives, however, tended to look different in isolation from their apperance when seen in their social context. Yet three incentives with a very definite character could be distinguished: the economic, the social, and the technical. Their relation to each other was very close; but in normal industrial life they were not coordinated: the economic incentive was of primary importance.

It seemed clear that in the course of the economic decline in the Eastern Valley the employment atmosphere underwent a change; conversations with workers who knew the periods of great prosperity always suggested this strongly. While the most important feature during a boom was pleasure of earning good money — implying a higher standard of living, more social acitivities, more variety in types of pleasure and amusement — the chief feature during a slump was economic pressure and continuous threat of unemployment. At such times constant anxiety for the future created a depressed social atmosphere, but did not alter the main incentives to have a job except by overemphasis on the economic incentive.

In good and bad times, the amount of money earned stood in the foreground; so much so, that any joy in the work process or any antipathy to it was only secondary as an incentive or hinderance.

Such a social atmosphere was in complete contrast to that developed by the work situation in the SPS. The occupation of the members there did not form the economic basis of their lives, which continued to be the unemployment allowance. The discontinuation of their activities in the Society was therefore not of vital importance to them. This was the outstanding difference between the SPS and any work scheme for the unemployed where the individual stood or fell by the results of his efforts.

The social atmosphere of the SPS was therefore not primarily a work atmosphere. This accounts for the fact that the majority of the members thought and spoke about their occupations not in terms of work but rather in terms of a pastime or a recreation. Besides the fact that the Society did not provide an economic basis of life, it offered no scale for measuring the value of a member to the community according to the work he put in; for there was no relation between the amount of work done and the amount of benefit. Further, there was no effective control of his efforts, of which either the individual or his fellows could be conscious. There was no grading of workers so as to distinguish between good, bad, and indifferent; there was no boss or manager by whose valuation of a member a money scale of value might be to some extent replaced. The individual had no hope of getting into a better position if he worked harder or better. Thus, all these more obvious and external factors which formed incentives to work during normal employment were eliminated. This situation had, at least one great advantage: it gave freedom for the appearance of less obvious incentives, and therefore permitted an investigation of whether or not such incentives existed or could be developed for men who had had a lifetime's experience of industrialism followed by several years of unemployment.

Such an investigation was important from the view point of the organisers of the Society; it had been their working hypothesis that a complete lack of compulsion would release the creative urge to work, which had until then been suppressed by the mechanical rhythm of normal industrialism, operating under motives of economic gain.

This lack of compulsion produced, however, as the first obvious reaction a certain irregularity in attendance at work. The few existing regulations asked a minimum of work from the members. Indeed, they did not even ask for a fixed amount of work, but only for an attendance of 30 hours a week. If a member did not keep this rule, he was still treated in just the same way as the others for a long time. I found that in an average week of five days that the 183 men working in the Brewery and at Beili Glas had an attendance of 696 days (76%) out of a possible 915; that meant that 139 members coming regularly would have put in the same number of working days. For the whole year of 1937 the loss of days over the whole membership amounted to 21%.

Allowance had to be made, however, for the fact that these figures as they stood, could not be compared with the attendance in normal industry. The composition of the membership was different from that of the personnel of a colliery. It included a high percentage of older men who had been unemployed for a period of six years on average, and who were having to get used to a new type of work at an advanced age.

If the intensity of work of those who did attend was considered, the Society compared still less favourably with normal industry. This was partly because the members did not care to work with their whole strength, partly because there was not always enough work to do for everyone in every department. The storekeepers, for example, said that when doing all they were supposed to do they still had about two hours out of their six hours per day in which they had no work. Those two hours did not form a single long interval, they were spread over the whole working day. This discontinuity in work created an atmosphere of leisure which was not easy to overcome when there was suddenly some work to do. It soon became a fixed habit with the members that there was no hurry over anything. Almost any small distraction was therefore sufficient to interrupt the continuity of work.

It was not always lack of work that was responsible for the slackness of the members. In many groups there was always something that could have been done; the weavers, for example, could generally have carried on without depending on any outside factor. At the time of the study they had nine members; their instructor who had had many years of experience in normal industrial life, believed that he could have achieved the same result as he was getting at that time with two paid hands. As there were some men in his group young enough to get the full benefit of the training given, some other factor must have been in operation to produce this lack of intensity.

The same held true for the group building the slaughter house. Twelve men were at work there under the supervision of two paid masons. The instructor said that he could have done the same amount of work without any of the members if he had had two more paid hands.

Other groups, however, gave a different impression: they worked intensively. The bakers for example, did not always keep to their regular dinner hour but postponed it voluntarily if there was still some dough to be moulded or bread to be taken out of the oven. Apparently the knowledge that the dough would have been spoilt or the bread burnt unless handled at the right time acted as an incentive. In other words, the work carried on in the bakery required a close and continuous adjustment between mechanical processes and human efforts, and the consequence of non-adjustment were at once obvious. Such work apparently exercised strong pressure upon individuals to maintain the required adjustment.

This incentive to work was, however, much more mechanical than the creative urge aimed at by the organisers. Individual inclination was not the effective incentive here but the rhythm of the work. Wherever such types of work existed in the Society the intensity of effort was higher than in those departments where conditions were different. It was notable that this kind of compulsion seemed to increase not only the intensity of effort but also joy in the working process.

I could not decide whether this result was due to a general human attitude or to a long period of training in normal industrialism. All the SPS members had had industrial experience, and there was no possibility of finding control cases in which this factor was absent. I can only state that, again and again, I had noticed that the existence of a mechanical rhythm exercising an external pressure proved to be an effective incentive to work.

One kind of work that was generally carried out with much reluctance and without any impulse of joy was the washing up of the dishes after the midday meal. Yet once, if the reports of all those who took part may be trusted, it became a fascinating and joyful occupation through application of a mechanical rhythm to the job. This happened at the big anniversary party given to all the members and their families. Six hundred people had to be served and all the dishes cleaned and put away within 40 minutes after the meal to make room for dancing. The organisation of this washing up was carefully thought out, everyone had his place and knew what to do. Work was carried out with a speed incredible to those accustomed to the normal tempo and everyone greatly enjoyed this period of intensive work.

There were, no doubt, exceptional situations or cases of emergency in which everyone submitted willingly to a work rhythm governed by external factors. These were, however, comparatively rare, and there were only a few types of work which showed a persuasive or compulsory rhythm like that of the bakery. The cloth was not spoilt if the weaver paused to smoke a cigarette, for each loom was geared separately to the electric motor and could be started or stopped at will by the weaver, who thus could decide for himself whether he worked continuously or not.

In brickmaking, the members worked in pairs at the hand-driven machine. Each pair was able to set its own pace. However another factor that made for intensity of work was demonstrated by the behaviour of one of the brickmakers. He was a man of 36, strong and able bodied. The first day at the brick making machine he restrained his fellow workers with the following words: 'Not so fast! We do not get a better dinner if we produce more'. Work was little more to him than avoiding getting bored by standing about. Some days later an insignificant event made him count how many bricks he had produced that day. The next day he counted again and found that he had produced in three hours as much as in five hours the previous day. Counting the bricks produced every day became a game for him. After a week the result was 520 bricks in three hours; before, it had been something like 200 a day. He had found a scale by which to measure his achievements: by this very simple means his intensity of work had considerably increased.

Such mechanical help from the outside would probably have been unneccessary for those who had a genuine interest in a particular job. This, however, was the case with only a few of the members; the others were dependent on some external factors, which unfortunately for the efficiency of the Society did not exist in every department.

In the Marienthal investigation into the effects of unemployment, it was found that the unlimited amount of leisure time enjoyed by the unemployed men prevented them from making any use of it. The behaviour of the brickmaker suggested that an unlimited amount of work raises the same difficulty, unless it is organised in some way.

Herein would have lain the importance of having a planned system of production, apart from the general economic importance of a plan in a large scale social experiment. Such a plan could have formed the basis of organisation for the work; it would have given a limited aim to be reached in a definite time, a direction for all efforts, and the satisfaction of completing each assigned task in turn. A plan, in fact, would have fulfilled two important social and individual functions: it would have brought a certain rhythm into the work and it might have replaced the system of evaluating a man according to the amount of money he made by an evaluation in accordance with his fulfillment of a plan. It certainly seemed as if the working out of a plan for each department of the SPS would have led to general improvement of the intensity of work.

It proved impossible to exactly measure the amount of work put in by each individual member of the Society because the individual output did not offer a suitable basis for comparison unless age and bodily fitness were taken into account. The output might have been the same if a man of 70 had put in all his strength or if a man of 30 had worked in a very leisurely way. The intensity of work depended not only on the rhythm of work and on the age factor, but also on the personal inclination a man had for his job. Every able bodied man, if he had had a free choice, might have found a type of work that interested him sufficiently to become the central activity of his life. The SPS might have provided unique opportunities for the exercise of such free choice by its members in many cases for the first time in their life, for normally, in the Eastern Valley, boys of 14 with no experience of work were compelled to take the job that was offered and later on the economic situation of the worker very rarely allowed for a fresh choice; they took what they could get.

The unemployed men joining the SPS were in a far better position than children leaving school; they already had experience of different types of work, and in the Society there was the possibility of realising their wishes to a greater extent, because the SPS gave them a choice among a large variety of different types of work. Yet, most of them, when asked their special inclination on joining the Society said that they were ready to take any job. If they expressed any special wishes, these were generally dictated by subsidiary motives. For example, one man wished to join a group where he had a friend, another a group which appealed to him because it worked indoors, or in other cases out of doors, and so on. Some preferred to take up work of which they happened to have previous experience; it was not possible to discover whether this previous experience had been gained by chance or by conscious choice. Now and again, however, one of the instructors or organisers gave time and attention to helping a man choose the kind of job that would give him personal satisfaction. Normally the needs of the organisation did not allow so careful a selection, although it would have been worthwhile in helping to make enthusiastic members of indifferent ones.

It is clear from what has been said above that neither common ideology nor a predilection for a particular kind of work was generally operative as an incentive to work in the SPS; a special inquiry was therefore made as to the incentives that were effective. A large amount of information was collected in about 100 individual cases. In each individual case there was, of course, a complex of incentives, and not a single one; however, three categories of incentives could be distinguished.

Technical incentives
Technical incentives were taken to be all those incentives which were in immediate relation to the work process or product. Such an appeal to work by the work itself had different aspects: 60% of the sample observed showed some degree of interest in their jobs; but this incentive was hardly ever isolated from other technical incentives, not to speak of economic and social ones. Interest in work was often an expression of the mere personal pleasure given by handling some material or tool. It was for some sublimated into an interest in the use which was to be made of the goods produced. This interest in the use as an incentive to work occurred only amongst those who had a developed sense of social relations. Frequently this incentive was effective only if a worker was producing for his own or his family's use; it operated, though with less effect, if he knew he was producing for an acquaintance or someone in the same local community. When, however, the relation between producer and consumer became anonymous, it was only consciousness of wider social relations that induced a man to work in the belief that his production would be of use to someone somewhere.

For 30% of the sample this consideration played a part in the complex of incentives to work. One such case was that of a boot repairer, who always took the children's shoes first, repairing them specially well to prevent the children getting wet feet on their way to school. In that case the technical interest in the product was combined with a social incentive. Something similar was noted in the case of the bakers, in whose work the symbol of the 'daily bread' played a great part. Their remarkable self-respect was due to their knowledge that they were producing something of good quality and also — a more social incentive — which was constantly used by everyone.

The last technical incentive to work was the organisation of the work process in accordance with certain compulsions inherent in the materials or machines. This incentive was effective for 38% of the sample, a figure which included almost 90% of all those who were taking part in work thus organised.

Economic incentive

It has been suggested that economic incentives are found to be most effective in normal industrial life. They could not operate in the same way and to the same degree in the SPS where no relation existed between the amount and quality of work done and the amount of personal benefit to the worker. Yet they played their part in the complex of incentives to work. The individual economic benefit a man drew from the SPS induced him to work, partly because the idea of an increase in the individual benefit, by an increased intensity of work, was strongly established in his mind. Sometimes this idea took the form of very vague hope that good work in the SPS may have led to a paid job there. Such a hope was not realisable for all those who shared it; and indeed all knew this very well, but merely through habit they continued to play with the idea; even when compelled to abandon this hope, they were still influenced by the incentive of individual benefit through their share of the products of the scheme. For 67% of the sample this incentive in one form or another played a part.

It was perhaps a sign of the strength of this incentive that many of the members restricted their activities by a very careful calculation so that they were able to avoid doing more than what they thought corresponded to the benefit they received.

There was still another economic consideration which formed an incentive to work: the desire to increase the total benefit available from the Society. This incentive operated with those who genuinely believed in the SPS and its economic possibilities. In 26% of the sample it played a part in making them work. Obviously social as well as purely economic incentives were involved.

Social incentives

Observations revealed three different kinds of social incentives operating in the SPS. The first was that sometimes a man worked because he was one of a team of working comrades, and would have felt himself out of the group unless he had worked. This social incentive was highly effective, because it prevented a man from yielding to every little personal indisposition or distraction. Work in the SPS groups in which this incentive operated kept a more regular tempo than any ividual working by himself. They continued the tradition of working in the mines, and brought something of the trade union atmosphere to the SPS. Such work groups had their organised pauses during work and strongly objected if anyone belonging to their group did not observe them. Less strongly but still with effect they objected to those who did not perform their share of the common work. Some types of work such as bricklaying and brickmaking, depended on collaboration. Whenever the opportunity arose in the Society for organising a work team, this worked much better in speed and effectiveness than a number of individuals working in isolation. For 34% of the sample, team work acted as an incentive to carry on and overcame their occasional inclination to do nothing.

Another social incentive that might have been of high importance was a common ideology. It has already been noted that this operated only with a minority of the members: 35% of the sample were found to work because they shared the common idea of the Society. If this percentage had been doubled, work would have been carried on in a very different way. Support for this was offered by some of the SPS members, who had reported that in Garndiffaith a 'community house' was to be built. The materials for this were provided by the Social Service Organisation; the work was carried out by four unemployed miners, three of whom happened to be members of the SPS. Although they got a certain benefit from the Society and none at all from work on the construction of the building, they put their strength and time wholeheartedly into the building of the club house — even time they were supposed to spend in the SPS. They were working for the idea.

It seemed therefore that the 'ideological' incentive in the Society did not operate side by side with the economic incentive. The workers in the Eastern Valley were obviously willing to do something in the service of ideas; but as soon as any question of the personal benefit arose, they fell back into the traditional attitude and began to worry about the amount of the benefit. Voluntarily they would have done many things; but for their own benefit, they wanted to have a choice and judge for themselves how much work this benefit was worth.

Most effective among the social incentives was the value of work in the SPS as a pastime; without it life would have been too monotonous. For 71% of the sample the strongest incentive in the whole social group was the wish to have a regular pastime. This wish could, of course, also have been satisfied by means other than work, e.g. by walking, discussions, games, etc. This explains why in the Society this incentive to work was often and easily turned into an incentive to do something else.

This analysis of the incentives to work in the SPS in isolation is not adequate, because none of them ever occured isolated as they appear here. Probably all of them were to a certain degree effective in each individual. The quantitative results given above are only useful in showing their relative influence on the whole of the membership at the time of the investigation. The technical incentives were more reliable in guaranteeing continuity of work; therefore any attempt to strengthen the incentives to work in order to increase the output of the SPS ought to have started with reorganisation of working conditions, for example, attempts to find the right type of work for each individual.

There were, however, other elements of the situation which paralysed some of these incentives. An exposition of these has been included here and there in the course of the whole chapter. Thus it was indicated that the conflict between traditions and new ideas prevented many members from putting their whole strength into the task. The organisers could have made their own task much easier and have increased the economic output by accepting traditional attitudes and habits; but the whole experiment would have lost much of its interest and value at once if they had done so.

In summarising these observations it must be said that it would not be fair to use them as a basis for a final judgement; they merely describe a real but changing situation. The development of the Society from the beginning had already gone a long way towards releasing the creative urge to work. Mistakes had been made, and some helpful measures neglected; but this was to be expected in an experiment of relatively short duration.

Conclusion

The attempt to represent a part of social reality in its dynamic development from a sociological and psychological point of view meets two main dangers: one is that reality may be forced into a framework of ideas which may perhaps influence the representation of facts; the other is that observations and representations of details may be accumulated without giving the possibility of generalisation. Both these dangers were not always avoided in this chapter, although the awareness of them was constant.

The method of combining a theoretical framework with results of practical fieldwork has to be much improved before it can influence social and psychological research in the direction envisaged here: namely, to represent social phenomena in a scientific way, which might help us not only to understand what we are experiencing in our present society but to find the means of altering it.

The general problems dealt with may be subsumed under the question of the relation between the social and individual determination of human beings. The interference of society with the psychological stages in life, the relation of 'ideologies' to external life, the question of group identities and the question of incentives to work — all form part of this larger problem. The answers given in this chapter did not pretend to be of general application; yet they threw some light on general problems, and therefore it may be useful to repeat them here in condensed form.

The interference of society in psychological stages in life in two different situations was dealt with. In each the effect of social and economic reality on the course of life, described in Charlotte Bühler's terminology, was presented. The social and economic phenomena in question were unemployment and the system of the SPS. In both situations it was shown that social interference did not cause a reaction away from the normal course of life. What could be, and actually was, changed by the influence of social forces was the extent and the tempo of the realisation of this normal course. The social and the individual determination in these cases were not co-ordinated forces, but represented systems working out of synchronism. The individual urge sought for realisation and in so doing encountered social hindrances like unemployment. These hastened or slowed down the individual course of development. Thus were created conflicts which formed — according to the special stage in which they occured — hindrances of various degrees of difficulty. The general course of development was, however, unchanged.

The recognition of this relation between social and individual determination allowed us to formulate what the individual had to expect from a wholesale economic reconstruction of society. At the foundation of most social experiments, and all Utopias, lies the longing for a form of society which would abolish social interference with normal individual development, or at least would restrict it within limits, which would leave the possibility of a free and full development of the personality. It may be noted that this aim has nothing in common with the hedonistic aim as usually formulated — that social changes should make mankind happy. The idea of happiness is not implied in that of a normal course of human life.

The SPS represented a small and limited attempt to compensate for the social interference of unemployment within the individual life; it aimed at realising, on a small scale, a common life having the character just now indicated. Its limited success in this line seemed to be due more to its limited economic possibilities than to any other cause. It succeeded, however, in providing a compensation for the effect of unemployment on individuals in the fourth and fifth stage of life.

The relation between ideologies and the external life, or as it has sometimes been called in this chapter, the problems of habits and traditions in thought, is extremely difficult to grasp, because what is commonly called thinking represents a mixture of elements determined by tradition, emotion, social conditions, and speech habits, of which only one thing is clear from the outset: it has almost nothing in common with the logical laws which often are supposed to determine our thinking.

Any attempt to bring some order in this variety has to distinguish two spheres of thought. The first sphere includes all thoughts which are not constantly confronted with, and corrected by, outward realities. These are on a level of abstraction which prevents the individual from seeing at once any discrepancies between them and the many minute details of daily life. All abstract catchwords expressing attachment to a political or social system — Socialism, Christianity, Fascism, and so on — belong to this sphere. Here also we find thoughts of the imaginative type, dreams, wishes, Utopias. No creative thought could ever be born unless the human mind were able to neglect concrete experiences to a certain degree and to raise itself above these in imaginative experience. Yet thoughts in this sphere are not fully independent of the world of realities from which they have become separated. In each generation they are either consciously taken over from previous generations as thought systems, or they develop less consciously in the individual under the influence of social traditions, especially in the early stages of the individual life and in connection with emotional experiences. Before they reach their more abstract form they come into existence in close relation to the second sphere of thought, e.g. the sphere which includes all thoughts in immediate relation to reality. This 'daily-life' thought has the function of directing actual behaviour and is related to all those limited and inaccurate abstractions and generalisations by which actual behaviour is justified. Thoughts in this sphere are continuously influenced and modified by reality and at the same time partake of all the limitations that individual experience of reality always exhibits.

In the first sphere are found all ideas and thought systems that arise from past economic conditions and social traditions. Its connection with, and application to, external reality is so complicated because a change in economic structure and activity or an external break with traditions does not immediately alter such ideas and thought systems; the process of adaptation takes time. Such a situation is still further complicated because reality does not wait until the adaptation is complete but changes continuously. If it were not for this comparative stability of traditional thinking the capacity of the human mind would probably be insufficient to deal with reality; without tradition and habits of thought the infinite variety of life would overwhelm us. But on the other hand its existence accounts for the discrepancy between ideas and behaviour and for the logical unreliability of a world in which the great majority of individuals is not capable of bringing behaviour and ideologies into harmony with one another. The coordination of both processes would be much easier, however, if the individual were more conscious of the non-logical elements which influence thinking.

The SPS members provided, in their attitude and behaviour, an excellent example for the study of these two spheres of thought. Each of them adhered to some system of thought which was more or less apart from external reality. They were trade-unionists, Socialists, Communists; they had their religious convictions; all these ideological systems appealed strongly to their considerable capacity for imaginative and systematic thinking. Almost everyone of them could give a clear description of what he thought the world ought to have been like. Quite apart from this they thought about the SPS or rather they justified by pseudo-generalisations their behaviour in the SPS. The gap between the two spheres has been described (p.37). Almost no attempt was made by the organisers to bridge this gap by a definite and continuous educational process. Hence the difficulty arose that the SPS ideology was not fully known or not known at all; this lack accounted for a good many of the human difficulties that the Society encountered in the Eastern Valley.

In connection with the necessary distribution of functions within the SPS we found the tendency to re-establish the old social contrasts in the new frame. This fact brought to the front the problem of the hierarchy of groups. Every individual participated normally in the life of several groups; to take only a few, he was a member of a family, a social class, a working group, a political group, and so on. Which of these gained a predominant influence over the individual? This question was not easy to answer simply; it seemed, however, that the traditional groups came in the upper levels of this hierarchy. The family group and social class were stronger in their influence than any other grouping, except the rarely found group that had a creative character, achieved something new, added a new element not found in the traditional associations. Thus in the Society the group of boot repairers had created a new element based on the personality of its leader; none of its members knew anything comparable to this community of friendship and continuous intellectual education before it existed. A model may have been found for this group in the family, e.g. in the relation of the father to the children; but to experience such a relation within an adult group was something new.

So far as the evidence of the fieldwork went, it seemed that those groups which were able to displace the traditional hierarchy came into existence spontaneously in consequence of an experience common to all their members. Thus the group of late-comers who were refused their dinner tickets, or the group of cooks who had eaten the puddings, were spontaneously built groups, not organised by the outside. These examples demonstrated at the same time that the creativeness of a group was not to be mistaken for a positive social element. Its creative character had no relation to its social purpose and content.

The fieldwork did not lead to further generalisations as to the function of the leader within a group. It only gave evidence of the fact that the existence of an acknowledged leader helped the definition of the group character, which had its personification in the group leader.

The question of incentives to work in the SPS was answerable only by contrasting them with the incentives to work in normal industrial life. Although there was no opportunity to study the latter during the fieldwork, the general description of the atmosphere of normal industrial work given earlier showed that there existed no isolated incentives but a complex work atmosphere which had compelling force. The economic, social and technical factors were in mutual relation, although the economic factor was certainly predominant for working class people. The effects of this complex work atmosphere were so far reaching that the question of withdrawal from its influence did not arise.

Such a work atmosphere did not exist in the SPS; working or not working there was not a matter of vital importance for the unemployed man. Work in the pit formed the basis of existence; work in the SPS raised the level of living, but did not form its basis. This fact probably accounted for the impression that the SPS seemed to lack social and economic reality in the eyes of its members; it had nothing which might have been compared with the compelling effect of the work atmosphere in normal industry. This was, however, no justification for those who maintained that without the element of private profit no continuous and effective form of production was possible.

Work in the SPS was carried on without this all important factor of a compelling work atmosphere. This had the advantage — from the research point of view — that it allowed a more detailed analysis of the isolated incentives than would have been possible in normal industry; but its disadvantages for the result of the experiment were obvious. Moreover the position in the SPS must not be oversimplified. It also had its complex of incentives. Among these, technical incentives seemed to be most important as a guarantee for continuous work. They were however, not so generally effective as the organisers may have supposed in holding their theory that the cessation of compulsion would release the creative urge in men. This was actually the case with only a few. Careful and continuous vocational guidance would probably have helped to strengthen the influence of the technical incentives.

The experiment has been presented in its development, in its connection with ideas and traditions, and in its effects on the economic, social, and individual sphere. It is difficult indeed to combine the economic with the human results in order to arrive at a final judement. Every social construction which has been commenced and has developed through sacrifices and in spite of difficulties compels respect and deserves an acknowledgement of its achievement. Neither respect for the results obtained, nor the fascination of so fine a social laboratory for the research worker, must prevent us here from looking deeper.

The question arises: What is the use of a social experiment like the SPS for society, apart from the fact that it provided an excellent opportunity for studying social phenomena? This involves the question of the methods appropriate for wholesale social changes. The SPS was created by men and women who shared the deep and genuine conviction that the prevailing social and economic system was wrong. What did they do, what were they able to do, to overcome this system?

Firstly, they developed in their thoughts and in their practice a method they opposed to the political method — be it the evolutionary or revolutionary one — of changing society. They called it the experimental method.

Secondly, they created an institution, the Subsistence Production Society, which — as all institutions — tended to follow its own lines and to become conservative. The organisers committed themselves to the idea of the SPS and as soon as this idea took shape in reality, they put themselves into it wholeheartedly; they were not in the position of a cool minded physicist who could give up a method if it did not work. They had created an experiment which they wanted to justify; partly out of the very human attitude of regarding their work as a mother regards her child; partly because they had involved in it several hundred human beings who found in it some benefit and some satisfaction, which they would certainly have missed if the experiment had been discontinued.

Behind the SPS were ideas; behind any large scale social experiment there have to be — besides ideas — social forces which back those ideas because they appeal to them and correspond to their needs; at least it seems that during the thousands of years of human history no social idea was ever realised unless it was backed by the needs and wants of a social class. The ideas of the SPS were meant to meet the needs and wants of the unemployed men, within the limits of the Means Test, but they were carried into the district from the outside, and were backed by social powers very different from the power of the working class.

Some of the SPS members always suspected that there had to be some sinister motive behind this support gained from those who had no obvious interest in the improvement of the living standards of unemployed men. There was indeed something behind it, but something far more complex than the suspicion of the unemployed men that somebody was managing in a mysterious way to make some private profit out of their work in the Society.

Humanism had added a new element to the technique of bringing about social changes. As a result of an ambivalent attitude towards present society, which made some of those who shared its advantages suffer from their sympathy with those subject to its disadvantages, some individuals or groups encouraged the attempts of the suppressed to get rid of this suppression, within certain limitations. It was interesting to note in this context that the Brynmawr boot factory was founded with the financial aid of two boot manufacturers from Birmingham. The organisers of the SPS shared this ambivalent humanistic attitude. They introduced an idea into the Eastern Valley which had not grown up in the social conditions there; they got the money for running the Society to a great extent from those whose obvious interests would have induced them to oppose the experiment; but they either had not realised that it intended to be more than charity for old unemployed men, or their sympathy or perhaps their bad conscience had concealed this conflict of interest.

It was comparatively easy for some to satisfy their social conscience by giving money. It was a much more difficult task for the organisers in the Society to preach the necessary idealism — the only means that had a chance of making the SPS really successful — to the unemployed men while in daily contact with them, if the standard of living of those organisers was high above the standard of the unemployed. Those men, whose main function it ought to have been to create a common 'ideology' in the SPS were employed there at normal rates of pay. Thus it was perhaps a welcome escape for those who did not wish to be conscious hypocrites if they neglected the problem of ideas and principles and concentrated on the economic efficiency and development of the SPS. The practical problems of the organisation were big enough to occupy all the attention in a conference of the organisers. The ideas that lay behind the external organisation of the SPS became a secret shared by a few and were already deep in that sphere of thought which was not constantly confronted or checked by reality.

Perhaps it was not possible to find among the unemployed themselves those highly educated and qualified persons who might have taken the whole responsibility in such a Society, or on the other hand, to find a sufficient number of idealists in other classes who would abandon voluntarily the advantages offered to them by their privileged position, but if so it meant that the experiment could not have been extended so widely as to affect the economic order. It could never have surpassed the limits of charity.

Does this mean that the carrying through of such an experiment must have been useless? No and yes. No, because the recognition of its charitable character made it unnecessary to take into account its economic difficulties. Nobody expected that money spent for charity should have produced a calculable profit. There was no reason to expect such a profit from the SPS. Money spent in the Society was partly returned in the form of benefit to the members. In addition it provided a possibility for some unemployed men to gain an amount of experience in the social technique of production, distribution, and consumption, which was normally the privilege of a few highly specialised experts in key industrial positions. The SPS was small enough to be understood in its general operation by every member, and big enough to provide an insight into various social processes and a comparison with normal industrial life. The colliery system with its problems of export, trade, and finance, extending over the whole world was far too complicated to allow the average miner to understand its working; the family unit or a handicraft job was too small for the same purpose in the modern world. The amount of collective social experience represented by the members of the Society was one of its main positive effects.

Moreover, the Society had one decisive advantage over and above all other organisations and institutions for the benefit of unemployed men: it really touched the problem of unemployment at its central point, while all the others with their various activities remained at the periphery. Therefore it was easier for them to escape criticism; their limited function did not provoke a careful analysis. The Society was a heroic attempt to tackle a problem at the right point. Heroic, because its means were insufficient and the attempt involved failure from the outset. Under the prevailing social conditions no experiment of similar type could ever have been successful in influencing the whole society. This was the justification for saying 'yes' to the question asked above. If one measured the Society on a scale in proportion to its ideas, one had to say the experiment had not succeeded; it would never have succeeded in changing the prevailing social system; for this purpose it seems to be wiser to rely on social forces than on charity.

Appendix

The weekend of a miner's family

The family consisted of husband, wife and four children. The father was 43 years old, and had been unemployed for five years. The mother was 39 years old; there were four children: Bill and Ted, 16 and 14 years old, worked underground, Eddy was eight years old and Margaret six years old. The table in the kitchen was only big enough for four. Therefore it would have been impossible for the whole family to eat together in the kitchen. There was a table large enough for the whole family in the sitting room, but this was only used for guests.

Saturday, 29th January, 1938, 4 p.m. The two boys came home from work, undressed and washed; first Ted, then Bill. Ted had his dinner, then Bill. Mother served the boys; now and again a word was spoken. Mother got ready to go to Abersychan to the cinema as she did every Saturday; left at 4.30 p.m. by bus. The boys dressed and went off with some friends to the same cinema as their mother. They preferred to go separately because — their mother said — they amused themselves afterwards with their friends and she did not want to interfere. The two little ones had left at 2.30 to walk down to Abersychan in a group of other children all going to the cinema; they came back about 5 p.m. Father was at home all the time, looking after the fire and playing the accordion. At 5 p.m. he started to make tea for the two little ones and for himself; they had tea and pancakes, which mother had prepared in the morning. The little ones went out and played with other children, the little girl taking her doll for a walk. Father sat again by the fire in the sitting room, left the lighted oil lamp in the kitchen and, in the dark, played the accordion. Then he went down to fetch Society milk from the Brewery; had a talk with a friend and with an unemployed man (not a member of the Society) who asked him to come to his house on Sunday morning and mend his wireless. Then he came home again.

All the others saw the same cowboy film. Mother first had her tea with her sister-in-law in Abersychan, then she went shopping alone, then had another cup of tea at Woolworth's; at 6 p.m. she went to the cinema. Afterwards she went to see a friend just for a couple of minutes, had a cup of ovaltine with her, which she never had tried before and enjoyed it very much; she came back by bus at 9.30.

How the boys spent their afternoon besides going to the cinema was not quite clear. Mother suggested that they walked about in Pontypool, teasing some girls. At 8.30 father walked down to see whether mother was coming with the bus. The house was now empty except for the observer; the little ones were still playing out of doors. At 9 p.m. they came in and brought a child friend. We sat by the fire, I told them a story. Some minutes later, Bill came in, lingered around, listened for some time to the story, then went into the dark room to play the accordion. At 9.30 mother came home with Ted whom she picked up on the bus. Father had gone to the pub, as he did every Saturday night. Mother prepared supper. She was very satisfied with the film she had seen; during her work she talked to the children about it. Supper consisted of fried bacon with tinned tomatoes, and tea. First the two little ones ate, then they were sent to bed without washing because it was too late. They took a candle upstairs because they were afraid of the dark. Then mother laid supper for the rest of us. The boys did not sit down when it was ready, so mother began her meal without waiting for them, and so did I. They never waited for all to sit round the table. After supper the boys went into the other room, sat in the dark; Ted took the accordion, they smoked cigarettes. Both obviously very tired, but refused to go to bed, although Ted had to get up at 4.30 a.m. because he was working a Sunday shift. At 11 p.m. father came home. The boys finally made up their minds to go to bed. Father had drunk a little too much; he was very animated, but not actually drunk and talked about some conversations with some chaps in the pub. Mother prepared his supper. She and I washed up while he was eating. He was a bit too noisy, she told him several times to shut up, but in a very controlled and cool way. After washing up we three sat together, had a talk about the Society and some of its members and organisers. At 11.45 they went to bed. At midnight everyone seemed asleep. It was a very nasty night, stormy and raining and I woke up because two cats were fighting in the garden, howling terribly; the storm blew. The little girl awoke, was obviously afraid, wanted to go in her mother's bed but was refused. For 15 minutes everybody was awake, the boys were making fun, the little girl crying. Then they fell asleep again. At 4.30 a.m. the alarm clock went. This awakened mother, she awakened father, who got up to get Ted out of bed. This was rather a hard job, but at last he succeeded, both went downstairs, father lit the fire and prepared tea, Ted was dressing. It was still very stormy. They decided that the weather was too bad for Ted to go over the hills; as he was not bound to do Sunday work, they got back to bed, after having a cup of tea, and slept. At 9 a.m. the little girl and Eddy came downstairs. No washing. They sat with me at the fire. At 9.30 mother came downstairs and prepared breakfast. While the kettle was heating, she washed hands and face and combed her hair. At 10 breakfast was ready for the children, mother and me. It was shredded wheat with milk, tea, bread and butter. Father came down during our breakfast. He waited until we had finished, then he had his. The boys were still in bed. They slept until 10.30 then one could hear them speaking, shouting, and making fun. They only got up at 1 p.m. in time for dinner. During the morning mother washed up, cleaned the rooms in a very superficial way, 'because it is Sunday'. Father cleaned the fireplace, the children went out to play. After father had finished he sat down, smoking a pipe, while mother prepared dinner. He left at midday to look at his friend's wireless, then went over to the pub to have his Sunday morning drink. At 1 p.m. dinner was ready. The boys, mother and I ate – pork, cabbage, potatoes, and gravy. As they had only two knives we used them in turn. There was no table cloth. The two littles ones had their dinner then we started to wash up. Father came home and had his dinner. Mother made an apple tart because they were expecting visitors for tea. At 2.15 the two little ones left for Sunday School in their best clothes. They did not come back after the class but played in the open air. Father was a bit more drunk than the evening before, therefore mother sent him off to sleep, he seemed to be very glad to go. The boys smoked cigarettes, sat about, then went out for a walk. Mother laid the table in the front room for tea with a white fresh table cloth, prepared bread and butter, tinned fruits and custard, and the apple tart, then she sat down for a moment and glanced through the newspaper *(The People)*. She looked for thrilling stories. 'I like a nice thrilling murder', she said. At 4.30 we had tea, father, mother, the little boy and I, but the visitors had not yet arrived. At 4.45 the visitors arrived: father's sister and her daughter, mother's nephew with wife and son (three years old). They were not invited to sit at the table. 'Don't bother about us, we'll just finish tea', mother said. After a while: 'Have you had your tea?' They were bound to say 'Yes'. 'Well, it is no good inviting you for tea, when you have already had it'. Some tension was noted, caused by the guests not being invited to have tea. This, however, soon disappeared. Mother's behaviour seemed to be unexpected to everyone. The nephew went with the boys who had just come home, to the kitchen to play the accordion. After tea the whole party was in the sitting room. Two more people arrived; there were 14 now in the small room and it was terribly hot and noisy. The nephew played the accordion, the women chatted, the children played and cried, and the cat yowled. Bill produced some card tricks. Then there was some dancing, but only the women danced, afterwards card tricks again, and smoking. The women talked about shopping and about some of their friends. Ted left at 5.30, went courting, as his mother explained. Mother didn't seem to enjoy the noise very much. Tried to stop the crying of the children, but this was hopeless. Father said: 'Let's offer some wine'. Mother: 'I don't care for it, but if you like'. She went and offered a home made wine, which was very much appreciated by everybody. At 7 p.m. the noise seemed to be too bad for mother's nerves. She sent the two little ones to bed who went with loud protests. Then it was a bit quieter. At 8 p.m. four of the party sat together to play cards. This lasted half an hour. In the meantime mother prepared supper for the guests: cold pork, bread and butter. They had supper in the kitchen, mother looked after them; it lasted about 20 minutes then they prepared to go home. They left at 9.20. Mother prepared supper for the family. As usual some began earlier than others. Supper was the same as for the guests. Ted came home at about 10. He seemed to be very satisfied with his afternoon. All sat at the table. They ate without a table cloth, and with only one knife. After supper mother read the paper and told about one of its stories. Father and the boys went to the other room, Bill read a cowboy story, Ted played a game of patience, Father did nothing particular, smoking his pipe. Now and again a word was exchanged between the three of them. After the strain of the afternoon everybody enjoyed the peaceful atmosphere. At 10.30 the boys went to bed after having been asked to do so several times. At last father took the poker — but just for fun — and chased them off to bed. Mother and I washed up. At 11.15 the parents went to bed. At midnight everybody was asleep.

References

BÜHLER, C. (1933). *Der Menschliche Lebenslauf als psychologisches Problem.* Leipzig: Hirzel.

ECROYD, H. (1983) 'Substistence Production in the Eastern Valley of Monmouthshire'. *Llafur, The Journal of Welsh Labour History, 3* (4), 34-37.

JAHODA, M., LAZARSFELD, P.F. and ZEISEL, H. (1972). *Marienthal: The Sociography of an Unemployed Community.* London: Tavistock Publications.

MANNHEIM, K. (1972). *Ideology and Utopia.* London: Routledge and Kegan Paul.

ORDER OF FRIENDS (1930). *An Account of Their Activities and Ideas.* (The exact reference is now forgotten).

PILGRIM TRUST (1938). *Men Without Work.* Cambridge: Cambridge University Press.

2

David Fryer

Monmouthshire and Marienthal: sociographies of two unemployed communities

'Incentives to labour ... tend to look different in isolation from their appearance in their social context' Jahoda (this volume).

The publication in this volume of *Unemployed Men at Work* half a century after the field work upon which it is based was carried out, is of great interest to students of employment in general and occupational and social psychologists in particular. It is certainly essential reading for students of motivation, group behaviour, leadership, life span development, organisational science and evaluation research. It constitutes an audacious and largely successful attempt at methodological triangulation and exemplifies proper, but seldom found, attention to social context, interacting individual and social change over time and the role of sociohistorical tradition in thought and action.

However, it is probably students of the psychological experience of unemployment who will be most intrigued by it. This is not only because of the insight it affords in itself into the psychology of unemployed people, nor even because it is one of the earliest investigations of a practical, yet psychologically sophisticated, attempt to ameliorate the experienced distress of being unemployed. Rather, the interest is likely to arise initially because of respect and admiration for Jahoda's earlier work, *Marienthal* (Jahoda *et al.* 1972), which occupies a paramount position in terms of esteem and influence in the field's literature. The contribution which this pioneering study has made to our understanding of psychological aspects of unemployment guarantees curiosity about a sister study. However, there is added cause for interest in that as the research in the Eastern Valley of Monmouthshire took place six years after that in Marienthal, it seems probable that it would reveal both continuities and discontinuities, development and change of direction, with the previous work — and leave intellectual legacies for future projects. This raises the possibility that careful reading of *Unemployed Men at Work* could simultaneously deepen our understanding of *Marienthal* and extend our understanding of both the experience of unemployment and the process of research upon it.

Finally, interest arises from the perspective of intellectual biography in the development of concepts during the years including and lying between these two major social psychological investigations. Because Jahoda's ideas have been so widely influential for half a century in social psychological research on unemployment, this chapter will also be an exploration of the history of ideas central to the field.

In this chapter I offer a comparative perspective on these two important investigations. This is attempted in terms of: a biographical orientation; a setting of the scenes where the tragic dramas were acted out; an introduction to the two communities; and comments on certain aspects of the fieldwork: authorship; research contribution; and timing. Finally I discuss parallels in methodology, findings, movements towards an explanation and routes of influence.

A disclaimer is necessary at the outset. Both studies are complex and multi-faceted. Definitive accounts, let alone comparisons, are out of the question. This comparative perspective is, then, very personal and selective.

Research in Austria and Wales: a biographical orientation

In 1930 a group of young researchers at the Psychological Institute, University of Vienna, where the Professors were Karl and Charlotte Bühler, resolved to forsake the laboratory and investigate pressing social problems in the field. This group included Marie Jahoda and Paul Lazarsfeld. Their 'branching out was at best condoned, rather than led, by the faculty members under whom they had studied' (Jahoda 1981, 205). They formed themselves into the Wirtschaftspsychologische Forschungstelle (WF) (Industrial Psychology Research Station: Lazarsfeld 1932). Amongst their earliest committed applied research projects were investigations into the standard of living of Viennese beggars, revealing a 'highly regulated professional organisation' (Jahoda 1981, 209). Limited financial support from the Rockefeller foundation, via a grant administered by the Bühlers, enabled them to cast their empirical net wider. Half an hour's train journey from Vienna was a small village whose labour market had for generations been totally dominated by the textile industry. In 1929 the industry had collapsed resulting in mass unemployment. In late 1931 a team of researchers from the WF began to collect 'all the available material relating to the conditions of life among the inhabitants' (Lazarsfeld 1932).

For a summary of the results, I quote from the earliest published English language account.

> 'If one were to attempt to summarise the result of the enquiry in a formula, it might be worded as follows: The psychologist finds that in spite of the extraordinarily low economic standard of life of the unemployed persons whose conditions we investigated, no actual *deroute* has yet occurred. This indicates that paralled [*sic*] with the narrowing of the economic scope of these people, their psychic life has contracted; a narrowing of the psychological sphere of wants occurs, so that the pressure of external conditions is not felt in its full force. We defined this psychic attitude as resignation and to describe it in its various forms is one of the principal objects of our inquiry. Yet it may be shown, from our material, that this contraction of wants has a limit which cannot be exceeded. If it is reached, and if the external pressure continues to increase, the result is a catastrophic physical and psychic collapse (ibid., 149).

By 1933, when the full report of these Marienthal investigations was published as a monograph in German, Marie Jahoda was Director of the WF and doing research on the phenomenological world of young girls and authority and leadership in the family (Jahoda 1981). However, sudden and brutal changes were soon to come. In 1936, whilst she was working on a study of 'the deep split in Austrian culture by comparing two types of joke then current' (ibid), jokes featuring urban Jewish intellectuals and naive Austrian aristocrats respectively, Jahoda was arrested and interrogated by the fascist Austrian State police. Released into exile only after appeals at the very highest level, she found herself in the UK where she was offered the opportunity in 1937–1938 to continue her work in Wales. Characteristically, she grasped the opportunity with both hands.

The Welsh study, in the Eastern Valley of Monmouthshire, took place six years after that in Austria, allowing plenty of time for reflection on the Marienthal study's strengths and weaknesses. Jahoda had had other research experience in the intervening years. She had also herself been through the trauma of arrest, interrogation, imprisonment and exile into an alien culture. The whole sociopolitical climate had undergone a profound change — in 1931 'National Socialism' was only just gaining a foothold in Marienthal; by 1938 the full horrors of Naziism, especially to an intellectual of a Jewish family still in Vienna, were tragically evident; the catastrophe of the Second World War was imminent and Marie Jahoda was living in the country about to enter into combat of awesome savagery with her homeland, Austria. Bearing in mind all these aspects of the individual and social context within which the Eastern Valley study began and unfolded, it would be remarkable if there were not marked contrasts with its predecessor in Austria. Any points of similarity would be all the more noteworthy for transcending these changes.

Setting the scenes

Marienthal was a village of some 1,486 souls a few miles into the flat, monotonous countryside to the south east of Vienna. The village, as drab as its surroundings with workers' housing built all to one pattern, clustered around the factory which dominated the village in every sense. Except for the former manor house, the multi-storey factory overlooked all other buildings, most of which, including the single storey workers' housing and the inn, it owned. The village also boasted two horsemeat butchers, a confectioner, a co-operative store, grocer, barber and a few other shops. It had a cinema but no church, despite the fact that the population was predominantly Roman Catholic. Marienthal had been in its time very active both socially and politically: no less than 22 social and/or political organisations existed.

Up until 1929 a large textile company had provided employment for virtually the whole population, however throughout the second half of that year parts of the works closed down one after the other. By February 1930 the only sign of activity in the factory was its own demolition. When the researchers went in, 77% of the families had not a single member in employment.

The Subsistence Production Society in the Eastern Valley of Monmouthshire, Wales, was a social experiment on such a grand scale that it almost beggars the imagination. The headquarters and industrial workshops of SPS Ltd were originally set up in a derelict five-storey building, originally a brewery, in 1934. Over four years the project blossomed into a diversified production, distribution and consumption centre.

The original core consisted of: woodworking, including furniture making and handicrafts, supplied by the SPS's own outlying woodwork shop complete with power machinery; boot repairing; and tailoring, supplied by SPS's own weaving and knitting workshops. A kitchen and canteen were added to provide midday meals. A bakery, provided with flour from the SPS's own grain cleaning plant and flour-mill, provided bread, cakes and the like for on-site consumption and sale to members. Meat, from the SPS's own piggeries and poultry farms, was slaughtered in the SPS abbattoir and jointed in the SPS butchery. Milk was provided by the SPS dairy herd of Ayrshires, grazed on SPS pastures. SPS farms, there were six in all, cultivated crops of vegetables, salad, fruit and honey. These provided raw materials for SPS jam and pickle production.

The infrastructure required to maintain this vast Society enterprise included workers' housing, offices, stables, lorries and garaging, boiler rooms, green houses, a reservoir, byres, a limestone quarry and a drift mine for coal.

In the autumn of 1937 when the membership of the Society stood at just over 300, Marie Jahoda entered the community to begin her second major social psychological field study of the psychological consequences of unemployment.

The two communities

The Marienthal and Eastern Valley communities, although geographically separated by half of Europe, with all the linguistic, cultural and sociopolitical differences implied, bear fascinating resemblances. Both find their very beginnings in paradox: Marienthal, homophonetically Maria's valley, lay on a flat plain in the Steinfeld region of lower Austria just outside Vienna. The Eastern Valley lay 'in the western part of the country ... in the extreme east of the South Wales coalfield ... (following) a north to south course'. As if to emphasise the effects of long term unemployment on identity and self-concept, even the very geographical settings seemed to betray a confusion about where and what they were.

There was a profound ambiguity in both communities as to whether they were urban or rural. Both stood on rivers but even these 'natural' features were constant reminders of the industrial tradition: the very river ran black, loaded with coal silt, in the Eastern Valley and the temperate Marienthal river was a power source, for all seasons, to the mills.

Both communities had pervasive reminders of their industrial heritage. In the Eastern Valley 'the most obvious signs of human effort in the landscape' were the colliery tips, with other signs of industry scattered all along the western ridge. However, paradoxically, the ridge on the other side of the valley gave a 'mainly agricultural impression'. Although few of the Eastern Valley dwellers had personal experience of rural life, 'being at the boundary of the coalfield, they had some connection with, and knowledge of, the agricultural area beyond'. There was also periodically to be found 'deep longing for participation' in 'the life beyond the hills'.

Marienthal, too, was continually reminded of its industrial inheritance. Only the factory chimneys, hospital and office block, apart from the former manor house, rose above the stone-built workers' houses; the shoddily built, mean huts, thrown up in a rush to house the workers during the boom times and crumbling factory walls. 'From their windows at home, the workers look out onto a heap of rubble, dented boilers, old transmission wheels and crumbling walls where once had been their place of work' (Jahoda *et al.* 1972, 14).

Indeed the whole region was, at the time of the investigations, in the grip of an industrial depression. The surrounding villages whose employment was based on industries as diverse as knitwear, glass or quarrying were mostly in decline. Again however, as with the Eastern Valley dwellers, the inhabitants of Marienthal did not perceive themselves as being an unambiguously urban community. In better times there was employment to be found with farmers in the surroundings, although in the hard times of the study there was hardly even seasonal employment to be had at harvest time. If the villagers were ambivalent about their urban/rural status, the investigators were not. Despite a century of textile production in Marienthal, the research team saw the community as a 'closed rural community' which had 'greater resistance against breakdown than the multitude of urban unemployment' (ibid.).

The researchers argued that the traditions of urban and rural life and the ambivalent position of the village on the boundary of agricultural and industrial landscapes had had a profound effect on the experience and consequences of unemployment. Thus they recorded a 'partial return to an agricultural existence, which the Marienthal industrial worker was able to make' which 'distinguishes him from the urban unemployed and alleviates his position to some extent' (ibid., 74). This return was reflected in the regular activities of the men: collecting firewood, cultivating vegetables in field allotments — by 392 out of the 478 families — and rearing rabbits — there were 150 independent rabbit breeders in the village. The rural unemployed people of Marienthal were also more affected by the changing seasons than urban unemployed people: 'The seasons of the year ... make themselves felt more strongly. The end of the need for lighting and heating, the relief afforded by the produce of the garden allotment and the possibility of occasional work on the land have attained a signficance they did not normally have in the household of an industrial worker' (ibid., 77).

The rural nature of the sample, in the eyes of the investigators, seems seldom to be fully appreciated by today's commentators but is worth bearing firmly in mind. The researchers' assumption that rural unemployment would be psychologically less destructive than its urban counterpart has been supported by high quality modern work by Gore (1978), although others suggest rural unemployment carries its own penalties (Into Work 1980). However, if true, it means that the distress discovered in Marienthal and the Eastern Valley, in so far as they were rural communities, and bad as it was, *under*stated the psychological distress caused by unemployment in more typical urban settings.

Both the Eastern Valley and Marienthal communities were dominated by single, monolithic, industries. In the Eastern Valley, coal mining and its attendant enterprises had been dominant for over 150 years. Only 100 years before the investigation whole families of mother, father and children of only six years old had been employed together in the pits. Things had improved but it was still true that 'for most of the boys the inevitability of working there as soon as the law permitted' remained. In Marienthal the textile industry, in which the majority of the community had been employed, had been established a century before the investigations began when in 1830 a flaxmill had been opened. At that time, too, young children had to work in the industry in three shifts of eight hours, as well as their mothers and fathers. Cotton spinning, weaving, bleaching and rayon production were gradually introduced over the next 100 years, with a peak of employment being reached only two years before the total closedown of the textile industry in the village in 1930.

Both communities had known the vicissitudes of immigration and migration: both causes and symptoms of social instability in themselves. Both had known an influx of workers, attracted by employment, from the mid 1800s onwards. Between the mid 19th century and the beginning of the First World War, the population of the South Wales coalfield counties trebled. There was a continuous trickle of migration from the Eastern Valley with improving educational standards, as the upwardly mobile moved to match their new aspirations with opportunities elsewhere, but migration became a haemorrhage after 1923 with jobs in coal dwindling. In Marienthal similar expansion occurred in the mid 19th century, with immigrants coming not only from Austria but also Bohemia, Moravia and Germany. There was also a siphoning off of the most pro-active people in the late 1920s: 'probably some of the most active and energetic families had already escaped the general fate by emigrating'.

Both communities had an ingrained tradition of trade union power. In the Eastern Valley the trade unions had maintained 'steadily increasing power' and 'through their unions the workers had carried on the struggle for an improvement of their standard of living'. Twelve years after the General Strike, in which they had participated, 'the unemployed men got excited in remembering those weeks of fighting for better conditions'. In Marienthal, trade union activity had begun in 1860. Thirty years later a strike crushed by the military had done nothing to inhibit trade unions' growing influence. In 1925, only a few years before the investigations began, the national textile workers' strike took place in Austria.

Neither community in which Jahoda's research on the psychological consequences of long-term unemployment was conducted, was an island entire of itself. Approaching Marienthal, 'a stranger to the district would scarcely notice the border between Grammat-Neusiedel and Marienthal', while the Eastern Valley merged into its surroundings to the east, west, north and south. In many ways both communities were more like their neighbouring regions than like each other. Nevertheless, each constituted a distinct community of people bound together by experiences and traditions: of urban and rural ways, industrial giants and developing collective strength. Into those complex, social atmospheres 'penetrated by conscious and unconscious forces' ... 'in which the employment rhythm mastered all others', where 'the industrial tradition, formed and handed down through several generations ... governed the attitude of the great majority' (Jahoda, this volume, 81), Marie Jahoda ventured, twice, to carry through her investigations of the psychological consequences of unemployment.

The field work

Who wrote the accounts?

The modern, English language, reader acquainted with *Marienthal* via the 1972 Tavistock 'translation', is likely to associate the study with three names: Marie Jahoda, Paul Lazarsfeld and Hans Zeisel, whose names appear on the book's spine. However, the orginal research monograph, published in German in 1933 under the title *Die Arbeitslosen von Marienthal (The Workless of Marienthal)* varies in its content in several interesting ways compared with the 1972 'translation'. Chapter 1 of the 'translation' is an amended version of what appears in the 1933 monograph as an introduction by Paul Lazarsfeld. Lazarsfeld in fact wrote an introduction to the German monograph; he subsequently wrote a new introduction for a second German edition of 1962 and yet another introduction for the 1972 'translation', which appears in it as '40 Years Later'. The changes in these introductions, and indeed in summaries of the study over the years is a fascinating topic in its own right but beyond the scope of this chapter.

The attribution of authorship is also of interest. In the 1933 monograph only Marie Jahoda and Hans Zeisel are referred to as authors (Verfasser). However, Jahoda, was given her, then, full name: Dr Marie Lazarsfeld-Jahoda (she was married briefly to Paul Lazarsfeld). Jahoda has indicated (personal communication) that, in fact, she alone was responsible for the writing of the main body of the monograph itself: 'When all of the material was in and we had had many discussions, chaired by PFL, I took the entire material, went into the country and wrote the report'. Since the material weighed about 66lb, this was no mean feat, even physically: intellectually the task was Herculean. Paul Lazarsfeld wrote in the 1930s only the introduction, i.e. what appears largely in 1972 as Chapter 1, and in 1971 added '40 Years Later,' although one should not minimise the effects of his leadership throughout. Zeisel alone wrote the historical appendix: 'Afterword'.

In other words, contrary to initial appearances of the tri-partite authorship of the 1972 version, Marie Jahoda alone can really be considered the author of the research on *Marienthal*. Jahoda was also, of course, the sole author of *Unemployed Men at Work*, at least in so far as there ever are such things as 'sole authors' of social psychological studies.

Research participants

If we are taken aback by the fact that there was one rather than three authors in the case of *Marienthal*, we are likely to be more astonished by the actual number of research personnel in the same study.

Jahoda has written (personal communication) that Paul Lazarsfeld was in Marienthal 'only very occasionally, Zeisel more often and I more regularly'. However, the success of the entire set of investigations was very much due, in addition to the guidance of Jahoda and Lazarsfeld, to a team of co-workers. Dr Lotte Danziger, was foremost amongst these. Although she is briefly credited in the 1972 version, the 1933 Monograph is more informative (pp.v/vi): 'The contribution of Dr Lotte Danziger was, above all, fundamental to the success of the whole enterprise. She negotiated access with great personal skill, and during the six weeks she lived in Marienthal, gathered all the basic data with diligence, expertise and sensitivity' (free translation of David Fryer). Apart from Danziger, moreover, there was a sizeable team of co-workers: Erich Felix, Franz Zdrahal, Marie Deutsch, Elfriede Guttenberg, Hedwig Deutsch, Karl Hartl and four medical doctors: Josefine Stross, Clara Jahoda, Kurt Zinram and Paul Stein.

Even if we make allowances for Marie Jahoda's intellectual generosity and assume that she understates her own empirical involvement and was rather generous in 1933 with apportioning the magnitude of the contribution by Lotte Danziger, it is clear that the Marienthal investigation was very much a large-scale team operation with a limited, if important, degree of 'hands-on' contact, (sich einleben), for Jahoda herself. This is very much in contrast with her research in the Eastern Valley. In Monmouthshire she was not only sole author but sole investigator very much involved in true participant observation, as well as the collection of 'objective' data, according to personal recollections of one of the SPS members (Ecroyd 1983).

Jahoda's involvement in, and thus her influence on, the actual day-to-day research in the Eastern Valley was more intensive, more thorough, more 'immersed' than her involvement in Marienthal. It is, thus, the quintessential Jahoda field study.

Fieldwork timing

Although 'preliminary work and discussions' began in the autumn of 1931, most of the actual fieldwork, upon which the Marienthal monograph and subsequent accounts was based, was conducted, between December 1931 and January 1932 in a period of just six weeks by Lotte Danziger. However, investigations involving the rest of the team of 14 continued less intensively until about mid May 1932. 'All in all', Jahoda writes (Jahoda *et al.* 1972, 9), 'we spent some 120 working days in Marienthal'. The data processing of course took much longer — about six months. Astonishingly, the number of woman-hours spent actually engaged in the field in the Eastern Valley of Monmouthshire was identical: 120 days: 'She spent four months in the Eastern Valley' (Ecroyd 1983). Crucially, however, each of these days represented 'hands-on' research by Marie Jahoda herself, rather than by one of the Marienthal team of 14.

In Marienthal the end of the textile era came in 1929. In July the spinning mills closed, in August the printing works were shut down and in September the bleaching plant was brought to a final standstill. The looms themselves ceased movement for the last time in February 1930. Within days demolition began. Thus when the field work began in December 1931, it was already about two years since mass redundancy had hit the community. In Wales the Subsistence Production Society was started up in March 1935. Jahoda's fieldwork commenced in autumn 1937, about two-and-a-half years after the phenomenon under investigation had become a reality in the valley. Moreover, unemployment, the leitmotif of the whole study, 'had, for many years, been the most important feature of life in the valley' (Jahoda, this volume), a baleful threat at least since 1921.

In both Marienthal and Monmouthshire, therefore, Jahoda began her investigations of already well established phenomena; in both cases a similar duration of fieldwork took place. As regards personal contact with the work in hand, however, the Eastern Valley was favoured.

Methods

Both the Marienthal and the Monmouthshire investigations are outstanding instances of thorough-going triangulation in action: 'In collecting the material it had to be borne in mind that it was necessary to avoid injuring the susceptibilities of the distressed population, that psychological self-observations cannot be expected of working-class people and that any report must contain as many exact data as possible' (Lazarsfeld 1932). Thus the researchers tried 'to find procedures which could combine the use of numerical data with immersion (sich einleben) into the situation ... to gain such close contact with the population of Marienthal that we could learn the smallest details of their daily life' (Jahoda *et al.* 1972, 1).

This latter statement of aims could as well have been a description by Jahoda of her Welsh fieldwork goals. And she achieved them to great measure: she lived in turn in the homes of nine Society members and worked for a week in each of twelve different departments of the Subsistence Production Society (Ecroyd 1983).

The fact that Jahoda actually laboured in the Society workshops as well as conducting research is again a telling symmetry with Marienthal. There the investigators had made it 'a consistent point of policy' that 'none of our researchers should be in Marienthal as a mere reporter or outside observer. Everyone was to fit naturally into the communal life by participating in some activity generally useful to the community' (Jahoda *et al.* 1972, 5). In Marienthal, free medical consultations were provided each week by a female obstetrician and a female paediatrician. Notes were kept on consulting room conversations and thus medical benefits for the patients and research benefits for the investigators had been combined: 'our medical service, like all our social work, aside from serving its own good purpose is part of our arrangement for collecting needed data' (ibid.,

34). Jahoda's attempts to contribute to the material success of the SPS as well as gather high quality data coalesced in her participant observation.

Findings

Both the Marienthal and Eastern Valley investigations demonstrate commitment to the production of substantive knowledge. This has been a dominant preoccupation of Jahoda in her work over the last half century, as she recently reaffirmed: 'What I am interested in as a social scientist is to know something about specified people and situations. That is what I call substantive knowledge' (Jahoda 1986, 13). This could not have been more clearly stated with respect to Marienthal: 'our concern was the unemployed manual labourer in a particular industry, in a particular village, at a particualar time of the year' (Jahoda *et al.* 1972, 3).

Although both pieces of research were done largely during the winter months in long-term unemployed rural/urban communities, when one considers the differences not only of industry and village but also country, language, culture and tradition, it is remarkable how many findings were similar.

The dominant finding in each community of unemployed people must surely be that of resignation. In Marienthal, 70% of the families had been placed in this category. The criteria by which this assignment had been made was summarised as follows: 'no plans, no relation to the future, no hopes, extreme restriction of all needs beyond the bare necessities, yet at the same time maintenance of the household, care of the children, and an overall feeling of relative well-being' (ibid., 53). In the Eastern Valley, too, 'the normal attitude amongst the unemployed might be described as resignation ... an almost complete cessation of any capacity to make an effort' (Jahoda this volume). Jahoda comments, however, that 'nothing worse than resignation was found in the Eastern Valley, in Marienthal despair and complete apathy were discovered' (ibid., 19). In fact, even in Marienthal these desperate extremes had been relatively rare reactions. The investigators estimated that a total of 2% were 'in despair'. These families were suffering from 'despair, depression, hopelessness, a feeling of futility of all efforts', although even these families did 'keep their households in order and looked after the children'. A total of 5% of families were estimated to be 'apathetic'. These exhibited 'complete passivity, absence of any effort. Home and children are dirty and neglected, the mental outlook is not desparate but simply indifferent'. Lamentable though the predicaments of these 7% of families were, they should be contemplated against the other extreme: the 23% of familes who were characterised by 'maintenance of the household, care of the children, subjective well being, activity, hopes and plans for the future, sustained vitality, and continued attempts to find employment' (Jahoda *et al.* 1972, 53).

Jahoda suggests that the omission of despair and apathy from the catalogue of attitudes characterising families of unemployed miners in the Eastern Valley 'may have been mainly because of the size and permanence of the unemployment allowance in Wales'.

This constitutes a very important convergence of the Austrian and Welsh investigations. The Marienthal monograph emphasises 'the connection between powers of resistance, income and previous life history' (ibid., 9). In particular, despair and apathy are described as 'probably but two different stages of a process of psychological deterioration that runs parallel to the narrowing of economic resources and the wear and tear on personal belongings. At the end of this process lies ruin and despair' (ibid., 87). This emphasis in the Marienthal study on the role of poverty in the genesis of psychological distress associated with unemployment is insufficiently appreciated by modern researchers who tend to attribute the distress more to the withdrawal of psychologically supportive features of employment structure, latent functions, than to the inability to earn a living, the manifest function of being employed. The original investigators themselves could hardly have been more explicit, in the full accounts of the investigations, about the relationship between 'broken' attitude and income. They established a connection 'between a family's attitudes and its economic situation' and were able to predict 'at approximately what point the deterioration of income will push a family into the next category', unbroken, resigned, in despair or apathetic (ibid., 81).

There were, in this connection, two crucial differences between the unemployed people of Marienthal and those of the Eastern Valley. In Austria, the unemployment relief laws meant that after a time unemployment payments were superceded by emergency relief, which was gradually reduced and eventually ran out altogther. Some families in Marienthal had no income whatsoever.

In Monmouthshire, the unemployment allowance was permanent and relatively more generous, though claimants still lived in penury. Subsistence Production Society members, whilst receiving no more in absolute terms of unemployment allowance than non-members, were able to exchange their allowance for more and better quality goods than non-members. These differences in consumption power, although small, may according to the Marienthal experience have been significant for psychological well-being. In Marienthal, we were told, the difference between having sugar as opposed to saccharin, or between children having shoes as opposed to bare feet 'meant also the difference between being unbroken, resigned, in despair or apathetic' (ibid., 82).

These factors go part way to explaining why unemployment, though extremely unpleasant, was less psychologically destructive in South Wales than in Austria or within the SPS than outside it. As Jahoda wrote of non-Society members in the Eastern Valley: 'it is as if the lower the standard of living, the less were they able to take any steps to improve matters' (Jahoda this volume).

In both communities, what may be called the financial imperative operated. This refers to the fact that, as poverty bites deeper, beliefs give way to monetary self interest as guides to action. As the Marienthal investigators put it with regard to club membership: 'The general conclusion is fairly obvious. As privation increases, organisation membership becomes less a matter of conviction and more a matter of financial interest' (Jahoda *et al.* 1972, 42). Against a background of general decline in club membership in Marienthal, three clubs actually prospered. These 'organisations offer their members more or less direct financial advantages' (ibid., 42). The Cremation Society, die Flamme, which provided help with funeral expenses, actually grew by 19% in membership in the four years to 1931.

In Marienthal, following the discovery that certain political parties offered forms of charity, 'a few men had actually become members of both politically opposed organisations' (ibid., 41). In the Eastern Valley symmetrical events were recorded. For example, 'There were many different reasons which determined the choice of newspaper, among them being the fact that newspapers offered benefits of various kinds to their regular readers. The political colour of a paper was often overlooked. In one family where the man was Labour, and the wife Liberal, *The People* was read on Sundays. Asked about its political outlook, the man said: 'it's socialist', the wife: 'it's liberal' (Jahoda, this volume).

There are many other more minor but still fascinating convergences of findings in the two communities. In both, Jahoda found evidence of financial irrationality. In Marienthal she had recorded people who had lived without any income at all for a year buying trinkets from doorstep pedlars, people unable to buy vegetables cultivating flowers on allotments and so forth. In the Eastern Valley she again found people desperately stricken by poverty buying 'novelties which did not rise above the standard of the cheapest shops' or elaborating complex and costly systems for winning the football pools. Jahoda suggested these behaviours might have been serving a cultural function for those 'who otherwise would have had no hope left' (ibid.).

In Wales she reported the 'swiping' of goods and materials from the Society for personal consumption, gifts or resale. But in Austria, too, she had documented the stealing of coal, theft of potatoes and cabbages from farms, poaching and even the abduction and eating of others' pet cats and dogs. Conventional morality proved as difficult to uphold under severe poverty in Wales as in Austria.

In the Marienthal monograph, Jahoda had written: 'to the extent to which Marienthal had been changed by unemployment, we had to learn something about what the atmosphere and life of the community had been during normal times'. In fact, the attention given to this in the Austrian investigation was modest. In this respect, however, the Eastern Valley study was exemplary: it could have only been substantially improved by a genuine longitudinal component in the research design.

What is particularly striking, however, is the extent to which what have come to be regarded as the classic psychological consequences of *un*employment are attributed instead in the Eastern Valley investigation to *em*ployment or community life outside the employment relationship altogether.

Thus feelings, even whilst still in employment, were said to be 'embittered', there was a 'continuous physical and mental tension during work in the pits' and 'during a slump ... constant anxiety for the future created a depressed atmosphere'. Depression was, also, a result of the material conditions of life. In Blaenavon, for example, the bad housing, busy traffic, narrow streets, over crowding and lack of open space 'created a most depressing atmosphere'.

Fatalism, which has come to be uncritically accepted as the last of a series of reactions to *un*employment, was in the Eastern Valley study in fact discovered to have been 'created by ... work in the pits' which had brought 'the people in the valley into daily contact with danger and death and had demonstrated to them how, without the possibility of foreknowledge by human beings, questions of life and death were decided'. Indeed, fatalism was described in the Eastern Valley as a characteristic attitude to everything unforseen or uncontrollable. With both the Aurora Borealis and the Eden crisis 'neither was foreseen. The reaction of the population was similar: in each case thinking turned from the normal rational course to a magical and fatalistic line' (ibid.).

If the trade unions, part and parcel of employment in the coal industry, 'represented and almost seemed to exhaust the collective effort of the workers' (ibid.), it was also clear that social forces in the community other than unemployment were working against that sense of solidarity and collective purpose. For example, the 'essentially individualist religion', in its own various sects, broke up 'the social life of the local community into various separate non-cooperating units' (ibid.). Admittedly, within these isolated units 'the Sunday services gave the opportunity for social contact' but this again only goes to show that in the Eastern Valley employment was not the only provider of what Jahoda was later to call the latent functions, nor unemployment the only social force undermining them.

A similar point might be made regarding fantasy. Jahoda has periodically cited Freud's insight that work is a person's strongest tie to reality. It is clear from the report however that in Jahoda's view national temperament can undermine that tie as effectively as unemployment: witness her references to 'the vivid fantasy life of the Welsh'.

Jahoda has suggested that 'employment imposes a time structure on the waking day' (Jahoda 1979, 313) and that part of the distress and disorientation of unemployment results from the cessation of this imposed time structure. In the Eastern Valley, however, this imposed time structure was found to be anything but the norm: 'work in the mines communicated a jazzlike rhythm to life in a miner's family and home. There was no fixed hour for getting up or going to bed nor even for meals as a consequence of the shift system in the pit, ... the house was kept under tension almost continuously day and night ... this irregularity was the normal way of living' (Jahoda this volume). It also proved to be the case that purposeful activity, work, in the Society sometimes failed to impose a time structure on the waking day with similar consequences for sense of time as unemployment. 'In the Marienthal investigations into the effects of unemployment, it was found that the unlimited amount of leisure time enjoyed by the unemployed men prevented them from making any use of it. The behaviour of the brickmaker suggested that an unlimited amount of work raises the same difficulty unless it is organised in some way' (ibid.).

Towards an explanation

Jahoda has become associated, within the field, with a particular line of explanation of the effects of unemployment. She has outlined this as an application of the notions of manifest and latent functions, due to Merton, to the accumulated evidence of the psychological experience of unemployment, (e.g. Jahoda 1979, 312). According to this explanation, the manifest or intended function of being employed for a person is to earn a living. Employment also however, Jahoda asserts, provides five latent or unintended functions for the employed person. In addition to imposing a time structure on the waking day (see above) employment is said to imply regular shared experiences and contacts with people beyond their families; link an individual to transcending goals and purposes; define aspects of personal status and identity and enforce activity. Implicit in these five functions is a sixth, which Jahoda has recently made explicit: employment has a 'control function' (Jahoda 1986, 110).

Merton's work was not published until 1949. It is exciting to discover in *Unemployed Men at Work* very clear traces of the developing conceptualisation which made Merton's work eventually appear appropriate to Jahoda as an ordering device.

Jahoda had touched lightly on some of these themes in *Marienthal*. The essential notions of manifest and latent function, for example, are implicit in her reference to the women of Marienthal: 'the women are merely unpaid, not really unemployed ... Their work has a definite purpose, with numerous fixed tasks, functions and duties that make for regularity'. These functions remained, in the monograph, largely implicit and undeveloped however. The major part of the explanatory burden fell on poverty, the lack of the manifest function of employment: an income.

Thus, the decline in social activity and contact in Marienthal was explained principally *not* by reference to the withdrawal of employment imposed contacts with people outside the family but by reference to financial privation: on 'just one quarter of the normal wages ... It is understandable that under these circumstances the fulfilment of social duties or of the most simple cultural needs is out of the question' (Jahoda *et al.* 1972, 31 and 32). As we read earlier, fall off in club membership was largely a 'matter of financial interest'.

In *Unemployed Men at Work* whilst the latent functions account is by no means fully developed, emphasis has started to be placed on the notions of intended and unintended consequences of employment and, in particular, collective purpose and compulsion. Thus, employment in the pit was said to have produced a 'complex social atmosphere in which the employment rhythm mastered all others ... *penetrated by conscious and unconscious forces* '[my emphasis] (Jahoda this volume). Work in the Society was said to aim to produce 'real goods in the sense that unemployed men and others could experience benefit from them' (ibid.). However, for many the Society 'was not quite real for them'. This was 'due to two factors: first, the economic benefit was not large enough to permit them to live a normal life, secondly their habits of thought did not permit them to envisage any development that did not imply enjoying normal wages and working conditions in the prime of their lives (ibid.).

As regards links to purposes and goals which transcended the individual: 'the amount of collective social experience represented by the members of the SPS was one of its main positive effects' (ibid.). A major failing of the SPS, however, according to Jahoda, was nevertheless the lack of a 'compelling work atmosphere'. The 'atmosphere of normal industrial work' did not consist in 'isolated incentives' but in 'a complex work atmosphere which had compelling force'. The Society, however, had nothing which might have been compared with this compelling effect of the work atmosphere in normal industry' (ibid.).

Finally, the core of Jahoda's explanatory model is the notion of withdrawal or deprivation. Employment is said to provide certain latent functions in a combination which is necessary for mental health. Unemployment is said to lead to the withdrawal or deprivation of this combination.

In Marienthal, the embryonic notion was there: 'cut off from their work and deprived of contact with the outside world, the workers of Marienthal have lost their material and moral incentives to make use of their time' (Jahoda *et al.* 1972, 66) but it is tempered with emphasis on the material, poverty related, factors. In *Unemployed Men at Work*, however, the notion has a more psychological, ideological, social historical emphasis: 'the thought system then current was rooted in the tradition of mining. Since the basis of the whole structure, i.e. employment in the mine, had been withdrawn, the whole system had lost its balance'.

The Eastern Valley investigation is a conceptual landmark on the way to Jahoda's eventual account of the distress of unemployment in terms of manifest and latent functions of employment and deprivation of them by unemployment.

Routes of influence

Applied to the Marienthal investigations the adjective 'seminal', often overworked so inappropriately, is for once entirely fitting. This Austrian field work, and the various reports and summaries of it, is without serious doubt the most widely cited and influential work in published psychological research on unemployment. It is true that the study was empirically surpassed in some respects in the 1930s by the work of Bakke (1933) and the Pilgrim Trust (1938) and in recent years in other respects by Kasl *et al.* (1975) and Warr's team (e.g. Warr 1984) — Jahoda herself maintained the investigations were 'technically primitive' (Jahoda 1979). However, *Marienthal* has not previously been approached by anything in the published literature for vision, ingenuity, decency or, except perhaps for Eisenberg and Lazarsfeld's ubiquitously cited 1938 review, influence. With the publication of *Unemployed Men at Work* that state of affairs is likely to alter.

How did the *Marienthal* investigation's influence spread? Recall that the fieldwork was conducted in 1930/1931. In the very next year the first published account emerged, it is retrospectively interesting to note, in English (Lazarsfeld 1932). The orginal full monograph was published in the following year in German as *Die Arbeitslosen von Marienthal* but in the same year (1933), the investigation received more publicity in another English language paper. The Save the Children International Union published in that year a series of enquiries into the effects of unemployment on children and young people. Part II, pp 115-135 was written by a certain Marie Jahoda-Lazarsfeld and included relevant data from the investigations in Marienthal and a neighbouring village in lower Austria, Donawitz, and Vienna. Two years later, Zawadski and Lazarsfeld (1935) published a description and psychological evaluation of a set of biographies of unemployed people collected by the Institute of Social Economy, Warsaw. This paper too found it useful to summarise the main findings of the Marienthal investigations: relating to attitudes.

Nineteen thirty eight saw the publication of Eisenberg and Lazarsfeld's influential review paper which referred repeatedly not only to the original monograph but to Lazarsfeld's own accounts of 1932 and 1935. By this time, according to the Pilgrim Trust (1938) the 'survey of unemployment carried out at Marienthal' was already 'well known', although their exaggeration of the role of Dr Gertrude Wagner, who helped with the Pilgrim Trust study and whom they mistakenly claimed was a member of the Marienthal team, suggests only a sketchy familiarity with the details. Of more interest here though in Pilgrim Trust (1938) is the extended discussion of the Upholland Scheme, prototype of the Eastern Valley Subsistence Production Society, together with a footnote concerning a 'second scheme in Monmouthshire where the experience gained during the first experiment has borne fruit'. The 'underlying assumption of Subsistence Production' was described by Pilgrim Trust as that 'idle hands can be trained to produce goods'. It is interesting in this connection that the dust jacket of the First Edition of Pilgrim Trust carried a photograph of a pair of idle hands inert on a table top. In any event this is the first reference in print I have found to the Eastern Valley Investigation.

Marie Jahoda herself published a brief account of the SPS study in 1942 (Jahoda 1942) but otherwise mention in print seems to disappear until 1981.

The same fate did not befall the study's elder sister, *Marienthal*. Via the original monograph (1933), Jahoda's Save the Children (1933) article or at least one of Lazarsfeld's papers (of 1932, 1935 and 1938), the investigation was publicised via Beales and Lambert (1934), Cantril (1934), Hall (1934) and Pilgrim Trust (1938). These early reports were long influential. Query (1968), for example, refers to the investigation via Zawadski and Lazarsfeld (1935). The ripple of influence spread far and wide.

There was, however, a second even more powerful surge of influence of the Marienthal study in the 1970s and into the 1980s. In 1972 an English language 'translation' of the monograph was published. Then in 1979 the text of Jahoda's Myers lecture was published in the *Bulletin of the British Psychological Society* (Jahoda 1979). This paper included both a brief summary of the Marienthal investigation and also for the first time, a clear statement of the manifest and latent functions account of unemployment distress. A more popular version of essentially the same paper also emerged that year in *New Society*. It seems likely that both these articles were based on ideas being worked out by Jahoda and Rush for a systematic exposition which emerged as a research paper next year (Jahoda and Rush 1980) and as a book two years later (Jahoda 1982).

This second wave of influence was virtually tidal in proportion. In brief, it is difficult to find a single prominent current researcher who has not cited in references one of these publications, with the 1972 version and the 1979 *Bulletin* paper the clear leaders in the field in terms of citation.

If the ripples of influence of the Marienthal investigation have been persistent and wide ranging, the impact of the Eastern Valley investigation — quintessential Jahoda research of great power and elegance — has been muted and subtle, permeating through her influential conceptualising but so *sotto voce* as to be virtually unattributable. After 1942 it disappeared from the published literature until Jahoda's paper of 1981, where the reasons for self imposed censorship rather than the material itself were the focus of attention. The following year a slightly fuller account of the investigation appeared (Jahoda 1982). Apart from the Pilgrim Trust (1938) allusion, in the very year the research was in progress, I am aware of no secondary citing. Now half a century after the original fieldwork was completed, the research report, with only minor alterations, is published.

References

BAKKE, E.W. (1933). *The Unemployed Man*. London: Nisbet.

BEALES, H.L. and LAMBERT, R.S. (1934/1973). *Memoirs of the Unemployed*. Wakefield, UK: E.P. Publishing.

CANTRIL, H. (1934). 'The Social Psychology of Everyday Life.' *Psychological Bulletin*, *31* (5), 297-330.

ECROYD, H. (1983). 'Subsistence Production in the Eastern Valley of Monmouthshire. An Industrial Experiment, 1935 to 1939'. *Llafur, The Journal of Welsh Labour History, 3*, 34-47.

EISENBERG, P., and LAZARSFELD, P.F. (1938). 'The Psychological Effects of Unemployment.' *Psychological Bulletin, 35*, 358-390.

GORE, S. (1978). 'The Effect of Social Support in Moderating the Health Consequences of Unemployment'. *Journal of Health and Social Behaviour, 19*, 157-165.

HALL, O.M. (1934). 'Attitudes to Unemployment'. *Archives of Psychology, New York, 25*, No. 165.

INTO WORK (1980). *Looking for an Opening* and *Working for Experience*. London: Lithosphere Printing Co-operative Ltd.

JAHODA, M. (1942). 'Incentives to Work — A Study of Unemployed Adults in a Special Situation. *Occupational Psychology, 16* (1), 20-30.

JAHODA, M. (1979). 'The Impact of Unemployment in the 1930s and the 1970s.' *Bulletin of the British Psychological Society, 32*, 309-314.

JAHODA, M. (1981). 'To Publish or Not to Publish?' *Journal of Social Issues, 37* (1), 208-220.

JAHODA, M. (1982). Employment and Unemployment: A Social-psychological Analysis. Cambridge, UK: Cambridge University Press.

JAHODA, M. (1986). 'The Social Psychology of the Invisible: an interview with Marie Jahoda by David Fryer'. *New Ideas in Psychology, 4* (1), 107-118.

JAHODA, M. (1986). 'In Defence of A Non-reductionist Social Psychology'. *Social Behaviour: An International Journal of Applied Social Psychology. 1*, 25-29.

JAHODA-LAZARSFELD, M. (1933). 'The Influence of Unemployment on Children and Young People in Austria'. In: *Children, Young People and Unemployment*, The Save the Children International Union, Part II, 115-137, Geneva.

JAHODA, M. and RUSH, H. (1980). *Work, Employment and Unemployment*, SPRU Occasional Paper No.12, ISBN 0 903622 13 0.

JAHODA, M., LAZARSFELD, P.F. and ZEISEL, H. (1972). *Marienthal: The Sociography of an Unemployed Community*. London: Tavistock Publications Ltd.

KASL, S.V., GORE, S. and COBB, S. (1975). 'The Experience of Losing a Job: reported changes in health, symptoms and illness behaviour'. *Psychosomatic Medicine, 37*, 106-122.

LAZARSFELD, P. (1932). 'An Unemployed Village'. *Character and Personality*, *1*, 147-151.

LAZARSFELD-JAHODA, M. and ZEISEL, H. (1933). *Die Arbeitslosen von Marienthal*. Leipzig: Hirzel.

MERTON, R.K. (1949) *Social Theory and Social Structure*. Glencoe, Illinois: The Free Press.

PILGRIM TRUST (1938). *Men Without Work*. Cambridge: Cambridge University Press.

QUERY, W.T. (1968) *Illness Work and Poverty*. San Francisco: Jossey Bass Inc.

WARR, P.B. (1984). 'Job Loss, Unemployment and Psychological Well-being. In: V. Allen and E. van de Vliert (eds), *Role Transitions*, New York: Plenum Press.

ZAWADSKI, B. and LAZARSFELD, P. (1935). 'The Psychological Consequences of Unemployment'. *Journal of Social Psychology*, *6*, 224-251.

3

Felicity Henwood and Ian Miles

The experience of unemployment and the sexual division of labour

Introduction: work, unemployment and women's lives

Research has repeatedly documented the material and social problems faced by unemployed people. There has been considerable debate about the nature of the relationship between ill-health and unemployment. The balance of research suggests that unemployment in Western societies contributes to a variety of physical health problems, although the evidence is somewhat confounded by the associations between unemployment and poverty and by the tendency of unemployment to be more concentrated among people whose previous jobs were of low quality (see Hayes and Nutman 1981, Jahoda and Rush 1980, Kelvin and Jarrett 1985, Macky and Haines 1982, Warr 1984a, b). There is strong support for job loss and unemployment being implicated in poor mental health, with various types of longitudinal and cross-sectional study tending to yield the same results. (For literature reviews see John *et al.* 1983b, Miles 1983b, Spruit 1983.)

Noting that the sorts of psychological problems reported among groups of unemployed men have been remarkably consistent over some 50 years — years in which the affluent society and welfare state have surely transformed the material circumstances of employed and unemployed alike — Marie Jahoda suggested that these problems do not stem from financial hardship alone (Jahoda 1979, 1982, Jahoda and Rush 1980). She argues that to have a job places one in a complex set of social relationships, going beyond the wage relation. Five experiences which are crucial to psychological well-being — social contacts, status, time structure, activity and being part of some collective purpose — are typically provided in our society by formal employment. These experiences may be gained through other means but the wage relation provides a rationale which impels people into social relations which usually involve these experiences. It does so in a way that may not encourage the development of skills for seeking them out and establishing them from scratch. With the decline of traditional forms of household production and community life and with an increasing proportion of the population participating in the labour force, employment has become increasingly the means of gaining access to these categories of experience.

Most claims about the negative consequences of separation from employment are based on research concerned with men and their experience of unemployment (and, in some cases, retirement). It is only recently that comparative studies including women, and detailed explorations of their experience of unemployment, have emerged (e.g. Adamson *et al.* 1978, Coyle 1984, Hall 1984, Hancock 1982, Warr and Parry 1982) and most of these studies are largely descriptive. Is Jahoda's analysis relevant to both men and women?

Why should the psychological implications of unemployment be any different for women? Before we can answer this question, we need to consider how the term 'unemployment' is defined and used. In common usage, 'unemployment' means not having a job. Why, then, is unemployment amongst women not seen to be much higher than it is amongst men? Whilst female employment has grown more rapidly than male employment over the post-war period, the proportion of women of working age in employment is still notably lower than that of men (Wainwright 1978). In addition, women form a greater proportion of retired people than do men (Abrams 1978).

Despite these 'facts', unemployment figures record men's unemployment as being much higher than women's (Joseph 1983, Allin and Hunt 1982). There are several reasons for this. Retired people and full-time housewives do not appear in the figures: unemployment statistics only include the 'economically active' (those employed, or looking for employment, in the formal economy) which means that these two groups, not regarded as economically active, are excluded.

Furthermore, unemployment statistics are compiled from those people actually registering themselves as available for employment. Large numbers of married women and/or women with children who are not in paid work do not register and therefore do not appear in official unemployment figures. These women do not register because they are, in social policy terms, defined as 'ineligible' for benefit, a term which, we would suggest, may reinforce amongst such women, the feeling that they are not really 'unemployed'.

The acceptance of a sexual division of labour which sees men as the breadwinners (expected to do paid work or, if unable to secure employment, to register as unemployed and claim benefit) and women as the carers (expected to perform a disproportionate share of unpaid domestic work and be financially dependent on men) is, thus, embodied in social policies and reflected in the official unemployment figures.

Women's experiences of unemployment are, then, likely to be very different from those of men, which raises the question as to whether the Jahoda analysis is generalisable across the sexes. For example, we might expect that non-employed women are less liable to be leading a life without work than are unemployed men. For a significant number of these women, housework and childcare are likely to take up a great deal of their time. Data from the 1983/1984 ESRC time-budget survey (Gershuny *et al*. 1986) demonstrate that the volume of domestic work carried out by unemployed men was considerably greater than that of employed men — at least on weekdays — but still fell far below that of the non-employed women they were living with (see also Laite and Halfpenny, this volume). Indeed, it fell below that of non-employed women and part-time employed women in general, although it was above full-time employed women on average (Thomas *et al*. 1985). What is not clear, however, is to what extent, and in what ways, this 'women's work' can be seen to compensate for the lack of formal employment. The research we describe below sets out, in part, to answer this question.

We shall present the results of a number of studies which bear on these issues. They represent tests of hypotheses derived from Jahoda's analysis. While we believe that the results generally support the hypotheses, and thus the analysis, they do not constitute proof of the analysis so much as confirmation that it is a fruitful direction for research. One major limitation of our studies is that we are dealing with cross-sectional data: while we can control for some of the differences between employed and unemployed people, we are not really able to trace the impact of change over time on any one person, and our ability to make inferences about causality is thus limited.

The first study which we shall describe (the 'Henwood' study) was actually carried out subsequent to the second (the 'Miles' study). We present them in reverse chronological order because the Henwood study involved both men and women, and it addressed what is logically the first of the hypotheses that concern us.

Employment, unemployment and ACE

Jahoda argues, first, that being in formal employment brings access to certain categories of experience (ACE) often denied to those not in formal employment; and, second, that having access to these categories of experience is important for psychological well-being. Both of Jahoda's claims have been given impressionistic support by a number of observers (e.g. Fagin and Little 1984, Seabrook 1983). The Henwood study, carried out in 1983, used rather simple measures in an attempt to investigate these two claims in a systematic fashion. It was based on a postal questionnaire distributed to a sample of Brighton residents and by a home visit, together with the recruitment of some unemployed interviewees at the Unemployment Benefit Office (rather few were located by the postal questionnaire). Some 117 men and 107 women eventually completed the set of questions (see Henwood 1983, for further details).

Seven groups of people form the great majority of the sample: full-time employed women and men, part-time employed women, unemployed (signing on) women and men; (self-defined) housewives, and retired people. Certain characteristic differences between the groups in our sample should be borne in mind when interpreting our results. Nearly all women in part-time employment were married (or 'living together' with men) nearly 75% had children for whom they were fully or in part responsible. Women in full-time employment were also more likely than not to be married, but they were younger and less likely to have children than part-time employees. Housewives were mostly married and approximately 50% had children; this rather low proportion relates to the fact that the sample produced a large proportion of older housewives, who do not remain responsible for children. Unemployed women, like unemployed men, were more likely not to be married, less often had children and tended to be younger than their employed counterparts. Of employed men, 75% were married and over 50% had children.

The questionnaire was a brief one, with single-item measures of each of the Jahoda categories. Responses to the items were all on 0—10 point scales, with the extremes being defined as 'this is not my experience at all' and 'this is very much my experience'. The items we used — drawing on an earlier Miles study — were:

Social contact	I meet a broad range of people in my everyday life.
Activity	The things I have to do keep me busy most of the day.
Collective purpose	I feel that, at this time in my life, I'm making a positive contribution to society at large.
Status	Society, in general, respects people like me.
Time structure	Much of the day, I have to do things at regular times

Our results showed a positive relationship between being in employment and ACE, as the Jahoda argument suggests. Both employed men and employed women scored significantly higher on all five main categories of experience than their registered unemployed counterparts, as predicted (Table 1). Thus cross-sectional evidence supports Jahoda's hypotheses that, for unemployed men and women, ACE tends to be depressed below the level that would be likely to be obtained if employed. There are no sex differences within the full-time employed and unemployed groups: employment and unemployment seem to be having similar consequences for this sample of respondents.

Table 1. Henwood's study of group differences in ACE

	Social contacts	Activity	Collective purpose	Status	Time structure
Full-time employed men	7.5	8.4	6.0	5.8	5.1
	(2.6)	(1.9)	(2.9)	(2.7)	(3.3)
$n = 56$					
Unemployed men	6.3	4.9	3.4	2.5	3.0
	(3.7)	(3.9)	(3.8)	(3.1)	(4.0)
$n = 35$					
Comparison: employed and unemployed men	FTE>U	FTE>U	FTE>U	FTE>U	FTE>U
Full-time employed women	8.2	8.9	6.3	5.9	6.3
	(1.90)	(1.8)	(2.9)	(2.9)	(3.4)
$n = 28$					
Part-time employed women	6.6	9.2	5.7	5.2	7.1
	(3.3)	(2.3)	(2.7)	(3.8)	(3.0)
$n = 16$					
Unemployed women	5.3	6.7	3.7	2.4	2.7
	(3.6)	(3.4)	(3.5)	(2.8)	(3.5)
$n = 20$					
Housewives	4.5	7.3	4.7	5.9	5.8
	(3.3)	(2.6)	(3.6)	(3.3)	(3.2)
$n = 20$					
Comparison: full-time employed and unemployed women	FTE>U	FTE>U	FTE>U	FTE>U	FTE>U

	Social contacts	Activity	Collective purpose	Status	Time structure
Part-time employed and unemployed women	n.s.	PTE>U	n.s.	PTE>U	PTE>U
Housewives and full-time employed women	FTE>H	FTE>H	n.s.	n.s.	n.s.
Housewives and unemployed women	n.s.	n.s.	n.s.	H>U	H>U

Figures are means with standard deviations in parentheses. Significant group differences are as indicated at the 0.05 level or below by *t*-tests; n.s. = not significant.

Housewives, retired people and ACE

If the loss/absence of particular categories of experience causes the psychological problems associated with unemployment, then how do all those women who remain housewives, lacking access to these experiences via formal employment, cope? Do any of the activities associated with being a housewife provide ACE – or does the absence of certain of these categories of experience explain, in part, the sense of purposelessness and depression experienced by many housewives? (Oakley 1974, 1976, Brown and Harris 1978). As part of the background research for this chapter we have engaged in some analyses of the national 'Quality of Life' studies carried out in the early 1970s, which give us representative samples of employed women and housewives (see Hall 1984). One of the instruments in these studies was a set of semantic differential scales and we were able to compare housewives and full-time employed women in terms of these. While the differences are not large in absolute terms, statistically significant differences were observable between the two groups (even when we controlled for the woman's age, household, social class and marital status/age of youngest child). The housewives were prone to give their lives scores that were further toward the end of the scales labelled as boring, miserable, tied down, empty, frustrating and unsuccessful; there were no differences in terms of fun, happiness, or the 'roughness' and 'hardness' of life.

So, even if the problems of housewives are not as marked (or markedly publicised) as those of unemployed people, it looks as if there is an issue here. How would we expect housewives to fare in terms of ACE, given that by definition they have domestic work responsibilities but no formal employment? Compared to unemployed women, domestic responsibilities would be likely to lead to higher levels of committed activity, time structure and — if servicing family needs is seen as 'collective' — collective purposes, but we would also except them to achieve lower ACE scores in general than their employed counterparts, as the semantic differential results hint. In particular, their social contacts are likely to be at a low level, like those of unemployed women, their sense of status may be higher (since the social role of housewife is defined in positive terms, the role of an unemployed person solely in negative terms).

The results partially bear out these expectations (Table 1). Housewives did not differ significantly from unemployed women in terms of social contacts and activity, while scoring significantly lower on these categories of experience than women in full-time employment. In terms of status and time structure, these housewifes resembled women in full-time employment, scoring significantly higher than unemployed women. For the fifth category of experience — collective purposes — housewives did not differ significantly from either employed or unemployed women, falling between the two groups. The differences between groups remained significant even when background factors like age and marital status are taken into account (Henwood 1983).

Housewives' low scores on *social contacts* confirms those studies recording the sense of isolation they often feel; and social contacts are a major non-financial reason for women wanting paid work. (The financial reasons are very strong, however; the idea of women's work as 'pin money' is largely a myth). In terms of *activity*, the difference found between employed women and housewives may have more to do with the very high score for full-time employed women, rather than housewives having particularly little access to this category of experience. Part-time employed women scored particularly highly on this category of experience: presumably this reflects the dual responsibilities of this group of women.

It is not surprising to find housewives to be more *structured in their use of time* than unemployed women. To be a housewife implies having particular tasks to fulfil which may need to be organised to fit in around the needs and timetables of children and/or husband. Exactly which aspects of the housewife role account for the self-reported status being similar to that of women in full-time employment and higher than that of unemployed women is not clear. Given that our sample of housewives were older and more likely to be married than women in full-time employment, the high felt status may be partially explained in terms of age and marital status/parenthood. In subsequent research, with a larger sample, we have used postal questionnaire methods and multi-item measures of ACE. Here again, we found housewives to report fewer social contacts than employed women and to resemble them in terms of activity as well as status; they fell between employed and unemployed women in terms of collective purpose and time structure. Group comparisons such as this may, however, be affected by the particular samples involved; we suspect that this was indeed a particularly active group of housewives (Miles and Howard 1984b).

Table 2. ACE and retired people in the Henwood study

	Social contacts	Activity	Collective purpose	Status	Time structure
Retired men	4.6 (3.3)	7.3 (2.8)	3.7 (3.1)	5.5 (2.7)	3.6 (3.7)
n = 16					
Contrast with:					
employed men	E > R	n.s.	E > R	n.s.	n.s.
unemployed men	n.s.	R > U	n.s.	R > U	n.s.
Retired women	4.2 (3.9)	7.6 (2.7)	4.6 (4.1)	6.4 (3.3)	3.7 (3.1)
n = 15					
Contrast with:					
full-time employed women	E > R	n.s.	n.s.	n.s.	E > R
housewives	n.s.	n.s.	n.s.	n.s.	n.s.
Unemployed women	n.s.	n.s.	n.s.	R > U	n.s.

Scores are means with standard deviations in parentheses. Group differences are assessed via *t*-test; n.s. = not significant.

Another group that we can look at is retired people, although our sample sizes here are quite small. No significant differences were found (in terms of our ACE measures) between retired women and retired men. The group whom retired people most closely resemble are housewives: only in terms of the former's reporting little time structure do they differ significantly. The fact that retired women report less time structure than do housewives fits our suggestion that housewives' time structure is to do with the organisation of time imposed by the working hours of husbands and/or the school hours of children. Like housewives, our retired sample were particularly low in terms of social contacts. In other respects they fell between the employed and unemployed samples, resembling unemployed people in terms of collective purpose and time structure and employed people in terms of status (Table 2). Given that we know from other sources that the range of activities in which retired people typically engage is rather limited (e.g. Abrams 1978, Henley Centre 1982, Miles 1984), the high self-rating on this activity scale is rather puzzling. Perhaps there is a lowering of expectations, or a sense of greater physical and social obstacles having to be overcome to engage in many activities.

ACE and well-being: a study of unemployed men

The earlier Miles study, carried out in Brighton in 1982, was not concerned with contrasting ACE across social groups. Instead, it sought to address the questions: how far, within a sample of unemployed men, are there variations in ACE; are there means other than formal employment for this group to achieve ACE; and do variations in ACE relate to psychological well-being? (For more details of this study, see Miles 1983a.) We interviewed some 300 men recruited after 'signing on' at the local Unemployment Benefit Office, using multi-item questionnaire measures of ACE and of well-being, such as the General Health Questionnaire (Banks *et al.* 1980).

The results of this study did indicate a wide span of variation in ACE scores among the unemployed men. Furthermore, some of the questionnaire measures — such as those of activity and social contacts — could be compared with other indicators. There were significant correlations between responses to such items as 'I meet a broad range of people in my everyday life' and measures of social participation derived from time budgets and from questionnaire inquiries into the frequency of different types of social contact. Thus we are inclined to believe that the ACE scores represent something more than response biases.

The men's reported access to each of the categories of experience through their social relationships were found to be positively correlated with measures of psychological well-being. A summary measure of ACE, based on all five of the specific scales, revealed considerable differences in well-being between unemployed men with preponderantly low and those with preponderantly high scores. While we cannot definitely rule on the causal processes here — perhaps men with certain psychological resources are both less prone to depression and more able to obtain ACE of their own accord — the results do suggest that different ways of using one's time after losing (or not finding) a job may be important determinants of one's well-being.

The sorts of activities which were found to be associated with higher reported access to the five categories of experience included sports, community work and some sorts of social and family activities. On the whole, they were the more active ways of spending time, as opposed to the more passive ones, for example TV-watching or long walks (often taken just to get out of the house).

With the fairly large sample, it was possible to control for a variety of background factors. The results described above remained statistically significant when such factors were taken into account. For example, age, family type, previous occupational level, reasons for leaving employment (including ill-health), and scores on the Work Involvement Scale (Warr *et al*, 1979) did not displace the relationship between ACE and well-being. (Indeed, we are inclined to see 'work involvement' as a reflection of one's sense of dependence on paid employment as a source of finance and ACE.) Some of these background variables were, however, related to ACE and social participation; notably higher money worries — concerns about the financial hardships imposed by unemployment — were associated with lower ACE. This suggests that poverty contributes to unemployed men's difficulty in establishing and maintaining the sorts of social relationships provided by employment. (A familiar tale told to us was that interviewees had felt obligied to drop out of social activities because they felt that they were financial burdens on their employed friends — the archetypal situation was being unable to purchase a round of drinks.) The length of time they had been unemployed and their prior occupational status had, by and large, no relation with the ACE measures (Miles 1984). But family type was related to experience of collective purposes and status. Separated men were low on each measure; members of couples with children reported high collective purpose; single unmarried men and members of childless couples reported higher feelings of status. Age was strongly related to social contacts (they declined consistently with age), and displayed a curvilinear relation with activity (which was lowest for middle-aged groups).

Analysis of recall and time-budget measures of social activities generally supported the results noted above — with the exception that engagement in a wide range of active pursuits, as assessed via time budgets, seems to decline with age. (This contrasts with the curvilinear trend suggested by the interview questions concerning the men's sense of business and fullness of time but it corresponds to trends revealed in the population at large through time budget studies.) The general picture to emerge applying to employed as well as unemployed men was that being separated tends to be associated with social isolation: single men tend to socialise more; members of couples are engaged in family activities to a greater degree and social contacts and active pursuits tend to decline with age. While these age-related trends are often interpreted in terms of biological ageing, we suspect that they involve various social processes that exclude not only the elderly, but a broad range of 'non-young' people, from our youth-oriented social institutions. In any case, it is clear that social circumstances condition access to the social relationships, the categories of experience, highlighted by Jahoda. This underlines the need to be aware of possible differences in the experience of the two sexes.

Women's well-being and the categories of experience

In the Miles study, a high correlation had been found between the General Health Questionnaire and a symptom-based measure of well-being, on the one hand, and a single-item measure of life satisfaction derived from the Quality of Life studies. Thus we determined to use this measure as the dependent variable in the later Henwood study. It simply asks respondents to answer the question: 'How satisfied or dissatisfied are with your life, in general, nowadays?' on an 11-point scale with 0 representing 'the lowest level of satisfaction' and 10 'the highest level of satisfaction'.

One approach to the Jahoda analysis involves relating our ACE measures to this well-being measure. If differences in well-being between employed and unemployed people are related to the differential ACE between the two groups, then we would expect to find a marked diminution in the former differences when we control for ACE. (Other factors — such as financial hardship — are likely to prevent the differences from disappearing completely.)

Taking both men and women, from the Henwood sample, there is the expected significant difference in life satisfaction between those in full-time employment (mean 6.5) and those unemployed (mean 5.4). We simply summed the five individual ACE measures to made an overall scale of access to categories of experience (CATEXP). For our 139 cases, under analysis of variance, CATEXP is highly associated (F-test significant below 0.000 level) with life satisfaction; and after controlling for CATEXP, neither sex nor employment status remained significantly associated with life satisfaction. (The significance levels were 0.256 and 0.172, respectively.) This result is not merely in line with our expectations — the disappearance of the association between employment status and satisfaction after controlling for CATEXP is more than we had bargained for!

However, a close inspection of the results suggests that things are rather complicated and that our measure of well-being is rather flawed. Our 139 cases consisted of 91 men and 48 women — due to the relative difficulty in locating full-time employed, and unemployed, women (as compared to men). When we replicated the analysis of variance within each sex, we found that the association between CATEXP and life satisfaction was still highly significant for men (below 0.000) but did not quite reach significance for women (0.084). In neither case was employment status associated with life satisfaction *after* controlling for CATEXP, but, furthermore, we found that without taking CATEXP into account, there was a significant difference between the life satisfaction scores of employed and unemployed men (a mean score of 6.7 and 5.5 respectively) but not between full-time employed and unemployed women (6.6 and 5.2).

To some extent this failure to substantiate our expectations may relate to the relatively small sample of women involved here, but we have also been led to reconsider the adequacy of our life satisfaction measure as a well-being indicator. One reason for this is the further result that our housewives do *not* fall between the employed and unemployed in terms of life satisfaction ratings in the way that their mixed pattern of ACE would have led us to expect. They actually awarded themselves the highest scores. (The mean self-ratings for women were: full-time employed 6.2, unemployed 5.2, housewives 7.2: there is a significant difference here only between the housewives and the unemployed women.)

In contrast to reports about feelings, symptoms or competences, the life satisfaction measure asks respondents to make an evaluative judgement about their living circumstances. Satisfaction is typically associated with accomplishment rather than with happiness; it refers to one's performance in terms of some standard of comparison (Mason and Faulkenberry 1978). Shin and Johnson (1978) argue that self-reports of overall happiness — as opposed to items that enquire into one's experience of feeling pleasure, misery, etc., are also based on an evaluation of performance against goals. For people who regard themselves as unemployed, this standard is likely to be their circumstances when they were employed; thus their evaluations are markedly depressed compared to those of employed people. Housewives, in contrast, may be making their evaluation in the light of the housewife role.

This life satisfaction measure was one of a battery of instruments used in the 1974 and 1975 Quality of Life surveys. For the Henwood study, it was chosen for its simplicity, its high correlation with more sophisticated measures in the Miles study and the availability of a national source of data in the Quality of Life surveys. These surveys asked a number of other well-being-related questions, including an investigation of health symptoms and used the Bradburn Affect Balance Scale (which enquires about the experience of a range of feelings in one's recent life). There were too few unemployed people in these surveys to make comparative analysis possible — but there were quite large samples of employed women and housewives. Table 3 displays the life satisfaction ratings of different groups of women, together with a number of symptom measures.

On this broader sample, housewives certainly do *not* appear to be more satisfied than the employed women. Satisfaction levels in general do appear higher in this national sample (the balmy 1970s?) but the housewives do report more 'psychological' symptoms, as we would expect in view of the research literature concerning the incidence of depression and tranquiliser use among different groups of women (e.g. Nathanson 1980). Likewise, there are higher levels of negative affect, and lower positive affect, among housewives. *Within* this national sample of housewives, we find highly significant correlations between life satisfaction scores and the reported incidence of these 'psychological' symptoms, and with the presence of negative and the absence of positive affect as measured by Bradburn's Affect Balance Scale. This is similar to our result in the study of unemployed men: *within* a group, life satisfaction correlates closely with well-being indicators but our suspicion is that it is less valuable as a way of comparing groups, at least in terms of well-being. If life satisfaction scores are influenced by respondents' sense of their situation compared to that of a reference group (e.g. employed women, housewives), then they will vary according to the reference group appropriate to the sample concerned. In order to make comparisons of well-being, it would seem to be much more appropriate to employ measures of symptoms, affect, and feelings about the self.

More recent studies (Miles and Howard 1984b) support this connection: here we find registered unemployed women to differ from their employed peers in well-being as well as ACE measures, in much the same way as unemployed and employed men differ. Our life satisfaction measure has not proved satisfactory itself in assessing variations in the well-being of the different groups of women — or in relating these to ACE but our simple assessment of ACE in the Henwood study does seem to represent a step towards accounting for variations in well-being such as those depicted in Table 3.

Conclusions

The Jahoda analysis appears to be a useful approach to understanding different people's experiences of unemployment. We here focused on gender differences in ACE and its relation to involvement in the formal and domestic economies. We have argued that these can be understood in terms of women's and men's relationship to work (both paid and unpaid) which is divided up along sex lines. Parental status, age and other such factors play important roles in facilitating or reducing ACE.

What are the policy implications of our analysis? Formal employment continues to be of central importance in the lives of most people. It remains important for women, despite the fact that the sexual division of labour operates in such a way as to define men as breadwinners and women as dependents and/or carers, thus causing many women to feel some ambivalence towards paid work as presently constituted. This leads us to conclude that any policies designed to create new jobs, or to redistribute the paid work that is available, should take into account the importance of this work for women, as well as for men.

This is only dealing with one side of the picture, however. Should not unpaid domestic work and childcare also be redistributed or reorganised? Our results on the absence of certain categories of experience amongst housewives — social contacts, in particular — suggests that more collective and supportive forms of childcare and domestic work would be valuable. In the case of childcare in particular, collective and supportive facilities would not only enable those taking responsibility for children to

Table 3. Life satisfaction and well-being in the Quality of Life Surveys

	Full-time employed	Part-time employed	Housewives	Retired women	Comparison of housewives and full-time employed women
Life satisfaction (0 – 10 scale)	7.9	8.2	7.7	8.1	0
Health satisfaction (0 – 10 scale)	8.2	8.4	7.3	6.9	2
Positive affect score	2.93	2.26	2.08	2.20	1,2
Negative affect score	1.06	0.89	1.35	1.20	1,2
Affect balance	1.87	1.37	0.73	1.00	1,2
Symptom incidence: (1 = not all, 2 = a little, 3 = quite a lot, 4 = a great deal)					
Colds/flu	1.67	1.46	1.68	1.71	0
Feeling dizzy	1.21	1.19	1.39	1.30	0
Aches/pains	1.71	1.68	1.88	2.24	1
Hands sweating	1.21	1.20	1.21	1.24	0
Headaches	1.76	1.58	1.71	1.52	0
Muscle twitch	1.13	1.17	1.32	1.46	2
Nervousness	1.73	1.50	1.81	1.83	0
Rapid heart beat	1.14	1.16	1.28	1.57	0
Short of breath	1.25	1.30	1.39	1.50	0
Skin rash	1.19	1.07	1.19	1.09	0
Upset stomach	1.33	1.26	1.38	1.61	0
Run down	1.69	1.55	1.76	1.71	0
Women's complaints	1.22	1.11	1.15	1.02	0
Trouble getting to sleep	1.61	1.50	1.79	2.09	0
Trouble staying asleep	1.35	1.28	1.61	1.76	0

Mean scores presented for each group. In far right column 0 = housewives not significantly different (0.05 level) from full-time employed women once age, household social class, age of youngest child and marital status controlled for; 1 = significantly different when age, household social class and age of youngest child controlled for; 2 = significantly different when age, household social class and marital status controlled for.

remain in close contact with friends and colleagues, but also increase the opportunities for women to take and retain paid work. These aspects of work might, then, also become imbued with a stronger tie to social contacts and collective purposes, perhaps leading more men to take an interest in them.

What is clear from our analysis is that many people lacking formal employment, whether formally unemployed or engaged in informal economic activities such as housework and childcare, are failing to gain access to important categories of experience which contribute towards a sense of well-being. It is a political choice as to whether governments and communities divert resources towards the creation of new jobs in the provision of a whole range of unmet social needs. Community-based activities of various kinds could also provide ACE, and, perhaps, alternatives to the 'community care' that leads to the increased isolation of many unpaid female domestic workers. Other measures include the expansion of opportunities in full- and part-time education so that more people have access to this form of work which also appears to provide ACE, as well as providing a sense of achievement and opportunities for personal growth (Miles and Howard 1984a). However, the reduction or abolition of childcare fees for those not in formal employment and the provision of adequate support facilities for all carers will be essential if such policies are not to reproduce the existing sexual division of labour.

Acknowledgements

This work was mainly carried out with financial support from the Joseph Rowntree Memorial Trust, to whom we would like to express our gratitude. Jill Howard contributed significantly to our work on this project. Our time-budget analyses have additionally been supported by the Economic and Social Research Council. For an accessable brief report, see Gershuny *et al.* (1986). John Hall of the Polytechnic of North London assisted our use of the Quality of Life data, and data tapes were efficiently supplied by the ESRC Data Archive at the University of Essex. The Quality of Life survey is described in Hall (1984). Reports of results of this survey include Hall (1976).

References

ABRAMS, M. (1978). *Beyond Three Score and Ten*. London: Age Concern.
ADAMSON, L. *et al.* (1978). *Unemployed Women: A Research Report* (Council of Social Service of New South Wales) New South Wales: D. West, Government Printer.
ALLIN, P. and HUNT, A. (1982). 'Women in Official Statistics' In Whitelegg, E. *et al. The Changing Experience of Women*. Oxford: Martin Robertson and Open University.

BANKS, M.H., CLEGG, C.W., JACKSON, P.R., KEMP, N.J., STAFFORD, E.M. and WALL, T.D. (1980). 'The use of the General Health Questionnaire as an indicator of Mental Health and Occupational Status'. *Journal of Occupational Psychology*, 53, 187-194.

BROWNE, G. and HARRIS, T. (1978). *Social Origins of Depression*. London: Tavistock.

COYLE, A. (1984). *Redundant Women*. London: Women's Press.

FAGIN, L. and LITTLE, M. (1984). *Forsaken Families*. Harmondsworth: Penguin.

GERSHUNY, J., MILES, I., JONES, S., MULLINS, C., THOMAS, G. and WYATT, S.M.E. (1986). 'Preliminary Analyses of the 1983/4 ESRC Time Budget Data, *Quarterly Journal of Social Affairs*, 2 (in press).

HALL, E. (1984). *Depression in Unemployed Swedish Women*. (Mimeo) Stockholm: Karolinska Institute, Stockholm University.

HALL, J. (1976). 'Subjective Measures of the Quality of Life in Britain, 1971 to 1975, *Social Trends*, no 7. London: HMSO

HANCOCK, M. (1982). 'Invisible Workers: women, redundancy and unemployment', *New Zealand Journal of Industrial Relations*, no 7, 173-178.

HAYES, J. and NUTMAN, P. (1981). *Understanding the Unemployed*. London: Tavistock.

HENLEY CENTRE FOR FORECASTING (1982). *Leisure Futures* (Winter 1982). London: Henley Centre.

HENWOOD, F. (1983). *Employment, Unemployment and Housework*, unpublished MSc dissertation, Service Policy Research Unit, University of Sussex.

JAHODA, M. (1982). *Employment and Unemployment: A Social Psychological Analysis*. London: Cambridge University Press.

JAHODA, M. and RUSH, H. (1980). Falmer, Brighton: Science Policy Research Unit, University of Sussex (Occasional Paper no 12).

JOHN, J., SCHWEFEL, D. and ZOLLNER, H., (eds) (1983). *Influence of Economic Instability on Health*. Berlin: Springer-Verlay.

JOSEPH, G. (1983). *Women at Work*. Oxford: Philip Allan.

KELVIN, P. and JARRET, J. (1985). *Unemployment: its social psychological effects*. Cambridge: Cambridge University Press.

LAND, H. (1981). *Parity Begins at Home*. London: SSRC/EOC.

MACKY, K. and HAINES, H. (1982). 'The Psychological Effects of Unemployment: a review of the literature', *New Zealand Journal of Industrial Relations*, no 7 (2), 123-135.

MASON, R.M. and FAULKENBERRY, G.D. (1978). 'Aspirations, Achievements and Life Satisfaction', *Social Indicators Research*, no 5, 133-150.

MILES, I. (1983a). *Adaptation to Unemployment?* Falmer, Brighton: Science Policy Research Unit (Occasional Paper no 20).

MILES, I. (1983b), 'Unemployment and Individual Well-Being in Britain.' Paper presented to WHO Workshop, Unemployment and Health, Dec 1983, Lidingo, Stockholm. Miles, Henwood and Howard (1984).

MILES, I. (1984). *Work, Non-work and Aging*. A report to the ESRC. (Mimeo) Falmer Brighton: Science Policy Research Unit, University of Sussex.

MILES, I. and HOWARD, J. (1984a), 'A study of Youth Employment and Unemployment'. In Miles. (1984)

MILES, I. (1984). *Work, Non-work and Ageing*. A report to the ESRC. (Mimeo) Falmer, Brighton: Science Policy Research Unit, University of Sussex.

MILES, I. and HOWARD, J. (1984a), 'A Study of Youth Employment and Unemployment'. In Miles (1984).

MILES, I. and HOWARD, J. (1984b). 'Categories of Experience and Well-being in Different Social Groups'. In Miles, Henwood and Howard (1984).

MILES, I., HENWOOD, F. and HOWARD, J. (1984). *Dependence, Interdependence and Changing Work Role*. A report to the Joseph Rowntree Memorial Trust. (Mimeo) Falmer, Brighton: Science Policy Research Unit, University of Sussex.

NATHANSON, C.A. (1980). 'Social Roles and Health Status among Women', *Social Science and Medicine*, *14*, 463-472.

OAKLEY, A. (1974). *The Sociology of Housework*. London: Martin Robertson.

OAKLEY, A. (1976). *Housewife*. Harmondsworth: Quartet Books.

SEABROOK, J. (1982). *Unemployment*. London: Paladin.

SHIN, D.C. and JOHNSON, D.M. (1978). 'Avowed Happiness as an Overall Indicator of the Quality of Life', *Social Indicators Research*, *5*, 475-492.

SPRUIT, I.P. (1983). *Unemployment, Employment and Health*. Leiden: Institut voor Sociale Geneeskunde, Rijksuniversiteit te Leiden.

THOMAS, G., WYATT, S. and MILES, I. (1985). *Preliminary Analyses of the 1983/4 ESRC Time Budget Survey*, A report to the ESRC. (Mimeo) Falmer, Brighton: Science Policy Research Unit, University of Sussex.

WAINWRIGHT, H. (1978). 'Women and the Division of Labour'. In P. Abrams, (ed.) *Work, Urbanism and Inequality: UK Society Today*. London: Weidenfield and Nicolson.

WARR, P. (1984a). 'Job Loss, Unemployment and Psychological Well-being '. In E. van de Vliert and V. Allen (eds) *Role Transitions*. New York: Plenum Press.

WARR, P. (1984b). 'Work and Unemployment'. In P.J.D. Drenth *et al.* (eds) *Handbook of Work and Organisation Psychology*. London: Wiley.

WARR, P. and PARRY, G. (1982). 'Paid Employment and Women's Psychological Well-being', *Psychological Bulletin*, *91*, 498-516.

WARR, P.B., COOK, J.P. and WALL, T.D. (1979). 'Scales for the Measurement of some Work Attitudes and Aspects of Psychological Well-being', *Journal of Occupational Psychology*, *52*, 129-148.

WESTCOTT, G., SVENSSON, P-G. and ZOLLNER, H.F.K., (eds) (1985). *Health Policy Implications of Unemployment*. Copenhagen: World Health Organisation.

WILSON, E. (1977). *Women and the Welfare State*. London: Tavistock.

4

Philip Ullah

Unemployed black youths in a northern city

Introduction

The term 'unemployed black youth' brings together three social categories which are socially and politically salient and in so doing creates a new category which is even more so. It conjures up images which overlap with an array of vexing social issues: the problems of the inner cities, rising crime, the despair of young people on the dole, racism, riots, police-community relations. The list is almost endless. Yet what is life like for young unemployed Afro-Caribbeans in Britain? How do they view their own joblessness and how do they cope, or fail to cope, with it?

This chapter describes a social psychological study which aimed to address questions such as these. An ethnographic approach was adopted in order to provide a qualitative account of the experiences of young black people in the labour market. This involved participant observation and informal interviews at youth centres catering for the unemployed. At the time of the study I was also working on a longitudinal survey of unemployed black, and white, youths. This survey enabled comparisons between blacks and whites to be made on measures of psychological well-being, job-seeking behaviour, various attitudes and social contacts and supports. Findings from this longitudinal study have been described elsewhere, (Banks and Ullah 1986, Banks et al. 1984, Ullah 1985, Ullah and Banks 1985, Ullah et al. 1985, Warr et al. 1985). In the ethnographic study to be described here, the focus of attention was shifted away from tests of hypothesised relationships between variables towards the social and psychological meanings of those variables for young blacks. It will be argued that their experience of unemployment needs to be viewed within the wider context of their individual and collective experiences of being black in a predominantly white society.

Although the details of the longitudinal survey have been published, the ethnographic study has not yet been fully reported. It is the aim of the remainder of this chapter to do this. However, in describing the study frequent references will be made to findings from the longitudinal survey in order to achieve a more complete understanding of the meaning and implications of some of the qualitative findings.

An ethnographic study

The setting

The ethnographic study was carried out in an industrial city in the north of England, which had at one time been internationally renowned for its manufacturing industries and the production of high quality wares. Although this reputation, and some of the larger firms, remained, there had been a steady decline in the manufacturing base of the city and in its spin-off occupations. At the time of the study (summer 1983) unemployment in the city stood at 14%.

The study consisted of a series of informal discussions with young black (Afro-Caribbean) people attending two youth centres, the Globe Caribbean Workshop and the Arrow Centre. Over a period of some three months I regularly attended these centres and gradually became known to a number of those present. The names of those taking part in these discussions have been altered to protect their identity, so too have the names of various places, streets, etc. However, many of the discussions were tape-recorded, and all quotations which appear in this text are strictly verbatim.

The Globe Caribbean Workshop is a small building which stands in the forecourt of a community centre near the centre of the city. Both buildings were originally part of a school and are of pre-war construction. In the Globe there is a small canteen area on the ground floor, where people can make hot drinks or toast. Adjacent to it are a few tables and chairs, and a table-tennis table. A larger room caters for group meetings and Sunday night discos. At the time of the study the walls were decorated with posters concerned with black political issues of the day: racist attacks on black families, apartheid in South Africa, and so on. On the first floor there is a staff office and a small adjoining room which is used to stock books and which is affectionately known as the library. Again most of the books are on black politics. Across the corridor there is a room containing stacks of plastic chairs and a television. This room is often used for group discussions as it provides a more cosy atmosphere than the larger room on the ground floor.

Although open during the day, the Globe centre was not well-attended during those hours. On a couple of mornings a week there was a mother-and-toddler group for local black women. Apart from that, most of the activity took place during the evenings, particularly at weekends.

However, on two days of the week classes in 'life and social skills' were held at the centre. These classes were attended by young blacks on the Youth Opportunities Programme (YOP). Each YOP placement entailed three days work on an employer's premises and two days of classes at the Globe. The Manpower Services Commission had arranged for staff there to act as supervisors and to find YOP placements for some of the young unemployed in that area. The staff (all black) had known many of those people prior to the start of the scheme and so were able to offer more personal counselling and placement procedures than might otherwise have been the case. They were also acutely aware of the specific needs of young blacks and the problems they were likely to encounter.

The Arrow Centre was in stark contrast to the Globe. The latter was quiet during the day, with very few people present other than the YOP trainees who were there every Thursday and Friday. By comparison, the Arrow Centre was a busy, noisy place, full of young people. The centre had been open for about four years, catering for the increasing number of unemployed young people in the city. During the first year it had been attended largely by young white males, most of them punks or skinheads. According to a member of staff there, many of these people were from very deprived homes and were frequently in trouble with the police. From about 1982 onwards more blacks began to attend the centre and at the time of the fieldwork about 95% of those attending were black.

The Arrow Centre is situated in an old building opposite the city's main Unemployment Benefit Office. It has a number of floors, including a basement, although most of the activity takes place on the ground level. In a large room on this floor there are three table-tennis tables and three pool tables. Adjoining it is a snack-bar area with a juke box and dividing both rooms is a canteen staffed by at least two women. Upon entering the building at the ground floor level one is immediately struck by the lively atmosphere. There are always four or five people around each of the games tables and against one of the walls a number of tables are used for playing dominoes. There are always at least six or seven people around each of these. The far side of the room is used for comparing and playing sound systems. Huge portable music centres are shown off by their proud owners, with several systems often being played at full volume at the same time. Reggae music is heard non-stop at the Arrow Centre.

Initial contacts with young black people were established at the Globe Centre. I had previously met the staff and discussed the possibility of conducting informal interviews with some of those attending the centre. It was agreed that I would introduce myself to the group of people attending life and social skills classes. At this meeting I described myself as a researcher working at a University. I told them that I was working on a project on youth unemployment and that this involved talking with young people to hear about their own experiences of being without a job. Although those present were not strictly unemployed, they had all experienced spells of unemployment. An important difference between youths and adults in the labour market is that the former have a range of options not open to the latter. The initial years after leaving school are often characterised by spells of unemployment, youth training, and further education as well as employment. Young people who at one particular moment in time are undergoing a training or work experience programme may not, therefore, be very different from others of a similar age who may be unemployed or in an insecure job.

The initial meeting proved to be a particularly difficult encounter and a great deal of hostility was expressed towards me by a few of those in the group. Most of the others remained silent, letting the most vocal among them act as spokesmen for the group as a whole. One of these 'spokesmen' was a young man called Steve. He was a tall, lithe person with a loud voice. Confident and extroverted, he was the sort of person who stood out in any group. Although he was initially very suspicious of my intentions, and viewed me with a considerable degree of contempt, he was later to become a valuable interviewee and a 'key informer'.

The process by which this change took place is significant because it reveals that entry into the particular subculture of these young people had first to be negotiated with them and allowed to take place on their own terms. Such entry is necessary if one is to recapture anything like the view of social reality held by those being studied. Otherwise one simply remains an outsider and is party only to the most superficial of their views and opinions. Gaining the confidence and acceptance of the interviewee is therefore an essential aspect of qualitative research. There were, inevitably, some people with whom a rapport could not be established. This was particularly true of some of the young women in the group, who were totally uninterested in talking to me about their experiences of unemployment.

The initial meeting with the group is worth reporting at some length because it also provides an insight into the way unemployment was looked upon by some of those present. These views may be taken as part of the content of the social representations of unemployment held by these people. The phenomenon of social representations is an increasingly popular and important topic within current European social psychology (Doise 1978, Farr and Moscovici 1984). Social representations are the versions of social reality which are held by particular social groups. They include cognitive phenomena such as concepts, attitudes and explanations. What distinguishes the study of social representations from the traditional social psychological approaches to these phenomena is that the former emphasises their *collective* nature (Moscovici 1981, 1982, 1984). Social representations thus involve the study of *social*, as opposed to *individual*, cognitions (Forgas 1981), attitudes (Jaspers and Fraser 1984), attributions (Hewstone *et al.* 1982) etc.

A study of the *meaning* of unemployment as it is experienced by black youths, of the explanations they offer for their own unemployment and that of those around them, their attitudes towards it and the images they hold of those whom they perceive to be influencing their lives, must almost by definition be concerned with the social representations held by young black people. The content of these representations will be unfolded during the remainder of this chapter.

Those aspects of representations which were revealed to me during the initial meeting showed how research into unemployment was looked upon by some of those present. This in turn was seen to be closely related to the role of the government in reacting to high levels of unemployment, particularly among the black population. Apart from myself, the discussion which ensued principally involved three people.

In addition to Steve there was another young man who felt it was his duty to speak for the group. His name was Sam; he was not on the YOP scheme but had simply called into the Globe to pass some time. There was also a member of staff present. His name was Clifton and he was the person responsible for finding placements for the people on this scheme and for dealing with any problems which arose. During the discussion it was clear that he felt some embarrassment at the hostile reception being given to me and attempted to defend me and my role as a researcher into unemployment.

Part of the hostility was because they thought research into unemployment was futile. Research of this type was seen as a palliative by the government and something which detracted from the real issues which needed to be dealt with. This type of attitude is clearly illustrated in the following comment by Steve:

> What can this survey do for us? It can't do nothing for me. Imagine, you: you have to live at home even if you don't want to; you get £25 a week, right; you're 17, you like to go out, buy things, buy clothes. How would you feel if you were only getting £25 a week? You don't have to ask me. You're human and I'm human. It's just the same feeling. How you'd feel, I feel. I don't want you to ask me questions, I want you to do something about it. Not *you* but them who are telling you to ask questions. I don't want them to ask questions, I want them to do something about it. Anybody knows how you feel when you're unemployed. You don't have to be unemployed to feel it.

At one point in the discussion an argument ensued between the three main protagonists. Both Sam and Steve felt that politicians would ignore the findings from research into unemployment, that these politicians were already aware of the problems faced by black people and that only mass action on the part of black unemployed youth could stir those in power into providing help for them. Clifton attempted in vain to provide some justification for the need for research and to quell more militant responses to unemployment. The argument began with Clifton suggesting that unemployed youth need to help themselves instead of relying on others for help:

Clifton: You've got to exert yourselves to do something about the situation that you're in. I know we're in a bad economic situation ......

Sam: But what can we do, personally? What can we do?

Steve: Make government know how we feel and that we are not going to stand for it. That's what we can do ... As you said, we ain't gonna get nowt, they ain't gonna give us nothing, unless we stand up and say 'We want it, and if you don't give it to us ...' Research don't do nothing. They *know* how we feel already, they *know*.

Clifton: But it helps if you have research to back up your argument.

Steve: Yes, but how much research do you need? I bet there's research .... there's people like him [the author] and whoever's employed him, spending almost a thousand pounds and it's something that won't do anything. It will just go to parliament, and they will just dash it away .... Paper ain't nowt.

Sam: Listen Clifton, paper is something to a certain extent, right. And if we're not getting nothing – then we have to do something about it. And that means action, doesn't it? Because it's alright saying 'Read this, read that', and they're reading it and saying 'Oh, black people – dash it down'. Until we stand up and say 'Right – were gonna do something about it' — *then* they will make a move. So we must do something about it.

Steve: History tells you that already. That's why I've got no confidence in paper. Sending this and that to parliament and they just dash it out.

Sam: I'm doing my best, but what can we do? Nothing – apart from scrounge this and scrounge that. And if we do thieve, we're not gonna win, because when we get caught up we're gonna get a lock put on our door. So, Clifton, *what* can we do, apart from riot and get together as one?

Steve: History tells you that you can't get now't without standing up and saying 'If you don't give us this, we're gonna do something bad'.

There are at least two important points which emerge from this brief description of that first meeting. The first concerns the way in which research into unemployment was looked upon by both Sam and Steve. Such research was viewed as a completely fruitless exercise, since it was obvious to all that unemployment was an unpleasant experience. What was the point, then, in researchers asking people what it felt like to be unemployed? This point was made very strikingly by Steve, when he said:

It's just like you walking down the street. You see a man on the road and he's been stabbed a hundred times. You don't go up to him and say 'How does it feel?'

Given such views it is not surprising that I was accorded an unfriendly reception. However, a more significant reason for their low opinion of me stemmed from the *intergroup* nature of their perceptions. This was the second, and perhaps the most important, finding to emerge from this initial encounter. One striking feature of the language used by both Steve and Sam is the 'we vs. they' framework in which it is expressed. They saw themselves as members of an oppressed minority group, whose life chances and experiences were being determined by a dominant outgroup. The latter corresponded to some vague notion of 'the white establishment' rather than any specific group within society. Thus although the Conservative government of the day was frequently criticised for its insensitivity to the problems of black people, neither Sam nor Steve attributed their unemployment to the policies of that government. Their antagonism extended to all political parties, with none of them being seen as genuinely concerned with the problems experienced by ordinary people:

Steve: I don't take no notice of them. They just talk rubbish, all of them.
Sam: They say something good and then when they get in power everything just changes, just like that.
Steve: Promises are comfort to a fool.

The distinction between 'intergroup' and 'inter-individual' behaviour is an important one within social psychology (Tajfel 1978). Once people begin to see their lives as being affected by their membership of a particular social category, rather than the individual qualities they possess, then *intergroup* behaviour is likely to emerge (Tajfel 1981). This entails the development of a sense of identification with the ingroup, along with a corresponding sense of hostility towards an outgroup. Solutions to the problems experienced by the ingroup are then seen to lie in *collective* action: in members of the group altering the status of their group as a whole rather than achieving individual gains through their own individual actions. This type of intergroup attitude can be seen in the responses to unemployment recommended by both Sam and Steve. Sam states that black people should 'get together as one' and at another point in the discussion Steve gives a grim and, in many respects, prophetic warning to the powers that be:

If you want something, you have to get it. And how the government treats us, the only way that we see that we can get that is by *fighting*. We talk to them every day and nothing is done. Only a fool carries on talking forever. You kick a dog every day: one day that dog's gonna jump up and bite you. But government should be wise and say 'We'll try and avert them things happening'.

It is important to emphasise that Steve was not simply making idle boasts in order to impress me. Although it is true that he did not belong to any radical group and that he was not in any sense an activist, he did display a remarkable depth of knowledge about the social and historical aspects of the oppression of minority groups. On a number of occasions he made references to the role played by history in shaping consciousness and in defining courses of action. And when Clifton suggested that giving money to the unemployed will not solve all of their problems, Steve's reply revealed a carefully planned and practical response:

> But I'm not talking about just giving us money, just like that. You put money *into* us instead. Instead of just giving a country money, or just giving them food, you make that country self-reliant. That way they will be able to carry on after.

The attitudes of both Sam and Steve towards me can also be explained if an intergroup perspective is adopted. Their antagonism cannot readily be seen to have arisen from any of my personal and individual qualities. Indeed I had hardly begun to speak before I was challenged by some of those present. Instead, their behaviour can be seen as being determined by their intergroup perceptions. I was not seen as an individual but as a member or associate of the group perceived to be oppressing them. Universities were seen as another white, middle-class institution. Given the strength and rigidity of this group perception, any expression of sympathetic understanding I made was met with contempt and derision, as the following exchange clearly shows:

> *P.U.*:   I feel bad about unemployment too.
> *Steve*:   You might, but we don't care.
> *P.U.*:   I feel bad when politicians don't act to prevent unemployment…
> *Steve*:   Anybody can say that. It don't matter to me. It don't mean nothing to me.

In order to overcome this barrier, it was necessary for me to attempt to differentiate myself from the group I was seen to belong to. I pointed out that I was not sitting behind a desk in a warm and comfortable office like many of my colleagues were at that moment, that I had not spent my life living in white middle-class communities isolated from the black population and indeed that I had myself attended an inner city school. I also pointed out that this was an opportunity for them to make their opinions known to those they were so antagonistic towards, since I was in a position to communicate those opinions. It was this latter point which sparked off a shift in the attitude of many of those taking part in the discussion. Largely as a result, and with the support of Clifton, they agreed that I could go to the youth centre on future occasions, observe what they were doing and saying, and ask them any questions I felt were important.

Establishing contacts and conducting interviews in the Arrow Centre was more difficult, partly due to the party atmosphere which always prevailed there. At first I attended the centre when I knew that people from the Globe would be there. I would ask them if they would introduce me to anyone they thought would be willing to be interviewed. This technique worked for the first few interviews, but after that it became clear that I was expected by Steve and his friends to establish my own contacts. This was always difficult, since when approached on an individual basis people were often suspicious of me and were reluctant to spare me any time. I often had the impression that I was being viewed with the same suspicion as originally at the Globe, although when I approached individuals they were never willing to voice these suspicions and so I was never able to reply to them. It was as if I was never allowed to go through the initiation ceremony which had enabled me to gain access to people at the Globe and so was always to remain more of an outsider at the Arrow. Despite this, I did manage to speak with a number of people at the Arrow and to tape-record most of these discussions and this material has been added to that from the Globe.

Young black people in the labour market
All of those people on the Globe's YOP scheme had left school about a year before I first attended the centre. Not one of the people interviewed had had a normal full-time job in that time yet a few of them attached any significance to this. When talking about their plans for the future, no-one mentioned the possibility of obtaining such a job. It appeared that they accepted the existence of YOP schemes, spells at college and periods of unemployment as part of their post-school 'careers', with employment being removed to some indefinable future period outside the range of their everyday plans and expectations.

This attitude was reflected in their chequered histories since leaving school. Most had been to college for a month or two, all had experienced at least one spell of unemployment and quite a few had already been on one YOP scheme. When asked what they intended to do when the present scheme ended, many said they wanted to go to college, even though some had already been to college and had left voluntarily before completing their course.

Roberts (1984) has stated that although many young people today are turning to further education, this is mainly to avoid entering the labour market and not necessarily because they value the experience of studying at college. This certainly seemed to be true of some of those at the Globe. Steve, for example, planned to go to college in the coming September to study for 'O' levels. When asked if he was looking forward to going he replied 'I didn't like it before, but... got no choice have I?' A similar fatalistic approach was adopted by a young woman called Mary. She had completed a three-week course at the Globe after leaving school and then spent six months working at the city's Housing Department as part of a YOP course. After that she went to college for a while and then started on the current course at the Globe. Each of these ventures had been interspersed by brief periods of unemployment. She had enjoyed the time spent at the Housing Department and was disappointed when they could not keep her on at the end of the six months. She left college before sitting any exams and now planned to return in the autumn for a City and Guilds foundation course in order to do a later course in fashion and design. She told me that she did not enjoy college but knew that it was necessary to enable her to do the fashion course. She regretted not having worked harder at school and not doing the current course as soon as she had left, 'but all I wanted was some money'.

Results from the longitudinal study have shown that this type of post-school 'career' is not uncommon. A total of 475 (41.3%) respondents had experienced at least one spell of YOP and at least one period of unemployment during their first year in the labour market (Ullah *et al.* 1983). A small number of these people had also spent some time at college, with blacks being more likely to have done so than whites. The qualitative material gathered from the ethnographic study suggested that this was seen by many young blacks as a perfectly normal career path after leaving school and that employment was not expected to form part of this route. In some respects this type of existence is similar to the notion of 'subemployment' suggested by Roberts *et al.* (1982) to characterise the numerous brief periods of employment and unemployment which young people today expect to experience in their first years out of school. However, it differs in the fact that employment was replaced by a YOP scheme or a further education college as the alternative to unemployment by many of those I spoke with. For example, one young man at the Globe, named Tony, said:

> ... when you're unemployed and you're my age, the most you'll get is a scheme. Anybody that leaves school — the most they'll get is a scheme. When my brother left school he had a full-time job, but nowadays, you leave school and you're on a scheme.

There was little support for the notion that the young will attempt to 'try out' a number of different jobs as a means of gaining experience or that they expect their prospects to improve with time, both of which are contained in the description of subemployment offered by Roberts *et al.* (1982). The following quotations illustrate this amply:

> Nobody's really interested in just doing a job to leave to go to another one. They want to do it for a certain period of time.

> I'd try my best to hang on to a job. You can't afford to be jumping from job to job in this day and age.

Well, look at all those people at University. They can't get jobs, so what chance is there that we can get a job?

In contrast to this, results from the longitudinal study showed that 82.5% of the initial sample agreed with the statement 'It's a good thing to try out a few different jobs after leaving school'. It is possible that many agreed with this in principle, although the realities of the labour market meant that few would actually consider leaving a job voluntarily. Instead it appeared that this type of behaviour was applied to a YOP scheme or further education college, with different courses being tried out for their suitability. For example, one young woman at the Globe said of her first YOP placement:

Eileen: First place was alright. I learned a lot there.
P.U.:   Why did you leave then?
Eileen: I don't know. Widen my experience I suppose.
P.U.:   Was it your decision to leave?
Eileen: Yes, I just left. It was my choice. I suppose I just wanted to see what other places were like.

During interviews with people at the Globe Centre I took advantage of the fact that they were all on a YOP scheme by asking them about their attitudes towards YOP schemes and their own scheme in particular. It appeared that the main reason for many of them starting the scheme at the Globe was the extra money which it paid them. Few thought it would increase their chances of getting a job. A young man called Linton told me:

It was more money but to me it was like everything else: you're not gonna learn much — just gonna be boring, that's all. Not much different from being unemployed. Only thing is you don't have to go an sign on.

Steve also reported going on the scheme to get extra money ('£25 as opposed to £18 – it's a big difference') and seemed amazed when asked if he would have attended the scheme if he had been getting £25 in unemployment benefit:

P.U.:   If it would have been the same money, do you think you would have still done the course?
Steve: I would have stayed on the dole.
P.U.:   Even though the course would have given you something to do during the day?
Steve: Fucking hell, I've got here (the Arrow) for nowt. I can come here any time I like. I don't have to be here for 9 o'clock. For the same money? No chance.

Research by Stafford (1982) has shown that participants on YOP courses exhibited lower levels of psychological distress than those who were unemployed and she suggests that this may be due to the latent benefits of employment which are provided by YOP (see Jahoda 1982). Tha above passage suggests that features such as shared social contacts, purposeful activity and a time structure may also be met by day centres such as the Globe and the Arrow Centres, leaving financial reward as the main, and often only, motivation for attending a YOP scheme. The suggestion that frequent attendance at a youth centre may help to alleviate some of the harmful psychological effects of unemployment is supported by cross-sectional results from the longitudinal study (Warr *et al.* 1985). In that study it was found that reports of the amount of time spent with friends, the amount of time spent out of the house and the amount of day-to-day variety were all significantly associated with measures of pyschological well-being among unemployed people. Those who reported the most activity and variety tended to have lower levels of psychological ill-health.

There were, however, several features of this particular scheme which aroused the antagonism of those attending it. These features tended to be those which were seen as introducing an element of unfairness into the course. For example, all participants were told that they would have nine days holiday over the six-month period of the scheme. Some time later they found that this included five bank holidays and this was greeted by many with a sense of having been deceived. Another feature which was not popular was the fact that different placements entailed different hours of work. Steve, for example, worked normal office hours at a solicitor's, while Tony just worked from 10 a.m. until 2 p.m. at a restaurant. According to Steve: 'It's not fair everybody getting the same wage. That's communism'. Such comments, centring on notions of equality, bear a striking resemblance to those given by the participants of the Subsistence Production Society described by Jahoda in this volume.

Perhaps the greatest source of hostility among these young blacks was the docking procedure, by which payment would be docked for lateness or absenteeism. Thursday mornings at the Globe Centre would largely be spent exchanging stories of who had been docked and by how much. It was not so much the principle which annoyed them but the fact that there appeared to be so little consistency in the procedure. Some were docked for being a few minutes late, while others would take a morning off and not be stopped a penny.

It is important to recognise that these young people had a sense of justice and fair play which they felt was not being reciprocated by the YOP scheme. With some justification they felt that several features of the scheme failed to recognise differences in the individual contributions of those attending and this in turn led to a sense of cynicism. Policy makers may need to be aware of such potential sources of hostility if they are to provide the type of scheme which does not alienate the young.

Another source of dissatisfaction lay in the unpleasant circumstances experienced by some in their placements with employers. The most serious of these concerned Tony, who worked at a restaurant. He complained bitterly that 'every day they make me do the same thing: peel fruit …. I ain't getting no learning 'cause nobody learns anything about how to peel potatoes! I know how to do that already, so why am I learning it? I'm telling you, I've not learned nothing 'cause there's nothing for me to learn.' After a few weeks Clifton, the member of staff who had arranged this placement, paid a visit to the restaurant to find out why Tony was being given such menial work to do and to ask if he could be allowed to do something more interesting. The outcome of the meeting was that Tony was taken off this placement and given a new one.

Problems such as this were inevitably seen by the young people at the Globe as the product of racist practices. Tony, for example, described how he was not allowed to wait on tables at the restaurant, yet white trainees there were allowed to do so. During a group discussion on racism, and after hearing of Tony's complaints, a young woman called Eileen told of being treated unfairly at her job: 'They always chuck the filing at me'. She added: 'We've got a new girl working at our place, and they give right good jobs to her'. At one point Clifton suggested that they were too quick to 'put things in racial terms', to which Tony earnestly replied 'Because it *is* in racial terms! It is, it is in racial terms'. Clearly then, the *intergroup* nature of these beliefs was firmly established and not prone to refutation.

Despite these problems, the scheme run by the Globe was enjoyed by most of those attending. Even Steve said he felt he had benefited from it, although he could not say in what way. This was in contrast to their attitudes towards the YOP schemes in general, which were extremely negative. In order to understand this combination of both positive and negative attitudes it is necessary to view them within the wider social and cultural context in which they occur.

There was no doubt in the minds of all those young people that YOP schemes in general were simply a form of cheap labour. One young man told me 'Most of them are crap. They're just using people for the money. I don't think they should work such long hours for that money..... Some of them you're just doing one thing, no experience, nothing out of it. You've got nothing to show. No experience or nothing, so I just think its crap.' During one group discussion at the Globe those attending the scheme were 'instructed' about this feature of YOP schemes by one of the staff, a Rastafarian called Thomas. He told them:

> You have to understand the whole concept of YOP and about the MSC. It's all about cheap labour. It is the opportunity for a firm to get a lot of cheap labour, through the YOP scheme and the MSC. That's what this course is all about. They're not learning you any skills or technical problems. They'd rather give you a floor to wash or a broom to sweep or say 'Carry these bags'.

At this subcultural level YOP was clearly defined as another act by the establishment designed to oppress young people. In reproducing aspects of this culture the young people at the Globe accepted this view unquestioningly. Yet their decision to enter into YOP schemes, given this hostile reaction to them, reveals the reproduction of a more central theme within the wider context of the working class culture they inhabit — that of instant financial gratification. Willis (1977) described a similar process amongst his sample of white working class youth. Although 'the lads' in his study assumed that all work was unpleasant, this was 'equilibriated by the overwhelming need for instant money' (p. 100). Black people today do not have the same opportunity to enter the world of labour through traditional patterns of employment and so it appears that this same process of reproduction now acts through youth training schemes. Hence at one level YOP schemes were seen as a form of exploitation, in much the same way as labouring was seen as menial by Willis' 'lads', and at another level it was desired as a means of increasing one's income. This ambivalence is clearly reflected in the fact that YOP schemes were seen principally as a form of cheap labour and yet the main reason for many of those attending the scheme at the Globe was the extra money it afforded them.

This suggests that the negative and hostile attitudes of these young people towards YOP schemes in general should not be taken as indicative of their attitude towards a scheme which they might be attending. Many of those at the Globe seemed to feel it was perfectly consistent to condemn YOP courses while admitting that they had made the right choice in attending the scheme at the Globe. Similar findings among white youth attending YOP schemes have been reported by Breakwell *et al.* (1982). They report that although YOP courses were seen by those people as a form of cheap labour and unlikely to increase their chances of finding real employment, they were nevertheless preferred to unemployment and did carry certain psychological benefits.

Analysis of the employment histories of those respondents taking part in the longitudinal study has shown that the proportion of time since leaving school which was spent in employment was higher among whites than among blacks. When blacks were not unemployed they tended to be on YOP courses rather than in jobs. Hence YOP courses may be acting as a substitute for employment among blacks. The findings from the ethnographic study suggest that this may also be true at a psychological level. The availability of YOP schemes and their short life meant they were often looked upon in the same way as were jobs in the secondary labour market when they were plentiful. Hence the notion of subemployment, where jobs are tried out for their suitability and then left, seems to have applied more to the YOP scheme than to employment. In a similar vein, the low pay of the YOP scheme in relation to the number of hours worked meant that it was viewed in a similar light to that of the unskilled manual jobs which YOP had largely replaced. However, there was still an element of active choice involved in the entrance of young blacks into the YOP scheme, as it provided an alternative to unemployment and a source of increased income to that obtained from unemployment benefit.

Where it was possible to elicit attitudes towards employment, they tended to reveal an ambivalence which has been suggested by quantitative analyses of the data from the longitudinal study. These analyses have shown that although employment commitment tends to remain high with continuing spells of unemployment, attitudes towards looking for work become significantly more negative. This pattern was observed in the interviews conducted with young blacks where, although employment was positively valued, there appeared to be very little desire to actively seek it. To the outsider this reluctance to engage in job-seeking may be interpreted as a lack of interest in obtaining employment. Yet such an interpretation would fail to acknowledge the complexity of labour market attitudes, where apparently contradictory positions are often maintained alongside one another. The ambivalence involved in this was often revealed when I asked about commitment to finding employment. For example, when one young man at the Globe Centre was asked if he was looking for a job he replied 'No, not at the moment. I was before.' He was then asked how important it was for him that he obtain employment, to which he responded 'Very important. Very important. But sometimes I just can't be bothered.' Another youth said: 'I'm not trying hard to get a job. No, not really'. When asked if it was important that he should get a job he replied, 'Yes, it is important, but there's none about.' The conflicting demands producing this desire for employment and the reluctance to engage in job-seeking are clearly illustrated in the following exchange with Linton at the Globe Centre.

P.U.:   How does being unemployed affect you?
Linton: I don't mind. I *am* bothered, but it's, you know, one of them things. Life.
P.U.:   Does it make you feel like not looking for work?
Linton: Well it does and it doesn't. It does, right, 'cause I want to get a job — bit of money and stuff, better living — and it doesn't, right, because I *know* that there ain't no jobs. When you go in the job centre there's just a bare wall. No vacancies anywhere. So there's no point in looking.

This section has shown how there might be a useful interplay between quantitative and qualitative approaches to the study of a single issue. This will be further illustrated in discussing the final set of findings from the ethnographic study, relating to differences in the experience of unemployment.

Variation in the experience of unemployment

The longitudinal study used various indices of psychological well-being to assess the effects of unemployment. Thus by quantifying these effects, it was possible to make comparisons between specific subgroups within the samples, e.g. between those people on temporary training schemes and those unemployed, or between high and low scorers on employment commitment scales. Although such comparisons are extremely useful, it is important to recognise that there may be important differences within the unemployed which are not so easily quantified. In particular, there may be responses to unemployment which differ *qualitatively* from each other and which may or may not have implications for the *degree* of psychological harm caused by unemployment. Such qualitative differences were found within the sample of young black people taking part in the ethnographic investigation. Three reasonably distinct patterns in the way unemployment was experienced emerged during the course of the study. It would not be correct to refer to these as *responses* to unemployment, since they represented ways of behaving and experiencing the social world which probably existed before the onset of joblessness. However, they nevertheless played a part in structuring the experience of unemployment and determining at least some reactions to it.

1. The disaffected.   The first of these three patterns of behaviour, and the most prominent, corresponded to the fairly widespread notion of young black people who are disaffected with British society. This type of behaviour was most vividly displayed by Steve and Linton and by a few of those people interviewed at the Arrow Centre. Typically, it entailed a resigned, almost dejected attitude towards their current situation. It also contained the aggressive rejection of white society which is commonly associated with black male youth (Cashmore and Troyna 1982a, Gaskell and Smith 1981). The important point to emphasise about those people who could be characterised in this way is that they perceived unemployment as simply another feature of the oppression which their minority status entailed. As such, it was seen as just another fact of life, in much the same way that being black was seen as a fact of life. For example, when asked of his feelings about unemployment, Linton replied:

> It's just one of them things. To me, being unemployed is just like being black. Just one of them things. You either are or you aren't.

The attitudes of these people towards unemployment were therefore couched in terms of a fatalistic acceptance of their predicament. At a later point in time Linton told me that he thought unemployment was 'just everyday life.... I've just accepted it', while Steve, when asked if he ever felt bad about being unemployed, replied: 'What, you mean depressed? It's a fact of life isn't it. Just accept it'. Similarly, when I asked a young man at the Arrow Centre whether being unemployed troubled him much, he replied 'Not really. Not any more. I've accepted it now.' The ability of these people to cope with unemployment in this way was something of which they were themselves fully aware. Steve, for example, told me: 'I might get a bit fed up. But it won't be a big thing. None of this committing suicide business.' Similarly, in a group discussion on unemployment, a young woman called Jackie said: 'It's not that I'm not bothered. I'd like a job, but I don't let it worry me.' Hence the response of these young black people to their unemployment was to accept it and not to let it get them down. Jackie, for example, warned: 'Never worry about getting a job. If you can't get one you don't worry.' In effect, these people appeared to be reducing the salience of employment in their lives. This is clearly shown in the following exchange with Eileen:

P.U.: Is it important to you that you get a job?

Eileen: It is important, but it's not *that* important. What I can't get I just do without. It's not that I don't try but if I keep trying and I don't get anything, I don't get upset or anything. If I can't get a job I just can't get one.

Results from the longitudinal study confirm that there is a relationship between psychological health and the importance of employment for the individual. Significant positive correlations were found between the measure of employment commitment and measures of psychological distress (General Health Questionnaire) and depression and anxiety (Zung 1965). Those unemployed respondents (both blacks and whites) who were most committed to obtaining employment were those who tended to have the highest scores (and therefore greatest ill-health) on these affective variables. The disaffected black people in the ethnographic study provide an illustration of the better psychological adjustment to unemployment which tends to accompany less importance being placed on obtaining a job.

Findings from the longitudinal study also suggest that if this is a way of coping with unemployment then it is one which blacks are quicker than whites to adopt. When interviewed one year after leaving school unemployed black respondents were found to be making significantly fewer job applications than similar whites. The black respondents also reported looking less hard for a job than did whites, were more negative in their attitude towards looking for work and had lower expectations of obtaining a job (Warr *et al.* 1985). What is equally important is the fact that, at that time, black respondents (both males and females) displayed lower levels of psychological ill-health than their white counterparts. Analyses showed that this was partly, though not wholly, due to their 'laid back' approach to job-seeking. However, to this must be added two further points. Firstly, the levels of psychological ill-health found among blacks in this unemployed sample were still much higher than those found among comparable employed samples. Blacks were still experiencing a considerable amount of distress, depression and anxiety as a result of not having a job. Secondly, when the sample was followed-up one year after the initial interviews, no significant difference was found between the level of psychological ill-health of unemployed blacks and that of unemployed whites. Neither was there any difference in their reported levels of job-seeking. Longitudinal analyses showed that white respondents, but not blacks, had significantly reduced their levels of job-seeking behaviour, their expectations of obtaining a job and had grown more negative in their attitude towards looking for employment (Banks and Ullah 1986). It would appear that young blacks in the sample were aware of the difficulties they faced in obtaining a job at a much earlier stage than were their white counterparts and that once the latter began to recognise their limited chances of obtaining employment then they too began to adopt similar coping strategies.

It is possible that this awareness among blacks develops well before they leave school and arises as they encounter the many obstacles which face black people in Britain today. The strategies which they use for coping with unemployment, therefore, may be those which have been developed over time for coping with the many inequalities which result from being black. This is certainly how some of the disaffected blacks in the ethnographic study perceived their abilities and in this respect they were quick to point to their superiority over those whites who had not learnt to cope with disadvantage:

> The white community does not know how to hustle like blacks, who have been hustling all their lives. And now we're in the situation where nobody has any money, the white community doesn't know how to hustle or to create anything to go and hustle it, right, to gain money or income.

In their introduction to their book on black youth, Cashmore and Troyna (1982b,4) state that the "twilight activities" of thieving and hustling are seen by some as "strategies of survival". This can be seen to be true of the disaffected blacks I observed. However, what also emerged in the ethnographic study was the clear sense of superiority this gave them over their white counterparts. This was further illustrated during a group discussion at the Globe Centre:

P.U.:   Would you say that unemployment is bad for you, that it makes you feel depressed or anxious?

Tony: Only if you want something. If you wanted to buy something and you knew you couldn't afford it.

Linton: That's where black people have got it over white people, because if we see something we want we just have to hustle for it.

P.U.:   So black people aren't as affected by unemployment as white people?

Linton: No, I'm not saying that. I'm just saying that we know how to use our heads more.

For these people, then, the experience of unemployment had been assimilated into the experience of being black. Hence one feature which differentiated the disaffected blacks from those others observed (to be described below) was the greater importance they attached to being black. It was this identity which was the most salient for them and which moulded and structured their experiences of everyday life. This is important from a social psychological perspective since it is also possible that unemployed black people might derive a sense of identity from their unemployed status. Social identity is typically defined as that which derives from knowledge of one's membership of a social category or group, together with the evaluative and affective significance of that membership (Tajfel 1981). As such it can be either positive (in the case of belonging to a group which is deemed important and which imparts a sense of pride) or negative (when one belongs to a low status group). Since being unemployed entails being assigned membership to a low status social category ('the unemployed'), it is possible that under certain conditions this becomes a salient and negative identity for the person concerned. However, as stated above, this was not the case for those blacks who could be described as disaffected. For them, their identity as black people was far more salient. Thus Steve once told me that 'If you're black, it's at the forefront of your mind. If you're white you might not think about it..... For them it might be something that's just under the surface, but if you're black – to me it's a major problem.' In contrast, an identity derived from being unemployed was much less salient for him: 'I don't really think of myself as unemployed.' This difference was made even more explicit at a later interview with Steve, when I specifically asked him which category, 'unemployed' or 'black', he tended to identify with:

P.U.:   Do you see yourself as having more in common with unemployed white people, or more in common with black people, whether they're unemployed or not?

Steve: More in common with black people, whether they're unemployed or not (laughing).

P.U.:   Is that a daft question?

Steve: It is.

P.U.:   What I'm trying to get at is whether, when you're unemployed, you think of all unemployed people as one group, irrespective of whether they are black or white.

Steve: Yes, I suppose so. But it's like saying 'When you're at school, do you think your class is one group?' Yes you do, but you don't have more in common with them than your own family.

The significance and salience attached to being black was closely related to the importance attributed to racism in Britain. Disaffected blacks appeared to be more aware of how their lives were influenced by racist practices than were other blacks I interviewed. Very often this influence

was seen as extending back into their childhood years. One young man
told me: 'I've had it against me all my life. It makes me feel that I want to
get something back at these white people.' Similarly, Eileen told of how, as
the only black girl at her primary school, she was constantly tormented: 'I
used to be frightened of them. Because they were white, I used to think
they were stronger than me.' Her own view of racism in Britain extended
even further into the past: 'It's been happening since before my mum
came to this country. She used to tell me what she's gone through and I
just think it's still happening.'

One common experience to emerge during the course of the interviews
was the way in which these people approached job vacancies with
apprehension. The possibility that they would face racial discrimination
was constantly in their minds on such occasions:

> *Tony*:   If you're in an interview .... you're always thinking about it.
> *Steve*:   Yeah, you're always thinking if he's gonna be racist.
> *Tony*:   And another thing, if they show you around a new job, always
> — I don't know why — always people are staring at you.

Similarly, a young man called James told me how being black affected
his experience of unemployment:

> It makes you more nervous going for a job, because you know that —
> people *are* prejudiced, that is obvious like — and you know that if there's
> white people going for the job, they're gonna take the white person.

Another young man recalled:

> I went for a job, like. Went to the reception place. And you *know*. You can
> see. You know these looks, what they mean. So I knew I wouldn't stand a
> chance.

The effects of such experiences on attitudes and on the willingness to
continue seeking employment are predictable, as the following exchange
clearly illustrates:

> *Woman*: Last week me and my friend went for this job, right, and there
> were only three of us applying for the job — just a dirty little
> restaurant place, right. And us two were black and the other girl
> was white. And I had as much experience as any of them two.
> The white girl got the job. And why? Because she's white.
> *P.U.*:   How does that make you feel?
> *Woman*: It makes me feel very aggressive.
> *P.U.*:   Towards whom?
> *Women*: Most white people. And to the authorities, government,
> everybody. What future is my kind going to grow up to?
> *P.U.*:   Does it ever make you feel like not bothering?

Woman: A lot of times I have given up. For the past three years I have not bothered to look for a job 'cause I know I'm not gonna get one.

Analyses from the longitudinal study have shown that black respondents who report having experienced job discrimination display significantly higher levels of disaffection than those who do not feel they have faced such discrimination (Ullah 1985). Disaffection was measured by a multi-item attitude scale and tapped negative attitudes towards the youth labour market and official agencies operating in it. In many respects it covered the notion of angry and resentful attitudes towards 'the authorities' expressed by this young woman. The analyses are only cross-sectional and so do not identify the experience of discrimination as a *causal* factor in the development of disaffection. As shown by the ethnographic material, those who were the most disaffected tended to perceive discrimination to be widespread. Hence it is likely that disaffection and the experience of discrimination influence each other. The longitudinal survey proves useful in confirming this association for a much larger sample of young unemployed black people than that which formed the basis of the ethnographic study.

These examples of the experience of racism have been quoted at length because they show the central role played by racism in the lives of the people taking part in the ethnographic study. Such experiences contributed to and reflected a *group* ideology which not only defined racism as the central obstacle in their lives but also defined their identity as that of members of an oppressed minority. Cashmore and Troyna (1982c, 26), have made a similar observation of young blacks in Britain today:

.... as young blacks become aware of their colour and realise that it can be depreciated and used as a basis for exclusion, they fuse this blackness with a new significance, incorporate it into their consciousness, organize their subjective biographies so as to include it, strike up allegiances and perceive adversaries on the understanding of it; in general, position themselves in relation to that quality of blackness.

It was this collective sense of identity, based on the common experience of racism, which characterised the young blacks have described as 'disaffected'. As such it differentiated them from those who displayed a more individualistic approach to unemployment. It is to these latter people that attention is now turned.

2. The unconcerned.   An alternative to the disaffected experience of unemployment was displayed by two young men who worked on the YOP schemes organised at the Globe Centre. In contrast to people like Linton and Steve, they seemed to be totally unaffected by their frequent periods of unemployment. In fact they appeared to be almost completely unconcerned about the uncertainty which unemployment and temporary schemes entailed for their lives. The two youths in question, Michael and Neil, did not appear to know each other. Michael had started his YOP scheme as soon as the Globe had started arranging placements, while Neil did not start until after Michael had completed his course. Yet despite this, both appeared to be remarkably similar in their behaviour and attitudes. Although theirs can hardly be described as a particularly common way of experiencing unemployment (I was unaware of any other blacks who could be characterised in this way), it was so distinctive that it deserves mention. A similar pattern of behaviour among black youths has also been described by Cashmore (1984), and so it may not be unique to the young people described here.

The way in which both Michael and Neil structured their lives was largely based on the articulation of style (Hebdige 1979). They both wore expensive and modern clothes and it was clear that their main concern was with their own appearances and not with unemployment. Neither displayed any evidence of having suffered psychologically from being unemployed.

Michael was present during my initial visit to the Globe Centre, in which I addressed the group and explained the reasons for my research. While both Sam and Steve were voicing their opinions of unemployment and their objections to the research, it was clear that Michael did not share their views. He could not understand why they were getting so angry about being without a job. Although others in the group were annoyed that he was contradicting their descriptions of the unpleasantness of unemployment, at the same time they were mildly amused and perhaps even a little impressed, by his indifference. He was obviously something of a character. A few weeks later, on a Thursday morning at the Globe and while those present were discussing how much money they had been docked, Michael breezed into the room carrying a bag containing an expensive pair of leather trousers. He showed them to a few people, who examined them with a mixture of envy and admiration.

Michael had been on two YOP schemes prior to starting the one at the Globe Centre. He left both of these schemes after only a very short time on each. His main reason for doing so was that they did not correspond to the type of work he thought was befitting of him. Thus his first YOP placement was in painting and decorating: 'That wasn't my style', he told me. He left that scheme and was unemployed for a while before starting another, this time in catering: 'I ended up washing a load of big pots and doing a bit of peeling potatoes. So I only did one day of that, then I came here.' His placement arranged by the Globe Centre was at a jean shop in the city centre. He enjoyed this immensely, since it appeared to fit his 'style' perfectly: 'The sort of work I like to do...and you get your clothes cheap'.

When asked about the times he had been unemployed, and why they had not caused him any great concern, Michael revealed the self confidence which characterised his way of life as a whole:

Michael: As long as I had a bit of money in my pocket, I wasn't bothered about anything. When I was on the dole I didn't have much money, so I used to be up at the sports centre every day, you know what I mean. It didn't bother me. I wasn't really bothered.

P.U.:   So you never went out looking for a job?

Michael: No, nothing like that..... I thought somebody would offer me one. I got that sort of thinking that one day somebody would just come up and offer me a job, know what I mean? I never worry about anything. I just take things as they come.

Although this degree of self confidence may appear to be somewhat extreme, it can prove to be beneficial. When I next saw Michael, some months later, he had a proper full-time job. I asked how he had obtained the job. Apparently, at the end of the YOP scheme, the manager of the jean shop came up to him and offered him a job there.

Michael's way of coping with unemployment entailed an active use of his spare time. Much of this was spent at a sports centre, making the most of the city council's free sports facilities for the unemployed. In this respect he differed markedly from the disaffected blacks described in the previous section, whose methods of coping with unemployment were passive rather than active. Results from the longitudinal survey confirmed that there was a significant association between this type of active behaviour during unemployment and lower levels of psychological ill-health.

A similar degree of confidence was displayed by Neil. He was aged 18 and had left school two years earlier. He went straight onto a YOP scheme, which he completed, and had then been unemployed until he started the scheme at the Globe. His main reason for starting the scheme was the extra money it paid compared with that received when unemployed and like Michael he cited lack of money as the worst aspect of unemployment. When I interviewed him he had a placement at a supermarket warehouse and appeared to like the way in which the scheme was organised by the Globe. However, this was not because it was a more attractive alternative to unemployment but simply because it suited him at that time to have some extra money. Unemployment still carried with it the attraction of freedom to do what he liked: 'You can do anything you want. Get up, go to bed anytime, don't think about work. If you're working you've got to think about time.' When asked how he had felt when he was unemployed he displayed the same kind of self confidence which had helped Michael through his periods of unemployment. He had never been depressed 'because I had somewhere to go.... when you go to the Arrow there's always something to do' and he had never let the fact of his unemployment cause anxieties about the future: 'I'm always sure of myself. I come before anything.'

Neither Neil nor Michael tended to identify themselves with the category 'unemployed'. This simply was not a salient aspect of their self-concepts. Similarly, the question of their unemployment was not an important one for either of them. Neil, when asked who or what he blamed for his unemployment, replied: 'I've never really thought about it to tell you the truth.' Unlike the disaffected blacks, however, this was not replaced by a powerful sense of identity derived from being black.

Although both Neil and Michael were obviously aware of their blackness and of the disadvantage this can bring, it did not carry with it the same ideology of oppression which it did for the disaffected blacks. Racism was not a big issue for either of them. For example, when asked if he experienced racism at work, Michael told of how he was watched very carefully by the manager of the shop, particularly when his friends came in to see him. He then added that this did not bother him too much because he would do the same if he was manager. Similarly, Neil did not attach a great deal of importance to the need to overcome racism, mainly because he did not experience it as a problem himself. This was displayed during a life and social skills class in which Clifton, the group leader, was holding a discussion on the nature of racism. Both Clifton and the others present were aggravated by the fact that Neil would not recognize racism as a problem:

Clifton:	Don't you think any of this is important?
Neil:	No. I don't think it is.
Clifton:	Why don't you think it is? I'm interested in hearing why you don't.
Neil:	What I don't know I never miss.
Clifton:	So you mean ignornance is bliss? But I tell you basically what this session is about: it's to raise your consciousness about things that's happening around you, that you don't even see.
Neil:	I feel no way in being black, 'cause I'm proud of my colour.
Clifton:	But it's not just people calling you black, it's how those people affect *your* life.

The awareness of oppression which Steve and others had displayed was thus not apparent in Neil or Michael. As such they did not possess a collective consciousness which placed their identity as blacks within a political and historical context of oppression and which defined this identity in these terms. Thus, although aware of the existence of racism, neither showed signs of having developed the powerful sense of ingroup identity which social identity theory predicts will result from this form of social categorisation. Michael, in fact, was quite keen not to be associated with the type of black youth who spends most of his/her time at the Arrow Centre:

I used to go to the Arrow Centre, but... I'm not into the same things as them. They're into reggae and all that. People think that you're a rogue if you go there.

Given the significance of reggae music as a cultural symbol of identity for blacks, there can be few more direct indications of the lack of importance attached to a black identity than the indifference towards reggae music voiced by Michael. For him and Neil, then, being black or being unemployed were not particularly salient identities. Their style of life may be seen as similar to the subcultural alternative to Rastafarianism which Cashmore (1984, 53) decribes as 'Jazzfunk':

This was a predominantly black form with the adherents eschewing any political influence: music, dancing and dressing were the important items.

According to Cashmore, a significant minority of young black people have opted for this particular subculture in preference to Rastafarianism. Hence it is reasonable to assume that the attitudes and behaviour of Michael and Neil form a coherent pattern which is not confined to this sample. As such this may be described as a second distinct way of experiencing unemployment to be found among blacks, in contrast to the disaffected experience. However, there was also evidence of a third pattern, quite different from the two already described.

3. The distressed.   A significant number of the people interviewed at the Globe and Arrow Centres showed all the signs of poor psychological health which form the basis of the standard response to unemployment. Had they taken part in the longitudinal survey they would have probably obtained high distress scores on the General Health Questionnaire. Theirs is the type of behaviour — depressed, low in self-esteem, lacking in confidence — which has led researchers to conclude that unemployment has a psychologically damaging effect on those unfortunate enough to be experiencing it. The people displaying this type of response to unemployment were each interviewed on only one occasion. This was because they were not regular attenders of the Globe and Arrow and so I never saw them again at either of those two centres. It is possible that their infrequent use of these day-time facilities for the young unemployed was itself a significant factor in their failure to cope with unemployment. They would not be part of the social networks which characterised the groups of regular attenders and would not possess the social support which comes from this. The longitudinal survey has confirmed that certain kinds of social support during unemployment are significantly associated with better psychological health (Ullah *et al.* 1985).

The material gathered from these interviews is thus somewhat sketchy and fails to recreate the depth of character which comes from material gathered over a number of interviews with the same person. Despite this it still conveys a vivid picture of the harmful psychological effects of unemployment.

These effects were clearly illustrated during an interview with two young men at the Arrow Centre. One of these, James, was a quietly spoken lad. With his short neat haircut and smart clothes he stood out from the crowd of typical Arrow regulars. He had had two jobs and had been on two YOP schemes in the two years since he left school. The last job had lasted for 14 months and had ended about six months prior to this interview, when he was made redundant. Since that time he had been on a YOP scheme, though he was unemployed again when I interviewed him. His friend Micky was a year or so younger and was studying for his 'O' levels on a part-time basis whilst registering as unemployed. He hoped to be able to join his brother in the Navy when he was 18.

Both James and Micky badly wanted a job, and this may partly explain why they appeared to be most affected by their unemployment. The longitudinal survey, along with a number of other studies, has clearly shown that those people most committed to obtaining a job tend to suffer greater psychological ill-health when unemployed. James and Micky provided flesh and blood examples of what has typically been expressed as a statistical relationship between two variables.

For James, the time he had spent in employment had made his current spell of unemployment even more difficult to bear:

P.U.:   How important is it to you that you get a job?
James: It's very important, 'cause having that job last year I'm used to getting up early. I like working.
P.U.:   And have you still been getting up early?
James: I used to, after I finished, but now I stop in bed 'till about eleven.

(later)

James: It's just like a routine every day; sign on, wait a few days 'till you've spent your money, then wait 'till you sign on again.
P.U.:   Have there been times when you've felt depressed?
James: Yes. You feel like not getting up in the morning. No point.
P.U.:   How do you get out of that feeling?
James: Play my records, that's all.
P.U.:   Is there anyone to help at all?
James: Yes. I come down town and see my friends. That breaks the boredom.

In addition to illustrating how the importance attached to obtaining employment can influence reactions to unemployment, the above passage also shows how this is compounded by the loss of some of the 'latent' benefits of employment (Jahoda 1982). This conversation with James suggests that two of these benefits, a time structure around which to organise the day's activities and variety, were lacking in his life when he was interviewed. Feelings of depression were only avoided when he made a concerted effort to gain access to a third of these five benefits: social contacts.

It has been suggested that the salience of the category 'unemployed' for the young blacks taking part in this study may characterise and explain some of the differences observed between them. For the disaffected blacks, the most salient aspect of their self-concept was the fact of their blackness. Being unemployed was seen simply as a product of being black in Britain today and did not in itself assume any significance. For the unconcerned, being black or being unemployed did not carry any particular significance. In contrast to the people in both of these groups, James and Micky both appeared to be very aware of their status as unemployed people. One possible effect of this was that the stigma attached to unemployment was much more of a problem for them than it was for others:

> *Micky*: I prefer to say I'm unemployed rather than say I'm on the dole. It just sounds better. If someone says 'you working?' and you say 'No I'm on the dole' – you don't want to say you're on the dole really. Just say 'No, I ain't got a job'.
>
> *P.U.*: Are there any things that you feel make you stand out as unemployed?
>
> *Micky*: Yes, the fact that you go down town all the time. People say 'Do you always go down town?' People down the road say to me 'Is that all you do all the time, go down town?' I mean, you go down Lower Cross (a shopping precinct) everyday. *That* makes you stand out. People say 'Oh, he spends all his time down Lower Cross.'

Quotations from other interviews confirm the picture of unemployment which has been drawn by results from the longitudinal study. Symptoms of depression and anxiety figure large in the accounts these young people give of their experiences of unemployment:

> I didn't worry about it at first. But after a couple of months of being on the dole I started worrying. All the jobs were for 17-year-olds or over... I just felt depressed, like 'cause I couldn't get a job, I didn't know what to do. Staying at home, I was bored all the time. I used to think 'I've got no chance of getting a job.' I use to think about the future. I might be a tramp or something.

> Depressed sometimes. I sit at home and think 'What am I gonna do today?', like, you know what I mean? You get frustrated sometimes, when you sit at home.

Everybody wants a future and I want a future. I won't mind if I get £100 a week on the dole, because £100 is a lot. It'll get a mortgage or buy a car. But if you're getting £20, you have nothing, because £20 to me: I go out and buy a pair of trousers – finished. But if I got £100 a week I'd say 'Right, I've got a future here' ..... Personally I'm feeling bad about my life. I'm getting nowhere in this life. And I've got brothers and sisters and they're about 21, 22, and they're buying houses, 'cause they're working; and I'm feeling useless. Because my brother John, right, he's buying a house for £18,000 and I'm looking at me and thinking 'I'm going nowhere in this life.'

Did you see that series 'Boys from the black stuff'? Yosser Hughes, right, he wanted a job. He wanted to do something but he couldn't do it. So he just cracked up... It made me think a bit: Where would I be? That's the situation we're in now. I could get like him.

The qualitative material gathered from these interviews can not give an indication of the extent of this third type of response to unemployment. However, the results from the longitudinal survey show that the mean level of psychological distress (as measured by the General Health Questionnaire) found among unemployed blacks is significantly higher than that found among those in the sample who had jobs. Hence it may reasonably be assumed that the majority of those unemployed exhibit similar symptoms of depression, boredom and anxiety about the future.

Discussion

The ethnographic approach adopted in this study differs quite radically from the more commonplace psychological approaches to the study of unemployment. The latter have typically attempted to quantify the harmful psychological effects of unemployment. In this respect they have provided accurate and important information. Yet they have not given any indication of the *quality* of this experience. The need for more qualitative research applies equally to research on whites and to members of other ethnic minorities (e.g. Asians) as much as it applies to black people. Psychologists have been slow to utilise ethnographic techniques in the study of unemployment, even though these are now well-established in other areas of occupational psychology (Van Maanen *et al.* 1982). Ideally, both quantitative and qualitative methods can be used to provide different types of answers to a pressing social problem like youth unemployment. An indication of such an approach has been given in this chapter. By frequently interpreting and comparing the findings from the ethnographic study with the findings obtained from the longitudinal survey, a greater understanding has been obtained than that provided by each of these studies on their own.

Perhaps the most important point illustrated by the qualitative approach adopted here is that the experience of unemployment needs to be understood within the wider social context in which it occurs. The reactions of those disaffected blacks towards their unemployment was shown to be part of a more general reaction to their status as black people in Britain today. Through gaining an understanding of their experiences of racism, of the significance which their blackness holds for them and of the ways in which they have had to learn to cope with disadvantage throughout their lives, it was possible to understand and interpret the way in which they responded to being unemployed. The *intergroup* nature of this response was revealed, in contrast to the individualistic picture which is often painted when one only considers a person's score on a measure of well-being.

A criticism which is sometimes levelled at qualitative research of this type is that it is difficult to judge the representativeness of the findings. In the present chapter this was partly addressed through references to the results obtained from the longitudinal survey. In this way it was possible to show that many of the patterns of experience observed in the ethnographic study were present among a much larger sample of black people and that some patterns were also present among unemployed whites. However, there are also examples of similar findings being reported in the research literature on youth subcultures. This lends further evidence for the suggestion that some of the present findings may not be limited to this particular sample or even to black people.

For example, several writers have reported on the significance of ethnic identity for young blacks and how this significance moulds and structures their experiences of the events in their lives. Small (1983, 45) has written of the black youths' which formed the target of his ethnographic research in London:

> In their spontaneous conversations it is clear that their racial origins are most central to the way in which they define themselves; they see themselves first and foremost as black, black British or West Indian and regard this as emphasizing their distinctiveness from indigeneous mainstream society.

Similarly Cashmore and Troyna (1982d, 77) have argued that it was 'the awareness that their progress would be ...retarded by their blackness (which) fused that blackness with a fresh symbolic meaning and social arrangements came to be organized around that meaning'. Such patterns of behaviour are consistent with social psychological theories of identity and need not be confined only to black people (Tajfel 1978). Individuals may structure their behaviour in terms of any group membership they possess, especially if they believe that that membership is being used by others in a discriminatory way (Turner *et al.* 1983).

One feature of youth labour markets which has attracted a considerable amount of research is the provision of youth training. Once again parallels can be found between findings from that research and those reported in this chapter. The similarity suggests that attitudes towards such training are equally negative among blacks and whites. Moreover, such attitudes appear to correspond in content as well as degree with youth training being seen principally as a form of cheap labour. Cashmore (1984, 96), in his study of young people in the labour market, reports that 'slave labour is the key term used time and again by youths involved, who feel they are exploited quite openly and, sometimes, ruthlessly by the programme'. Similarly, Stokes (1983) argues that most of the unemployed youths in his sample showed little interest in joining YOP schemes and quotes one youth as saying 'You're cheap labour for six months then you're dumped back on the dole' (p. 28). Such expressions bear a striking similarity to the opinions voiced by the black youths described in this chapter. The similarity is extended further when the specific experiences of youths following youth training schemes (YTS) are compared. Roberts and Kirby (1985, 3), in their research on young people who have rejected or left YTS, quote one person as saying:

> I'm not learning nothing at all. I'm not doing owt in horticulture. You know, planting some daffodils, we went down there with all these daffodils and that was about it. It isn't hard to plant daffodils.

This is almost identical in manner to Tony's description of his experiences of a YOP scheme, quoted earlier in this chapter, ('I ain't getting no learning, 'cause nobody learns anything about how to peel potatoes! I know that already, so why am I learning it?'). As shown here and elsewhere, then, youth training can often offend the sense of natural justice which many young people, both black and white, possess. The feelings of being exploited, of not receiving proper training and of not having enhanced one's long-term job prospects, do not appear to be restricted to the young blacks who have formed the basis of this chapter. Such feelings appear to be equally common amongst white youths.

A similar conclusion may be drawn concerning the fatalistic stance adopted by blacks towards their unemployment. Although Cashmore and Troyna (1982c, 33) also describe how a 'mood of fatalism is rife in the black community', Cashmore (1984) refers to similar processes occurring among white youths who fail to escape the unemployment queue. The suggestion made in the present chapter that such a response represents a way of coping, albeit passively, with unemployment is supported by Stokes' (1983) findings. He reports that the unemployed youths (mainly whites) in his sample experienced an apparent improvement in their psychological health towards the end of the six-month observation period but adds (p. 29) that this was not a genuine improvement, since the unemployed had come to terms with their situation by restricting their potential... They had become resigned to their privation. Hope for the future was restricted and fatalistic apathy permeated everyday life.

As an example of this fatalism, Stokes quotes one youth as asking: 'What's the point in worrying? I accept that I haven't got a job and probably never will have'. A 17-year-old girl is also reported as saying: 'I'll probably get a job one day. But until that day comes I'm not going to bother myself'.

There are of course, issues which have not been adequately covered here. In particular, young black women have not received specific attention. Although I interviewed a number of black females and some of their comments have been reproduced, the ways in which their experiences of unemployment differed from those of black males have not been explored. Their experiences of racism, their fatalistic attitude towards being unemployed and their experiences of jobs and youth training schemes have been conveyed as part of a general response revealed by many of the blacks described here. These are areas in which there were few important differences between males and females. However, those aspects of black females' experiences which related specifically to their gender were not so readily conveyed to me. It is possible that detailed ethnographic study of those aspects would be more successfully conducted by a female researcher.

Another issue which has not been dealt with in any great detail in this chapter is the role played by Rastafarianism. Once again this is because any influence it may have had was not immediately obvious to me. Cashmore (1981) has drawn a disinction between those black people who wholeheartedly embrace the doctrines of Rastafarianism and those who adopt its cultural symbols but not its central tenets. The former believe in the reincarnation of Christ in the form of the Ethiopian Emperor Haile Selassie. Such commitment requires the adoption of a very different form of social reality to that which is the dominant social reality in Britain today (Cashmore 1979). The majority of young black people may not be described as committed Rastafarians. However, they are still very much aware of their oppression under the influence of a dominant ideology of white racism and many take great pride in their African origins and wish to emphasise the distinctiveness of their cultural traditions. For this reason young blacks who are not prepared to become Rastafarians may borrow many features from that culture. They wear their hair in dreadlocks, believe they are the victims of racial oppression and emphasise their distinctiveness from the dominant British culture by incorporating the Ethiopian colours of red, gold and green into many aspects of their dress. Thus in the words of Hebdige (1979, 43), the generation of British-born blacks have developed their own unique style of Rastafarianism, 'stripped of nearly all its original religious meanings'. Similarly, Small (1983, 49) has stated that 'in Britain today... it is the non-religious cultural symbols and practices of Rastafari which have had the most pervasive influence'.

A number of the black people taking part in this study had adopted the cultural symbols of Rastafarianism, yet none fitted the strict definition of a Rastafarian. Steve was a prime example in that he wore his hair in dreadlocks and always managed to include the Ethiopian colours in the clothes he was wearing, even if only in the form of a wristband or badge. He once spoke to me of his belief in the Rastafarian prophecy of 'the fall of Babylon' (white racist society destroying itself in its own decadence): 'That means me and you can just sit back and say "It don't matter, 'cause this is supposed to happen"'. However, when I asked him if Rastafarianism provided some sort of comfort to him, through defining and explaining the position of black people and offering a course of action for them, he replied 'At this present time it's not helping me. And if I want help, the only thing that I can rely on to give me that help is me, so I know the prophecy is being fulfilled but right now that is no benefit to me.' Rastafarianism, then, provided a subcultural style for some of these young people to adhere to. It was a style which was free of any white influence or of any commercial influence. However, Rastafarianism did not offer any magical solutions (Brake 1973) to the everyday problems of poverty, unemployment and discrimination experienced by many of these people. As such it did not intrude into their lives to the extent that would have allowed it to feature prominantly in this report.

Finally, and by way of concluding this chapter, what are the implications of this research for social psychological approaches to the study of unemployment? Although a number of works on unemployment are labelled as being social psychological (e.g. Fraser 1980, Jahoda 1982, Kelvin 1980) one has to look hard to find in them instances of social psychological theories being applied to the study of unemployment. They are certainly psychological approaches and they are focussing on a social issue, but this itself does not make them social psychological. What then, should a social psychological approach to the study of unemployment look like and how does the material presented in this chapter measure up to such a description?

It has been suggested that 'social psychology can and must include in its theoretical and research preoccupations a direct concern with the relationship between human psychological functioning and the large scale social processes and events which shape this functioning and are shaped by it '(Tajfel *et al.* 1984, 3). If one accepts this then much of the research carried out into the psychological effects of unemployment can be said to fit this description. Unemployment certainly is a large-scale social process and researchers have so far looked for its effects on many different aspects of psychological functioning. However, it will be argued here that in order for the study of unemployment to be truly social psychological, both unemployment and the psychological features of the person experiencing it need to be studied in an altogether different way than has typically been the case. Specifically, both need to be approached from an explicitly *social* perspective. It will be suggested that the study described here gives some indication of what this might look like and how it might be achieved.

If one begins with unemployment, then it is clear that psychologists have tended to treat this as a given feature of the environment. It is simply one value of an independent variable, employment status, which is used to divide up a sample. There is no analysis of its features and the question of how such features might differ for different people is rarely addressed. Psychologists may not wish to offer detailed descriptions of the objective features of a period of unemployment, such as benefit levels and how these change over time, eligibility for specific schemes, and so on, but they can say something about the subjective interpretation of unemployment and how this may differ across social groups and categories. This need is only partly met by measuring aspects of a person's psychological health while he or she is unemployed. Instruments such as the General Health Questionnaire (GHQ) tell the researcher whether the respondent has been losing sleep with worry, has been unable to concentrate or has been feeling under strain. But they do not say anything about how that person views their unemployment, how they explain it or what meaning they attribute to it. Studies which have sought to elicit explanations for unemployment typically do so with the aim simply of dividing respondents up into 'externals' (those who attribute it to forces outside their control) and 'internals' (those who see it as their own fault); or sometimes into categories of those offering fatalistic or societal explanations. On the whole, the *meaning* which unemployment has for different people has not been explicitly studied, possibly because it is seen as being too subjective and unreliable. In this way the social psychological aspects of unemployment have been largely omitted from empirical investigation. Differences in the perceptions, views, explanations, interpretations, etc, of people experiencing unemployment and how these in turn modify the ways in which they react to it are all obscured when unemployment is treated as an objective condition which unites them all.

In the study described in this chapter some attempt was made to explore the meanings which unemployment held for the young black people taking part in the investigation. In this way differences within them were allowed to emerge. It has been shown that for some being unemployed was simply another feature of being black, in much the same way that bad housing and limited educational opportunities are. For others, unemployment assumed even less significance. For some, it was probably the worst thing to happen to them. In quoting the words they used when talking to me, the quality and the content of these differing experiences have been conveyed in a way they are not if the psychological effects of unemployment are quantified on a scale measuring well-being.

Support for such an approach within social psychology can be found in an article dealing with some of the problems of studying the social representations of social groups (Potter and Litton 1985). Two specific problems which are outlined by the authors of the article relate firstly to the relationship between groups and social representations and secondly to the level at which these representations are shared within a particular group. With regards to the first of these, Potter and Litton criticise researchers for relying exclusively on objective indices of group membership, since 'satisfying one index of membership, however objective, does not entail that the individual will identify with, or act in terms of, the specified group' (p. 83). Their point is similar to the one made above: defining a collection of people as a group (such as the unemployed) on the basis of a shared objective characteristic may obscure important differences between those people in terms of their own representations of that group. Instead, Potter and Litton suggest that researchers should attempt to discover whether 'the participants are actually identifying with the categories to which they are assigned' (p. 84). In the study described here, it was shown that many of the black people did not strongly identify themselves as unemployed, even though they would normally be categorised in this way by researchers. Furthermore, Neil and Michael did not strongly identify themselves with other black people. Yet once again standard research techniques would require that blacks be treated as a single category, with the result of obscuring potential differences in their identification with that group. By focussing on the representations, interpretations and perceptions of the young blacks taking part in this study, some of the complexity of the relationships between social groups and the group identifications of their members has been illustrated.

Potter and Litton's second point takes up these issues in more detail. They suggest that the degree of consensus within a group (in terms of the beliefs of its members) is often assumed rather than demonstrated. This is often compounded by the use of certain research procedures, since by presenting results in terms of mean scores possible intragroup differences are not able to emerge. The qualitative approach used here, in contrast to one which might simply examine the mean scores on certain variables of the whole sample of blacks, has highlighted rather than obscured such intragroup differences in the experience of unemployment.

In addition to treating unemployment as a social phenomenon, and being alerted to the different meanings it may have for those experiencing it, the researcher needs to view the unemployed individual from an equally social perspective. Although unemployment may physically isolate a person from his or her peers and friends, this does not necessarily imply that he or she will cease to exist as a social being. Turner (1982), for example, has argued for a cognitive definition of the social group rather than the affective definition which has been so dominant in social psychology. He points out that large scale social groups sometimes develop without the attraction or interaction of all their members. The sufficient condition for the emergence of such group behaviour seems to be the recognition and acceptance of some self-defining social categorisation. According to Turner, 'what matters is how we perceive and define ourselves and not how we feel about others' (1982, p. 16). It is important, therefore, that the cognitive and not just the behavioural or attitudinal dispositions of the unemployed are considered. Viewing the unemployed person as a social rather than individual being requires that the researcher seeks to discover how that person sees and defines him or herself and this may or may not be in terms of their unemployed status. In this way unemployed people are shown to be social beings rather than just collections of individuals. Thus Steve's initial reaction to me, whom he saw as a member of the white establishment, and his opinion of that establishment were in part determined by his sense of identification with the black population of Britain. As such he was acting almost exclusively as a member of a social group and not simply as an individual who happened to be unemployed.

The overall conclusion to be drawn from this study is that it points to the importance of considering the social context in which the experience of unemployment occurs. In order to understand something of the ways in which unemployment is experienced by young black people, it is necessary to understand how they live and organise their lives, the importance they attach to their blackness, how they view British society in general, the way in which racism has impinged on their life chances and their own interpretations of this, and many other features. Hopefully the study described here has made some progress towards providing such an understanding, and in so doing given an example of how unemployment research might proceed.

Acknowledgements

This research was supported by a grant from the Department of Employment. I am grateful to the Department's Liaison Committee for advice and guidance in the conduct of this study. The views expressed, however, are my own and I accept full responsibility for them.

References

BANKS, M.H., ULLAH, P. (1986). 'Unemployment and Less-qualified Urban Youth: a longitudinal study'. *Employment Gazette*, *94*, 205-210.
BANKS, M.H., ULLAH, P. and WARR, P.B. (1984). 'Unemployment and Less Qualified Urban Young People.' *Employment Gazette*, *92*, 343-346.

BRAKE, M. (1973). *The Sociology of Youth Culture and Youth Subcultures.* London: Routledge & Kegan Paul.

BREAKWELL, G., HARRISON, B. and PROPPER, C. (1982). 'The Psychological Benefits of YOPs.' *New Society, 61,* 494-495.

CASHMORE, E. (1979). *Rastaman: The Rastafarian Movement in England.* London: George Allen & Unwin.

CASHMORE, E. (1981). 'After the Rastas.' *New Community, 9,* 173-181.

CASHMORE, E. (1984). *No Future: Youth and Society.* London: Heinemann.

CASHMORE, E. and TROYNA, B. (eds) (1982a). *Black Youth in Crisis.* London: George Allen & Unwin.

CASHMORE, E. and TROYNA, B. (1982b). 'Introduction.' In E. Cashmore and B. Troyna (eds) (1982a).

CASHMORE, E. and TROYNA, B. (1982c). 'Black Youth in Crisis.' In E. Cashmore and B. Troyna (eds) (1982a).

CASHMORE, E. and TROYNA, B. (1982d). 'Growing Up in Babylon.' In E. Cashmore and B. Troyna (eds) (1982a).

DOISE, W. (1978). *Groups and Individuals: Explanations in Social Psychology.* Cambridge: Cambridge University Press.

FARR, R. and MOSCOVICI, S. (eds) (1984). *Social Representations.* Cambridge: Cambridge University Press.

FORGAS, J. (ed) (1981). *Social Cognition: Perspectives On Everyday Understanding.* London: Academic Press.

FRASER, C. (1980). 'The Social Psychology of Unemployment.' In M. Jeeves (ed.) *Psychology Survey No. 3.* London: Allen & Unwin.

GASKELL, G. and SMITH, P. (1981). 'Alienated Black Youth: an investigation of "conventional wisdom" explanations.' *New Community, 9,* 182-193.

HEBDIGE, D. (1979). *Subculture: The Meaning of Style.* London: Methuen.

HEWSTONE, M., JASPERS, J. and LALLJEE, M. (1982). 'Social representations, social attribution and social identity: the intergroup images of "public" and "comprehensive" schoolboys.' *European Journal of Social Psychology, 12,* 241-269.

JAHODA, M. (1982). *Employment and Unemployment: A Social Psychological Analysis.* Cambridge: Cambridge University Press.

JASPERS, J. and FRASER, C. (1984). 'Attitudes and Social Represetations.' In R. Farr and S. Moscovici (eds) (1984).

KELVIN, P. (1980). 'Social Psychology 2001: the social psychological bases and implications of structural unemployment.' In R. Gilmour and S. Duck (eds). *The Development of Social Psychology.* London: Academic Press.

MOSCOVICI, S. (1981). 'On Social Representations.' In J. Forgas (ed.) (1981).

MOSCOVICI, S. (1982). 'The Coming Era of Representations.' In J.P. Codol and J.P. Leyens (eds). *Cognitive Analysis of Social Behaviour.* The Hague: Nijhoff.

MOSCOVICI, S. (1984). 'The Phenomenon of Social Representations.' In R. Farr and S. Moscovici (eds) (1984).

POTTER, J. and LITTON, I. (1985). 'Some Problems Underlying the Theory of Social Representations.' *British Journal of Social Psychology, 24,* 81-90.

ROBERTS, H. and KIRBY, R. (1985). 'Y.B. on Y.T.S.? Why not?' *Youth and Policy, 4,* 1-5.

ROBERTS, K. (1984). 'Youth Unemployment.' Paper presented to Dept. of Sociological Studies, University of Sheffield, 1984.

ROBERTS, K., DUGGAN, J. and NOBLE, M. (1982). 'Out-of-School Youths in High Unemployment Areas: an empirical investigation.' *British Journal of Guidance and Counselling, 10*, 1-11.

SMALL, S. (1980). *Police and People in London: II : A Group of Young Black People*. London: Policy Studies Institute.

STAFFORD, E.M. (1982). 'The Impact of the Youth Opportunities Programme on Young People's Employment Prospects and Psychological Well-being.' *British Journal of Guidance and Counselling, 10*, 12-21.

STOKES, G. (1983). 'Out of School – Out of Work: the psychological impact.' *Youth and Policy, 2*, 27-29.

TAJFEL, H. (1978). *Differentiation Between Social Groups*. London: Academic Press.

TAJFEL, H. (1981). *Human Groups and Social Categories: Studies in Social Psychology*. Cambridge: Cambridge University Press.

TAJFEL, H., JASPERS, J.M.F. and FRASER, C. (1984). 'The Social Dimension in European Social Psychology.' In H. Tajfel (ed.). *The Social Dimension: European Developments in Social Psychology*. Vol I. Cambridge: Cambridge University Press.

TURNER, J.C. (1982). 'Towards a Cognitive Redefinition of the Social Group.' In H. Tajfel (ed.) *Social Identity and Intergroup Relations*. Cambridge: Cambridge University Press.

TURNER, J.C., SACHDEV, I. and HOGG, M.A. (1983). 'Social Categorization, Interpersonal Attraction and Group Formation.' *British Journal of Social Psychology, 22*, 227-239.

ULLAH, P. (1985). 'Disaffected Black and White Youth: The role of unemployment duration and perceived job discrimination.' *Ethnic and Racial Studies, 8*, 181-193.

ULLAH, P. and BANKS, M.H. (1985). 'Youth Unemployment and Labour Market Withdrawal.' *Journal of Economic Psychology, 6*, 51-64.

ULLAH, P., BANKS, M.H. and WARR, P.B. (1983). 'Social and Psychological Effects of Unemployment upon Young People. *MRC/ESRC SAPU* memo No. 577.

ULLAH, P., BANKS, M.H. and WARR, P.B. (1985). 'Social Support, Social Pressures and Psychological Distress During Unemployment.' *Psychological Medicine, 15*, 283-295.

VAN MAANEN, J., DOBBS, J.M. and FAULKNER, R.R. (1982). *Varieties of Qualitative Research*. London: Sage.

WARR, P.B., BANKS, M.H. and ULLAH, P. (1985). 'The Experience of Unemployment Among Black and White Urban Teenagers.' *British Journal of Psychology, 76*, 75-87.

WILLIS, P. (1977). *Learning to Labour*. Farnborough: Gower.

ZUNG, W.W.K. (1965). 'A Self-rating Depression Scale. *Archives of General Psychiatry, 12*, 63-70.

5

Kenneth Cooke

The living standards of unemployed people

Introduction

One of the persistent myths about unemployment is that it is no longer, as it was in the past, a cause of hardship. Compulsory insurance benefits now exist to provide protection against poverty during interruptions of earnings, but in a number of respects social security provision for the unemployed has become increasingly out of step with trends in the structure of unemployment. The benefit system was not designed to cope either with high levels or long durations of unemployment. Insurance benefits were framed in anticipation of virtually full employment, essentially to meet needs arising from temporary spells of unemployment in a generally buoyant labour market. National insurance benefits make no special provision for the long-term unemployed as they do for the long-term sick. The increasing numbers both of the long-term unemployed who have exhausted their entitlement to contributory benefits (after 12 months) and of unemployed young people with no contribution record, and therefore no entitlement, have created a massive dependence of the unemployed on the basic rates of means-tested supplementary benefit.

In the case of families with children, insurance benefits are simply inadequate to provide financial security without additional recourse to means-tested benefits (Deacon and Bradshaw 1983). This is not new; its origins lie in the post-war government's failure (Deacon 1982) and the failure of every government since, to set insurance benefits at a level sufficient not to require means-tested supplementation. Most families with dependent children are entitled to (but do not necessarily claim) supplementary benefit in addition to unemployment benefit, especially since the abolition of earnings-related supplements to unemployment benefit in 1982.

The outcome is that roughly two-thirds of unemployed people are now dependent on supplementary benefit, either alone or as an addition to unemployment benefit (DHSS 1986, table 1.36). No matter how long they are without a job, the unemployed have no right to the higher, long-term rate of supplementary benefit which is available to all other groups after 12 months. The gap between the basic and long-term rates has widened over the years, allowing the living standards of the long-term unemployed to fall behind those of other long-term beneficiaries.

There has also been a growing gap between benefits and average earnings. The 13% average rise in real earnings since 1979 has not been matched by similar improvements in social security benefits (indexed only to prices). The Child Poverty Action Group, in its pre-budget submission to the Chancellor of the Exchequer (Lister 1986) estimated that over the period since 1979 unemployment benefit for a two-child family has fallen from 45% to 40% of average net male earnings and supplementary benefit from 46% to just over 44%.

Sinfield (1981) has suggested that the obsession with work incentives and the moral panic fuelled by the popular press about supposedly work-shy claimants (Golding and Middleton 1982) has enabled attention to be deflected away from questions about poverty and hardship in unemployment. The increasing numbers of the long-term unemployed, however, have provoked a concern to refocus attention on the living standards that the unemployed are able to afford and whether these are adequate in individual and relative terms (Field 1977, Lister and Field 1978, Burghes 1981, Piachaud 1981).

The numbers of the unemployed on means-tested benefits present a static picture of the pool of the unemployed at any one time, which does no justice to the fact that, although durations of unemployment have generally lengthened, by no means all of those who experience unemployment are out of work for long periods and the impact of unemployment may differ considerably between the short and long-term unemployed. This dynamic element is important because we need to know more about the impact of increasing durations of unemployment on living standards, and whether the return to work either carries the unemployed out of poverty or is merely the continuation of poverty by other means. Most studies have been cross-sectional (Sinfield 1970, Clark 1978, Marsden 1982) and not surprisingly have tended to focus on the long-term unemployed.

The few studies that have been longitudinal in design (Daniel 1974, Daniel and Stilgoe 1977, Moylan et al. 1984) have focused on a narrow range of indicators, particularly income, which provide only a partial representation of living standards. Current income clearly has an important place as an indicator of livings standards, but it is not their only determinant. Previous income, particularly through savings and previously acquired assets, the ability to borrow money and access to credit can all contribute to current living standards and a wider range of indicators may reveal changes in livings standards even though current incomes remain constant.

It is also important to consider the living standards of the unemployed in relation to those of other low-income groups in order to attempt to assess the impact of unemployment on living standards which is not simply that arising from low income but results from unemployment itself. For this purpose the best comparison is with families with incomes from employment which fall within the same range as those of the unemployed.

Analyses of data from the *Family Finances Survey* and *Family Resources Survey* (Knight 1981) have enabled some of the limitations of earlier research on the living standards of the unemployed to be overcome.

Family finances and family resources surveys

The *Family Finances Survey* (FFS) was carried out between the last quarter of 1978 and the third quarter of 1979 and followed the model of *Family Expenditure Survey* (FES) — a large national household survey of income and expenditure carried out every year by the Department of Employment. While there are always households containing an unemployed head (and other low-income households) in every year's FES sample, even in times of high unemployment there are too few for detailed analysis. The *Family Finances Survey* differed from the standard FES by being restricted entirely to low-income households, defined as those whose resources did not exceed 140% of their supplementary benefit entitlement, including housing costs. This definition has been frequently used in research (Townsend 1979, 161–166) as a means of identifying families in or on the margins of poverty, taking account of differences in family size and composition. The sample is also restricted to families with at least one dependent child.

Twenty-seven per cent of fathers in two-parent families in the FFS were unemployed, 60% were in work and most of the remainder were out of work through sickness or were permanently sick or disabled. Although this survey included a far greater number of families with an unemployed head than any single year of the FES, because of the income ceiling, the sample is only representative of families in about the bottom quartile of the income distribution. However, while some families with an unemployed head will undoubtedly have been excluded by the truncation of the sample, it is likely that most of the unemployed dependent on social security benefits are represented in the sample, even those who were receiving maximum earnings-related supplement (still in existence when the survey was conducted).

The families in the sample were re-interviewed 12 months later in the *Family Resources Survey* (FRS) and so, despite the limitations mentioned above, these data provided an opportunity both to compare cross-sectionally the living standards of the unemployed and the poorest families in work and also to examine changes in living standards over a period of 12 months and relate these to changes and continuities in employment position.

Living standards

Living standards are not easy to define or measure, nor is there any agreed normative minimum level against which actual living standards can be compared. However it is possible in these surveys to assess a number of indicators of living standards including income, expenditure, possession of various consumer durables, use of credit and the extent of indebtedness.

Income can be characterised as a measure of the resources available to families and the opportunities open to them for various kinds of consumption. However, in addition to being compressed in this study within a narrow band, income has the disadvantage of taking no account of purchasing power derived from, for example, the use of savings or credit. For this reason, expenditure is generally considered an important complementary indicator which captures the element of consumption in living standards more adequately than income. There is also another form of household consumption — that represented by durable goods — which takes place over an extended period of time, for most of which there may be no current expenditure, but which continues to contribute to standards of living. Consumer durables are therefore a third important indicator. Where durable goods are owned outright they may also be considered as a component of the household's asset wealth, which is a store of value that can be realised for cash. However there are no data on the actual value of these assets and their resale value may in fact be very small. Indebtedness and credit use are more complex measures when treated as indicators of living standards, and these have been analysed separately by Parker (1986). Parker's analysis suggests that there is a significantly higher incidence of money problems among the unemployed than among low income families in employment, fuel and housing arrears being particularly common. This analysis focuses on the extensiveness and intensity of credit use and debt, rather than on subjective feelings and responses to financial problems which have been the subject of psychological studies of unemployment (Warr and Jackson 1984).

None of these indicators is sufficient in itself to measure living standards, but taken together they give a more complete picture of the relative living standards of the employed and unemployed and changes in living standards over time than has been possible in other studies.

The sample

In this analysis a number of households included in the original sample have been omitted. The data presented here are based on single tax unit households (parents and their dependent children). Multi-unit households have been excluded for two reasons: first, because, like the FES, these surveys are unable to take account of sharing between different family units in the same household; and second because some expenditure data (fuel expenditure, for example) are collected on a household basis and there is no exact way of apportioning expenditure between two or more families in one household. One other concern was that the relationship of families in the sample to the labour market should be consistent, that is, that all heads of households should be economically active — either in employment or unemployed and looking for paid work.

The analysis is carried out both cross-sectionally in the FFS and longitudinally between two surveys. In the cross-sectional analysis, the FFS sample was divided into five groups by employment status: the short-, medium- and long-term unemployed and the short- and long-term employed. The three durations of unemployment corresponded to up to 13 weeks, 14–52 weeks and more than 52 weeks. There are no universally accepted definitions of these categories, but periods of longer than a year are often taken to represent long-term unemployment because by then any entitlement to unemployment benefit is normally exhausted. The short- and medium-term unemployed were divided at 13 weeks. The rationale for this was partly to secure an adequate number of cases in each group, but also to create a short-term group who had been unemployed for longer than a period of 'frictional' or job changing unemployment.

The short-term employed were defined as those who had had their present job for six months or less and had received either unemployment or supplementary benefit in the previous year. The long-term employed were those who had had their present job for more than six months and had received neither benefit in the previous year. Employed families were divided in this way in order to separate those in relatively stable employment from those with some recent history of unemployment, but the placing of the division at six months was determined by the data set.

In the longitudinal analysis, families were classified according to their position in both surveys. Six groups were identified, which fell into three pairs: one pair consisting of households who were unemployed in both surveys, either continuously unemployed or with a spell of employment in between ('intermittently unemployed'); a second pair containing households 'continuously' and 'intermittently' employed where the latter had a spell of unemployment between the FFS and FRS; and a pair consisting of households whose employment status in the FRS was different from its employment status in the FFS.

Table 1 shows that between the FFS and FRS continuities in employment status were far more frequent than changes. Only one-fifth of these households were in different employment positions in the FFS and FRS and the majority of households whose employment status was the same in both surveys had been in that position continuously throughout the 12 months separating the two surveys.

Table 1. Continuities and changes in employment status.

FFS employment status	FRS employment status	n	%
Employed	Employed 12 months	355	58.5
	Employed less than 12 months	21	3.5
Employed	Unemployed	22	3.6
Unemployed	Employed	94	15.5
Unemployed	Unemployed 12 months +	72	11.9
	Unemployed less than 12 months	43	7.1
			100.0
In the same employment position in FFS and FRS	– throughout 12 months	427	70.3
	– with some change during 12 months	64	10.5
In different employment position in FFS and FRS		116	19.1
			100.0

Most of the change in employment status between the FFS and FRS is accounted for by households moving from unemployment back into work. Of 398 households who were employed in the FFS only 22 (6%) were unemployed 12 months later. In contrast, of the 209 households who were unemployed in the FFS 94 (45%) had returned to work in the FRS.

Only those who continued to be in two-parent, single tax unit households in the FRS were included in the longitudinal analysis and so the numbers in the longitudinal data set (607) are smaller than those in the cross-sectional analysis of the FFS (873). The most significant point to note is that over half of those who were unemployed in both surveys had already been unemployed for more than a year at the time of the first survey. Similarly, the majority (in fact, nearly all) of those who were in work in both surveys had been in long-term employment at the time of the first survey. So the stability of the two groups whose employment status has remained the same in fact extends over a considerably longer period than the 12 months separating the two surveys.

Results

Cross-sectional comparisons of income and expenditure
Table 2 compares various measures of income and expenditure between

the five groups in the FFS. Current disposable income (gross income less deductions for tax and national insurance) differs substantially between the employed and unemployed groups, even within this constrained sample. The results suggest that the unemployed as a whole are considerably poorer even than very low wage earners. This might be expected in the long-term unemployed group, who are virtually entirely supported by supplementary benefit (and therefore their incomes as a proportion of supplementary benefit not surprisingly cluster at about 100%, while the incomes of the employed vary up to the limit at 140%). Only 12% of wives in this group were in paid employment. However the other two unemployed groups have incomes which do not substantially differ from those of the long-term unemployed, despite the fact that only about half (53% of the medium-term and 46% of the short-term unemployed) had any supplementary benefit income, and nearly a quarter (23%) of wives in the short-term unemployed group were in paid work. So despite this difference in the sources of income and the apparent (see conclusions) withdrawal of wives from employment, cross-sectional analysis suggests that lengthening durations of unemployment have little impact on living standards as measured by disposable income.

One of the problems that arise in these simple comparisons of means is that they take no account of differences in the number of children dependent on incomes of a given size and that, in the case of social security benefits which vary with the number and ages of children, apparent differences in living standards may simply be a function of different family compositions. One method of controlling for these differences is to apply an equivalence scale to the distribution of income. Briefly, an equivalence scales is a set of factors for families of different compositions which purports to represent the extent to which their incomes need to be raised or lowered to achieve a common standard of living. Equivalent current disposable income is also shown in the table using the DHSS equivalence scale (van Slooten and Coverdale 1977). This much more comparable measure of disposable income continues, however, to show the same pattern of results.

As has been said, the level of expenditure may be a better indicator of living standards than disposable income and is also shown in the table. For all groups total expenditure exceeds disposable income. This is a normal occurrence for low income households in each year's FES and, at least in part, reflects the margin of consumption which is sustained through the use of savings, credit or borrowing. The interval between income and expenditure is smallest in the two stable groups and largest in the short-term unemployed, and declines between the short-term and long-term unemployed. The progressive alignment of income and expenditure may reflect the depletion of savings or more difficult access to loans or credit, or a reluctance to take on (further) loans or credit. A one-tailed test of significance shows that the mean expenditure of the long-term

Table 2. Income and expenditure in FFS

	Long-term unemployed	Medium-term unemployed	Short-term unemployed	Short-term employed	Long-term employed
Current disposable income (£ per week)	47.91	50.20	48.08	59.13	72.25
Equivalent current disposable income (£ per week)	29.63	32.54	31.59	38.11	47.44
Total expenditure (£ per week)	52.24	56.31	59.72	65.79	75.39
Excess of expenditure over disposable income (£ per week)	4.16	6.11	11.81	6.66	3.14
Proportion of total expenditure taken by food, fuel and housing (%)	65.7	59.6	60.2	57.2	55.5
Base (= respondents)	126	131	85	54	477

F ratios

All groups (d.f. = 4:868)
Current disposable income — 106.2*
Equivalent current disposable income — 118.3*
Total expenditure — 23.2*
Proportion taken by food, fuel and housing — 15.6*

Unemployed groups (d.f. = 2:339)
Current disposable income — 1.2
Equivalent current disposable income — 6.8*
Total expenditure — 2.3
Proportion taken by food, fuel and housing — 7.8*

* $p < 0.001$

unemployed is significantly lower than that of the short-term unemployed, implying a significant downward trend ($z = 1.91$, $p < 0.05$). Therefore, although the current incomes of the unemployed groups are about the same, their expenditure level suggests that living standards fall with lengthening unemployment.

There are also differences between the groups in patterns of expenditure. Housing, food and fuel might be characterised as 'necessities', and what families have left after expenditure on these commodities is a measure of the access they have to others which affect their standard of living. The proportion of expenditure devoted to necessities, shown in Table 2, also indicates that the living standards of the long-term unemployed are lowest and those of the long-term employed are highest.

Regression analysis carried out with disposable income and expenditure as the dependent variables (Bradshaw *et al.* 1983) confirmed the independent association of these variables with employment status, controlling for other differences in the characteristics of the groups.

Changes in resources over time
Expenditure data were not collected again in the FRS and so longitudinal analysis has to be confined to income. In this analysis, the measures are current disposable income as before, but also the 'relative net resources' (i.e. proportion of SB entitlement) measure used in the initial section of the sample to restrict the FFS to low income households. The 'relative net resources' measure (RNR) has three particular advantages. First, because only those whose relative net resources were not greater than 140% of their SB entitlement were included in the sample, the RNR measure can be used as an indicator of the numbers of families who move out of poverty (so defined) between the FFS and FRS. Second, unlike current gross and disposable income, RNR is 'equivalent' in the sense that account is taken of the numbers dependent on different levels of income by relating them to SB entitlement and so RNR takes account of any changes in family composition between the FFS and FRS. Third, the RNR measure is based on benefit levels that are up-rated annually in line with movements in the Retail Prices Index (RPI) and so the effects of inflation are automatically taken into account in comparisons of RNR over time. These factors make RNR both a more convenient and a better indicator of changes in living standards than simple comparisons of diposable income. However such a comparison has been included here in Table 3 in order to give a more immediately appreciable assessment of changes over time in actual incomes rather than in proportions of a given standard (which is what RNR is).

Table 3 shows that, in real terms, the incomes of the unemployed in the FFS who were also unemployed 12 months later remained virtually constant. The incomes of the employed–unemployed group fell (by 16%),

Table 3. Current disposable income

Current disposable income in:	Continuously unemployed (n = 72)	Intermittently unemployed (n = 43)	Continuously employed (n = 355)	Intermittently employed (n = 21)	Unemployed employed (n = 94)	Employed unemployed (n = 22)
FFS Mean*	57.20	55.75	85.31	70.89	57.92	72.60
(SD)	(12.82)	(12.93)	(22.05)	(15.39)	(15.11)	(17.80)
FRS Mean	57.66	55.66	107.17	86.46	96.16	60.64
(SD)	(12.54)	(16.02)	(35.30)	(17.07)	(32.78)	(15.05)

All unemployed

FFS Mean*	57.21	
(SD)	(13.96)	
FRS Mean	57.51	
(SD)	(14.10)	

All-employed

FFS Mean*	83.85	
(SD)	(21.91)	
FRS Mean	100.28	
(SD)	(34.37)	

* Incomes in the FFS were uprated by 18.4%, which represents
the increase in the general RPI between January 1979 and January 1980.

which is consistent with the findings presented earlier which indicated that the incomes of even the short-term unemployed are lower, on average, than those of the poorest working families. The same feature can be seen in the fact that those who returned to work from unemployment had an increase in disposable income, but in this case the difference was much greater (66%). And the incomes of the continuously employed group rose also (by 20%).

Table 4 expresses these movements in terms of the RNR measure and enables something to be said about movements out of poverty rather than merely changes in levels of income. All households in the sample had RNR of no more than 140 in the FFS. Table 4 shows how many households in the sample had resources above this level in the FRS.

The findings indicate that there were movements out of poverty for two groups in this sample. The incomes of those who moved from unemployment into employment increased dramatically, but it is important to bear in mind that this increase was from the low base-line of income in the FFS. Mean RNR in the FRS was 171% for this group and so on average movements out of poverty were of relatively limited range. This was also true of the continuously employed group. Half of this group had RNR greater than 140% in the FRS but the mean for the group was only 155%.

This aggregate assessment of group means and movement across a particular threshold conceals a considerable amount of variation in individual incomes. In all groups there were both gainers and losers and only the net effect is shown by the group mean; and there were also movements in incomes which did not cross the threshold level, and so do not appear as changes in Table 4. Table 5 presents a fuller picture of the direction and magnitude of changes in resources over time based on a comparison of RNR in the FFS and FRS for each case in the sample. The table serves to illustrate the diversity in both direction and magnitude of change which is disguised by mean scores for groups as a whole.

Briefly, 60% of the continuously unemployed became poorer during the year separating the two surveys, although the majority did not become very much poorer. (Similarly, the majority of the 40% whose resources improved did not become very much better off during the year.) Twenty-seven per cent of the continuously employed group became poorer (most only sightly poorer), but 21% increased their resources by 50% or more. About 9% of those who returned to employment appeared on the RNR measure to be poorer in work than they had been in unemployment, and 28% of those who became unemployed appeared to be better off than in employment, but not much better off, and most were considerably worse off.

We can begin to see what accounts for these movements (or lack of movement) in incomes by examining the components of gross incomes in the FRS shown in Table 6. The incomes of the continuously unemployed

Table 4. Relative net resources in FRS

Relative net resources (% of SB entitlement)	Continuously unemployed (n = 72) %	Intermittently unemployed (n = 43) %	Continuously employed (n = 355) %	Intermittently employed (n = 21) %	Unemployed employed (n = 94) %	Employed unemployed (n = 22) %
Up to 140	99.5	97.7	51.2	54.5	33.0	95.4
141 – 200	0.5	2.3	33.5	29.1	43.6	4.6
201 +	—	—	15.3	16.4	23.4	—
Mean	92.9	96.2	154.8	146.5	171.4	95.4
SD	(10.1)	(27.3)	(58.4)	(42.3)	(60.8)	(20.9)

	All unemployed %	All employed %	Total %
Up to 140	98.3	47.6	59.1
141 – 200	1.7	35.4	27.7
200 +	—	17.0	13.2
Mean	94.3	154.8	
SD	(18.7)	(58.6)	

Table 5. Changes in RNR between FFS and FRS

% change in RNR	Continuously unemployed (n = 72)	Intermittently unemployed (n = 43)	Continuously employed (n = 355)	Intermittently employed (n = 21)	Unemployed employed (n = 94)	Employed unemployed (n = 22)
Fall	total = 59.7	total = 48.4	total = 27.5	total = 21.2	total = 8.7	total = 72.3
50 +	—	5.0	1.0	—	1.1	4.6
40-49	—	—	0.9	—	—	1.5
30-39	3.2	1.5	1.4	—	2.3	13.8
20-29	4.6	3.8	3.8	1.6	—	43.2
10-19	15.0	7.6	8.4	7.4	1.4	6.1
1-9	36.9	30.5	12.0	12.2	3.9	3.1
No Change	—	3.0	0.2	—	—	—
Gain	total = 40.3	total = 48.6	total = 72.2	total = 78.9	total = 91.4	total = 27.7
1-9	26.2	29.5	13.0	15.5	6.6	4.6
10-19	6.5	8.4	12.4	6.5	7.1	13.1
20-29	5.3	2.3	11.8	—	5.0	4.6
30-39	—	0.8	7.9	21.1	9.4	5.4
40-49	1.4	—	6.0	9.7	8.5	—
50 +	0.9	7.6	21.1	26.1	54.8	—
RNR (FFS)						
Mean	95.8	96.2	122.2	113.2	100.6	116.5
(SD)	(12.7)	(27.3)	(19.9)	(23.1)	(19.7)	(21.6)
RNR (FRS)						
Mean	92.9	96.2	154.8	146.5	171.4	95.4
(SD)	(10.1)	(27.3)	(58.4)	(42.3)	(60.8)	(20.9)
% Change	-3.0	0.0	26.7	29.4	70.4	-18.1

Table 6. Components of current gross income in FRS

Component RNR	Continuously unemployed (n = 72)		Intermittently unemployed (n = 43)		Continuously employed (n = 355)		Intermittently employed (n = 21)		Unemployed employed (n = 94)		Employed unemployed (n = 22)	
	% of gross income	% with source	% of gross income	% with source	% of gross income	% with source	% of gross income	% with source	% of gross income	% with source	% of gross income	% with source
Earnings of husband and wife												
Total	2.6	6.9	6.3	11.6	85.5	99.7	87.0	100.0	89.0	98.9	6.3	22.7
As employers (total)	2.6	6.9	6.3	11.6	85.5	99.7	86.3	100.0	88.7	98.9	6.3	22.7
Husband	—	—	1.9	2.3	79.9	99.4	82.3	100.0	80.7	98.9	—	—
Wife	2.6	6.9	4.4	9.3	5.3	27.9	4.0	23.8	8.0	29.8	6.3	22.7
As self-employed	—	—	—	—	0.3	7.3	0.7	19.0	0.3	8.5	—	—
Social security												
Total	96.6	100.0	92.3	100.0	8.4	99.4	10.2	100.0	8.5	100.0	90.4	100.0
Unemployment benefit	2.1	10.1	39.8	58.1	0.1	0.6	—	—	—	—	46.9	72.7
Supplementary benefit	74.7	100.0	34.0	62.8	—	—	0.4	—	—	—	26.5	56.5
FIS	—	—	1.1	11.6	0.2	4.2	—	—	—	2.1	0.3	4.5
Child benefit	19.7	100.0	17.4	100.0	7.8	99.4	9.2	100.0	7.9	100.0	16.7	100.0
Other	0.1	30.6	—	7.0	0.3	4.2	0.6	4.8	0.6	9.6	—	—
*Other**	0.8	11.1	1.4	7.0	6.1	74.9	2.8	47.6	2.5	43.6	3.3	31.8

* Includes: pension, annuities, imputed income from owner occupation, income from sub-letting, earnings of household members other than husband and wife.

stay more or less constant because so much of them are provided from social security, principally supplementary benefit. All of the continuously unemployed and two-thirds of the intermittently unemployed are SB recipients. The original sampling procedure of the FFS excluded the unemployed with any substantial income from sources other than social security and the means-testing of SB allows beneficiaries only limited access to other income. One of the main contrasts between the groups is in the proportion of employed wives — 7% in the continuously unemployed group (contributing less than 3% to family income) compared with 28% in the continuously employed group.

Table 7 shows changes in the employment status of wives in the six groups between the FFS and FRS. The table shows that the incomes of the continuously unemployed remain fairly constant not only because they are largely derived from social security but also because the employment position of wives hardly changes. A small number of wives obtained work and some withdrew from the labour market but for 94% their employment position remained unchanged.

The large increase in the incomes of the unemployed–employed group is clearly partly due to income from employment replacing income from benefit for the head of household but it is also probably due to the increased contribution of earnings from wives. Table 7 shows that 18% of wives in this group joined the labour force between the FFS and FRS and the previous table shows that this group had the highest proportion of working wives in the FRS and the highest proportion of gross incomes made up of wives' earnings.

Table 7 also shows that the fall in incomes of the employed–unemployed group is probably cushioned to some extent by additional earnings from wives. None of the wives in this group left jobs (although a small number changed from full-time to part-time work) and 14% of wives obtained jobs.

The largest proportion of wives joining the labour market is in the continuously employed group and this increased participation by wives partly contributes to the increase in the incomes of this group, but the increase is also partly accounted for by husbands increasing their earnings.

Table 8 shows that the gross earnings of heads of households in the continuously employed group increased about 10% and most of this was probably accounted for by job changing between the two surveys. The table also shows that not only were there three times more employed wives in this group in the FRS than in the FFS but also the average earnings of those employed had increased by 88%.

So the evidence suggests that over a 12-month period, the living standards of the unemployed decline after the onset of unemployment while those of the employed are more likely to improve. Let us now see to what extent these findings match those obtained using consumer durables as an indicator of living standards. The data in these surveys take three forms, which are discussed in turn.

Table 7. Changes in wives' employment status

Change in employment status	Continuously unemployed (n = 72) %	Intermittently unemployed (n = 43) %	Continuously employed (n = 355) %	Intermittently employed (n = 21) %	Unemployed employed (n = 94) %	Employed unemployed (n = 22) %
Obtained employment	4.2	7.0	22.3	15.0	18.1	13.6
Left employment	1.4	4.6	2.5	5.0	5.3	—
Full-time to part-time employment	—	—	0.6	—	—	4.5
Part-time to full-time employment	—	—	0.6	—	—	—
No change	94.4	88.4	74.0	80.0	76.6	81.8

Table 8. Changes in gross incomes of the continuously-employed group

	Same employer	Different employer	All
Gross earnings of head of household			
FFS Mean	89.42	83.79	88.34
(SD)	(81.97)	(32.27)	(75.55)
FRS Mean	96.03	105.16	97.54
(SD)	(34.95)	(47.79)	(37.56)
% increase in gross earnings of head of household	7.4	25.5	10.4
Gross earnings of wives			
FFS Mean			11.68
(SD)			(7.98)
FRS Mean			21.95
(SD)			(19.04)
% increase in wives' gross earnings			87.9
% of wives working in - FFS			10.4
FRS			30.0

Presence of consumer durables in the household

Information was only collected on a small number of consumer durables in the FFS and FRS. There are countless other consumer durables which might also have been included and the importance of durable goods as an indicator of living standards is recognised in the cohort study being conducted by the Office of Population Censuses and Surveys, in which data on a much wider range will eventually become available.

The assets included are: telephone, TV, washing machine, fridge/freezer, car and central heating. Central heating is somewhat different from the other assets in that it may be acquired in the short-term but it is not something that can readily be disposed of in the short-term, and in fact is likely to be associated with the type and tenure of housing which the family occupies. The proportion of households in the FFS with each asset is shown in Table 9. Generally, the long-term employed were the best provided with these assets and the long-term unemployed the worst provided. Logit analyses were also undertaken (Bradshaw *et al.* 1983) in order to test whether these differences were in fact associated with employment status independently of other characteristics of the groups. These analyses showed that the long-term unemployed were less likely than the other groups to have each of these assets. However, the effects of short-term unemployment and short-term employment were more variable, suggesting that a change in employment status does not

Table 9. Availability of consumer durables in FFS

Consumer durables	Long-term unemployed %	Medium-term unemployed %	Short-term unemployed %	Short-term employed %	Long-term employed %	χ^2 (all groups) d.f. = 4	χ^2 (unemployed) d.f. = 2
Telephone	25.5	37.1	46.0	35.9	59.6	60.9***	9.9**
Television	97.2	98.1	98.2	94.7	97.3	2.0	-†
Washing machine	75.3	76.1	81.6	83.6	88.3	19.8***	1.05
Any Fridge/Freezer	80.3	84.8	84.5	94.1	96.8	50.6***	1.2
(Freezer)	14.6	20.6	31.1	36.3	45.9	61.1	7.6*
Car	11.0	30.1	34.6	51.1	66.7	157.9***	20.0***
Central heating	33.1	41.9	37.4	47.1	53.3	16.3**	2.0
Base (= respondents)	126	131	85	54	477		

* $p < 0.05$;
** $p < 0.01$;
*** $p < 0.001$.

† Three out of six cells had expected frequencies less than five

necessarily have an immediate impact on the presence of assets in the household. The results were by no means as clear cut as with income and expenditure, and this is perhaps not surprising given that the availability of consumer durables is likely to reflect long-term living standards.

This conclusion is also confirmed by longitudinal analysis, presented in Table 10. The difference in the availability of consumer durables between long-term unemployed and long-term employed which was seen in the FFS can also be seen in longitudinal analysis between the continuously unemployed and the continuously employed. However, there was no marked difference in the average number of assets where employment status had changed between the surveys. Nor did availability of consumer durables seem closely related to changes in RNR. While there were net gains of consumer durables in those groups whose RNR had increased, the same was also true where RNR had fallen. Examination of changes in each consumer durable individually shows little consistent pattern and the general stability in the average number of assets in all the groups suggests that much of the change is in the form of substitutions of one asset for another.

The data available in the FFS and FRS are far from ideal. In particular, the mere presence or absence in the household of a mere six (very commonly possessed) consumer goods is not a very sensitive indicator of living standards. We do not know anything about the value of these goods and it is possible that while they continue to be present in the household, cheaper versions may be substituted for more expensive ones, they may deteriorate in their quality and functioning, or indeed, may not work at all. Where goods appear to have been lost between the two surveys we do not know whether they were sold under the pressure of making ends meet (or repossessed or returned if on HP or rented), or disposed of for other reasons. And the small number of consumer durables included in the surveys may have left undisclosed substantial changes in the possession of other assets. However, these data can be supplemented by information in two other forms: on expenditure and on felt needs.

Expenditure on durable household goods
The only other information in the FFS on consumer durables is weekly expenditure data. This covers expenditure on all durable goods, not just the ones shown in Tables 9 and 10, and is collected, along with other expenditure data, by means of weekly expenditure diaries. Some of this expenditure will take the form of recurrent payments of rent or HP but some will be single, lump-sum payments which are converted into weekly amounts. When these data are compared, as they are in Table 11, between subgroups of the sample, they are subject to considerable sampling errors.

In all cases the standard deviation is greater than the mean and the amount of variation is particularly noticeable in the long-term employed

Table 10. Changes in availability of consumer durables over time

	Continuously unemployed	Continuously employed	Intermittently unemployed	Intermittently employed	Employed– unemployed	Unemployed– employed
Telephone						
% gained	4.1	11.6	10.2	—	4.6	8.7
% lost	2.8	0.8	8.6	6.5	1.5	3.9
net gain (%)	1.3	10.8	1.6	-6.5	3.1	4.8
TV						
% gained	2.3	1.9	—	—	—	1.1
% lost	1.8	0.3	—	—	8.5	0.7
net gain (%)	0.5	1.6	—	—	-8.5	0.4
Washing Machine						
% gained	13.7	3.5	13.3	5.7	4.6	5.5
% lost	4.1	6.5	12.5	5.7	—	1.6
net gain (%)	9.6	-3.0	0.8	—	4.6	3.9
Fridge/Freezer						
% gained	10.4	1.7	14.9	6.5	5.4	5.3
% lost	3.0	0.3	5.9	—	4.6	2.1
net gain (%)	7.4	1.4	9.0	6.5	0.8	3.2
Car/Van						
% gained	5.1	3.5	10.6	11.3	8.5	10.3
% lost	0.9	2.0	3.9	9.0	-9.2	4.8
net gain (%)	4.2	1.5	6.7	2.3	-0.7	5.5
Central heating						
% gained	7.2	6.8	9.4	—	18.4	4.4
% lost	0.5	2.3	2.8	4.9	10.0	3.9
net gain (%)	6.7	4.5	6.6	-4.9	8.4	0.5
Mean number of durables available						
FFS	3.2	4.7	3.3	4.0	3.6	4.0
FRS	3.5	4.9	3.5	4.0	3.8	4.2
Base	72	355	43	21	22	94

Table 11. Expenditure on durable household goods in FFS

	Long-term unemployed	Medium-term unemployed	Short-term unemployed	Short-term employed	Long-term employed
Mean (£ per week) (S.D.)	2.73 (5.73)	2.27 (3.98)	2.87 (4.93)	3.80 (5.98)	4.62 (10.44)
Proportion of total expenditure (%)	4.3	3.6	4.8	5.1	5.4
Base	126	131	85	54	477

Table 12. Estimated expenditure on furniture and household goods in preceding year

	Continuously unemployed	Continuously employed	Intermittently unemployed	Intermittently employed	Employed-unemployed	Unemployed-employed
Calculated mean (£ per week)	1.86	3.85	2.15	3.01	3.81	3.73
Base	72	355	43	21	22	94

group. What differences there are between the groups are small in relation to the standard deviations. However, the results suggest that the unemployed groups spend less than the employed groups, both in absolute terms and as a proportion of total expenditure.

Expenditure data on durable household goods which were collected in the FFS were not collected again in the FRS, but respondents were asked to give an estimate of how much they had spent on furniture and household equipment in the last 12 months. The answers were coded in ranges of expenditure and so a mean expenditure per week was estimated, based on the mid point of these ranges. The continually unemployed group spent least on furniture and household goods, followed by the intermittently unemployed.

Self-perceived needs

As has been said, the particular consumer durables that have been examined here by no means constitute an exhaustive list. Other assets may have shown a different pattern of availability among the employment groups. Although data were not collected on stocks of other durable goods, families in the FRS were asked two questions which give an indication of the extent to which the possession of assets varied more generally between the groups. Respondents were asked a general question about essentials which they found difficult to afford. In Table 13a it can be seen that over half of the continuously unemployed group mentioned at least one item which they found difficult to afford, compared with less than a third of the continuously employed group. The table also shows the proportion of those in each group who mentioned items of furniture or household goods. About 15% (a higher proportion than in any other group) mentioned these items, compared with only 4% of the continuously employed group.

Second, a question was asked specifically about items of furniture or household equipment that respondents needed but could not afford. The results are shown in Table 13b. The proportion mentioning more than one item suggests that the greatest needs are in the unemployed families in the FRS and the proportion is lower in the continuously unemployed than among those with recent experience of employment. It is important to bear in mind that these results are of *self-perceived* needs, which may reflect attitudes as much as the impact of employment status. In this particular case, it may be that the continuously unemployed have different aspirations or expectations than the other groups. The particular items mentioned showed few differences between the groups. Broadly the same items, particularly furniture, floor coverings, curtains and electrical appliances, were mentioned by all of the groups.

Table 13. Durable goods: self perceived needs

	Continuously unemployed %	Continuously employed %	Intermittently unemployed %	Intermittently employed %	Employed-unemployed %	Unemployed-employed %
a) 'Essentials' which respondents found difficult to afford						
Proportion mentioning at least one item	55.0	30.6	41.4	40.7	20.3	30.4
Proportion mentioning furniture and household goods	14.7	3.9	12.5	11.5	0.0	5.2
b) Essential items of furniture or household equipment urgently needed but which respondents felt they could not afford						
Proportion mentioning at least one item	32.1	21.5	28.2	26.0	22.3	37.1
Proportion mentioning more than one item	38.8	12.6	43.7	29.2	50.0	19.0
Base	72	355	43	21	22	94

Conclusions

The conclusions of this study are two-fold. First, among the general population of low-income familes with children at any one time, a considerable proportion are poor because the main breadwinner is unemployed. In this instance (1978/79) the proportion was just over a quarter but would be higher in a more recent sample. Many of these will already be long-term unemployed and are likely to remain unemployed for at least another year. Their lives are characterised by incomes derived wholly or largely from social security which are substantially below those of even the poorest working families in employment and material living standards declining over time. This casts serious doubt on the ability of social security benefits to preserve an adequate standard of living, especially over the long durations of unemployment that have become increasingly common.

These findings are based on data collected in late 1978 and 1979. Since then, while real earnings have improved, social security policy has been dominated by a desire to sharpen employment incentives and this has included the taxation of benefits and the ending of earnings-related supplements. It has been persuasively argued (Layard *et al.* 1978, SSAC 1982) that in practical terms, at current benefit levels and particularly during the recession, reducing benefits is hardly an appropriate way of improving incentives. As a matter of urgency, far greater attention should now be given to the adequacy of the living standards of families in unemployment, particularly the long-term unemployed.

Second, low income families do not necessarily remain in poverty for long periods (although they may continue to have low incomes). Layard *et al.* (1978) have estimated, on the basis of General Household Survey data, that the number of poor families would treble but for the contribution of wives' earnings. The results presented here underline the importance of secondary earnings as a major factor enabling movements out of poverty to take place. Most of the poor working families included in the FFS fell within this range of income either because they had only one earner or a wife with very low earnings. However, for many this appeared to be a relatively transitory state. Moreover, the unemployed who return to employment do not necessarily remain poor, although many *do* remain poor. In this study about a third did so. For the remainder, wives' earnings made a contribution to enable this movement out of poverty to occur.

The position of those who remain unemployed is much more constrained. Not only do the unemployed themselves have no access to earnings but the wives of unemployed men also appear to be discouraged from entering (or staying in) the labour force. The reasons for this are not entirely clear (see Cooke forthcoming) but it is thought that the stringent earnings limits in social security may be an important factor discouraging secondary earnings which might otherwise keep unemployed families out of poverty (Bradshaw 1985). The somewhat more generous levels of disregarded earnings for the long-term unemployed proposed in the White Paper (DHSS 1986) following the recent social security reviews may, therefore, make some contribution to increasing the economic welfare of this group and also enable larger numbers to maintain some contact with the labour market.

However, as Bradshaw (1985) has suggested, the time may now have arrived to undertake a much more fundamental reappraisal of the assumptions about patterns of employment in social security and, in particular, to find ways to break down the constraints imposed by the rigid distinction (much more in evidence in British social security than in many other countries) between unemployment and employment. It may then be possible to give families greater freedom to exploit what employment opportunities (including part-time work) are available. This development is not a substitute for adequate maintenance benefits. Its purpose would be to change the character and function of benefits, in ways that are consistent with the demand to reduce the stigma that now attaches to the unemployed, by making social security less of a prison and more a floor on which the unemployed can build.

References

BRADSHAW, J. (1985). 'Social Security Policy and Assumptions about Patterns of Work'. In R. Klein and M. O'Higgins (eds) *The Future of the Welfare State*. Oxford: Martin Robertson.

BRADSHAW, J., COOKE, K. and GODFREY, C. (1983). 'The Impact of Unemployment on the Living Standards of Families.' *Journal of Social Policy*, *12* (4), 433-452.

BURGHES, L. (1981). 'Unemployment and Poverty' In L. Burghes and R. Lister (eds) *Unemployment: Who Pays the Price?* London: Child Poverty Action Group.

CLARK, M. (1978). 'The Unemployed on Supplementary Benefit.' *Journal of Social Policy*, *7*, (4), 385-410.

COOKE, K. (forthcoming). 'The Withdrawal from Paid Work of the Wives of Unemployed Men: A Review of Research.' *Journal of Social Policy*.

DANIEL, W.W. (1974). *A National Survey of the Unemployed*. London: Political and Economic Planning.

DANIEL, W.W. and STILGOE, E. (1977). *Where Are They Now? A Follow-Up Study of the Unemployed*. London: Political and Economic Planning.

DEACON, A. (1982). 'An End to the Means Test? Social Security and the Attlee Government.' *Journal of Social Policy*, *11* (3), 289-306.

DEACON, A. and BRADSHAW, J. (1983). *Reserved for the Poor*. Oxford: Martin Robertson.

DEPARTMENT OF HEALTH AND SOCIAL SECURITY (1986). *Social Security Statistics*. London: HMSO.

DEPARTMENT OF HEALTH AND SOCIAL SECURITY (1986). *The Reform of Social Security: Programme for Action* (Cmnd. 9691). London: HMSO.

FIELD, F. (1977). 'Unemployment and Poverty.' In F. Field (ed.) *The Conscript Army*. London: Routledge and Kegan Paul.

GOLDING, P. and MIDDLETON, S. (1982). *Images of Welfare*. Oxford: Martin Robertson.

KNIGHT, I. (1981). *Family Finances*. Office of Population Censuses and Surveys, Occasional Paper 26. London: HMSO.

LAYARD, R., PIACHAUD, D and STEWART, M. (1978). *The Causes of Poverty*. Royal Commission on the Distribution of Income and Wealth, Background Paper 5. London: HMSO.

LISTER, R. (1986). *A Budget to Unite a Divided Britain*. London: Child Poverty Action Group.

LISTER, R. and FIELD, F. (1978). *Wasted Labour*. London: Child Poverty Action Group.

MARSDEN, D. (1982). *Workless*. London: Croom Helm.

MOYLAN, S., MILLAR, J. and DAVIES, R. (1984). *For Richer, for Poorer? DHSS Cohort Study of Unemployed Men*. London: HMSO.

PARKER, G. (1986). 'Unemployment, Low Income and Debt.' In I. Ramsey (ed.) *Debtors and Creditors: Socio-Legal Perspectives*. London: Professional Books.

PIACHAUD, D. (1981). *The Dole*, Discussion paper 89, London: Centre for Labour Economics, London School of Economics.

SINFIELD, A. (1970). 'Poor and Out of Work in Shields.' In P. Townsend (ed.) *The Concept of Poverty*. London: Heinemann.

SINFIELD, A. (1981). *What Unemployment Means*. Oxford: Martin Robertson.

SOCIAL SECURITY ADVISORY COMMITTEE (1982). *First Report of the SSAC 1981*. London: HMSO.

TOWNSEND, P. (1979). *Poverty in the United Kingdom*. Harmondsworth: Penguin Books.

VAN SLOOTEN, R. and COVERDALE, A.G. (1977). 'The Characteristics of Low Income Households.' In *Social Trends No. 8*. London: HMSO.

WARR, P. and JACKSON, P. (1984). 'Men Without Jobs: some correlates of age and length of unemployment.' *Journal of Occupational Psychology*, *57*, 77-85.

6

Stephen P. McKenna and James McEwen

Employment and health

Introduction

It is an accepted fact that for many unemployment is deleterious to health and well-being, and this is amply illustrated in other sections of this book. What is also generally accepted is that employment is good for individuals and for society more generally. For example, Doyal (1985) has recently reported that now more women are gaining employment outside the home and that this has had a positive effect on many women's health. Despite this, the article then continues to explain that women are now coming into contact for the first time with hazardous dusts, chemicals and fumes. Consequently, they are becoming more likely to develop serious diseases, even though they are not working in the most dangerous industries. This chapter will provide an overview of the health and safety problems associated directly or indirectly with employment, and will question the accepted wisdom that work is good for most or all people, most or all of the time. Only by clarifying the standard against which the experience of unemployment is usually compared can we begin to understand that experience fully.

The scale and nature of employment-related health and safety problems

Ill-health may develop directly as a result of employment or indirectly through the 'side effects' of the process of production. Four major sources of either directly or indirectly caused ill-health can be identified:
   (a) occupational stress,
   (b) environmental pollution,
   (c) occupational accidents,
   (d) occupational disease.

Stress is not, as frequently supposed, limited to senior management but is common in all categories of workers. Such stress is increased at times of high unemployment, when greater productivity is demanded and fear of redundancy is at its highest. It is difficult to estimate with any accuracy the impact of occupational stress on the nation's health. Similarly, it is difficult to determine the costs of pollution, either to the environment or in terms of associated ill-health. Stress and pollution are considered further later in the chapter.

We do have some information about the frequency of accidents and occupational disease in Britain but even this is suprisingly imprecise. The latest reliable statistics are for 1982 when there were 675 fatal accidents reportable under the Health and Safety at Work legislation. Health and safety statistics are also available for deaths which resulted in successful claims for death benefit (i.e. a subset of those that occur). In 1982 this figure was 1,349; made up of 556 accidental deaths and 793 deaths resulting from prescribed diseases. In the same year there were 388,000 spells of incapacity of at least three days following injury and 6,382 resulting from prescribed diseases. (Figures are provided by the Royal Society for the Prevention of Accidents.) These figures are likely to be underestimates and it is hard to determine trends, as frequent changes occur in the definitions of accidents and in the number of employees included in the statistics. It is estimated that in 1982, 15 million days were lost from work as a result of accidents and prescribed diseases and that the cost to employers was over £1,100 million (RoSPA 1984). It is clear that there is a considerable risk of injury and disease as a result of being employed, a factor which should be considered when assessing the value of employment.

The recognition of occupational hazards

Early awareness of occupational hazards
The recognition, both of the benefits and the ill-effects of work go back to the ancient civilizations (Hunter 1962, 1-58, Schilling 1973, 1-23). Some of the world's religions speak of the importance of work in the overall life of a community and of the benefits and burdens to the individual. The ill-effects of work were first documented well in Greek and Roman times when, in particular, the hazards of mining and metal working were recognised. Although there may have been some early attempts at reducing hazards, the practical solution to the problem depended on the use of expendable slave labour in such dangerous occupations.

As Hunter notes, 'throughout the medieval period there were no contributions to the subject of occupational diseases' (p.23) and it was not until the 16th Century that we find definite information relating to diseases of miners and workmen in dangerous trades. It was in the middle of the 16th Century that two remarkable men, Agricola and Paracelsus, wrote on the subject of miners' diseases, and at the close of the 17th Century came the classical work of Rammazzini, 'the Father of Occupational Medicine', who introduced the vital concept of asking the patient—'what is your occupation?'.

It was with the Industrial Revolution in England that doctors first began to assume responsibility for the health of the worker in industry. The specific task of investigating health hazards in various occupations began in the early 19th Century when Charles Turner Thackrah in Leeds decided to devote his life to preventive medicine of a new kind (Hunter *op cit.*).

As the recognition of hazards developed, so did the opposing view of the benefits of work which was frequently associated with the protestant religion (Argyle 1972). Within psychiatry, the therapeutic aspects of work were incorporated into certain treatment regimens. Perhaps the workhouses associated with the Poor Law System may be regarded as the extreme application of these views.

An examination of morbidity and mortality records associated with occupation may suggest a relatively minor problem, when compared with ill-health in the community at large. However, the records provide a very inadequate picture of the overall burden of ill-health resulting from work. Many cases, even the more severe ones, are not recorded or not attributed to occupation, and much of the burden of less severe chronic ill-health is accepted as part of life. While it is difficult to obtain the total picture, the recognised problems point to the less visible part of the 'iceberg' of occupational ill-health and the need for further effort to clarify the problems and to identify the best forms of intervention.

The role of the medical profession

Although medical practitioners have been relatively unsuccessful in the promotion of health, they have generally been more competent in the recognition of ill-health. In many diseases they have been responsible for the initial suspicion of an occupational factor being associated with a particular disease. However, medical care is essentially individually based and unless a doctor has a high index of suspicion and is fortunate enough to see several cases of a rare disease in a selected occupational group, it is unlikely that an association will be suspected.

One of the best known examples is that of Percival Pott and the recognition of scrotal cancer in boy chimney sweeps. Normally a disease of older men, Pott realised that to produce the disease in a much younger age group some special influence must have occurred. Thus, from his own clinical work, he was able to lay the foundation block in the now well known and extensive field of occupational carcinogenesis. Similar work in relation to textiles and mining, with the recognition of respiratory problems and the acute and chronic toxicity of many metals, laid the foundation for the present knowledge of occupational disease and the practices of occupational medicine and occupational hygiene.

The detection and verification of hazards
The first part of this process is usually the epidemiological approach, which attempts to find a proven association. Toxicology textbooks provide exhaustive lists of substances where one or two clinical cases of disease were ascribed, sometimes in only one country, often many years ago, but where no further well planned research studies have been possible or have been attempted.

Full details of epidemiological methods exist in most textbooks of community medicine, but in industry it is often difficult to obtain sufficient numbers of employees with different levels of exposure, over a sufficiently long period, to demonstrate significant differences between exposed and normal populations. While retrospective studies are easier and quicker, they will not provide proof of a casual association, but may provide the justification for more expensive prospective studies. Collaborative studies involving different industrial organizations in various parts of the country and the relevant trade unions may be required to overcome the difficulties of occupational and geographical mobility and uncertainty over exposure.

Other methods which can be used to confirm epidemiological association, such as laboratory testing for carcinogens, may be used without this large epidemiological process, to screen or eliminate potential carcinogens prior to introduction in industry.

Problems in the recognition of hazards
The recognition of an occupational hazard has not usually been welcomed by employers, as it has implications for costs. Such recognition might require the search for a safer substitute, the expense of comprehensive environmental control systems, the burden of compensation claims or the possibility of a process or factory being closed down. Government, management, unions, health professionals and other experts, may all be involved in discussions on risk, its control and the consequent cost. Frequently, there is disagreement about what can be regarded as acceptable risk, and the quality of proof is often debated. This highlights the problems in the existing system. Government, management, unions and professionals all lack positive policies and a sound theoretical basis for taking decisions. There is no agreed comprehensive approach and there often seems to be a lack of the commitment and resources necessary to investigate suspected hazards or to find effective controls of recognised occupational hazards.

While it is relatively easy to suspect links between occupation and disease, this is just the beginning of the process of prevention. A proven association between a disease and a particular substance or process may require many years of detailed research work. Even the clinical suspicion of a link may arise long after the disease process has started. It is important that the reader be aware of some of the difficulties involved in the identification of hazards in occupational settings. Without such an awareness, an unfair assessment might be made of the valuable work which has been done by clinicians, toxicologists and other professionals concerned with occupational health and safety. This section discusses some of the problems involved in identifying hazards.

Occupational health is primarily an observational discipline, experimental studies being difficult to conduct (Olsen 1981). Because of this, problems arise due to the possibility of uncontrolled factors influencing or contributing to the observed findings.

One of the major problems concerns the 'healthy worker effect'. The fact that workers are employed full time implies that they are in a reasonably good state of health. If a job is physically demanding or one that requires a pre-employment medical examination, it is clear that employees will initially be healthier on average than a random sample of the population and that they will be more resistant to subsequent disease. If this is not taken into account, there may be an underestimate of the harmful effect of exposure to the suspected toxic substance or hazardous process. Further, some health-related attrition of the work force studied is likely to occur, resulting in a relatively less disease-prone or 'safer' cohort of workers.

The problem of healthy worker selection is particularly important when the disease under investigation has a long latent period before clinical diagnosis can be made. The state of the labour market also plays a part insofar as it influences the likelihood of changing one's occupation for reasons of health.

Information bias is a problem in prospective studies or surveys which rely on self-reported data of subjective symptoms. Information collected from the exposed group may be influenced by a 'collective awareness' of the significance of the research. The group awareness may alter the individual's perception of the disease and their awareness of its cause. Such a situation arose with the widespread reporting of the dangers of asbestos and may have led to workers overestimating their exposure to the substance.

It is possible that exposed groups of workers will have medical service support while non-exposed workers will not. The consequent screening function may lead to false-positives or the early detection of health problems, both of which may lead to biases, particularly where the disease under study may have a natural history that could be overlooked and consequently remain undiagnosed in the control group.

Bias may also occur as a result of unequal access to medical services, resulting from employment status, distance to medical facilities or the availability of child care. Powell *et al.* (1971) showed that the frequency of accident reporting was directly related to the distance the worker had to travel to the factory's medical facilities.

Three further problems hinder the early detection of possible occupational hazards:

(a) the presentation of the disease may be the same whether or not occupationally produced (for example, lung cancer),

(b) the scattered nature of similar industrial processes and the problem of occupational mobility may lead to delay in recognising the links,

(c) many occupational diseases have a long latent period. Even after heavy exposure there may be a delay of 20, 30 or 40 years in occupational cancers.

The asbestos-related diseases provide an excellent illustration of some of these problems. Commercial use of asbestos began about 1880 and increased rapidly. The first case of asbestosis was observed in 1900 and was described by Murray in 1907. However, this was not accepted at that time as an industrial disease under the Workman's Compensation Act. The story gradually unfolded and its complexity became apparent in the first half of the 20th century. Regulations were introduced in the 1930s to control asbestosis and some years later evidence indicated that these control measures had been effective. However, in the 1950s, the first suggestion was made that cancer might be associated with exposure to asbestos. This triggered a great deal of research into the links between lung cancer and asbestos, resulting in new regulations prohibiting its use (Health and Safety Commission 1979).

Care of the employed

The economic value of workers and fighting men, even slaves, was recognised in Greek and Roman times and this resulted in certain instances in policies to ensure adequate nutrition and sleep. However, this message seems to have been forgotten and it was not until the work of the Social Reformers in the 19th Century that efforts were made to look after employees. Four related aspects of this new concern are recognizable: public health, occupational health, the setting of environmental standards and health and safety legislation

The Public Health Movement
This movement, which commenced about the middle of the nineteenth century, sought to consider the widest aspects of the prevention of ill-health in relation to the environment. It sought through social policy change: to reduce the pollution that existed, to provide clean water supplies, to build better houses and to improve working conditions. These

changes were followed by developments in education and personal behaviour change designed to improve health and to prevent ill-health, particularly the spread of infectious disease. In some instances enlightened employers, such as Robert Owen, sought to provide a better and healthier working environment, for example in the New Lanark Mills (Schilling *op cit.*). Advances in medical therapy lead to further improvements in health, but it is recognised that the major influence on health was socioeconomic rather than medical (McKeown 1979).

Occupational health

Individual factories sought to establish services for their workforce. Although there is some uncertainty as to who was the first occupational health nurse, it is possible that the first industrial nurse was Sister Mary Rachel Jaques, who attended to men injured at the Middlesborough Iron Works in 1858. She had been trained in Kaiserwerth where Florence Nightingale had received her nursing education some years previously. Another claimant is Phillipa Flowerday who was appointed by J & J Colman of Norwich in 1878 (Dixon and Price 1984). It is possible that the retail trade can claim the credit for the appointment of the first medical officer in 1872 when the Army and Navy Stores recruited a part-time doctor.

From these beginnings, gradual expansion took place producing a wide variety of approaches which included first aid care, clinics, convalescent homes and sun ray treatment. Comprehensive occupational health schemes were set up and in some instances, small hospitals and physiotherapy, chiropody and dental services were provided. Despite these developments in selected companies, the type of services provided depended on the interests and enthusiasm of the doctor and management, and the commitment of the company, there being no statutory requirements to have an occupational health service and no clear guidance as to what would comprise such a service.

There have been few recent national surveys of occupational health provisions but the one carried out for the Employment Medical Advisory Services discussion document—*The Way Ahead* (HSC 1977) showed that 85% of all firms in the industries surveyed, employing about 34% of the workforce, have no occupational health service other than first aiders employed less than 10 hours per week in that capacity.

Legislation

Although the Health and Morals of Apprentices Act of 1802 is always quoted as the first act on health and safety, its importance lies not in its achievements, which were virtually non-existent as there was no effective system of enforcement, but in the fact that it indicated that the state had a right to legislate on health and welfare for those employed in private industry. Out of this eventually developed the current legislation, which established the enforcement powers and advisory aspects of the Health and Safety Executive.

Environmental standards

For many years it has been accepted that the most appropriate way to reduce occupational ill-health is by ensuring that exposure to hazards is limited and that there is effective environmental monitoring to achieve this. Often it has been necessary to set environmental standards on very limited evidence and to renew these later in the light of new research. In 1984 the Health and Safety Commission produced the consultative document *'Control of Substances Hazardous to Health'* in an attempt to improve the situation. In the same year, a new guidance note, *EH40 Occupational Exposure Limits* was issued.

The regulations aimed to ensure that exposure to all substances hazardous to health was adequately controlled, by taking measures appropriate to the risk involved, and that the general health surveillance should be expanded to include all workers. The new guidance notes seem to separate substances into a small group where there are control limits and a much larger group where there are recommended limits. Approaches vary in different countries and the philosophy underlying such differences seems to be crucial. Is the aim to produce a working environment where there are no hazards or to recognise the difficulties and aim for what is reasonably practicable? Some concern exists that the new approach will lead to a weakening of standards and that there is an insufficient enforcing presence to make the approach effective (Grant 1985). It should be noted that recruitment into the factory inspectorate has been curtailed in recent years.

In recent years there has been a significant contribution to health and safety through the trade union movement and individual unions. This has involved providing comprehensive and detailed information for members on hazards such as cancer (see Fox *et al.* 1982), in some unions the appointment of qualified advisers and the institution of safety representatives in occupational settings (LRD 1985). Unions were relatively late in developing a commitment to health and safety and there remains considerable opportunity for them to make a greater contribution— although this is hindered in the present economic climate, which has considerably reduced the bargaining powers of the unions.

The following sections consider some of the major problems resulting from employment and the manufacturing process.

Occupational stress

Stress is one area of occupational health which has been widely researched but which still lacks an adequate theoretical basis. Stress may be self imposed, for example where one is striving to reach a high standard of performance, or imposed from outside—by an employer or the environment in which one works.

Poulton (1971) listed some of the factors which could cause stress at work. The first was 'too much to do at once'. Clearly, someone who is expected to undertake two activities at the same time will be unable to give full attention to both. A person in such a situation may either slow down—increasing the pressure of work—or make errors or sustain an accident.

The working environment can also lead to stress. Continuous loud noise increases a person's level of arousal and decreases ability to concentrate. Inadequate illumination or flourescent lighting may also cause stress—as will high or low temperatures.

Factors within the worker can also cause problems. Lack of sleep or the use of tranquillisers or alcohol will reduce arousal, while excessive consumption of tea and coffee will increase arousal. Poulton argues that there is an optimum level of arousal for the efficient performance of particular jobs, complex tasks requiring lower levels of arousal. Stress can have the effect of increasing arousal to a level at which the job is carried out inefficiently or unsafely.

Cooper and Roden (1985) argue that while stress research has concentrated on 'stress risk' jobs such as air traffic controllers and bomb disposal experts, little attention has been paid to groups of workers undergoing social and technological change, such as secretarial, legal and accounting related services. They studied stress among tax inspectors, a group which was experiencing rapid introduction of sophisticated computing systems for handling income tax returns and which appeared to be a 'high risk' group in terms of stress-related ill-health effects. Results from a battery of tests showed that the tax inspectors did appear to be more vulnerable to the pressures of their job and/or work environment than comparable groups of workers. They had lower job satisfaction than similar workers and 15-25% (depending on the measure used) fell within the psychoneurotic outpatient norm category. Tax officers who felt they were not valued, not consulted, not rewarded and that they had little autonomy or decision making influence, were more dissatisfied with their job. In contrast, individuals who felt overloaded, pressured by work targets and deadlines and who got little support to reduce their mounting caseload, were at risk of mental ill-health. This was exacerbated by such qualitative aspects of their work as 'communicating with tax payers', 'dealing with computerisation' and 'not feeling adequately trained for the job'. With the rapid introduction of technology in Britain's manufacturing and service sectors, it is not surprising that general levels of stress appear to be rising.

Payne (1979) has proposed a model of stress which considers the impact of job demands, sources of support, and constraints upon action, to account for differing responses to stress. Social support has been shown to reduce the effects of stressors in occupational situations (House *et al.* 1979). However, sources of support can also constrain or make things more difficult for the person experiencing stress (Payne *et al.* 1984). For example, fellow employees may act both as a support and as a constraint, depending on their attitude or personal stress levels.

Stress, while being a problem itself, may lead to the development of disease. The study by Cooper and Roden illustrated the likely link between stress and psychosocial diseases. Finlayson and McEwen (1977) investigated the links between coronary heart disease and a number of factors including stress. They followed up the families of 76 married men of working age admitted to Dundee hospitals in the early 1970s, who survived a first myocardial infarction (heart attack). Interviews were conducted with the men and their wives and follow up continued for four years after the attack.

One analysis undertaken was of the relationship between potential areas of stress at the time of the first interview and outcome assessed at the time of the second interview. Outcome was determined by whether or not the man had returned to work and whether his wife judged that his illness was over. Five areas of potential stress were identified, one of which was difficulties likely to arise for the husband at work or in getting back to work.

There was a clear relationship between the number of areas of potential risk evidenced at six months and outcome assessed after four years. Of the sample, 63% were judged to have employment as a potential area of stress. The authors concluded (pp. 144-145) that

> 'assessment of areas of potential stress at the time of hospitalisation, coupled with information on age and socio-economic status, could help to indicate men likely to have less successful outcomes. Such assessment could be undertaken by medical social workers or by health visitors who would then be in a position to collaborate with general practitioners in initiating and sustaining programmes of intervention'.

It would follow from this that screening for potential risk of coronary heart disease might be undertaken by occupational health services, where they exist. Such health screening could well prove cost effective in terms of reducing sickness absence and the costs of training inexperienced replacements for temporarily or permanently absent employees. In 1982, 88,716 men died from ischaemic heart disease in Britain, representing nearly one-third of all deaths. In addition, nearly 29 million working days were lost on account of the disease.

While we are far from fully understanding the nature of occupational stress, what is abundantly clear is that employment is a major source of the high levels of stress in present day society. As with occupational health and safety, the recession of the last decade has lead to an increase in the levels of stress and a reduction in willingness to reduce this burden on the well-being of employees.

Public safety

When examining the effect of employment on health it is important to include wider issues than simply the health of employees. In particular, the health and safety of the general public must be considered, especially when one remembers such disasters as Flixborough, Seveso and Bhopal and the more invasive problems of industrial pollution.

The Robens Committee (HMSO 1972) addressed itself to this issue and noted that many hazards of industrial origin could have serious consequences for members of the public. It was noted that there was a long established and deep seated reluctance on the part of the administering departments and the inspectorate to accept any explicit responsibility in relation to the safety of the public. A public inquiry into a crane accident at Brent Cross, Hendon in 1984, in which seven coach passengers were killed, recommended that the Factories Act should be amended to bring the public directly within its scope; but no action was taken on the recommendation. Similarly, the Aberfan Tribunal drew attention to the limited responsibilities of the Mines inspectorate in regard to the problem of controlling unstable colliery tips, but the intended improvements to the safety of persons within the vicinity of mines was effectively avoided.

Modern technology has lead to a rapid increase in the storage and use of intrinsically dangerous substances with highly explosive, flammable or toxic properties. Disaster-potential can be increased by entirely new developments, a change of use or process, or by an increase in the size and scale of existing operations. Potential hazards of new compounds or new processes may never be fully known and may only be indicated by an accident. There had been small scale accidents in Germany and Derbyshire during the production of trichlorophenol, but the hazard was not fully appreciated until the Seveso plant exploded.

The Robens Committee recommended that a cordon of safety be established between potentially hazardous activity and nearby residential areas. To a certain extent this is happening in Britain, in particular with the siting of nuclear power stations, but there is now a tendency for industrialized nations to export such hazards to developing countries where such precautions are not taken.

An editorial in *Public Health* (Editorial 1985) remarked that had the Bhopal leakage of methyl-isocyanate occurred in Western Europe, fewer people would have died, but if the Flixborough disaster had happened in Bhopal, the death toll could have been immense. Moore (1985), asking how many died at Bhopal, reports that the official death toll was 3,000;

that one politician said he would not argue with a figure of 12,000 but that another observer put the figure at 30,000—based on the level of medical services provided and interviews with medical staff.

The Robens Committee also recommended that,

> 'Local authorities should have an explicit duty to take account of the public safety implications of all applications for planning permission and to consult the central authority responsible for industrial safety in any case where they are in doubt'.

The importance of such controls was soon demonstrated by the Flixborough disaster in 1974 (HMSO 1975). The Court of Inquiry commented that siting of hazardous processes should depend on both the risk of disaster and the size and nature of the disaster envisaged. The greater the risk of disaster and the greater the potential disaster, the more important it is that the plant should be away from any populated areas—as Flixborough was. The disaster occurred at 4.53 p.m., on a Saturday and the works were virtually demolished 'by an explosion of warlike dimensions'. Twenty-eight people on site were killed but on an ordinary working day many more would have died. Outside the works injuries and damage were widespread with 1,821 houses and 167 shops and factories damaged. Fortunately, the immediate neighbourhood of the works consisted largely of farms and had a very low population density—the perimeter being surrounded by fields.

The *Public Health* editorial argued that economic pressures will lead to ever increasing risk to life and health (through the switch from small scale labour intensive processes to larger scale highly automated and sophisticated plant) and concluded (p.66) that,

> Only restriction of scale of plant and prevention of excessive concentration of dangerous processes in the vicinity of large populations can ensure that unforeseeable accidents do not lead to horrific consequences such as that of the Mexico City refinery blaze and the Bhopal leakage.

There are many potentially hazardous industrial sites in Britain which do not have such a 'cordon of safety' and to a large extent we are dependent on good fortune for the safety of the general public.

Pollution

All industrial processes produce pollution. Pollution may take many forms, ranging from toxic and radiological emissions to disfigurement of the environment. Like occupational disease and accidents, pollution started with the industrial revolution two centuries ago. In those early days the costs of production were those that the entrepreneur could not avoid paying (Ward and Dubos 1972). The use of air and waterways as giant sewers for effluents aroused little concern and natural systems were treated as 'free goods', as they appeared to be cost free cleaners. Some improvements were made in the time but the 25 year boom following 1945 exacerbated the situation once more. The scale of effluents and materials for disposal increased dramatically, leading to a vast increase in the strain on the air and rivers, which continued to be used as 'free goods'. Furthermore, the character of these effluents was changing with the rapid increase in chemicals employed.

Even today, modern industrial systems do not include in their costs the emission of effluents and used materials into the air, water or onto land. Instead, the costs fall on taxation, public spending, the destruction of amenities, or in the form of ill-health.

Ward and Dubos (1972, 97) suggest that Man should be thought of as,

> a new species of centaur—half man, half automobile— and it is the heavy breathing of his motorized half that pollutes the air, invades the lungs and builds up smog in cities.

The main source of industrial air pollution is combustion, and the two major sources of this are the generation of electricity and the motor car. In the United States about one ton of pollutants are emitted into the air every year for each of its 200 million inhabitants. When such emissions are dispersed by wind they can fall elsewhere as 'acid rain'—a form of sulphuric acid. Air carrying dirt and toxic substances damages organisms in addition to buildings and trees; it is breathed by people and leads to respiratory diseases. Over 3,000 people died following the last lethal smog in London in 1952. Measures have been taken to improve the situation and more could still be done to reduce such pollution, but the necessary actions tend to be expensive. Similar pictures can be painted of water pollution and the dumping of waste on land, each of which sooner or later lead to ill-health or at least to a reduced quality of life.

Recently the world has been shocked by the explosion at the nuclear power station at Chernobyl in the Ukraine. It is too soon to determine the magnitude of the disaster—indeed, the full implications for health will not be known for many tens of years. What is certain is that the radioactive pollution reached the majority of Europe and has led to the whole issue of nuclear power generation being called into question. Arguments for nuclear power have concentrated on such issues as its economic viability, lack of pollution and on the increasing scarcity of fossil fuels. Many of these arguments are now clearly debatable. In particular, are construction costs (even those quoted for power stations with elaborate safety systems) a true reflection of costs, or do they treat human survival as a 'free good'? (see Ward and Dubos 1972, 186–196).

When considering the advantages and disadvantages of employment it is necessary to look at the effects on society at large in addition to those at the individual level. No one would claim that we have not benefited as a society from the development of technology, but we must accept that high technology has its costs—human and environmental—and that these costs must be met at the stage of production.

Inequalities in the distribution of disease

Both occupational and non-occupational ill-health are unevenly distributed among employed people. Clearly, certain workers are exposed to greater risk of accident or disease through the nature of the work they do. However, the inequalities in health cannot be explained simply in terms of exposure to risk.

The Registrar General's classification of five occupational classes range from I–professionals, through to V–unskilled workers, although the allocation of types of job to one of the five classes appears somewhat arbitrary.

Clear-cut gradients exist across the five classes for almost all types of illness, accidents and mortality. For example, in the early 1970s, men and women in social class V had two-and-a-half times as great a chance of dying before reaching retirement age as did professional men and women (OPCS 1978). Such gradients occur at all ages, being particularly marked at birth and during childhood. Up to the age of one month, the risk of death in families of unskilled workers is double that of professional families (see Townsend and Davidson 1982). Boys in social class V have ten times the chance of dying from fire, falls or drowning as those in class I. In adulthood, rates of death from accidents, infections, disease, cancer, heart and respiratory disease show marked class differences. Various surveys have shown similar patterns for morbid experience, with 'limiting long-standing illness' (as defined in the General Household Survey) being three times as high among unskilled manual workers as amongst professional workers. Sickness absence from work also shows class gradients, with ratios (of unskilled to professional workers) being approximately 2:1 for absence due to disease of the respiratory system and for influenza, 4:1 for bronchitis and 6:1 for arthritis and rheumatism (Ministry of Pensions 1965).

Hunt *et al.* (1985) in a study of 2,173 individuals who completed the Nottingham Health Profile (a measure of perceived health) found strong associations between social class and perceived health problems —particularly in the domains of pain, sleep and physical mobility. Four times as many of those from social class V (21%) had difficulties with their employment resulting from their health problems as did those from social class I and the equivalent ratio for social life problems was 3:1, and for hobbies and interests 2:1.

This brief overview indicates that with almost any type of measure of health there is a strong class gradient. One has to ask why this should be the case, and to date no adequate explanation has been proposed. Part of the difference may be explained by relative incomes—with the higher social classes generally having higher incomes. Hunt *et al. (op cit.)* postulate a modern version of Marxian 'immiseration' where health is affected by a kind of spiritual and social impoverishment rather than by gross poverty or grinding labour. They claim that poverty is a relative concept and that the inability to fulfil social and occupational expectations may be felt more keenly by those who are striving in the face of poorer facilities and inadequate resources. Such an hypothesis would be supported by Maslow's hierarchy of needs, particularly in a society like that in Britain where the basic necessities of life are available to all.

When considering the association between social class and health it is important to note the criticisms of social class analysis made by Jones and Cameron (1984). They argue that the Registrar General's classification has been engineered to conform to 'the prejudices of narrow-minded professionals' and that 'the whole tradition of social class analysis in health is a massive tautology', insofar as the classifications have been manipulated to produce smooth mortality gradients. Thus those members of society who can buy the best food, housing and recreation and have the education to use the health and social services have the best health statistics. However, what must not be overlooked is that there are real inequalities in health whatever type of classification is adopted, and any society which accepts such a situation without question and without a genuine concern for change must stand condemned. Even if one accepts that the social classification is inadequate, as it almost certainly is, it is still interesting to consider whether individuals moving to a higher grouping gain the benefits of improved health. A similar issue is whether the high rates of ill-health associated with unemployment could be reduced either by an increase in available resources or by a change in the status with which the unemployed are endowed at present.

McKenna and Payne (1984) investigated the effects of unemployment on perceived health status as measured by the Nottingham Health Profile. Their findings indicated that men who had been unemployed between six and eighteen months had greater problems than workers re-employed after unemployment of a similar period, in the areas of physical mobility, energy, sleep, emotional reactions and social isolation. The unemployed also had higher scores for depression and anxiety—as measured by the General Health Questionnaire (Goldberg 1978). The re-employed workers had similar scores to a control group of long term employed workers, with significantly better percieved health in the areas of physical mobility, social isolation and emotional reactions. Thus it would seem that regaining employment has a marked beneficial effect on the health status of unemployed males.

The effect of reducing time spent in employment

Once the specific risks associated with certain types of work have been taken into account, we have identified two further causes of ill-health and poor well-being; that due to employment and that due to unemployment. It is possible to think of these causes as too much and too little employment. In Britain today, with between three and four million people unemployed and unable to gain employment, the most logical answer would seem to be to spread out the work which has to be done among all those available to do it. However, job sharing is still relatively rare and employers generally prefer to allow high levels of overtime to be worked rather than to employ more people. While it is clear that many jobs could only be done by suitably qualified and experienced people, the scope for work sharing is still immense.

McKenna and Fryer (1984) reported on the perceived health of groups of workers during lay off and early unemployment. They interviewed people from two factories, one of which was making its workforce redundant, and one which had introduced a system of rotating lay-offs. The latter case was particularly interesting as lay-offs had been negotiated between unions and management as an alternative to compulsory redundancies. The shop floor employees were split into three groups, each group being laid off in turn for seven weeks before working for 14 weeks and then being laid off again. In fact, for the lay-off group studied, factory shutdowns meant that they worked only one week in a 12 week period and many of those studied took this off as extra holiday.

The redundant workers had worse perceived health than the laid off workers and a comparison group of employed workers. The percieved health of the laid off workers (five weeks after lay-off) was as good as, if not better than that of a matched group of employed workers. The authors argue that this difference was not due to available resources (the redundant group having received relatively large redundancy payments) but because they knew that their period of unemployment was temporary and for a fixed length of time.

It was found that in most cases the laid off workers had planned for their lay-off—buying in advance, food and materials necessary for doing the jobs they intended to do. Nearly all of the respondents were very active and completed the tasks and activities they had set themselves. These plans included house and car repairs, gardening, taking holidays and partaking in sporting activities, frequently ones which had not been tried before. Financial planning similarly proved effective, with no serious financial problems being reported.

Knowing when they would return to work was a crucial factor in their planning and the major jobs could be undertaken without the uncertainty and distraction of having to look for another job, or the possibility of being required to start a new job at short notice.

In contrast, a greater proportion of the redundant workers were inactive and talked about sitting around all day watching television and of being bored. This planning is part of future orientation, a topic neglected by many researchers. Most of our efforts are directed towards distant goals; we plan for Christmas and holidays and even some (or other) things we dread.

Concern for the future was mentioned frequently by the redundant workers. Even though some had made financial plans, few could think of anything in the future to look forward to, other than somehow finding another job.

The laid off workers were more self-motivated and active. Some worked much longer hours than when employed, while others had active and inactive periods related to their needs and preferences. However, it should be noted that a minority of the laid off workers, often frustrated by bad weather or lack of money, found the lay-off period like a prison sentence with time passing slowly both day-to-day and week-to-week.

Despite this, for the lay-off group as a whole, their perceived health improved after five weeks of lay-off and improved still further on return to work. This is clear evidence that reducing the amount of employment can have beneficial effects and health and is worthy of further study. However, the associated reduction in income could have cumulative effects and the number of 'do-it-yourself' jobs may well be stretched by a series of lay-off periods. Further, the costs to the employer of operating such a scheme would undoubtedly be taken into consideration when making decisions as to whether or not to instigate lay offs more widely throughout industry. However, set against this are the savings in social security payments made by central government, and the minimal cost of creating 'more' jobs in this way.

Conclusions

This chapter has considered some of the disadvantages associated with employment. Efforts have been made to reduce the levels of occupational disease and accidents and this has been reflected in improvements in the well-being of employees. Improvements have also been made in the control of pollution and in safeguarding the general public. However, the overall picture must be one of dissatisfaction. The processes of detection and notification, the legislative and enforcing systems and the prevention and curative health services are patchy, inadequate and frequently ineffective. The present economic climate has led to higher levels of stress, fears of redundancy and limitations on managements' willingness to reduce hazards and trade unions' ability to fight for improved working conditions.

It is not possible here to make an analysis of the costs and benefits of employment. In our society we are expected to undertake worthwhile employment, often in manufacturing industries. Too little attention has been paid to questioning the value of this employment. Do we really need much of what is produced and could it be manufactured in a safer way? Consumers should be prepared to pay more in order to buy safer or less polluting products, for example, lead-free petrol.

Unless there is a considerable change in the attitudes of government, management, unions, health professionals and the public, which results in new policies, it is difficult to envisage an improvement in the present situation in which employees are injured, killed or incapacitated by disease, the general public is exposed to potential industrial disasters and we risk destroying the environment for future generations.

Perhaps it is time to consider at what stage the costs of industrialization outweigh the benefits of the consumer society. Widespread unemployment is not the only alternative to the present capitalist system; there will always be work to be done in a caring society.

References

ARGYLE, M. (1972). *The Social Psychology of Work.* Harmondsworth: Penguin.

ASTMS (1983). *Occupational Stress.* An ASTMS Policy Document. London: ASTMS.

BERAL, V., INSKIP, H., FRASER, P., BOOTH, M., COLEMAN, D. and ROSE, G. (1985). 'Mortality of Employees of the Atomic Energy Authority 1946-1979'. *British Medical Journal, 291,* 440-447.

CHAMBERLAIN, G. (ed) (1984). *Pregnant Women at Work.* London: The Royal Society of Medicine, and Macmillan Press.

COOPER, C.L. and RODEN, J. (1985). 'Mental Health and Satisfaction among Tax Officers'. *Social Science & Medicine, 21,* 747-752.

DIXON, W.M. and PRICE, S.M.G. (1984). *Aspects of Occupational Health.* London: Faber and Faber.

DOLL, R. and PETO, R. (1981). 'The Causes of Cancer: quantitative estimates of avoidable risks of cancer in the United States today'. *Journal of the National Cancer Institute, 66,* 1191-1308.

DOYAL, L. (1985). 'Is Work Good for You?' *World Health,* April, 4-7.

EDITORIAL (1985). 'Industrial Disasters'. *Public Health, 99,* 65-66.

FINLAYSON, A. and McEWEN, J. (1977). *Coronary Heart Disease and Patterns of Living.* London: Croom Helm.

FOX, J., GREEN, D., JAMES, D. and LEON, D. (1982). *Cancer and Work — Making Sense of Workers' Experiences.* London: City University.

GMBATU (no date). *An A-Z guide for GMB Safety Representatives.* London: GMBATU.

GOLDBERG, D. (1978). *Manual for the General Health Questionnaire.* Windsor: National Foundation for Educational Research.

GRANT, S. (1985). 'The Inspector's Story. The Health and Safety Executive-its capabilities and limitations'. *Hazards Bulletin, 5,* 6-7.

HARRINGTON, J.M. and SHANNON, H.S. (1976). 'Incidence of Tuberculosis, Hepatitis, Brucellosis and Shigellosis in British Medical Laboratories'. *British Medical Journal, 1,* 759-762.

HEALTH AND SAFETY COMMISSION (1977). *Occupational Health Services. The Way Ahead.* London: HMSO.

HEALTH AND SAFETY COMMISSION (1979). *Asbestos.* Final report of the advisory committee. Vols I and II. London: HMSO.

HEALTH AND SAFETY COMMISSION (1984). *Control of Substances Hazardous to Health.* Consultative document. London: HSE.

HMSO (1972). *Safety and Health at Work.* Report of the Committee on Safety and Health at Work. CMND 5034. London: HMSO.

HMSO (1975). *The Flixborough Disaster.* Report of the Court of Inquiry. London: (Department of the Environment), HMSO.

HOPE, Y.M., CLAYTON, M., HAY, R.J., NOBLE, W.C. and ELDER-SMITH, J.G. (1985). 'Foot Infection in Coal Miners: a re-assessment.' *British Journal of Dermatology, 112,* 405-413.

HOUSE, H.S., McMICHAEL, A.J., WELLS, J.A., KAPLAN, B.H. and LAUDERMAN, L.R. (1979). 'Occupational Stress and Health among Factory Workers.' *Journal of Health and Social Behaviour, 20,* 139-160.

HUNT, S.M., McEWEN, J and McKENNA, S.P. (1985). Social inequalities and perceived health. *Effective Health Care, 2.* 151-160.

HUNTER, D. (1962). *The Diseases of Occupations.* 3rd Edition. London: English Universities Press.

INTERNATIONAL LABOUR ORGANISATION (1983). *Accident Prevention.* Geneva: International Labour Organisation.

JONES, I.G. and CAMERON, D. (1984). 'Social Class Analysis - an embarrassment to epidemiology.' *Community Medicine, 6,* 37-46.

LABOUR RESEARCH DEPARTMENT (1985). *Safety Reps in Action.* London: Labour Research Department.

McKENNA, S.P. and FRYER, D.M. (1984). 'Perceived Health During Lay-Off and Early Unemployment.' *Occupational Health, 36,* 201-206.

McKENNA, S.P. and PAYNE, R.L. (1984). *Measuring the Perceived Health of Unemployed and Re-employed Men.* Memo No. 696. Sheffield: MRC/ESRC Social and Applied Psychology Unit.

McKEOWN, T. (1979). *The Role of Medicine - Dream, Mirage or Nemesis.* Oxford: Blackwells.

MOORE, R. (1985). 'How Many Died at Bhopal?' *Medical Sociology, 10,* 30-33.

OFFICE OF POPULATIONS CENSUSES AND SURVEYS (1978). 'Occupational Mortality 1970-1972.' London: HMSO.

OLSEN, J. (1981). 'Some Methodologic Problems Encountered in Occupational Health Research'. *Scandinavian Journal of Social Medicine, 9,* 19-24.

PAYNE, R.L. (1979). 'Demands, Supports, Constraints and Psychological Health'. In *Response to Stress: Occupational Aspects.* C. J. McKay and T. Cox (eds). London: International Publishing Corporation.

PAYNE, R.L., WARR, P.B. and HARTLEY, J. (1984). Social Class and Psychological Ill-health During Unemployment. *Sociology of Health and Illness 6,* 2, 152-174.

POULTON, C. (1971). 'Skilled Performance and Stress'. In *Psychology at Work*. P.B. Warr (ed.). Harmondsworth: Penguin.

POWELL, P.I., HALE, M., MARTIN, J and SIMON, M. (1971). *2001 Accidents*. London: National Institute of Industrial Psychology.

ROYAL SOCIETY FOR THE PREVENTION OF ACCIDENTS (1984). *Occupational Safety Yearbook 1984/5*. Birmingham: The Royal Society for the Prevention of Accidents.

SCHILLING, R.S.F. (1973). 'Developments in Occupational Health'. In R.S.F. Schilling (ed.). *Occupational Health Practice*. London: Butterworth.

THEISS, A.M. (1984). 'The Modern Chemical Industry'. In *Recent Advances in Occupational Health 2*. J.M. Harrington, (ed.) Edinburgh: Churchill Livingstone.

TOWNSEND, P. and DAVIDSON, N. (1982). *Inequalities in Health: The Black Report*. Harmondsworth: Pelican.

WARD, W. and DUBOS, R. (1972). *Only One Earth*. Harmondsworth: Pelican.

7

Paul R. Jackson and Susan Walsh

Unemployment and the family

Introduction

Despite widespread concern recently about unemployment and the future of the family as an institution in Britain, little systematic research has been done to assess the ways in which families are affected by the unemployment of one of their members. Rather, psychologists have consistently described and evaluated individual responses to unemployment. This chapter is an elaboration of our belief that personal responses to unemployment cannot be adequately understood without recourse to the social context of the families within which most people live. Moreover, a family approach to unemployment research can avoid the narrow assumptions implicit in much research that both employment and unemployment are more important to men than to women.

Our concern for research on unemployment and the family is also a reflection of the number of people not themselves registered as unemployed whose lives are nevertheless implicated in unemployment. In 1983, 61% of unemployed married heads of households had dependent children, (OPCS 1985) and 1.3 million children under 16 live in households whose head is unemployed (Labour Force Survey 1984). As well as this, the wives of unemployed men are much less likely to be in paid work than the wives of employed men — 30% vs 61% according to the 1983 General Household Survey (OPCS 1985). Many of these women do not themselves register as unemployed because they are not eligible for supplementary benefits and they cannot claim unemployment benefit unless they have been employed consistently for long enough to have made appropriate national insurance contributions. Unemployed wives of unemployed men are among the hidden unemployed.

Increases in the incidence of divorce, cohabitation and one-parent families make it easy to argue that the nuclear family of married couple and dependent children is no longer typical. Nevertheless, the 1983 General Household Survey shows that six out of ten people (58%) live in households of a married couple with children and a further 21% are married couples who probably have had or will have children. Thus, at any one time, about 79% of all people live in households headed by a married couple. Of the 8% who live alone, most are the elderly widowed, and the remainder are young people who are likely to get married in later life. Chester (1985) concludes from this evidence that the demise of the family is a myth, arising from the misinterpretation of large-scale surveys.

Many accounts of unemployment have fallen into the trap of describing 'the unemployed' as an homogenous group, and it is just as tempting to think in terms of effects of unemployment on 'the family'. The reality of course is that there is no single kind of family. Inferences about the death of the family ignore the individual's position in the life cycle and fail to capture movements in or out of marriage and parenthood. Families vary enormously in their structures, their dynamics and their histories and it is unrealistic to expect valid generalisations to arise from portraits of 'typical' families at a single point in time.

In this chapter we aim to present a framework for understanding unemployment as a *family* experience rather than simply as a *solitary* event and in this way to establish what we call the social intelligibility of family unemployment. We hope that such a framework will allow a productive research effort to grow on a topic which we believe to be of great importance. At the same time, we hope to show that the devastating effects of unemployment can be felt keenly by others in a family where one member is unemployed. We have chosen to illustrate the main points of our argument with the verbatim comments of some of the people we have interviewed as part of a study of family constraints on active coping with unemployment. Since the study is not the main focus of this chapter, we will not present any details of its design and findings. A detailed account may be found in Walsh (1986) available from the authors.

Unemployment as a family experience
At one level of analysis, it is possible to account for personal responses to unemployment in terms of their meaning within the social context of the family. From this perspective the personal meaning of unemployment to an individual depends on such things as the change in household income brought about by job loss, or the extent of demands on family resources from a young family. These direct effects of unemployment are well summarised by Warr (1984) and Fryer and Payne (1986). However at a second level, unemployment can also have indirect or hidden effects which superficially appear to have no direct bearing on the original job loss. Job loss may well *happen* to individuals, but there are a host of hidden costs which are borne by the members of the unemployed person's family and also by the larger community. These 'knock-on' effects of unemployment

on other members were described by two of the men we interviewed, Arthur and Roy.

Arthur is 41 years old. He has been unemployed for three-and-a-half years after having spent most of his working life in various jobs in the steel industry. He has been married for 13 years and has four sons who vary in age from 2 to 12 years. He is an active member of an Angler's Workshop near his home, the majority of whose membership are unemployed. He is very concerned about how his children are affected by his unemployment:

> I think children suffer in more ways from unemployment in material things than do adults, because I can always go without. I can say I'll not buy a packet of fags today, I'll not go fishing next week, but I can see in a week or two when I've paid that bill, I can go again. A kid doesn't look like that – he thinks *now*! 'I can't do that, I can't have that *now*'. Terrible, your life's useless...And when you see a 12-year-old kid who knows I'm out of work, who knows the money is limited, but when his mate is going to France (with the school) and to see the look on his face when I say I can't do it, it's cruel.

Roy has been married for 30 years and is now 55 years old. He is a skilled electrician by trade but has been unemployed for six years. He has two children, 16 and 18 years old. He is trying to set up a nature reserve on a spoilheap near his home. He has always regarded himself as the wage earner in his household and he feels it particularly hard when he has to turn down his children's requests for things — 'they can't rely on you' he said. He described to us his wife's nervous breakdown following his unemployment and commented: 'She's always been used to a regular wage and a nice little carry-on, no problems or anything like that'. He feels his children are affected outside the home too — 'Your youngsters go to school and it affects them there, and sometimes the teachers throw it at them.' He concludes 'It really does affect family life'.

An emphasis on the family as a context for understanding individual experience needs also to be combined with a focus on individual experience as a means of understanding the family. Seeing unemployment as a family event leads to an analysis of the psychological processes involved in intra-family and family-environment dynamics brought about by unemployment. Changes in relationships within families have been examined by Fagin and Little (1984) and Komarovsky (1940) who presented a careful analysis of shifts in the locus of authority within the family resulting from the unemployment of the male head of the household. Madge (1983) also refers to possible explanations for child abuse in terms of alterations in the relative status of father and mother when the father is unemployed. The relationship between the nuclear family and both extended family and the larger community has also received some attention (e.g. Binns and Mars 1984, Balloch *et al.* 1985), but psychologists have to a large extent ignored unemployment as a family experience.

Unemployment as a male issue

A family approach to unemployment research has been further hampered by narrow assumptions about the relationship between employment and unemployment for men and for women. Employment is still treated primarily as a male domain and, likewise, research on the psychology of unemployment is centered around the unemployment of men. Thus we find studies with titles: 'Health of Unemployed Middle-aged Men in Great Britain' (Cook *et al* 1982); 'Men Without Jobs: some correlates of age and length of unemployment' (Warr and Jackson 1984); *Men Without Work* (Pilgrim Trust 1933); and *The Unemployed Man: a Social Study* (Bakke 1933). Reading many studies it is hard to avoid the implicit assumption that men are the only ones to suffer both emotional and financial deprivation. Overall we must conclude with Kelvin and Jarrett (1985,65) that 'though women do feature in the literature of unemployment, they do so first and foremost as the wives of unemployed men, and as the mothers of such men's children'.

Naturally, there has been some dissatisfaction with this approach and there is now some research (for example, Brown and Harris 1978, Coyle 1984, Martin and Roberts 1984, Miles and Henwood this volume, Warr and Parry 1982) exploring the issue of work and non-work for women, which has helped to establish that the female employment in a family is not simply of secondary significance to that of the male. This is of particular importance since joint employment of both partners is becoming the norm in our society: in over half (52%) of all married couples of working age, both husband and wife are working (OPCS 1985). Just as for the husband then, there are important psychological and social issues involved when the wife has a job.

Arthur recognised the reality of the loss associated with unemployment for women as well as for men. He told us:

> I think working women it sometimes hits harder than it does a bloke. Working women who, say, are made redundant—lose their jobs—although they've got their home and family, that was only a small part of their life. It didn't used to be said that women work, a lot of them, because as well as needing to, they want to. I think it's a myth about pin money, that's gone.
>
> Women work because they need to, not for the money—for their own satisfaction, for their own pride shall we say, like working blokes need to work.

Peter is 42 years old and he and his common law wife have been together for 12 years. They have one child who is six years old. Peter is a qualified teacher, but has been unemployed for four years. He is now a local councillor and has seen the resentment many women feel about the assumptions others make when they lose their jobs:

I know women who have worked and who are now unemployed, and they get very angry because people just don't realise, they say 'you've got your family, well now you can look after your house properly'. Women are breaking out.

Research effort dedicated either to one sex or the other, tends to underemphasise the extent to which people live their lives together. A more wholistic analysis of the effects of unemployment must attend to the mutual experience of job-loss for both men and women within family relationships. In the next section we review two theoretical approaches which include the whole lives of family members.

Unemployment and theories of the family

The two approaches we describe here are drawn from very different domains of social science research. The first, a life course perspective on the family, is taken from family sociology and has the strength that it emphasises the dimension of time in understanding the family. The second approach is taken from the clinical literature on family therapy, and has a strong emphasis on the family system as the unit of analysis. What the two theoretical approaches share is the assumption that individuals in a family are interdependent: the experience and behaviour of one family member cannot be fully understood except by reference to the experience and behaviour of other family members. We believe that a combination of both approaches can enrich and extend our understanding of responses to unemployment.

Lifecourse perspectives on unemployment

Research on the family, particularly within sociology, has tended to follow one of several perspectives (Elder 1984). An *age-based perspective* locates families in an historical context fixed by the birth year of the head. Family patterns are constructed through age-related events such as school leaving, marriage, child rearing and retirement, and emphasis focuses on developmental changes and differential timing of events within the family life-course. Fagin and Little's (1984) analysis of unemployment by family life-cycle stage demonstrates the usefulness of this approach. However, Elder suggests that developmental models of the family life cycle are more suited as explanations in times of stability than in times of change since they are strongly prescriptive in their assumptions about the processes that 'normal' families go through. In times of rapid social change, many different kinds of family structure exist: single parent families, reconstituted families where children of more than one marriage live together, and so on. Normative models are much less useful in such circumstances.

The second perspective on family research is the *kinship approach,* which broadens the analysis to include more than one generation. Here, the concern is with the process whereby one generation replaces another, and individual experience is understood in terms of generational positions (child, parent, grandparent etc.). Kinship studies examine socialisation processes and the transmission of values from one generation to another and are beginning to look at how events in one generation can impinge directly on the well-being of other generations.

An alternative which synthesises these contrasting approaches is a *life course perspective,* which incorporates both age and kinship as two complementary views of time within families and individuals (e.g. Bühler 1933, see Jahoda, this volume). Elder describes three different views of the meaning of time within the family. First, *lifetime* or position in the ageing process refers simply to chronological age. In the unemployment literature, lifetime has been studied in terms of age subgroups which are differentially vulnerable to unemployment and other kinds of economic change (e.g. Jackson 1985, Jackson and Warr 1984). The meaning of economic change depends in turn also on chronological age and it is important to specify what variables are represented by the lifetime meaning of age. For example, Warr and Jackson (1985) report results of a study of working class unemployed men which show that age is related to income change (from employment to unemployment), employment commitment, marital status, number of dependants, and financial strain. They conclude (p.84) that age is a proxy variable for 'processes and states that require elucidation'.

The *social* meaning of time in the life course of the individual links age-patterned sequences of events to social roles and expectations. For the individual, the social meaning of age includes such things as norms for the timing of training, age-related prejudices against older unemployed workers and age hierarchies in vulnerability to being made redundant. In broader terms, 'family time' includes age-related social expectations about the timing of marriage and child rearing and options for participation in employment. A normative notion of family time defines an appropriate time for leaving home, having children and so on, which may influence how both men and women are treated in the labour market. For example, women's unemployment has often not been taken seriously since, it is argued, they can return to full time childcare in the home.

Finally, *historical time* locates the individual within the larger process of social change. Birth year and year of leaving school define a cohort and fix the point of entry into the labour force as well as the point of leaving it at retirement. Recent changes such as the replacement of the Youth Opportunities Programme by the two-year Youth Training Scheme and the removal of the requirement of men over 60 years of age to register as unemployed in order to claim benefit, have led to significant alterations in the meaning of unemployment for some unemployed people now compared with people the same age five years ago.

The lifecourse perspective includes all of these multiple meanings of time and age. It locates an individual and a family in three dimensions (see Elder 1984, fig.1) where historical time fixes an individual by birth date, generational time defines relationships with other family members, and lifespan accounts for changes which occur through a person's life. Since a family consists of people who differ in age, it is a meeting point for a diversity of life experiences.

From a lifecourse point of view, a family unit consists of a number of interlocking life trajectories or careers which differ in needs, options and resources. The significance of a period of unemployment for a family member will thus depend on a number of factors. In terms of an individual's personal lifecourse, unemployment means entirely different things at the start of working life compared with the same event towards the end of working life. The consequences of his or her unemployment for the rest of the family will depend on where they are in their own lifecourse. Sometimes it will be possible for parents or spouse to support an unemployed member financially and emotionally; at other times unemployment may be insupportable.

Systems theory approaches within family therapy
There are many approaches to therapy with families (see, for example, Nichols 1984), but many of them share a basic orientation in terms of the family as a system of interdependent elements. From this point of view, families are made up of a number of overlapping subsystems involving marriage partners, parent-child and sibling relationships. Boundaries between subsystems define where one subsystem ends and another starts. They may distinguish between, for example, parents and children, or may indicate other relationships such as alliance between mother and daughter, or an eldest child adopting a parental role. The family as a whole is also part of a larger system which includes extended family, community and neighbourhood systems; as well as being involved in areas of daily life to do with employment, education, religion, politics and health care. Family boundaries between sub-systems need to be clear, but also permeable enough for interactions to take place across them so that changes may occur in the ways in which a family is organised.

Another key concept within systems theory is homeostasis, that is, a system will work to maintain itself in a steady state. In relation to families, this means that families will develop characteristic and habitual ways of dealing with everyday living which become taken-for-granted and highly valued. Once the family has developed such lifestyles they will be resistant to change in them and will attempt to find ways of dealing with demands from their environment which allow them to maintain the family system intact as it has always been. The problem which unemployment poses for many families is how to achieve stability and continuity in severely constraining circumstances, when the separate but interdependent life course of family members may be in conflict. As early as 1960 Bakke gave an account of the impact of unemployment in similar terms, as a process of re-adjustment for the whole family. He described adjustment to unemployment as requiring a re-evaluation of 'the practices and attitudes upon which family relations are built' (p.112).

The foundation of our conceptualisation is the interdependence of identity between the family and the individuals that make it up. Laing and Esterson (1964) look on the make-up of the individual as constructed from the social norms and expectations of the family. They argue that social relationships condition a person's view of him or herself, and to some extent at least, individuals in a family are built of the roles that they play within the family. Thus each individual derives their identity in part from their family. When large changes occur in one member of the family, such as job loss for the primary wage earner, then the identity of every member of the family is altered and such changes may be felt as intensely threatening. The precise nature of these identity threats depends on the internal dynamics of each individual family; the basic point is that change within the circumstances of a single family member reverberates through the whole family system and challenges everyone in the family.

The rest of this chapter presents an account of aspects of the way in which families cope with unemployment, within a broad lifecourse perspective. Our argument is based on two key assumptions: the interdependence of individuals within a family, and the strong investment of families in stability and continuity. Both stability and change have to be worked out and managed and we argue that job loss is experienced as threatening because it produces substantial structural disorganisation in the family system. The third section of the chapter elaborates on this theme. The fourth section presents some of the ways in which families may actively respond to this structural disorganisation with adaptive coping strategies whose aim is to reintroduce stability into the family.

Structural disorganisation

Theoretical developments within the sociological literature on family stress have been dominated by a model generated in a study of wartime separation and reunion, the ABCX model (Burr 1982). This model describes the antecedents of crisis in a family system jointly in terms of stressful events in the environment and the resources of the family to cope with the event. The amount of crisis depends on the 'amount of disruptiveness, incapacity or disorganisation of the family social system' (ibid.,7). Thus, a stressor is an event which produces a change in the family social system (its boundaries, structure, goals, processes, roles or values). Some events are not stressors under this definition and may not lead to a crisis in a family if they do not lead to changes within the family system.

The term 'structural disorganisation' is an attempt to describe for the family the disruptive effects of unemployment which have often been noted for individuals (for example, Warr 1984, Warr and Payne 1983 and Kilpatrick and Trew 1985 have all described the ways in which individuals' life styles, their day-to-day activities, change when they become unemployed). Unemployment makes many aspects of daily family habits either impossible to continue or inappropriate, and our argument is that these changes in family daily living will have direct implications not only for the unemployed individual but for every other family member as well. So what exactly does losing a job mean for the family? We suggest that there are three important changes.

Financial disruption
First and most important, we have financial disruption. Most households can expect to be receiving half or less of their pre-employment income (Bradshaw *et al.* 1983, Warr and Jackson 1985). It is no surprise therefore that money worries for the families of unemployed breadwinners are also very high (Bradshaw *et al.* 1983, Jackson 1986a). Despite the fact that the British social security system was originally designed to ensure that everyone should have an income adequate to cover basic needs, there is no doubt that severe financial hardship is common during unemployment (Cooke this volume).

Hardship shows itself in many ways, such as not being able to buy new clothes and not being able to live up to normatively prescribed family roles (for example, grandparents or parents not being able to buy Christmas presents). Everything feels as if it comes down to money in the end: when you've got money then you have choices. As Roy put it:

> You can go and buy a suit, buy your shoes, you can buy dresses, and you know as well as I do that if a woman goes to the hairdresser and has her hair done she feels different.

Many options like these are just not available to the unemployed family.

The most obvious way in which unemployment effects and the family are tied together is concern with money. The British Supplementary Benefit system bases its calculations about entitlements on the family as a unit; an unemployed person receives benefits in order to support his or her dependants, conditional on satisfying complicated criteria concerned with family resources, In a large scale study of unemployment and the family life cycle, Jackson (1986a) found that the biggest proportional drop in income compared with pre-unemployment level was for younger married men without dependants, who said that they were getting less than half of their previous income as a household. This contrasts sharply with the group of married men with pre-school children who reported the lowest proportional drop, receiving about two-thirds of pre-unemployment income. Since this group also reported the greatest level of worry about money, it seems likely that families with young children were living in poverty before unemployment so that even a small drop in income has dramatic effects on household budgeting problems. Only one in ten of the wives of those men with pre-school children were in paid employment outside the home, compared with 65% of the wives of those men under 35 years who were without dependants.

Social relationship changes
Many friendships are lost along with the loss of a job and unemployed people tend to become isolated. The basis of this isolation is more than simply the inability to socialise which lack of money brings. Other more personal factors are well described by Kelvin and Jarrett (1985): the felt stigma of being unemployed, the feeling of having nothing to say when a group discuss the jobs they have and the desire to avoid embarrassment of having to answer questions about whether one has a job yet.

The most direct effect of unemployment on social relationships is the loss of that contact with others which is an immediate consequence of doing the job itself., John describes the way in which friends he met through his work just drifted away when he became unemployed. Losing a job has meant the loss of relationships which were very important to him:

> It's not only work you miss, it's the great chunk out of your life—knowing people, meeting people, having somebody to talk to other than the family.

Although it's different for old school friends, he says, or people he has known all his life, more superficial relationships have changed dramatically during his unemployment. He described problems when employed and unemployed men engaged in leisure activities together:

> If a bloke's working and, say, going fishing, and he's got a friend who's become unemployed and can't go fishing as often; people lose interest very quickly. Because you can't carry on at the level you could (when you had a job), and they can, they don't want to know you anymore.

There seems to be an important element of inertia offered by previously established levels of social intimacy with workmates. When the necessity of interaction around work activity is taken away, social contact during unemployment is only likely when close relationships are well established.

Evidence to support this point comes from two large-scale surveys of unemployed men. In the first study of 954 men (e.g. Warr and Jackson 1985), 83% of those unemployed at the second interview said that they now spent almost no time with former workmates. The second study of the social support networks of unemployed men aged between 25 and 45 years (Jackson 1986b) found similarly that 65% of men spent no time at all with former workmates now that they were unemployed (a further 10% reported spending almost no time with them).

The importance of the social traction imposed by the task structure of the job itself is emphasised by the finding in the second study that over half of this sample of men (56%) said that when they were employed they had spent almost no time with workmates outside normal working hours. For two-thirds of the sample, there was no change in the amount of social contact with workmates (defining social contact as that which occurs outside working hours). The level of non-work related social contact with former workmates therefore is no different from what it was before job loss. It is not particularly surprising then, that new patterns of social contact are rarely established in response to unemployment, given the other problems that unemployed people have to face. Once work-based social contact is broken, many unemployed family men become socially invisible; they are cut off from others in new and unfamilar ways, and many are reluctant to join support groups set up to help the unemployed.

Important too are the ways in which financial hardship changes how family members relate to each other. Binns and Mars (1984) showed in a study in Glasgow that previously dormant extended kin ties are reactivated by unemployment. Jackson (1986b) has shown that the family of unemployed men is the most important source of both expressive and instrumental support. Goodin (1985) has recently argued, more broadly, that 'self-reliance' (a virtue often applauded these days) in practice means dependence not only on the State but also on extended families. So there exists an interdependent relationship between the financial adjustments that have to be made and social relationship change.

At the same time, reliance on extended kin brings tensions and the possibility of reassertion of control of household functioning by parents and in-laws. Unemployment can thus force a regression to previous' patterns of dependence on parents which were severed when an independent household was established. This tension built into a renewed dependence on extended kin has been relatively little discussed in the literature on unemployment, although the consequences for family identity and integrity can sometimes be profound. For example, likely problems are inter-generational conflicts over role allocation between husband and wife, as well as tensions over childcare principles.

However, these social relationship changes are not just a loss for the male: a man's unemployment can also amount to a very great social loss for his wife. Paid employment gives access to a larger social world; indeed this is an important reason why many women are now choosing to take paid employment alongside caring for young children. As well as this, many wives enjoy vicarious participation in their husbands' work world and his loss is her loss too. Bill and his wife, Margaret, have been married for 29 years and they have two grown-up children. This is how they described the way in which they shared his work-world:

Bill: It's not just the work, it's the companionship as well.
Margaret: It's the other people's lives, it is.

Bill:	I mean, I miss working with the chaps at work, we used to have, you know, a laugh.
Margaret:	Oh, he's come home and told us some right things.
Bill:	You know, we used to have some good fun.
Interviewer (S.W.):	Doesn't that go on any longer
Margaret:	No because he's not with anybody.
Bill:	You can't afford to go for a drink (with anybody) apart from the wife.
Margaret:	And I can't talk the same language as him (Bill).

A husband's unemployment can have a dramatic effect on the social world of his wife as well. Jane is 32 years old and has been married for ten years. Both she and her husband Paul are unemployed; he is a chemist and has been out of work for five years. They have two children aged four and six years. She is a member of a parents' group and on the committee of a local knitting-machine club. Jane describes how she felt that Paul's presence in the family home during the day was a direct intrusion into her world:

I had this friend; for two to three years we saw each other every day — we were extremely close. And then, I don't know I've seen very little of her these past two years. I think it's more since he's been at home all of the time. With Paul being at home she doesn't come round so I don't see her.

The disruption to personal relationships did not stop there, for family rows became common:

Immediately after he (Paul) was made unemployed he was very moody. Him and my mother were the worst. It got to the point that every time my mother walked in (she said) 'I'm going home I'm not going to be talked to like this'. And the other way (he said) 'she's not coming again'.

Many other kinds of relationship disruption are reported in the unemployment literature and by our respondents and we do not have the space to document them here. Rather, what we have set out is an overview of how extensive and far-reaching unemployment can be in its effects. Psychological hardship is propagated through the social networks of the unemployed, their families, friends and neighbours; and we need to know a great deal more about how far the effects of unemployment spread.

Personal changes

The third kind of structural disorganisation involves personal change and we focus on one aspect of personal identity that is particularly salient to the family: authority changes resulting from unemployment.

The work of Komarovsky in the mid 1930s, discussed in her book *The Unemployed Man and His Family* (1940), addressed one set of issues centred around the authority which the husband derives from his employment status. Authority is defined not primarily in terms of coercion but as 'relative power exercised by one individual over another' (p.9). Madge (1983) points to studies which show a high proportion of unemployed fathers among parents of victims of child abuse and suggests that such abuse may be an assertion of the father's threatened authority within the family.

The breadwinner status which many men derive from their jobs is an integral part of the expectations, not just of husband and wife, but also of other family members. Brian told us how strongly such ideas are bounded into the identity of each member of his family. He has been married twice, his current marriage has lasted ten years and he has six children. He has worked in mining and the steel industry and has been unemployed for 15 years after being injured in an accident at work. He said:

> It's just one of those things, you grow up in a family like I have — working class, a miner's family — that it's bred into you that the man works. Woman's got her role and man's got his role. I'm not being a male chauvinist pig, but that's the attitude you're brought up in, in mining families.

Jim has been unemployed for five years since he was 54 and faces a difficult process of coming to terms with the likelihood that he will never be paid to work again.

> What's hanging over my head is that I'm unemployed, that I'm not the person I've been brought up to be as a wage-earner and head of family.

When a man's status as a worker and provider for the household is taken from him, then the source of many of his 'privileges' is also threatened and his position may well be challenged by other family members (Fagin and Little 1984). For example, there may be problems between husband and wife over the 'ownership' of benefits. Unemployment and Supplementary Benefit have an ambiguous status compared with Child Benefit (which is easily seen as the property of the wife) and take-home pay (which is easily seen as the husband's property). Fagin and Little (1984, 96–97) describe John and Mary Stride as an example of how the male head of household can have little more than token authority when he is unemployed:

> Throughout the first interview John did most of the talking, with Mary making sniping comments at him to us. John tended to ignore it and only reacted in a defensive way when Andrew (their son) commented on their relationship. It was clear that there was a lot of tension in the family; Mary and the children were allowing John to appear to be head of the household, but in fact he had very little real power.

For this family, the husband's employment allowed him to maintain an image as head of the household though everyone knew that his wife had the real authority. Unemployment took away the means available to him of legitimising his position in the family and the resulting disturbance in the functioning of the family caused problems of many different kinds for all of the family members.

The wife of an unemployed man may also have gained self respect and other psychological privileges from her husband's job and so there is a shared threat to identity and a shared feeling of stigma when he loses his job. Jane describes how devastated she was when her husband Paul lost his job as a chemist:

> My husband's unemployment does upset me, I suppose it's the shame.
> Nobody I'd ever known had got the sack. The shame of it all!

Chappell (1982,77) suggests that wives of unemployed men feel an obligation to reassure and support their husbands, but that no one reassures the wives. She quotes Maureen Adkin, a marriage guidance counsellor in Scunthorpe who said 'when the man in a marriage is unemployed, women feel insecure, unloved and unfeminine'.

To summarise this section on structural disorganisation, it is clear that the consequences of unemployment are far-reaching, for husband and wife, for parents, grandparents and children, for extended family members and for friends and neighbours. Although we have described financial, social and personal factors separately, they are in fact interdependent. Most fundamentally, the unemployed are poor, with everything that follows from it. At the same time though, unemployment threatens both personal and social identity and we have tried to elaborate on how this may occur. We turn now to the adaptation processes which families adopt in response to the disruption of losing a job.

Family adaptation processes

In the previous section, we described some of the ways in which unemployment can disrupt whole families over and above the damaging effects which can be seen for individual unemployed people. In this section we describe the responses that families (as opposed to individuals) may make to unemployment: how families adapt to the problems that unemployment brings.

Our use of the term 'adaptation' here implies an active rather than a passive response, for we regard it as important to think of families as essentially active agents in reconstructing family lives which have been in many cases severely disrupted by unemployment. It is tempting to think of the family as passive in the face of unemployment, using terms such as 'disrupted' or 'threatened' or 'assaulted' by unemployment. To some extent this is true of course, since one of the most important characteristics of unemployment is that it severely limits the discretion that families have (financially, socially and personally, as we have seen above). But this is to underestimate the extent to which unemployed men and women are able to find opportunities for positive action in unemployment and to reconstruct their lives together. This is our focus of attention in the last part of this chapter.

For some families, adapting to unemployment means active efforts during unemployment to return family organisation to its prior state so that the family system can remain unaltered. This would be to imply that unemployment is never more than 'time-out' of the real world of traditional full-time employment; like measles or chickenpox, it is a nasty but temporary experience to be endured and then forgotten. For many adults today, however, unemployment is either the prelude to what may be a life without paid work or is likely to be an experience of years rather than months. As changes in the economic fabric of society lead to changes in patterns of employment, it will increasingly be the case that families can expect to have to live with long periods during which the primary breadwinner is not in paid employment. Consequently, rigid maintainance of habitual family organisation patterns may become severely dysfunctional for the family as a whole and for individual members.

The real problem of unemployment for many families is how to change the family system in order to allow constructive lifestyles outside paid employment. Here, we concentrate on two aspects of the problem: the ways in which pressures towards homeostasis mean that the family imposes constraints on constructive coping (we may call this the family as having a *disabling* function as regards coping efforts); and the possibilities for change which enhance constructive coping (we may call this the family as having an *enabling* function). Hansen and Johnson (1979,584) note the possibility of this enabling process as follows: 'families are often observed "accepting" disruptions of habit and tradition not so much as unwelcome problems, but more as opportunities to renegotiate their relationships'. Several studies have described instances of individual proactivity. For example, Fryer and Payne (1984) discuss a sample of 11 men and women who have used unemployment to pursue activities that they valued highly and Fineman (1983) and Thomas et al. (1980) report similar findings in studies of unemployed professionals. Detailed attention now needs to be paid to the family context within which such proactive coping occurs.

In thinking about coping with unemployment it is important to recognise that coping is a process rather than a state and that families are not static. As we have seen above, families contain interdependent individuals whose lives change in response to normative events such as a child starting at a new school or an adolescent leaving home. Such events occur to some extent independently of unemployment within the family, although it may be that many such decisions within a family will be either delayed or provoked by unemployment. Family needs and demands from the environment will often conflict. Indeed, active coping efforts of one family member will sometimes increase tension and problems elsewhere in the family. Roy's case, referred to earlier, illustrates how this can happen. He took on the management of a nature reserve after several years of unemployment, but his wife was unable to accept this as a constructive alternative and suffered mental health problems which led to her eventual hospitalisation.

Lazarus and Folkman (1984) present an analysis of individual coping in terms of two main coping strategies. Coping which is directed towards regulating emotional responses to a problem is called emotion-focused coping; while coping which is directed at managing or altering the problem itself is called problem-focused coping. At the level of the family, a similar taxonomy of adaptive coping is given by McCubbin and Patterson (1982). They distinguish between stimulus regulation, a process of filtering environmental demands, and active environmental control, which seeks to alter the environment in order to change the demands it makes on the family. Here we follow a somewhat different way of organising discussion of forms of coping. We distinguish between coping responses to unemployment which retain present family systems intact, and responses which change the structural organisation of the family. McCubbin and Patterson (1982) refer to these two kinds of coping as assimilation and accommodation. Both may involve elements of emotion-focused and problem-focused coping.

Assimilation responses to unemployment
Assimilation means incorporating new demands of unemployment into unchanged family structures and habitual ways of functioning. The changes associated with this type of coping correspond to what have been described by Watzlawick *et al.* (1974) as first-order change: a substitution of one state for another, where the family system does not change. Thus assimilation responses do not involve radical changes in the way the family is organised. We draw from our own and others' research to illustrate this kind of adaptation to unemployment.

Some of the men interviewed by Jackson and Warr (1984) had found unemployment to be a regular experience; they had built their life-styles around seasonal employment with regular spells of unemployment. For them, unemployment was 'normal' such that another period of unemployment involved no major changes to household budgeting, daily life-style or employment patterns for other family members. Among the men interviewed were some who had been employed on a seasonal basis in the building trade as labourers and men living in the north east of England who, in 1982, were able to work offshore on oil rigs for a few months in order to subsidise several months of non-employment until their money ran out.

Johnson (1981) presents a case of the family of Betty Morgan and Jack Brown with whom he worked as part of his job at Wandsworth Family Service unit. Their relationship appeared complicated and confused, but he shows how both partners were using employment and unemployment as means of maintaining their relationship. Jack had been unemployed when first contacted by the Family Service Unit and he had stayed at home since the birth of their baby, taking primary responsibility for her care. Betty had been diagnosed as schizophrenic since adolescence, and Jack was insistent that he could not trust Betty to care properly for the child. Johnson (p.109) describes the ways in which both partners sought to resist change:

> To the outsider their relationship system was complex, confused and contradictory: a world of unpredicatable events. At another level their relationship was stable: rigidly stable in its instability. This was demonstrated in the homeostatic response of their system to the threat of change. For example, when Jack seemed intent on finding employment, Betty broke down sobbing inexplicably outside the job centre, which vetoed further progress. When Jack arranged full-time employment at the fish and chip shop, Betty coincidentally decided to leave him, only to return when the idea had been dropped.

Although they acknowledge that the evidence is sparse, Kelvin and Jarrett (1985,67) say 'to hold a job still does not appear to be as central to the social psychological situation of a woman as of a man'. Part of this reduced centrality may be assimilated into existing family life-styles. The argument is that the women who are made redundant can re-adopt the housewife role rather than seek alternative paid employment. Many of the very traditional workers in the study by Nowack and Snyder (1984), both male and female, reported this as the reason why redundancy of female workers was less disruptive than redundancy of male workers. Nowack and Snyder show that the majority (though not all) of the husbands of women made redundant saw the event as of little significance within the family. These men felt that their wives could return to a role that was more appropriate for the women to occupy. Conversely, Coyle's (1984) study of women made redundant from two textile factories in Yorkshire shows that such views are not shared by women whose redundancy led to material and psychological hardship for them and their families.

A further way of maintaining existing family structures intact during unemployment is by unemployed people substituting other forms of regular daytime activity for the paid work that they are no longer able to do. One way in which this may happen is by involvement in the 'hidden' or 'informal' economy, where skills and services are exchanged with other households in the neighbourhood either for cash or on a barter basis. In interviews conducted in four locations throughout England (Jackson *et al.* 1985), we found that many male respondents spent a great deal of time in car maintenance, DIY repairs, gardening and similar activities. As a result, the home remained the domain of the wife, and the husband retained a more or less regular set of daytime habits which kept him out of the home for long periods. There has been much discussion of the informal economy as a means whereby families may maintain their income during unemployment; but recent studies of the Isle of Sheppey (Pahl 1984) have demonstrated conclusively that working for undeclared earnings is overwhelmingly a practice of the employed rather than the unemployed. The kinds of informal work activity that we have seen are not done to earn money; rather they seem to serve other functions within the family. They seem to allow a family to continue to live together while not being together too much.

Accommodation responses to unemployment
More radical coping responses to unemployment require changes to the ways in which families are organised, and accommodation means changing the family system in response to the new demands. It corresponds to what Watzlawick *et al.* (1974) call second-order change. Most families can be expected to resist major systemic changes at first, and it may be some time before a family recognises that prior patterns of organising their transactions with the world are no longer viable. In reality, accommodation involves the individual accepting very long periods of unemployment (and possibly the prospect of never working again in traditional full-time paid employment) as offering possibilities for positive experience.

One example of an accommodation response to unemployment is the adoption of the sick role by the unemployed person. Fagin and Little (1984, Ch.7) present a set of parallels between the sick role and the unemployed role. The main feature of the sick role is that it exempts the person from social obligations and commitments; furthermore, the sick person cannot be held to be responsible for his or her condition. They use the Brown family as an example of how a family can accommodate to long-term unemployment in this way. After being unemployed for 14 months, Phil Brown was diagnosed as having an hereditary disease and this led to dramatic changes in the relationship between Phil and his wife, Wyn. He became much more dependent upon her and she became much stronger. She managed to overcome the threat that she had previously felt from being the primary breadwinner in the household; he in turn took on more domestic duties and learned to accept his dependence on his wife.

Some families find that they can redefine the respective roles of marriage partners in order to deal effectively with prolonged unemployment. For example Fagin and Little (1984, 83–88) describe the Howard family where Mike and Kay Howard established a pattern of alternating getting up to prepare their two children for school and domestic tasks were shared. A second example is the experience of one of our respondents, Brian, who we described earlier in the chapter. He recounts how he and his wife made real efforts in this direction:

> Well, we just sat round the table and discussed it. She put her points, I put my points and at the end of the day we just decided that if I can't get work then she's going to have to be the breadwinner. I didn't expect her to come home then and do housework, so gradually I was doing bits and then it just built up and I took the role on.

For most families, however, real role reversal is unlikely to be a realistic option given the long socialisation of both men and women in traditionally differentiated domestic roles.

Active efforts to alter environmental demands include involvement in support groups and drop-in centres for the unemployed; though these are only useful for a relatively small proportion of the unemployed. Walter (1985) describes an approach to unemployment based on personal agency (see also Fryer and Payne 1984) which encourages unemployed people to assert themselves rather than remain passive in the face of their unemployment. The road towards active, positive unemployment for a family is hard and fraught with difficulties, but our respondents show that it is possible to find a worthwhile style of living while being unemployed. Consider Arthur's conclusion after being unemployed for over three years:

> When I was working, I was happy with my lot.. I'd got my car, I'd got my fishing, I'd got my holidays, a nice family, a decent home.. why should I complain? Although being unemployed can be, and for too many people (and I think, the majority) is, a depressing, boring, useless life; it needn't be. There is an alternative.

He continues:

> I don't know whether you can say my story has been a success of unemployment.. I suppose it has, but I don't believe we're exceptional. If they (the unemployed) would only realise that if they got over the depression, the illnesses that unemployment causes; if they got over that and substitute something else like we've done, then your life can be just as meaningful. In fact, it's more meaningful and more full now than it ever was when I was working.

Other families have many more problems in adapting to unemployment. We have already referred to the problems in Roy's family which resulted from his conscious abandonment of the breadwinner role as a workable source of individual identity. For Jane and Paul, the first two years of Paul's unemployment was a very painful experience. Jane said that she would have walked out on him many times if her mother would have allowed her back. She look back on it now:

'Having stuck it out, now I think we're closer than we've ever been. Those first two years were very bad and I wouldn't like to go through them again. But having gone through them I think that we're better people for them.'

A crucial element in this process of active coping is autonomy, both for the individuals in the family and for the family as a whole. In relation to unemployment, individual and family efficacy is constrained to a large extent by a number of contextual factors. Notable among these are the State benefit system which penalises wives of unemployed men for employment and also the husband for doing any paid work to supplement state benefits. Even unpaid work above a small number of hours is discouraged because it affects his notional 'availabililty for work'. Family pressures to conform to traditional roles within the family may also be very strong. There are signs though that some of the families we have talked to are beginning to find positive and creative solutions to the immense challenges that unemployment brings.

Conclusion

When we started our research on unemployment and the family, we were very aware that the costs of unemployment and its challenges are not solely the concern of the unemployed themselves. In the first part of this chapter we have tried to show how the financial, social and personal costs of unemployment are felt as much by the husbands and wives of the unemployed, their children and their extended families. In getting to know these people we have been impressed with their courage, persistence and ingenuity in the face of near overwhelming difficulty. The important question is not so much 'how do they cope?' but 'why haven't they given up hope for themselves and their children?'

The second half of the chapter complements this analysis by describing a number of ways in which families have made efforts to cope with a life outside the comforting structures of paid employment. We have seen how some families can be remarkably resistant to change, preferring well-worn habitual lifestyles; while other families have struggled hard to build new lives for themselves. Every family faced with the prospect of long-term unemployment has the problem though how to maintain a balance between the twin needs for stability within the family and for change to meet the demands of an often hostile environment. Research on unemployment cannot afford to ignore these processes, for the individual and the family are interdependent: 'people are changed through change in families and families are changed through change in people' (Elder 1984, 111). Family change occurs as individuals grow and develop within the family: they have different resources to offer the family and make different demands upon it. Change also occurs in other ways when job-loss makes it impossible for the family to continue in the same way as before.

Our research has been concerned with families who are caught up in fundamental changes in the structure of our society. We have much to learn from them.

References

BAKKE, E. W. (1933). *The Unemployed Man: A Social Study*. London: Nisbet.

BAKKE, E. W. (1960). 'The Cycle of Adjustment to Unemployment'. In N. W. Bell and E. F. Vogel (eds), *A Modern Introduction to the Family*. New York: The Free Press.

BALLOCH, S., HUME, C., JONES, B. and WESTLAND, P. (1985). *Caring for Unemployed People*. London: Bedford Square Press.

BINNS, D. and MARS, G. (1984) 'Family, Community and Unemployment: a study of change'. *The Sociological Review, 32*, 662–695.

BRADSHAW, J., COOKE, K. and GODFREY, C. (1983). 'The Impact of Unemployment on the Living Standards of Families.' *Journal of Social Policy, 12*, 433–452.

BROWN, G. W. and HARRIS, T. (1978). *Social Origins of Depression: A Study of Psychiatric Disorder in Women*. London: Tavistock.

BURR, W. (1982). 'Families Under Stress'. In H. I. McCubbin, A. E. Cauble and J. M. Patterson (eds), *Family Stress, Coping and Social Support*. Springfield, Ill: C. C. Thomas.

CHAPPELL, H. (1982). 'The Family Life of the Unemployed'. *New Society, 62*, 14th October, 1982.

CHESTER, R. (1985). 'The Rise of the Neo-conventional Family'. *New Society, 72*, 9th May, 1985.

COOK, D. G., CUMMINS, R. O., BARTLEY, M. J. and SHAPER, A. G. (1982). 'Health of Unemployed Middle-aged Men in Great Britain'. *The Lancet, 3*, 1290-1294.

COYLE, A.(1984). *Redundant Women*. London: The Women's Press.

ELDER, G. H. (1984) 'Families, Kin, and the Life Course: a sociological perspective'. In R. Parke (ed), *Review of Child Development Research*, Vol. 7, *The Family*. Chicago: University of Chicago Press.

FAGIN, L. and LITTLE, M. (1984). *The Forsaken Families*. Harmondsworth: Penguin.

FINEMAN, S. (1983). *White Collar Unemployment: Impact and Stress*. Chichester: Wiley.

FRYER, D. and PAYNE, R. L. (1984). 'Proactivity in Unemployment: findings and implications.' *Leisure Studies, 3*, 273-295.

FRYER, D. and PAYNE, R. L. (1986). 'Being Unemployed: a review of the literature on the psychological experience of unemployment.' In C. L. Cooper and I. Robertson (eds), *International Review of Industrial and Organisational Psychology*. Chichester: Wiley.

GOODIN, R. E. (1985). 'Self-reliance versus the Welfare State.' *Journal of Social Policy, 14*, 25-47.

HANSEN, D. and JOHNSON, V. (1979). 'Rethinking Family Stress Theory: Definitional Aspects'. In W. Burr, R. Hill, F. Nye and I. Reiss (eds), *Contemporary Theories About the Family* (Vol. 1). New York: The Free Press.

JACKSON, P. R. (1985). 'Differential Vulnerability and Psychological Health in Unemployment'. *The Statistician, 34,* 83-91.

JACKSON, P. R. (1986a). *Unemployment and the Family Life Course.* MRC/ESRC Social and Applied Psychology Unit Memo. No. 746.

JACKSON, P. R. (1986b). *Personal Social Networks and Unemployment.* MRC/ESRC Social and Applied Psychology Unit Memo. No. 777.

JACKSON, P. R. and WARR, P. B. (1984). 'Unemployment and Psychological Ill-health: The moderating role of duration and age.' *Psychological Medicine, 14,* 605-614.

JACKSON, P. R., KARSAZKY, A., WALSH, S. and ULLAH, P. (1985). *An Exploratory Study of Long-term Unemployment.* MRC/ESRC Social and Applied Psychology Unit Memo. No. 793.

JOHNSON, R. (1981). 'Help Me, Don't You Dare!' In J. Miller and T. Cook (eds), *Direct Work with Families.* London: Bedford Square Press.

KELVIN, P and JARRETT, J. E. (1985). *Unemployment: Its Social Psychological Effects.* Cambridge: Cambridge University Press.

KILPATRICK, R. and TREW, K. (1985). 'Lifestyles and Psychological Well-being among Unemployed Men in Northern Ireland.' *Journal of Occupational Psychology, 58,* 207-216.

KOMAROVSKY, M. (1940). *The Unemployed Man and His Family.* New York: Dryden Press.

LABOUR FORCE SURVEY 1984. (1986). Department of Employment, London: HMSO.

LAING, R. D. and ESTERSON, A. (1964). *Sanity, Madness and the Family.* London: Tavistock.

LAZARUS, R. S. and FOLKMAN, S. (1984). *Stress, Appraisal and Coping.* New York: Springer Publishing Company.

MADGE, N. (1983). 'Unemployment and its Effects on Children'. *Journal of Child Psychology and Psychiatry, 24,* 311-319.

MARTIN, J. and ROBERTS, C. (1984). *Women and Employment: A Lifetime Perspective.* London: HMSO.

McCUBBIN, H. I. and PATTERSON, J. M. (1982). 'Family Adaptation to Crises'. In H. I. McCubbin, A. E. Cauble and J. M. Patterson (eds), *Family Stress, Coping and Social Support.* Springfield, Ill: C. C. Thomas.

MINUCHIN, S. (1974). *Families and Family Therapy.* Cambridge: Harvard University Press.

NICHOLS, M. (1984). *Family Therapy: Concepts and Methods.* New York: Gardner Press.

NOWACK, T. C. and SNYDER, K. A. (1984). 'Job Loss, Marital Happiness and Household Tension: do women fare better than men?' Paper presented at Annual Meeting of the Society for the Study of Social Problems, San Antonio, Texas.

OFFICE OF POPULATION CENSUSES AND SURVEYS (1985). *General Household Survey 1983.* London: HMSO.

PAHL, R.E. (1984). *Divisions of Labour.* Oxford: Basil Blackwell.

PILGRIM TRUST, (1933). *Men Without Work.* Cambridge: Cambridge University Press.

THOMAS, L. E., McCABE, E. and BERRY, J. E. (1980). 'Unemployment and Family Stress: a reassessment'. *Family Relations, 29,* 517-524.

WALSH, S. (1986). *Family Contexts for Personal Efficacy in Unemployment.* MRC/ESRC Social and Applied Psychology Unit Memo. No. 794.

WALTER, T. (1985). *Hope on the Dole*. London: SPCK.

WARR, P. B. (1984). 'Job Loss, Unemployment and Psychological Well-being.' In V. Allen and E. van de Vliert (eds), *Role Transitions*. New York: Plenum Press.

WARR, P. B. and JACKSON, P.R. (1984). 'Men without Jobs: some correlates of age and length of unemployment.' *Journal of Occupational Psychology, 57*, 77-85

WARR, P. B. and JACKSON. P. R. (1985). 'Factors Influencing the Psychological Impact of Prolonged Unemployment and of Re-employment'. *Psychological Medicine, 15*, 795-807.

WARR, P. B. and PARRY, G. (1982). 'Paid Employment and Women's Psychological Well-being.' *Psychological Bulletin, 9*, 498-516.

WARR, P. B. and PAYNE, R. L. (1983). 'Social Class and Reported Changes after Job Loss.' *Journal of Applied Social Psychology, 13*, 206-222.

WATZLAWICK, P., WEAKLAND, J. and FISCH, R. (1974). *Change: Principles of Problem Formation and Problem Resolution*. New York: Norton.

8

Julian Laite and Peter Halfpenny

Employment, unemployment and the domestic division of labour

Introduction

A growing body of research shows that the domestic division of labour is influenced by the labour-market participation of conjugal partners (Young and Willmott 1973, Berk and Berk 1979, Pahl 1984). This chapter contributes to that work by analysing the relations between household employment structures and domestic divisions of labour in two towns in the North-West of England. It compares the experiences of employment and unemployment in the two towns, particularly in relation to the employment of women, considers the reasons for both the levels of performance of domestic tasks and variations in those levels for different tasks and discusses husbands' views of those tasks. In particular, the activities and views of the unemployed are highlighted and compared to those of the employed, in order to establish whether there are significant differences. The central question addressed here, then, is whether participation in the labour-market affects the domestic division of labour. The answer is that it quite clearly does.

Explanations of the performance of domestic tasks by conjugal partners may be characterised as either pragmatic or cultural (Vanek 1980). On the one hand, a clear statement of the pragmatic approach is given by Becker (1976, 205-250) who advocates a human capital approach in which conjugal partners make decisions about the allocation of domestic time dependent on such resources as education, skills and wage-levels. On the other hand, a clear statement of the cultural approach is given by Oakley (1980, 7-8), arguing that the study of housework 'is an attempt to reverse the accepted order of concepts and values'. The aim here is not to resolve the theoretical differences in these approaches, but rather to draw on aspects of both to explain different features of the domestic division of labour. The overall level of domestic tasks performed by women is explicable in terms of capitalist development (Oakley 1974), but variations in the performance of tasks are due to conjugal partners assessing the allocation of resources in the light of their circumstances, as well as their prior attitudes.

Young and Willmott (1973) demonstrated that the nature of a wife's participation in the labour-market influences the nature of a husband's participation in the domestic duties. In their study of adults in London boroughs only 9% of wives who were employed full-time received no help from their husbands, compared to 22% of non-employed wives. Pahl (1984) also demonstrates this, showing that the domestic division of labour is most egalitarian when both the male and female are in full-time employment and least egalitarian when the female partner is non-employed. Pahl further analyses these activities in terms of age and child-bearing, which are discussed below.

Oakley (1980) and Young and Willmott (1973) relate changes in family relations and the domestic division of labour to general features of capitalist development, or post-war changes in British employment structure. Oakley points to the domestication of women and the perceived inferior status of women's work. Young and Willmott argue that the move to a symmetrical family, characterised by increased egalitarianism, is due to reductions in the age of marriage and family size and an increase in the number of part-time jobs available for women, 'owing to the restoration of part-time work, marital symmetry has been enhanced' (p.121). They also observed that if unemployment continued to rise then the growth in the numbers of women employed part-time could be reduced. Whilst Oakley (1980) is correct to draw attention to general features of capitalist development to explain general characteristics of the domestic division of labour, it is necessary to investigate local labour market conditions to understand variations in those characteristics.

For over a century the textile towns in the North-West of England have had very high labour-market female participation rates, to the degree that it is not useful to speak of a recent general 'domestication' of women. From the 19th century until the 1950s young women were employed full-time in the textile industry, some leaving to have children, many returning when their children were older and many staying. From the 1950s the decline in textiles has to some extent been accompanied by increasing job opportunities for women in the service sector, although again this has varied between different towns. Nor is it useful to speak of post-war part-time employment in the North-West as being taken up by previously non-employed female 'pioneers' (Young and Willmott 1973). The changes are more complex. Women move between full- and part-time employment during the course of their lives and current moves by women into part-time employment may be from previous full-time employment. Moreover, the growth of male unemployment has not necessarily led to an overall decline in women's employment.

Given these features of their labour-markets, and particularly the wide variation in their constituent household employment structures, the North-West textile towns provide ideal locations in which to study the precise links between the structure of employment in local labour-markets and the structure of the domestic division of labour. In the Autumn of 1983, a household survey was conducted in Macclesfield, Cheshire (Courtenay 1984) and in the Winter of 1984 a survey of electors was conducted in Blackburn, Lancashire (Halfpenny *et al.* 1985). Both surveys dealt with a wide range of issues, but both contained similar questions on the domestic division of labour and the employment structure of households and it is the data from those questions that form the basis of this chapter.

Macclesfield, 20 miles south of Manchester and separated from it by Cheshire farmland, is a small, free-standing town of 46,500 inhabitants (OPCS 1982). Originally a market town, the silk and button industries were established there in the 16th century. In the mid-18th century silk factories were built and by the mid-19th century the silk industry predominated, employing a high proportion of females. After the First World War, due to the development of artificial fibres, the textile industry emerged as the largest employer in the town and the demand for female labour was maintained. The textile industry has declined during the post-Second World War period, but employment has expanded in the service industries such that the demand for female labour has continued. Of those residents of Macclesfield aged 16 or over, 43% of those in employment are women, and 48% of all women are employed, compared to 72% of all men (ibid.). Compared to other North-West towns, Macclesfield has not been so severely hit by unemployment. In 1971 unemployment in the town was around 3% and in 1983 it was around 10%, below the average for Britain as a whole (12.5%). So, Macclesfield has relatively high levels of female employment and relatively low levels of unemployment (Laite *et al.* 1986).

Blackburn, 20 miles north of Manchester, and separated from it by moorland, has a population of 106,000 (OPCS 1982). Administratively, it is part of the Borough of Blackburn, made up of Blackburn itself, the smaller town of Darwen (population 30,000) to the south, and several small villages in an extensive rural area. It is a typical North-Western cotton town, growing rapidly with the development of the cotton industry and the factory system in the 19th century and reaching its economic peak in 1929–1930 when Blackburn and Darwen had 221 fully operational spinning and weaving mills. (Blackburn Borough Council Planning Department, [no date] 1). There are now fewer than a dozen mills working and employment in textiles has fallen from 63% of the workforce in 1929 to less than 3% (ibid.) The decline of the town was ameliorated in the 1950s and 1960s with the growth of new industries, including electronics, plastics and chemicals. During this period of relative prosperity, there was a large influx of Asian immigrants, who took the remaining poorly paid jobs in the textile industry. Blackburn now has about 16,000 people (11.5% of the Borough population) originating from the New Commonwealth and Pakistan, which is the highest concentration in Lancashire (OPCS 1982). Unlike Macclesfield, Blackburn does not have a large or expanding service sector. However, it does have a high level of female employment. Of those residents of Blackburn aged 16 or over, 41% of those in employment are women, and 42% of all women are employed, compared to 65% of all men (ibid.). The current recession has affected Blackburn badly, with unemployment reaching over 16.5% of the workforce in the travel to work area by the end of 1985 (ibid.). The Asian community has been particularly adversely affected, with male unemployment now standing at nearly 50% (Halfpenny *et al.* 1985).

There are, then, two major differences between the Macclesfield and Blackburn labour markets, despite both being characterised by high female employment rates. The first is the markedly higher overall current unemployment rate in Blackburn, higher than the national average, whereas for Macclesfield the rate is lower than the national average. The second is the high number of Asian households in Blackburn, whereas there are virtually none in Macclesfield. Both these differences are instructive when investigating the relationship between household employment structures and the domestic division of labour and this is the primary reason that the two towns are examined separately in this chapter.

Methods used

The two surveys

In November 1983 the Economic and Social Research Council funded a survey of Macclesfield residents, carried out by Social and Community Planning Research. The aim was to collect data on the relationship between household structures and household labour-market strategies. Information was collected on a wide range of matters relating to both employment and household work. A random sample of heads of household aged 20–60 years old, resident in the six wards of Macclesfield town, were selected from the 1983 Electoral Register. The final achieved number of usable interviews was 669, representing an estimated 68% response rate from those eligible and in scope. Full details of the survey are presented in Courtenay (1984).

The Borough of Blackburn obtained funding in its 1984–1985 Urban Programme for an unemployment survey and commissioned the University of Manchester Centre for Applied Social Research to do the research. The aim was to obtain data on changing patterns of employment and unemployment, along with data on a wide range of employment related matters. Those currently employed and non-employed (see below) were also surveyed to provide comparison groups with the unemployed. The sample was designed to include relatively high proportions of informants in Asian origin households and of unemployed informants.*

A four-stage stratified sample was selected in December 1984 using as the sampling frame the draft Electoral Register due to be introduced in February 1985. Pilot interviews were conducted in December and mainstage interviewing in January and February 1985. The final achieved number of usable interviews was 449, which represents an estimated 79% response rate from those eligible and in scope. When re-weighted to take account of the designed oversampling of Asians and unemployed and the screening out of three-quarters of the employed, the sample consisted of a weighted total of 678 informants representative of 16- to 65-year-olds in the Blackburn and Darwen Urban Programme area. All results presented in this chapter are based on this weighted total. Full details of the study are presented in the technical appendix to Halfpenny *et al.* (1985).

Employment status
In both surveys, informants were asked about their employment status during the week preceding the interview and classified according to whether they said they were full-time employed, part-time employed (less than 30 hours per week), unemployed — i.e., registered as unemployed at an Unemployment Benefit Office or Job Centre or regarding themselves as someone who was looking for paid employment — or non-employed. The last category includes those who are retired from work altogether, unable to work through sickness or injury of a longstanding nature, keeping house or looking after their family, in full-time education or on a full-time training course, or taking a holiday or break, excluding paid leave from their normal job. The distinction between unemployed and non-employed is obviously important, especially for women.

Household employment structure
Of the 669 households surveyed in Macclesfield, 529 contained two members married or living as married, and of the 678 informants in Blackburn, 582 lived in households containing a married couple. Even with just four employment status categories for each partner, it is possible to construct 16 household employment structure categories for married couples, ranging from both partners being in full-time employment, through part-time employment and unemployment, to both being non-employed. Yet it is obviously impractical to compare all 16 at once and the relatively small size of the two surveys limits the distinctions that can be made, for there are very few cases of several of the household employment

*The field-work on the Blackburn Survey was supervised by Iain Noble, Research Associate in the Centre for Applied Social Research at Manchester University; he was also involved in schedule design and preliminary data analysis.

structure types. In what follows, a number of simple but important contrasts will be made, for example between the stereotypical traditional household in which the man is in full-time employment and the woman non-employed, the dual-earner household where both partners are in full-time employment and the reverse roles household in which the husband is unemployed and the wife is in full- or part-time employment.

Ethnicity

Informants in Blackburn were asked about their birthplace and that of their father and in addition which language they regarded as their first (the one in which they were most fluent). Where either the informant or his or her father was born in the Indian sub-continent or East Africa, or spoke as their first language Gujurati, Punjabi or Urdu, they were classified as being a member of an Asian household. Given that the Electoral Register includes only citizens of Britain, the Irish Republic and the Commonwealth, Indian and Bangladeshi families were fully included in the sample but there may have been some under-representation of Pakistanis.

The domestic division of labour

In the Macclesfield study, informants were asked who usually does four domestic activities — cook a meal for the household, the main food shopping, tidy or vacuum the home and wash clothes—and five tasks to do with caring for children — taking a child to the doctor, looking after a child who is sick at home, taking a child out to sports or music or dance lessons or for walks, meeting a child from school and washing, bathing or putting a child to bed. In the Blackburn survey, interviewees were asked who last did seven domestic tasks — cook the meal eaten by the whole or most of the family, do the main shopping for the household, tidy the house or flat, vacuum the carpets, do a reasonably large amount of washing for the family (either sheets or clothes), wash the dishes and clean the windows outside — and who would do six child related tasks — go with the child to the doctor, look after a child if it were ill at home, take the child out to a sporting event or to the pictures or something similar, collect the child from school, bath a child under five years old and see the school teacher about the child. (That the extent, style and wording of these questions in the two surveys was different is a secondary reason for analysing the two towns separately. In particular, asking who last, rather than who usually, did the household tasks in Blackburn resulted in few responses stating that both spouses did the tasks.) Both studies asked, in addition, who would usually carry out minor maintenance on, and who would do a major repair to, a car or van if someone in the household owned or had regular use of one. In the Macclesfield interviews only, husbands were also asked if they thought they did as many things around the home as their wives and if they thought they did their fair share of the housework.

It is the answers to these questions that provide the information on the domestic division of labour in this chapter. The analysis focuses on who performs the activities, and whether the activities and husbands' views about them vary by household employment structure, age of the married couple, their occupational class, the presence of children in the household, and the ethnicity of the household.

Results

Employment status

In Macclesfield, data was collected on the social and economic status of all household members. For the 669 households, this revealed that 63% of residents were in full-time employment, 13% in part-time employment, 5% unemployed and 18% non-employed. In Blackburn, 51% of those interviewed were in full-time employment, 19% in part-time employment, 11% unemployed and 19% non-employed. The last group includes housewives and those looking after families (13% in Macclesfield and 12% in Blackburn), those suffering from long-term sickness or injury (0.3% in Macclesfield and 3% in Blackburn), the retired (1% in Macclesfield and 3% in Blackburn) and those in full-time education (4% in Macclesfield and 1% in Blackburn). The figures for the unemployed are based on the proportion of the total population, whereas unemployment rates are usually calculated on the base of those economically active, that is, those in employment plus the unemployed. On this basis, the unemployment rate in the Macclesfield sample is 6%, much lower than the rate of 14% in the Blackburn sample.

Turning to the men and women living as married couples in the two towns, the distributions of the social and economic statuses of husbands and wives are only marginally different from those in the whole sample, with slightly more married men being full-time employed rather than unemployed and slightly more married women being non-employed rather than full- or part-time employed. For both the whole sample and couples, men are much more likely than women to be in full-time employment, while the reverse is the case for part-time employment. More married men (97% in Macclesfield and 94% in Blackburn) are economically active than married women (72% in Macclesfield and 69% in Blackburn), though these rates for married women are comparatively high. Where married men are not employed, they are more likely than married women to be unemployed. Married women are more likely to describe themselves as non-employed, that is, as housewives or as looking after the family. Yet a high proportion of these non-employed married women have been employed in the recent past, and move on to employment in the near future (Halfpenny *et al.* 1985)

Household employment structure

By cross-tabulating the employment statuses of husbands by those of their wives, it is possible to construct 16 different household employment structure types (see Table 1).Overwhelmingly, couples live in households where the husband is full-time employed (92% in Macclesfield and 75% in Blackburn) and where the wife is full- or part-time employed (70% in Macclesfield, 58% in Blackburn). In Macclesfield the largest household employment structure type is the dual wage-earner one, where both partners are in full-time employment, comprising 37% of households, and surprisingly, given the higher unemployment rate, this is also the case in Blackburn, comprising 27% of couples. In both towns this category is closely followed by the one and a half wage-earner household type in which the husband is in full-time employment and the wife in part-time employment (30% of couples in Macclesfield and 25% of couples in Blackburn). Only 24% of couples in Macclesfield and 20% of couples in Blackburn live in the stereotypical 'traditional' household where the man is employed full-time and the woman is non-employed, and a further 1% in Macclesfield and 3% in Blackburn where the woman is instead unemployed. A tiny 2% of households in Macclesfield and 4% in Blackburn are of the role reversal type where the wife is full- or part-time employed and the husband unemployed or non-employed. Commoner in Blackburn (18%) is the non-wage-earning household, where both husband and wife are non- or unemployed, though only 5% of households in Macclesfield have this structure. So few couples (1% in Macclesfield and 3% in Blackburn) occupy households in which the male is part-time employed that this household employment structure type will not be examined in this chapter.

The domestic division of labour

In both Macclesfield and Blackburn households containing married couples, the domestic activities of tidying, vacuuming, cooking and washing are overwhelmingly performed by wives (Table 2). In 70%–80% of households, wives alone do these tasks, whereas in less than 15% of households do husbands alone undertake these activities. Shopping is done mainly by women alone (in 51% of households in Macclesfield, 48% in Blackburn) or shared by husbands and wives (40% in Macclesfield, 25% in Blackburn). Contrary to popular myth, even dishes are washed mainly by wives (61% in Blackburn), though husbands do contribute more here than to any other domestic task (22%), with other family members also taking a significant share (14%). Outside window cleaning is done mainly by window cleaners (42%), though when it is done by household members, it is wives (33%) who do it in far more cases than husbands (19%).

Table 1: Wife's employment status by husband's employment status
(a) Macclesfield (percentages of total sample)

Wife's employment status	Husband's employment status				
	full-time employed	part-time employed	un-employed	non-employed	row total
	%	%	%	%	%
full-time employed	37	1	1	0	39 (204)
part-time employed	30	0	1	0	31 (168)
un-employed	1	0	0	0	1 (7)
non-employed	24	0	3	2	29 (150)
column % total	92 (486)	1 (5)	5 (23)	2 (15)	(529)

$\chi^2 \, p < 0.000$

Table 1: Wife's employment status by husband's employment status
(b) Blackburn (percentages of total sample)

Wife's employment status	Husband's employment status				
	full-time employed	part-time employed	un-employed	non-employed	row total
	%	%	%	%	%
full-time employed	27	1	1	0	29 (169)
part-time employed	25	2	2	1	29 (170)
un-employed	3	0	3	0	5 (32)
non-employed	20	1	11	4	36 (209)
column % total	75 (433)	3 (20)	16 (95)	6 (32)	(579)

$\chi^2 \, p < 0.000$

Table 2: The domestic division of labour

Household activities / Vehicle activities

	tidy M	tidy B	vacuum B	cook M	cook B	wash M	wash B	shop M	shop B	dishes B	windows B	minor mntnce M	minor mntnce B	major repair M	major repair B
	%	%	%	%	%	%	%	%	%	%	%	%	%	%	%
wife	69	76	75	78	76	84	81	51	48	61	33	–	1	–	2
husband	3	10	12	4	14	4	10	7	18	22	19	63	85	31	56
both	23	3	2	17	2	9	1	40	25	1	2	–	3	–	0
ofm	1	9	9	1	7	0	7	0	5	14	4	*3	10	*0	11
other	5	2	2	1	1	3	1	0	3	2	42	34	1	69	32
N (=100%)	(524)	(568)	(570)	(524)	(570)	(524)	(569)	(524)	(570)	(423)	(559)	(454)	(376)	(454)	(272)

M = Macclesfield; B = Blackburn; ofm = other family member * For Macclesfield, includes wife.

Children related activities

	bath Under 16 M	bath Under 5 B	take to doctor M	take to doctor B	when ill M	when ill B	collect from school M	collect from school B	see teacher B	take to sports M	take to sports B
	%	%	%	%	%	%	%	%	%	%	%
wife	18	59	67	58	70	75	35	43	30	17	15
husband	3	16	4	16	3	3	2	22	25	16	32
both	37	16	27	20	22	12	9	11	38	53	36
ofm	42	9	2	3	3	7	47	12	5	3	7
other	0	0	0	3	2	3	7	12	2	11	10
N (=100%)	(307)	(177)	(307)	(307)	(307)	(307)	(277)	(231)	(266)	(303)	(273)

In contrast, vehicle acitivities are performed by men or firms. In only 1 or 2% of households do wives do even minor maintenance on cars, whereas husbands do minor maintenance work in 63% of households in Macclesfield and 85% in Blackburn. In the more prosperous and middle-class town, Macclesfield, many more households employ outsiders to do both minor maintenance (34%) and major repairs (69%) compared with Blackburn (2% and 32% respectively). In households where the work on cars is not done by husbands or firms, it is done by other household members, presumably mainly sons. Since the vehicle tasks, when done by household members, are almost exclusively done by husbands, with very little variation, the following discussion focuses on the gender differences in the performance of domestic activities.

The introduction of children into the household increases the range of domestic tasks to be performed. In the majority of households in Blackburn wives alone are responsible for bathing children (59%). In Macclesfield, however this is more of a shared activity (37%). The Macclesfield figures for bathing children refer to children under 16 — rather than the under five year-olds in Blackburn — and so include many children who bath themselves. Looking after children when they are ill at home is overwhelmingly the wife's task in both towns (70% in Macclesfield, 75% in Blackburn) as is taking them to the doctor (67% in Macclesfield, 58% in Blackburn). It is wives rather than husbands too, who collect children from school (35% in Macclesfield, 43% in Blackburn). Where wives do not undertake these activities alone, they are mainly shared by spouses. Only in a minority of households do husbands alone perform these tasks. Husbands play a somewhat fuller part in seeing teachers about their children: in 38% of households in Blackburn spouses share this activity, in 30% the wife does it alone, and in 25% the husband alone. Taking children to sporting events and suchlike is mainly shared by spouses (53% in Macclesfield, 36% in Blackburn) or undertaken by husbands alone (16% in Macclesfield, 32% in Blackburn), with wives alone doing this task in only a small proportion of households (17% in Macclesfield, 15% in Blackburn). With all child-related activities, in a significant proportion of households couples rely on other family members and non-household members to assist with the tasks. This ranges from 6% of households in Blackburn where others take the child to the doctor to 54% collecting a child from school.

Variations by age, class and ethnicity
Although it might be expected that the division of domestic activities between spouses varies with the age of the couple, their class, and whether the household is an Asian one, there is little systematic evidence for this in Macclesfield or Blackburn. The couples were divided into those in which the husband was under 40 years old and those in which he was 40 or more. (This division between young and old in the cross-sectional data could be

taken as a surrogate for changes over time in the domestic division of labour.) In Macclesfield, 60% of the couples were in the younger age group, in Blackburn 47%. There are only minor differences between the two groups. In general, among younger couples the husband alone does more of the household tasks and spouses share a little more, and among older couples other family members do more, this probably being a contribution by children. Although several of these variations are statistically significant at the 1% level, they have little impact on the highly disproportionate distribution of household activities between husbands and wives. In effect, wives, young and old, still overwhelmingly do the household tasks, but older husbands hand over what they did do to their children. The differences between the sex distribution of the performance of the child related activities among the young and old couples are also minor. Moreover, they are not uniform over the activities, and the differences are not generally statistically significant at the 1% level. (The same findings hold when the couples are divided in two groups by the age of the wife rather than of the husband.)

The couples were categorised as manual or non-manual according to the occupation of the husband. In Macclesfield, 61% of the couples were in the non-manual category, and in Blackburn 27%. As with age, although there are some minor variations, occupational class has little impact on the domestic division of labour. (The same is true when the couples are divided into manual and non-manual categories according to the occupation of the wife.) For example, there is some evidence that manual husbands are more ready to share the vacuuming and that manual wives do more of bathing a child and caring for it when ill but less of taking the child to the doctor. However, these findings are not statistically significant.

Informants living in Asian households made up 18% of the Blackburn sample. Two features of the Asian population stand out. Firstly, 47% of Asian males are unemployed compared to 10% of non-Asian males. Secondly, a far higher proportion of Asian women (67%) describe themselves as non-employed than do non-Asian women (13%). Yet, again there are only minor variations in the domestic division of labour between Asian and non-Asian households. Asian wives do much the same domestic chores as non-Asian wives, but Asian husbands do less than non-Asian husbands. Rather, the tasks are performed by other family members in Asian households. Asian wives do less of the shopping than their non-Asian counterparts, with rather more being done by Asian husbands. Indeed, Asian wives perform less of the out of home duties with respect to the children, such as seeing the teacher or taking a child to the doctor, than non-Asian wives. Conversely, Asian wives alone carry out more of the in-home tasks with respect to children than do non-Asian wives. So, although analysis revealed some differences between Asian and non-Asian households, yet again these were not as great as those between household employment structures.

Variations by household employment structure type

In contrast with age, class, and ethnicity, the employment structure of the household has a major influence on the domestic division of labour, even though all activities are still predominantly performed by women in all the household types (all but one of the differences by household type are statistically significant at the 0.001 level). A number of features emerge. One is that in the symmetrical employment structure households — the dual-earner and the non-earning households — husbands contribute more to tidying, cooking, washing, shopping and washing the dishes, than in the traditional and the one and a half earner households. That is, it is when men and women share the same employment status that men do more of the household tasks. A second is that women in one-and-a-half earner households do more of the tidying, vacuuming, cooking, washing and cleaning windows than women in traditional households and in dual-earner households. That is, when a woman undertakes part-time employment, she does more of these activities than when she is non- or un-employed and when she is full-time employed. A third feature is that there is a substantial redistribution of all household tasks from wives to husbands in reverse role households, but that even here, women still do more than men. (The figures for reverse role households must be interpreted with caution because of the small number in this category.)

Table 3 shows how great are the differences in the domestic division of labour between the various types of household. It also shows that there is a consistent difference between the two towns in that wives in Blackburn do more than their counterparts in Macclesfield, for most activities and most household employment structures. Wives in traditional families and in one-and-a-half earner families (78% and 86% in Blackburn, and 83% and 79% in Macclesfield) do more tidying than do wives in the other households. Sharing of cooking or the husband alone doing the cooking is much higher in dual earner, non-employed and reverse role households (29%, 32% and 30% in Macclesfield and 25%, 19% and 42% in Blackburn) than amongst traditional families or in one-and-a-half earner families (11% and 16% in Macclesfield, 8% and 9% in Blackburn). Shopping is mainly a husband's or shared activity amongst the non-employed households (58% in Blackburn and 76% in Macclesfield). Whilst this activity is shared to some extent by the other family types, only amongst the non-employed and the reverse role families are the husbands alone so much involved. Washing clothes is an activity mainly done by women whatever the employment status and whichever the town.

It was seen above how the introduction of children into the household increases the range of domestic tasks. Data from the Macclesfield survey shows that their presence also increases the frequency of the performance of these tasks. In general, the introduction of children leads to both men and women doing more tasks, but it does not alter the distribution of tasks between men and women. Indeed, the evidence suggests that women do

Table 3: The domestic division of labour by household employment
status type: household activities (a) Macclesfield

Household type	*Tidy*					*Cook*				
	dual	1 + 1/2	trad	non	reverse	dual	1 + 1/2	trad	non	reverse
	%	%	%	%	%	%	%	%	%	%
wife	53	79	83	64	46	69	84	86	68	69
husband	3	1	4	12	23	5	2	3	8	15
both	33	18	12	24	31	24	14	8	24	15
other	12	3	2	0	0	2	0	3	0	0
n (= 100%)	(196)	(158)	(132)	(25)	(13)	(196)	(158)	(132)	(25)	(13)

Household type	*Wash*					*Shop*				
	dual	1 + 1/2	trad	non	reverse	dual	1 + 1/2	trad	non	reverse
	%	%	%	%	%	%	%	%	%	%
wife	79	88	89	80	85	46	59	56	24	46
husband	4	3	4	4	15	7	5	5	12	15
both	14	4	5	16	0	44	34	35	64	39
other	3	5	3	0	0	3	2	4	0	0
n (= 100%)	(196)	(158)	(132)	(25)	(13)	(196)	(58)	(132)	(25)	(13)

$x^2 p < 0.001$

Key to household employment status types:

dual = dual wage earner (husband full-time employed and wife full-time employed)
$1 + \frac{1}{2}$ = one-and-a-half wage earner (husband full-time employed and wife part-time employed)
trad = traditional (husband full-time employed and wife un- or non-employed)
non = non wage earning (husband un- or non-employed and wife un- or non-employed)
reverse = reverse role (husband un- or non-employed and wife full- or part-time employed)

Table 3: The domestic division of labour by household employment status type: household activities (b) Blackburn

Household type	*Tidy*					*Cook*				
	dual	1 + 1/2	trad	non	reverse	dual	1 + 1/2	trad	non	reverse
	%	%	%	%	%	%	%	%	%	%
wife	72	86	78	71	73	72	88	79	69	59
husband	12	6	10	13	22	22	3	8	18	42
both	3	4	0	5	0	3	6	0	1	0
other	14	4	12	12	5	3	3	13	13	0
n (= 100%)	(155)	(138)	(131)	(100)	(21)	(155)	(138)	(131)	(100)	(21)

Household type	*Wash*					*Shop*				
	dual	1 + 1/2	trad	non	reverse	dual	1 + 1/2	trad	non	reverse
	%	%	%	%	%	%	%	%	%	%
wife	76	90	80	78	100	48	52	53	31	51
husband	17	3	6	11	0	17	10	16	32	49
both	0	0	3	02	0	27	32	21	26	0
other	8	7	11	10	0	8	6	10	12	0
n (= 100%)	(155)	(138)	(131)	(100)	(21)	(155)	(138)	(131)	(100)	(21)

Household type	*Windows*					*Vacuum*				
	dual	1 + 1/2	trad	non	reverse	dual	1 + 1/2	trad	non	reverse
	%	%	%	%	%	%	%	%	%	%
wife	27	43	29	33	16	74	90	74	70	44
husband	12	28	16	24	8	8	9	13	18	27
both	3	0	4	2	0	3	1	0	1	20
other	59	28	51	42	76	16	0	14	12	10
n (= 100%)	(155)	(138)	(131)	(100)	(21)	(155)	(138)	(131)	(100)	(21)

Household type	*Dishes*				
	dual	1 + 1/2	trad	non	reverse
	%	%	%	%	%
wife	39	62	77	68	52
husband	49	14	8	17	33
both	0	4	0	2	0
other	12	20	15	13	15
n (= 100%)	(155)	(138)	(131)	(100)	(21)

$x^2 p < 0.001$

Table 3: The domestic division of labour by household employment status type: children related activities (a) Macclesfield

Household type	Take child to doctor					Look after child when ill				
	dual	1 + 1/2	trad	non	reverse	dual	1 + 1/2	trad	non	reverse
	%	%	%	%	%	%	%	%	%	%
wife	61	73	69	65	29	45	77	88	47	14
husband	3	1	3	24	14	7	1	0	6	27
both	31	25	27	12	43	30	20	11	47	57
other	6	1	1	0	14	18	2	1	0	0
n (= 100%)	(71)	(114)	(98)	(17)	(7)	(71)	(114)	(98)	(17)	(7)

Household type	Take child to sporting event					Collect child from school				
	dual	1 + 1/2	trad	non	reverse	dual	1 + 1/2	trad	non	reverse
	%	%	%	%	%	%	%	%	%	%
wife	16	20	11	24	14	16	41	48	6	14
husband	15	14	12	35	43	0	0	1	25	0
both	47	54	63	35	14	11	8	7	19	0
other	22	11	13	6	29	73	51	44	50	86
n (= 100%)	(68)	(114)	(97)	(17)	(7)	(63)	(105)	(86)	(16)	(7)

Household type	Bath under 16-year-old				
	dual	1 + 1/2	trad	non	reverse
	%	%	%	%	%
wife	13	14	24	29	29
husband	1	5	3	0	0
both	23	35	51	41	0
other	63	46	22	29	71
n (= 100%)	(71)	(114)	(98)	(17)	(7)

$x^2 p < 0.001$

Table 3: The domestic division of labour by household employment status type: children related activities (b) Blackburn

	Take child to doctor					Look after child when ill				
Household type	dual	1 + 1/2	trad	non	reverse	dual	1 + 1/2	trad	non	reverse
	%	%	%	%	%	%	%	%	%	%
wife	74	64	66	32	29	87	73	84	65	19
husband	7	4	14	41	48	3	0	3	5	10
both	13	27	14	23	24	0	11	5	26	71
other	7	4	7	5	0	10	16	9	5	0
n (= 100%)	(62)	(90)	(77)	(65)	(11)	(62)	(90)	(77)	(65)	(21)

	Take child to sporting event					Collect child from school				
Household type	dual	1 + 1/2	trad	non	reverse	dual	1 + 1/2	trad	non	reverse
	%	%	%	%	%	%	%	%	%	%
wife	14	21	19	6	10	36	64	55	14	12
husband	18	26	37	54	19	14	6	16	56	18
both	46	44	29	15	71	9	12	3	12	71
other	21	9	16	26	0	41	18	26	19	0
n (= 100%)	(56)	(86)	(65)	(55)	(11)	(44)	(66)	(61)	(51)	(9)

	Bath under five-year-old					See teacher about child				
Household type	dual	1 + 1/2	trad	non	reverse	dual	1 + 1/2	trad	non	reverse
	%	%	%	%	%	%	%	%	%	%
wife	57	17	66	74	42	48	35	33	10	10
husband	29	50	9	5	0	9	2	40	59	0
both	14	0	21	14	47	35	58	23	19	91
other	0	33	3	8	11	9	5	5	12	0
n (= 100%)	(28)	(24)	(64)	(44)	(10)	(46)	(86)	(66)	(57)	(11)

$x^2 p < 0.001$

proportionately more. However, there is some variation in the performance of tasks between different household types, with the introduction of children. For vacuuming and tidying the house, the introduction of children results in a reduction of the woman alone doing this task for all three household types in which the male is employed full-time and no change in those in which he is non-employed. A significant number of dual-earner households with children have paid domestic helpers. To some extent, the washing of clothes varies with the introduction of children. Again, for the households in which the woman is non-employed or full-time employed, or the man is non-employed, the proportion of the woman's performance of washing either falls or remains unchanged with the introduction of children. However, when the woman is employed part-time and the man is employed full-time, the introduction of children results in a rise in her performance of various domestic duties.

The figures in Table 3 relating to child care activities need to be interpreted with some caution due to the inclusion of the response category 'the child him/her self' in Macclesfield but absent in Blackburn. However, some comparisons are clear. In Macclesfield, taking the child to the doctor is the responsibility of the wife alone in 69% of the traditional households and 73% of the one-and-a-half earner households, higher than amongst the other household types. Sharing this task is highest in the role reversal households (43%), and the contribution of husbands alone is highest in non-employed households (24%). In Blackburn the picture is similar for the one-and-a-half earner households, in 64% of which the wife alone undertakes this activity. In traditional households the husband does more alone (14%) and shares less (14%) than in Macclesfield (3% and 27%). Even amongst dual earner households in Blackburn, 74% of wives are responsible for taking the child to the doctor. This is again the case for looking after the child when it is ill, with 87% of wives in dual-earner households in Blackburn responsible for this. Only amongst the reverse role households in Blackburn do husbands share this activity to a large degree (71%), whereas in Macclesfield sharing is the case amongst 30% of the dual earners, 47% of the non-employed and 57% of the role reversal households. It is in taking the child on walks or to a sporting event that the husbands in both towns eventually take a full part. For all groups, in both towns, the proportion of spouses sharing or husbands alone doing this activity rises to around 70%. Interestingly it is amongst the traditional families in Macclesfield that the highest proportion (75%) of husbands are involved in this activity (singly or jointly), while in Blackburn it is amongst the role reversal households that husbands are most involved (90%).

It is mostly in the traditional and one-and-a-half earner household rather than the other household types that the wife meets a child from school, and again this is more the case in Blackburn (55% and 64%) than in Macclesfield (48% and 41%). Of course, there is a relation here between family structure and household employment structure. It is from those households containing children old enough to see themselves home from school that women go out to work full-time. In both towns it is the unemployed husbands from the non-wage earning families who most take on this task, if not at the school gate then at least by being in when the children come home. However, these unemployed men do not take on the task of bathing children. In Macclesfield these men will share this task (41%), otherwise it is full-time employed men with part- or full-time employed wives who will either share or do the task. Once more, this is less the case in Blackburn, and it is the children in the dual-earner households who are old enough to do it for themselves. In Blackburn it is the unemployed husbands in non-earning households who most see the teacher about the child's education (59%). Amongst one and a half earner families the task is shared (58%), whilst amongst dual wage-earning families it is split between wife (48%) and husband (35%). It is clear that, for some tasks, the particular employment structure can lead either to the sharing of tasks or to the separation of responsibilities for tasks.

Husbands' views of the domestic division of labour
Questions were asked in Macclesfield about husbands' views of the domestic division of labour — whether they did as many things around the home as their wife and whether they did their fair share. Only half the men in these households think they do as much as their wives, although 60% of these husbands think they do their fair share. The group that claimed most to be doing their fair share were the husbands in traditional households — fully employed men whose wives were non-employed — even though 61% admitted that they did not do as much as their wives. The tables show that the traditional households have the most unequal domestic division of labour. This reveals that what traditional husbands think of as a fair share is not an equal share in the domestic division of labour. In their view, their non- or un-employed wives should do much more of the domestic tasks than they themselves do. This contrasts with the symmetrical household types, where the husbands are more likely to interpret a fair share as an equal share. Being in the same employment status as their wives moves husbands to some extent to equalise the domestic division of labour. The tables show that the traditional households have the most unequal domestic division of labour.

The introduction of children changes the distribution of activities and in two cases husbands' perceptions change in line with changed activities — as the wife does more, so it is recognised. The exception, however, is in one-and-a-half earner households. Here the same proportion of men claim to do as much as their wives, irrespective of the presence of children, yet the tables show that when women are employed part-time, the introduction of children raises their share of the domestic division of labour. In households in which the husband is non-employed, there is a tendency for wives with children to do less, and husbands more. However in these households, with the introduction of children, more men systematically claim that they do less than women and less than their fair share. The highest percentage of men claiming that they do their fair share are those employed men with children and non-employed wives, 68% claiming this even though they have one of the most unequal domestic divisions of labour. There is a small group of non-employed men with children who feel that they do more than their fair share around the house.

Although age and occupation did not affect activities, they do affect some perceptions of activities. Nearly half the young traditional husbands thought that they did as much as their wives, compared to only 30% of older such men. More older unemployed men say that they do not do as much as their wives, but more of them feel that they do their fair share. Occupationally, it is the manual workers who systematically claim more that they do as much as their wives. Of older manual men with fully employed wives, but no children, 70% said that they did their fair share of domestic tasks, a proportion matched only by the non-manual traditional husbands, who least claimed that they do as much as their wives, yet most claim that they do their fair share. During interviews middle-class men with high paying jobs explained eloquently and forcefully that they were the mainstay of the family and their careers came first. The wife's role was as support and this was an equitable division of labour. Such statements usually produced extensive domestic discussion

So, two features emerge. Firstly, over all household employment structure types, many men think that they do their fair share of the household tasks, even though nearly all men do less than women and many men also know this. Secondly, it is in the symmetrical employment structure households, the dual earners and the non-earners, that men are more aware that they might not be doing as much as their wives.

Discussion

At this point we may turn to the reasons for these levels and variations in the domestic division of labour. The proportion of domestic work performed by women is high, despite Macclesfield and Blackburn having a long history of employed women and despite the women studied having themselves experienced full- and part-time employment, as their current statuses and life-histories reveal. This high level and the variations between the towns, require further explanation, beyond the scope of this chapter, but the domestication of women is not in itself a satisfactory reason in this case. Variations in the level of participation in the domestic division of labour are due to the employment and age structures of households, with some further variations in perceptions related to age and occupational groups.

The variations in activities by household type are a function of the resources available to the household, the way they are distributed over time and the concepts and values informing that distribution. Dual wage earners allocate household tasks into time batches, for example, shopping and vacuuming less often, and can sometimes afford to buy in labour to undertake domestic tasks. The non-employed are constrained by the cost of activities. Traditional wives have time available and spend it shopping. The increase in activities due to the arrival of the children means that the husband has more to do, but even though he thinks he is doing proportionately more, he is in fact doing proportionately less, the increased burden falling on the wife, or being passed to the children as they get older.

In terms of the distribution of activities, it is the wife's full-time employment or the husband's non-employment which have the most effect. These survey findings are reinforced by follow-up interviews. The dual wage earners redistribute their activities due to changes in their daily schedules, attitudes and income. As Berk and Berk (1979) observe, precisely when each partner is in the house importantly affects task performance. Several Macclesfield couples said that, 'He gets in first, so he puts on the tea.' As for the shopping, there is more money to spend, under joint supervision, and shopping is an opportunity to spend time together, making decisions jointly about the home—an outing.

Amongst the symmetrical households there is evidence that it is the husband who takes responsibility for extra-mural activities involving the children, such as taking the child to the doctor. This is also the case amongst Asian households. This may well be because such activities give unemployed men a sense of purpose and because Asian men speak better English than their wives, as well as being the ambassadors for the household. More than these, however, this finding reveals that household symmetry can have two different outcomes. On the one hand it can lead to more conjugal sharing of tasks as spouses spend time together, whilst on the other hand it can lead to greater task segregation as partners take individual responsibility for the different jobs that need to be done.

With both partners fully employed the man no longer has available to him the uniqueness of his status as a legitimating reason for not performing household tasks. His employment is no longer grounds for exemption. He may, and does still, claim it but the claim is now received differently. Firstly, it may be contested by employed wives, increasing domestic tension between couples whose total household time is shorter. Secondly, it may fall on deaf ears for the woman is out at work and there are household jobs to be done. In terms of the domestic division of labour the woman's full-time employment is a *fait accompli* — she is just not there. When she is there, and in part-time employment, then her position can become even more imbalanced than that of the traditional housewife.

Amongst the unemployed there is also some re-negotiation of the domestic division of labour. Unemployed husbands are those who most do the cooking, shopping and tidying. This evidence seems contrary to that of other studies (Bell and McKee 1986), but it must be remembered that many of the men interviewed in the North-West had been out of employment for over a year and some for several years. In the return interviews it was pointed out by the couples that since the man was around all day for so long he perforce did several of the household chores. In Macclesfield, where there is paid work available for women, it is also the case that some wives might be out say, distributing leaflets, whilst the husband stays in to meet the children from school.

Mothers who are employed part-time, shop and cook proportionately more than other women. In-depth interviews revealed that they do the shopping as they commute, feel that they are busy people, are home earlier than their husbands and put on the tea for the children. Several such women commented that they disliked being around the house all day and did more since they had gone back to work. Their counterparts without children wait to share the preparation of the meal with their husband when he comes in.

Dual wage-earner, non-manual households have paid helps to do the vacuuming and tidying. They earn more than the manual households and so can afford such help. Their houses are larger. When a manual woman goes out to work it may well be to clean the house of the non-manual dual wage earners. Yet there may also be cultural reasons for the differences between the classes over paid help. On the one hand, some middle-class women may find it quite normal to employ help, since their mothers and friends do so. On the other hand, it may be that the middle-class are more prepared to commercialise household relations than the working class. Is it that the working-class, subordinate in the market place, do not want that market penetrating their homes? Or, could it merely be that the geographically mobile middle-class have no local kin to call on for help? Yet the surveys have shown that, for the manual households, it is the husband who helps, rather than kin.

Amongst dual wage-earners with children, it is the manual husbands who most help to prepare the meal. This may be due to a difference in the type of meals eaten, between the social classes, with middle-class meals taking more preparation. Or, it may be that manual workers 'brew up' for themselves at work and do not have secretaries to do it for them. Pahl (1984) cites the RAF experience of his informants, when they learnt how to cook. Conversely, husbands in non-manual, dual wage earning households do more of the caring for a sick child at home, probably because they have more control over their conditions of employment than do manual workers who cannot get time off.

Traditional husbands do least around the house, but 75% claim they do their fair share. They take the view that they are the ones employed and there is a justified unequal division of labour. Yet this attitude changes as women's employment status changes and children arrive. The husbands of women employed part-time admit that they do not do their fair share and so perceptions change across the household employment spectrum until unemployed males claim either that they do as much as their wives or that they do not do their fair share.

Throughout this discussion reference has been made to the 'traditional' household structure in which the man is full-time employed and the woman is non-employed. This term has been deployed as a convenient shorthand, although it does echo previous views of household structures. Two things are clear, however. One is that less than 25% of households have this structure. The other is that this structural arrangement, like the others outlined above, is not a fixed position, but a stage through which some households may pass, and to which some may return, as households form and dissolve through the emigration of children or divorce. The involvement of women in employment in the North-West has been such that during the interviews it was clear that many women saw their current position as a temporary stage and their activities as contingent rather than 'traditional' ones. Similarly for both unemployed men and women there is a re-arranging of schedules and activities as the search for employment progresses and when employment is taken up.

The evidence presented here suggests that men's domestic activities and perceptions change either due to their wives' full-time participation in employment, or due to their own exit from employment. Given the changes occurring in the socioeconomic structure of Britain it is the former which will have more impact than the latter. That is to say that changes in men's domestic activities and attitudes will be brought about mainly through women's labour-market activities and women re-negotiating the domestic division of labour through those activities.

References

BECKER, G.S. (1976). 'A Theory of Marriage'. In Becker, G.S. (ed.) *The Economic Approach to Human Behavior*. Chicago: University of Chicago Press.

BELL, C. and McKEE, L. (1986). 'His Unemployment, Her Problem'. In Allen, S. *et al.* (eds) *The Experience of Unemployment*. London: Macmillan.

BERK, R.A. and BERK, S.F. (1979). *Labour and Leisure at Home*. Beverly Hills: Sage.

BLACKBURN BOROUGH COUNCIL PLANNING DEPARTMENT. (no date). *UK Regional Development Programme*. Blackburn Town Hall.

COURTENAY, G. (1984). *Macclesfield Survey*. London: Social and Community Planning Research, Northampton Square.

HALFPENNY, P., LAITE, J. and NOBLE, I. (1985). *The Blackburn and Darwen Labour Market*. Manchester: Centre for Applied Social Research, Faculty of Economic and Social Studies, University of Manchester.

LAITE, J., HALFPENNY, P. and STRAW, P. (1986). *The Macclesfield Labour Market*. Manchester: Centre for Applied Social Research, Faculty of Economic and Social Studies, University of Manchester.

OAKLEY, A. (1974). *The Sociology of Housework*. New York: Pantheon.

OAKLEY, A. (1980). 'Prologue: Reflections on the Study of Household Labour', In Berk, S.F. (ed.) *Women and Household Labour*. London: Sage. 7–14.

OFFICE OF POPULATION CENSUS AND SURVEYS (1982). *Census 1981*. London: HMSO.

PAHL, R.E. (1984). *Divisions of Labour*. Oxford: Basil Blackwell.

VANEK, J. (1980) 'Household Work, Wage Work, and Sexual Equality'. In Berk, S.F. (ed.) (ibid) 275-291.

YOUNG, M. and WILLMOTT, P. (1973). *The Symmetrical Family*. London. Routledge & Kegan Paul.

9

John T. Haworth and Stephen T. Evans

Meaningful activity and unemployment

Introduction

The experience of unemployment
In reporting on a number of studies into unemployment and mental health, Warr (1984a) notes that in the UK over a third of those registered unemployed have been without a job for more than 12 months, and that

> the large majority of people out of work nowadays are clearly employable and clearly want a job.

He stresses that

> In respect of men, research has clearly demonstrated a significant deterioration in psychological health caused by unemployment.

In referring to several studies asking people whether their health had changed since job loss, Warr comments, in respect of psychological health, that changes are typically described in terms of increased anxiety, depression, insomnia, irritability, lack of confidence, listlessness, inability to concentrate and general nervousness. He also notes that deterioration has been reported in 'psychophysical' conditions, namely dermatitis, eczema, headaches, high blood pressure and ulcers. However, he states that

> it is important to note that around 15% of men in these studies are likely to report an improvement in their health since becoming unemployed.

Although there are justifiable methodological and conceptual criticisms of research into unemployment (e.g. Hartley and Fryer 1984), it is not in serious dispute that research shows that unemployment can impair psychological health for many people. However, it is important to examine the experience of unemployment for different groups and individuals. Unemployment is not an homogeneous problem. For example, some groups in society are more prone than others to long-term unemployment. Glyptis (1983) reports that in 1982 when 36% of the unemployed had been out of work for over a year this was true of 52 % of the unemployed over 50 years of age. She also notes that young people are more prone to unemployment than other subgroups, but that they are most likely to find employment subsequently.

Within groups of people there are individual differences in the experience of unemployment. In young people, for example, Roberts *et al.* (1982) indicate that boredom and lack of money were the main complaints but that confidence and self-respect were rarely devastated. Roberts (1986) points out that the more flexible youth labour markets of the 1980s could be offering new opportunities for experiment and self-assessment. Stokes (1983), however, found that a large percentage of his sample of young people had become lethargic and apathetic and disinclined to participate in society.

It is perhaps fair to say that within any group of people some individuals are not psychologically devastated by unemployment and some can overcome the initial experience of negative symptoms (Evans 1986a), though the permanence of this may be an open question.

Factors moderating the experience of unemployment

Individual differences in the experience of unemployment are not unexpected since there are many factors which moderate the impact of unemployment. Warr (1984a) discusses eight principal factors which can be shown statistically to moderate the negative effects of unemployment. These are employment commitment, age, length of unemployment, financial strain, level of activity, social class, gender and personal vulnerability. He also reviews (Warr 1984b) other mediating variables such as social support, local unemployment levels, attendance on schemes, personal counselling and attributed cause of unemployment.

One factor which could be a focal consideration in moderating the negative psychological effects of unemployment is engagement in personally meaningful activity. Several studies have indicated the importance of engagement in activity for moderating the negative psychological impact of unemployment. Hepworth (1980), studying a sample of 78 unemployed men of varying ages and occupational statuses, found that the best single predictor of mental health was whether or not a man felt his time was occupied. Although she could not specify the direction of causal links, in that men who can fill their time with meaningful activity may be less likely to show a deterioration in mental health, or poor mental health, such as depression or anxiety, may inhibit a man from engaging in positive activities. Brenner and Bartell (1983) in a further analysis of her data using structural modelling (LISREL) supported the hypothesis that initially what is important is whether or not a man perceives his time as occupied.

Swinburne (1981) found that activity has a moderating effect on the negative aspects of unemployment. Of the 20 managers and professional men interviewed, 19 stressed the importance of keeping active. The study by Fryer and Payne (1984) of 11 people of different ages and socioeconomic backgrounds deemed to be coping well with unemployment showed that all the sample had a high level of personal activity and the capacity to structure time. Feather and Bond (1983), in their study of the moderating factors of unemployment in a sample of graduates, showed that time structuring and purposive activity were important. Miles (1983), in a study of 300 unemployed men aged 21 or over showed that unemployed people with greater access to the five categories of experience delineated by Jahoda (e.g. 1982), including activity, scored higher on measures of psychological well-being than did unemployed people with less access (see also Henwood and Miles this volume). Kilpatrick and Trew (1985), investigating variation in how the unemployed spend their time in a sample of 121 unemployed men in the 25–45 age range, found a significant relationship between psychological well-being and life-style with a progressive decline in mental health being paralleled by decreasing activity and withdrawal into the home.

Warr (1984c) indicates that amongst a sample of 399 unemployed men there was a correlation of 0.55 between measures of problems in filling time and propensity to mental ill health. Importantly, he also cites results indicating that the more passive behaviour is reported to have increased since job loss, the lower was psychological well-being (Warr and Payne 1983). For both middle- and working-class men in this study, spending more time on 'domestic pastimes' and 'other pastimes', such as watching the television (but not for study), was correlated with psychological distress. Obviously for some individuals, not any activity can moderate the negative symptoms associated with unemployment.

The nature of meaningful activity

Work

In several of the studies previously cited indicating the importance of activity as a moderating variable of the negative consequences of unemployment, the activity undertaken was either job search or activity which has been construed as work. Jahoda (1984, 289) considers that

> modern men and women have deep seated needs for structuring their time use and perspective, for enlarging their social horizon, for participating in collective enterprises where they can feel useful, for knowing that they have a recognised place in society and for being active.

In commenting on Fryer and Payne's (1984) sample of 11 proactive people, Jahoda states (p.298):

These needs are met in work, as Fryer and Payne's study so beautifully demonstrates: all of their 11 cases have, out of their own initiative, found work in informal institutions to satisfy these needs.

Jahoda stresses the importance of the role played by formal and informal institutions in relation to human needs. She agrees with Fryer and Payne that human beings are '... active, coping, interpreting agents', but she stresses (p. 298) that

> The degree to which these basic tendencies can be expressed depends on the nature of the environment which can be encouraging or repressing their manifestations. In complex human societies there are formal and informal institutions that affect the degree to which people have to exert themselves in meeting their basic needs ... The supportive character of many institutions is so taken for granted that it becomes visible only when they break down, as in unemployment.

Regarding the institution of employment she considers that for the past 200 years this institution has been the dominant place where work is performed and hence where the needs that work satisfies are met.

On Jahoda's analysis, work is an important meaningful activity, one which is undertaken in the institution of employment by the majority of post-school, pre-retired males. It is an analysis which receives some support from surveys into preferences for staying in employment for non-financial reasons.

For example, a study by Warr (1982) of a representative sample of 2,419 men and 1,206 women in mainland UK indicated that, in absolute terms, large numbers of people want full-time employment, even if they don't need the money (e.g. 55% of men, and 52% of women in the 45–64 age bracket). At the same time, however, the study indicated that many people would appear not to want employment in the absence of financial need (e.g. 27% of men, and 36% of women in the 45–64 age bracket).

Warr notes in this study that it would be valuable to assess the demand for part-time work for non-financial reasons. Some pointers to this can be gained from a study by McGoldrick (1983) of early retired men who were a 'healthier' and wealthier group than the retired in general. She reports that while 80% were pleased with their retirement, many of them intended to take part-time employment as a way of filling time and as a supplementary source of income.

Of course work is not synonymous with employment. McGoldrick found that 25% of respondents found increased participation in societies and committee work a major advantage of retiring early. Other members of her sample participated in voluntary work and others in intensive further education.

Grossin (1986), discussing research conducted in France, has also reported similar behaviour in the early retired and people who retired at

60, the now statutory retirement age in France. He considers, however, that usually the people who benefit from retirement are members of the middle classes who have been able to find creative, cultural or social pursuits in which they discover a new meaning for their lives to replace that which the absence of 'productive work' (i.e. employment) has sometimes removed. He notes (p. 100) that

> They have created their own temporal obligations: they have a function to fulfil, a sense of responsibility; they are expected to be available at certain times to arrange meetings. In this way they can continue to juxtapose and interrelate work time with free time and to benefit from the interaction of the two.

Leisure

Participation in clubs, societies and cultural pursuits has, of course, been classified as leisure by many research workers. However, Jahoda (1981, 189) states that

> Leisure activities, from television to sports to self-improvement, are fine in themselves as a complement to employment, but they are not functional alternatives to work, since they lack its compelling manifest function.

Earning a living, the manifest function of employment, is clearly important. People have to get up, get organised and participate in society in order to earn a living. Employment thus provides traction. The latent consequences of employment are then a consequence of being in employment. The job may not be enjoyable. It may even be detrimental to mental and physical health. But as Jahoda (1981) notes, it is a tie to reality and

> we all need some tie to reality so as not to be overwhelmed by fantasy and emotion

It may be, as Jahoda (1979) claims, that the psychological input required to gain access to the latent consequences of employment, or categories of experience, on a regular basis under one's own steam entirely is colossal. Nevertheless, some people manage this, as Fryer and Payne's (1984) sample shows. While these may be exceptionally proactive people, research into the early retired shows examples of less proactive people coping well (McGoldrick 1983). Some of these people appear to be engaged in what Stebbins (1982) has called 'serious leisure', activity which has an element of obligation and hence traction, built into it. Stebbins (1981) has studied participants committed to activities outside their employment, such as astronomy and archaeology. He notes (Stebbins 1982) that people engaged in serious leisure, whether as amateurs, hobbyists or volunteers are more obliged to engage in their pursuits than their 'unserious' counterparts while being less obliged than breadwinners to follow their occupation.

Stebbins characterises serious leisure by: the occasional need to persevere at it, the development of the activity as in a career; the requirement for effort based on specialised knowledge, training or skill; the provision of durable benefits including feelings of accomplishment, enhancement of self-image, social interaction and belongingness; the production of an ethos and social world; and the identification of the person with an activity. Thus modern amateurs, according to Stebbins, gain durable benefits from leisure by refusing to remain a player, dabbler or novice. The activity is transformed into an avocation in which the participant is motivated by seriousness and commitment as expressed in regimentation such as practice or rehearsals and in systematisation in schedules or organisation. In the case of amateurs there is also a strong link with professionals. Serious leisure has costs as well as benefits. It may, for example, affect the family. It requires the development of skills and knowledge, the accumulation of experience and the expenditure of effort, a background which has to be acquired. Stebbins quotes Roberts (1981, 61):

> Leisure is not always a good time. Freedom to choose never guarantees happiness. The growth of leisure does not automatically enhance the quality of life. It merely bestows the opportunity and thereby underlines the urgency of enquiring how individuals can be assisted to derive maximum benefit from their scope for choice, and why leisure sometimes fails to deliver the promised fulfilment.

Serious leisure obviously can provide access to the categories of experience which Jahoda associates with employment. It can also provide some obligation or traction. While there are many factors which can influence commitment to activity, some of which are highlighted in Haworth (1984, 1985, 1986), one which is important in the context of obligation and traction is the concept of 'side-bets' introduced by Becker (1960). For instance, he considers that the committed person has staked something of value on being consistent in his/her present behaviour. The consequence of inconsistency will be too expensive. In some cases side-bets are made for a person because of the existence of generalised cultural expectations. Accepting the vice commodore's office in a sailing club, for example, may carry with it the expectation that the holder will subsequently take on the position of commodore. The presentation of an image of oneself through involvement in a pursuit may also necessitate continued commitment to maintain the image. Becker notes that a person finds they have bet their appearance as a responsible participant in interaction on continuing a line of activity. He points out that some commitments result from conscious decisions, while others arise subconsciously. A person sometimes becomes aware of commitment only at some point of change and seems to have made the commitment without realising it. He also suggests that commitment may come about through a whole series of minor decisions over time.

Buchanan (1985) also points to the potential importance of side-bets in studying commitment to leisure behaviour. Amongst the indicators of side-bets he notes have been used are, equipment owned, organisational membership, money invested and the length of training. He also advocates the study of 'leisure social worlds' defined as

> diffuse sets of actors, organisations, events and practices that have coalesced into spheres of interest and involvement for participants.

These could, perhaps, have similar functions to the informal institutional organisations which Jahoda sees as important as a setting for work undertaken outside employment.

It may be argued, of course, that serious leisure is work with another label. If one takes a broad enough view of work, this may be the case. A danger, however, is that work is viewed in a restrictive manner, one which focuses primarily on purposive activity and neglects enjoyment or intrinsic motivation, a factor which Csikszentmihalyi (1981) believes is of prime importance for both quality of life and the socialisation of individuals. Graef *et al.* (1983) have shown that intrinsic motivation can occur in almost any situation, including obligated ones, and that individual perceptions are important in this respect. Their research using employed people has been supported by a small study undertaken with unemployed people at Manchester (Haworth and Millar 1986). Using time diaries to sample the everyday life of nine unemployed people in the 18 plus age group, this study found that intrinsic motivation was correlated with the unemployed person's subjective assessment of well-being but not with the degree of purposive activity undertaken; the latter being assessed using a scoring method validated by independent raters. The study showed that intrinsically motivated individuals could respond to unemployment not by seeking opportunities to replace employment by 'work', but by taking the opportunity to do things which although not purposeful as conventionally defined, they enjoy.

Enjoyment is perhaps more traditionally associated with leisure than with work, at least for many people. Yet we also have to make a distinction between enjoyment and pleasure. Unlike pleasure, enjoyment, according to Csikszentmihalyi and Larson (1984), is not just hedonistic sensation but also encompasses skill development, promoting personal growth.

It can be seen that leisure is a complex phenomenon, particularly if one uses definitions pertaining to quality of experience rather than time free after employment. Yet leisure in its more traditional definition of activity undertaken outside employment does not, for many people, appear to compensate for lack of employment.

In a study to ascertain whether the activities which unemployed people pursue in their 'leisure' provide an alternative to the psychological functions claimed to be provided by employment, Kelvin *et al.* (1984, 1985, 1) concluded that

It is quite clear from our findings that at this point in time the 'leisure' activities do not provide the kind of structure both social and practical provided by employment.

They add however,

One crucial factor ... is that unemployment also means financial hardship. It is by no means clear whether the failure to pursue 'satisfying leisure activities' when unemployed stems from 'social psychological consequences' of being out of work or mainly from a lack of material resources.

The study by Kelvin *et al.* (1984) investigated the use of time by both unemployed females and males ranging from school-leavers up to, but not including, retired people. Overall results showed that the mean amount of time spent out of the home was five hours, most of this being spent on entertainment, followed by shopping, then active leisure which took up only one hour per day, most of it spent walking around the shops. The remaining 19 hours per 24 hour day were spent in the home, most of this time, excluding sleep, being spent on passive entertainment, including TV watching, followed by housework. The authors consider that for most of the unemployed, activities were mere palliatives for boredom, this being the most common negative aspect of unemployment along with financial hardship.

It is important to note that this study is concerned with the general state of things rather than with whether or not some employed individuals use their time satisfactorily. However, as the authors point out, the mean data on time spent on activities, even for particular subgroups, has large standard deviations, indicating that some people in the sample may be very active in their 'leisure'. Yet despite these qualifications regarding individual differences, the study indicated that for most people leisure, or indeed any activity, did not compensate for the lack of employment.

This conclusion is not contradicted by the findings of Warr and Payne (1983) showing statistically significant increases in some recreational activities in unemployed men. This study of 203 middle-class and 196 working-class unemployed men aged between 25 and 39, showed that a substantial proportion of both classes did more gardening, hobbies, home repairs and walking. A study by Warr (1984d) of 954 unemployed working class men also reported similar findings. It may be that these activities were merely palliatives. However, it is also important to note that whereas the increase in passive and domestic activities was associated with higher levels of psychological distress, anxiety and depression as measured by the GHQ, this was not the case for increases in recreational activity. Warr and Payne (1983) make the point that social intervention to reduce personally negative behavioural changes after job loss are clearly desirable. They suggest that sustaining activity levels through the provision of free facilities for unemployed people has a great deal to recommend it, at least during the present extended economic depression.

This could particularly be true if it is done in a manner which recognises individual differences and changing requirements over time. Certainly the potentially ameliorative quality of leisure, viewed in its broadest sense, could be important. Miles' (1983) study of 300 unemployed men over age 21 showed that those with the greatest access to Jahoda's five categories of experience had better psychological well-being than those with less access, and that access came from participation in games and sports, visits, voluntary activities, car maintenance and home activities. While the psychological well-being of the unemployed group with the greatest access to Jahoda's five categories of experience was less than a group of people in employment, it must be noted that the employed group had a higher socioeconomic status (see also Henwood and Miles this volume).

Life-styles
Distinguishing the activity of the non-employed in terms of 'work' and 'leisure' is not always easy and the consideration of life-styles can be useful. Kilpatrick and Trew (1985) in studying how 121 unemployed men in the age range 25–45 spent their time, identified four distinct life-styles. Using cluster analysis on time diary data they found significant differences between time spent on behaviour which they considered were typical of active, social, domestic and passive life-styles. A significant relationship between psychological well-being (as measured by the GHQ-12) and life-style type was identified with a progressive decline in mental health being paralleled by decreasing activity and withdrawal into the home.

The 'active' life-style was typified by large amounts of time spent on active leisure and work-related activities such as job interviews. Social activities and travel was greatest in the second cluster, labelled 'social'. The third cluster 'domestic' was typified by more time spent at home and on domestic chores. The fourth cluster, 'passive', was characterised by an extremely large amount of time spent on passive leisure in the home and considerable time spent on child care activities.

The 'active' and 'social' groups, which had similar well-being scores (Trew and Kilpatrick 1984) were able to spend significantly more time out of the house than the 'domestic' and 'passive' groups. The 'active' group had more job interviews and did more sport and walking. The 'social' group did more visiting pubs and clubs and participating in games there, betting, and visiting friends. However, an examination of typical time-budget diaries tabled in Trew and Kilpatrick (1984) does not easily distinguish between the 'active' and 'domestic' group on the basis of extent of non-passive activity undertaken. Yet the 'domestic' group has significantly worse psychological well-being. Since how an individual perceives activity is important (Haworth 1986), the study of intrinsic motivation in conjunction with time diaries would have been very useful. It would also have been useful to have a wider range of measures and a more detailed analysis of the different dimensions of psychological well-being (Warr 1984c).

Kilpatrick and Trew (1985) also point to a number of factors which may have influenced the relationship between activity and psychological well-being. The 'active' group contained the highest percentage of short-term unemployed. It also had the largest percentage of men with working wives, which could help to relieve financial problems. The 'social' group contained the largest percentage of single men, who probably had less worries. Those in the 'domestic' group tended to be married with young families, as did those in the 'passive' group which also contained more long-term unemployed and fewer men with working wives.

It is apparent that life-style, including responsibilities and resources, and activity tend to be intertwined in these groups. Resources which may suffice for one group may not be adequate for another. An 'active' life-style may be psychologically beneficial, but different resources may be required for people in different circumstances.

Life-styles other than those described by Kilpatrick and Trew (1985) may also be beneficial. A life-style in and out of employment may provide an intermeshing of employment and leisure and a resource baseline for some groups. The study by Roberts *et al.* (1982) of 551 young people showed that many young people preferred periods out of employment, even though this resulted in boredom, than a continuous series of unsatisfactory jobs.

Studies from the 'retirement end' of the labour market have also suggested the importance of flexible employment-leisure life-styles. As previously mentioned, McGoldrick (1983), and Grossin (1986) indicate the importance of this for some early retired people. Long and Wimbush (1985, 88) in a study 129 males just prior to and after retirement at 65, state

> A major coping strategy appears to be to extend or intensify those parts of life that offered roles and satisfactions similar to those gained from work (e.g. feeling needed, purposeful, useful, helping others)

They also state

> Just as Jahoda has identified different categories of experience associated with work, a number of categories of experience (some similar to Jahoda's) can be identified beyond work

These are: mixing socially; helping others, feeling needed, being committed, being creative, filling time, relaxing; getting out, going away; exercising, keeping fit; learning, and keeping mentally active.

Long and Wimbush note that having regular commitments, either work-like (e.g. part-time job, social and voluntary work, committee work) or from other sources (e.g. family/domestic duties, leisure fixtures) assisted ready adaptation to retirement. On life satisfaction scores almost half had improved after retirement, while almost a third had decreased, though the authors point out that this sample may underrepresent those who are not satisfied with retirement. Factors associated with a drop in life satisfaction were declining health and mobility, lower finance, financial problems, missing social contacts, needing something else to do, time on hands, and not having a routine. Those experiencing increased life satisfaction were predominantly healthy with no financial problems, and although they had a routine they either engaged in activities or had a reflective life-style.

In considering the factors important for adapting to retirement, the authors state there was a general consensus that keeping an interest or staying active in retirement was essential for adaptation, but that there was considerable variation in attitudes towards the desired level of such activity or interest. While adaptation to retirement means different things to different people, it is interesting to note the main advice given by respondents to those about to retire, namely: keep physically active (33% of respondents), keep mentally active (28%), don't worry/enjoy it (23%), financial planning (22%), take up a recreational activity (20%), take it as it comes/live a normal life (16%), and get a job/don't retire (10%).

In concluding this section on life-styles it is worth noting that in the Long and Wimbush study, those respondents who participated in a large number of leisure activities in retirement tended to be those who had done so before retirement. Grossin (1986) also suggests that an integrated employment-leisure life-style prior to retirement is important for successful adaptation to retirement. However, successful forms of life-style need further research.

Given adequate financial resources there may be some benefits from the 'in and out of employment' style when one is young and single, but perhaps less so if one is married with children when some security of life-style may be more important. The more integrated employment-leisure life-style may be beneficial in terms of adaptation to change, but the appropriate balance will vary for different individuals and within each life history.

Issues

This review of 'work', 'leisure', and the life-styles of the non-employed raises a number of questions which could be fruitfully studied in research into the experience of unemployment and the nature of personally meaningful activity. For example, are there major differences in the experience of unemployment within various groups of unemployed people? Can activity moderate negative psychological consequences of unemployment, and if so, to what extent and in what way? What is the nature of this activity, is it solely purposive activity, i.e. 'work' in informal institutions, or can leisure, including social interaction, be important? Are individual perceptions of activity important and, if so, in what way? Is intrinsic motivation or enjoyment an important dimension of personally meaningful activity, particularly for some unemployed people? What form do beneficial life-styles take in different groups of unemployed people? Is personally meaningful activity confined to 'proactive' individuals, or can activity develop over time? What is the role of personal agency and situational factors (formal and informal institutional support) in generating and sustaining personally meaningful activity?

The following selective report of a study into activity and unemployment in the 18–30 age group tackles some of these questions.

Activity and unemployment in the 18–30 age group

There has been little research into the experience of unemployment in the 18–30 age group. Yet with entry into the labour market now being delayed in Britain, this could be an important stage of life for many people.

Evans (1986b) conducted a study which examined the moderating effect which activity can exert on the psychological well-being of a sample of unemployed young adults.* A total of 36 people were interviewed in their own homes having initially been contacted outside unemployment benefit offices. This quota-based sample was predominantly single, with a mean age of 21.5 years. Several psychological scales and measures of well-being were administered and in-depth interviews were conducted during which patterns of time use and the experience of unemployment were discussed.

The results obtained by Evans (1986b) confirm the findings of previous research which show significantly poorer psychological well-being amongst the unemployed. When compared to a matched sample of employed young adults (n = 36), his unemployed sample had significantly higher scores on the GHQ-12 (unemployed mean = 13.25, employed mean = 9.11†), indicating greater susceptibility to minor psychiatric disorder (t = 3.19, p = <0.001). Levels of self-esteem were also significantly lower for the unemployed, particularly with respect to negative self-esteem (unemployed mean = 3.65, employed mean = 4.21; t = 3.21, p <0.001), though positive self-esteem was also significantly worse (unemployed mean = 3.99, employed mean = 4.23; t = 1.83, p<0.05).

---

* This research was conducted by Stephen Evans whilst studying for a PhD (ESRC funded) at Manchester Universtity; the research being supervised by John Haworth.

† The mean scores cited in this section refer to the scale score in the case of the GHQ-12 results (range = 0–36), and the item score for the other scales (self-esteem scales: item range = 1–5; life satisfaction scales: item range = 1–7).

Similarly, overall satisfaction with life in general was substantially less for those without jobs (unemployed mean = 4.00, employed mean = 5.53; t = 5.45, $p < 0.001$), as was satisfaction with a variety of aspects of everyday life (unemployed mean = 3.97, employed mean = 4.92), such as standard of living, feelings of accomplishment and social life (t = 5.26, $p < 0.001$).

However when this unemployed sample was divided into two groups (median split) according to self-rated levels of personal activity, the more active group reported GHQ-12 scores which were not significantly different from those obtained from the comparison group of employed people. This group of active unemployed young adults however remained worse off in terms of the measures of self-esteem and life satisfaction. This finding was confirmed when the unemployed were similarly categorised by independent judges using the same measure of activity level; the judges rating written accounts of in-depth interviews conducted with the unemployed (Evans 1986c).

When another set of judges rated whether or not the unemployed had a particular activity or interest which they felt played a significant part in the life of the person concerned, a different pattern of results emerged. This time, the group of unemployed people who were judged to be more likely to have such a main activity were not significantly different from the employed group in terms of either their positive self-esteem or their negative self-esteem. This grouping of the unemployed sample, however, had significantly poorer levels of mental health in comparison to the employed when assessed by the GHQ-12 and by the measures of life satisfaction.

These results highlight two important issues in this area of work. Firstly, whilst it may be convenient to use generic terms such as mental health and psychological well-being, it is nevertheless important to differentiate between various aspects of well-being and the assorted scales and measures used to assess them. This is necessary as reported changes in well-being may be due to the effect of some specific set of circumstances (e.g. life-style change) on a particular component of well-being, without having any discernible influence over other aspects of well-being. This independent operation of different facets of well-being has already been observed. For example, Bradburn (1969) reported that positive and negative affect are statistically independent; though the interpretation of this finding remains an open question (Warr *et al.* 1983). In the area of unemployment research, Warr and Jackson (1983) found that for a sample of young people, employment status significantly affected levels of negative self-esteem, whilst no such influence over positive self-esteem was observed. Although this finding may well be a methodological artifact, they suggest that perhaps some form of psychological uncoupling may occur between positive and negative self-conceptions. Warr (1984c) has also made the distinction between measures of psychological well-being which assess the more constant features (self-esteem measures), and those which describe less constant aspects of well-being (measures of susceptibility to mental illness; GHQ-12).

The second issue arising out of the work by Evans (1986b) is concerned with the way personal activity is said to moderate the detrimental impact of unemployment. The findings suggest that being generally active (as assessed by the measures of level of activity) is beneficial in terms of the more volatile dimensions of mental health (as measured by the GHQ-12), but that structured, purposive or personally meaningful activity (as assessed by the measure of extent of a main activity) is necessary for sustaining the more stable aspects of psychological well-being (as indicated by the results obtained with the negative self-esteem scale).

Case histories

Selected case histories will now be briefly sketched in order to demonstrate the range of life-styles adopted by young people in this study and the variety of their experience of unemployment. Examples are given of life-styles which differ in terms of level of activity and in the extent to which they incorporate meaningful activity. Descriptions of main activities are given which demonstrate how they can range from more 'work'-like activities, to more 'leisure'-based activities. Some cases are illustrative of more proactive life-styles whilst others detail more passive life-styles.

The importance of being generally active
The following two case histories demonstrate the way generally active life-styles can, to some extent, aid adaptation to unemployment. Neither of these individuals were rated as having a discernible main activity, though they were judged to be generally active.

Peter and Helen*
At the age of 22, Peter had been unemployed for just one month, never having been without work before. Since leaving school with four 'O'levels, he gained an HNC in business studies and spent over four years working in the cost accountancy department of a large electrical company. On becoming unemployed, he quickly learnt that for him, life without a job required the adoption of some sort of routine if he was to avoid getting depressed:

> For about the first ten days (of unemployment) I felt really sort of down because I came from a busy office environment, and when I actually had so much time on my hands, I didn't know what to do with it. And then after about ten days, I knuckled down and thought, if you want to sort it out, at least try and discipline your day; which is what I've tried to do since.

* All Christian names and place names have been changed to maintain anonymity.

This took the form of becoming involved in a variety of activities, such as having informal guitar lessons on a daily basis with a friend living nearby and going swimming every morning. However, his reasons for engaging in such activities often appear more to do with their efficacy as palliatives rather than any intrinsic merit:

> Often it's not necessarily things that you want to do, but that you can force yourself to do. You haven't got as much time to feel sorry for yourself ... I started doing some art work the other day, just for a laugh. Just to keep myself occupied. I also potter in the garden and do odd jobs ... I can't bear the thought of just sitting down and vegetating.
> [SE: And when you do these things, do you get pleasure out of doing them?]
> Not always. But I get pleasure out of the fact that I'm doing something more constructive than just sitting around. I don't enjoy gardening particularly, but it's constructive.

In a similar way, going for a walk has more to do with getting away from the house, rather than any pleasure or enjoyment inherent in the act itself; more a case of an act of 'avoidance' rather than one of 'approach' (Haworth 1984):

> I try not to spend the whole day in the house. You get so accustomed to the four walls and that becomes depressing. So even if it means strolling into town to have a look round or to buy a paper ... it makes it a little less boring.

Whilst the type of life-style adopted by Peter may well serve a psychologically protective function in the short term (his GHQ-12 score was comparable to those in employment), the effectiveness of this strategy during a protracted spell of unemployment is debatable. Peter himself was in doubt as to how long he would be able to maintain such a way of living.

> I don't know if in ten or eleven weeks, if I'm still unemployed, whether I'll see it the same, but I'll do my damnedest to try and keep myself occupied.

It is interesting to note that when Peter was visited briefly six months later, he reported that he had not maintained this pattern of activity involvement. Instead he described how he had developed an overriding interest in stained-glass inlay work and, recognising its commercial potential, had successfully applied for a grant (MSC Enterprise Allowance Scheme), enabling him to start up his own business.

Unlike Peter, Helen (21) had been unemployed for a long time; over two years when interviewed. Prior to this, she had worked for six months on the provisions counter of a large supermarket; having been previously employed there on a part-time basis whilst she was studying for 'O' levels at school and sixth form college. At the start of her current spell of unemployment, Helen lived at home with her parents. However, when she started becoming bored and apathetic, tensions arose within her family and she decided to leave home:

> When I first left work it was a novelty; staying in and doing what you want. And then I got really fed up with myself. I tried looking for a job and I got so many knock-backs. I got fed up of doing that and I didn't do anything, and my Mum and Dad got really annoyed. So I left home and I rented a bed-sit and that's when I felt really depressed. It was in Fern Bank (a deprived inner city area, adjacent to a red-light district) and that didn't help. I couldn't go out at all during the day (as) I got followed in cars.

Fortunately for Helen, she soon moved into an unfurnished rented house in a different part of the city. Apart from living in a better area, this change involved her investing a lot of time in gradually decorating and furnishing her new home and her quality of life appeared to improve substantially:

> Since I've moved here, my time was taken up in decorating and saving up for carpets and things like that, so I just seemed to snap out of it after that; I had a lot to do in the house and that. And me and my Mum and Dad patched it up and it was all alright.

Besides settling into her new house, Helen also spent a considerable amount of her time with her mother. On weekdays, she would cycle the few miles to her parents' home and spend the day with her either shopping or visiting relatives. Helen also sees a lot of her sister who also lives nearby. Most evenings she spends with her fiance, and shares his interest in motorbikes. At weekends, they usually go for a ride on his bike with other members of his motorcycle club.

Thus whilst not having any particular main activity, Helen's generally active life-style appears to be one which does not present her with any time filling problems:

> I can't say that I'm bored, because I'm not. I always find something to do rather than stay in and get bored.

Examples of main activities
With respect to the unemployed who were rated as having a main activity, the extent of the variety of the activities reported was considerable, as can be seen from the case histories described below. Other examples (not cited below) include training for, and competing in, marathons, doing a home-based correspondence course in computer programming, compiling a low-budget cookery book and being involved with a fringe theatre company.

This variety emphasises the fact that potentially any activity could be developed into a 'meaningful' one by an individual during unemployment, with the way it is perceived by the person concerned being of fundamental importance. Such activities may well be 'employment'-like in nature (e.g. generating income), whilst others may be more 'leisure-based. However, the essential supportive characteristics of such meaningful activities have more to do with psychological factors (e.g. investment of self, sense of commitment) rather than with aspects of the activity (e.g. sport *vs* music).

'Work' as a main activity

Mary, John and Terry

Mary, a 28-year-old single parent led a busy life which was largely centred upon her interest in Irish music. This mainly manifested itself in the form of busking; playing her violin about three days a week in busy shopping precincts, usually earning about £50. However, she also attended an evening class in Irish dancing and was also trying to form her own ceilidh band. This case demonstrates how commitment to a particular activity can often entail the uptake of related activities (such as attending night classes) which facilitate the broadening and further development of the person's interest. Also, people sometimes report that having a main activity predisposes them to becoming involved in other unrelated activities. For example John (20), who had been unemployed for over a year, described how he became deeply involved with his local Labour party, having initially led an inactive and unsatisfactory life on the dole. He found that as he developed a more active life-style through his political involvements (committee meetings, leafletting and organising demonstrations), he also channelled a 'new found energy' into different areas and started using his local leisure centre on a regular basis. This was something he had never done before when he had more time and less commitments.

In a similar fashion, Mary also had interests outside music. She was a member of an informal group which met at a local college one night a week where they would discuss philosophy and related topics. Interestingly, she felt that her interest in philosophy had made her aware of how important it was for her to keep active whilst she was without employment:

> It teaches you to re-direct energy that you might put into being depressed, and wasting time being depressed ... You re-direct it in a positive way; usually at a physical level. You just get up and do something ... you can do anything.

As with Mary, Terry (22) supplements his State benefits with undeclared earnings in the informal economy. He has been involved in the construction trade for the last six years, having done building work for various employers, on a self-employed basis, and on an 'unofficial' basis during previous episodes of unemployment. When interviewed, he had been unemployed for four months and was busy doing house improvement work for 'customers', as well as his mother. He hoped to eventually get enough work to enable him to make a successful attempt at being self-employed and sign off the dole.

Terry has many friends who are also unemployed and he often goes drinking with them in the evenings. At one time when he was unemployed, he saw a lot more of these friends during the day. However, when he reflected on that period on the dole, he vividly commented on how his building work provided him with a sense of purpose and achievement which starkly contrasted with the aimlessness inherent in that period of unemployment when he pursued a more self-indulgent life-style:

> I used to be heavily involved in the drug scene, but I've kicked that in the head because I wasn't getting anywhere ... (Now) I spend a lot of time going round fixing what other builders have done wrong. I go round and fix it, and it gives me a right ego boost. Certainly a lot better than doing nothing ... If I didn't have that outlook, I'd still be in the fucking drug farm.

'Leisure' as a main activity

Mark, Andy and Stephanie

Listening to, and playing music is a commonly cited leisure interest of many young adults. It was therefore not unexpected to discover several people who further developed this interest whilst unemployed. Even though the opportunities or necessary abilities to be financially successful with music are few, musical aspirations can provide the vehicle for the development of meaningful activity for some unemployed young adults.

Mark (23), for example, is a well-qualified electronics engineer (having gained an MSc) and, whilst at university, played guitar as a hobby in a rock band. Having been unemployed for six months, Mark spends all his days writing words and music, rehearsing songs and recording demostration tapes. He does this with his two flat-mates who share his musical interest (they too are unemployed), and uses his technical skills in electronics to build and repair their equipment cheaply. Being disillusioned with their general employment prospects, Mark and his friends decided to try and earn a living from music and had given themselves a further six months to make a go of it and get a recording contract:

> It's fairly serious now (music interests). I didn't take it seriously when I was at university because I was after an engineering job. But after all this rejection, I decided to think seriously ... It's a serious commitment now ... It was only 'fun' originally. Now I'd like to turn it into work ... if I get the chance.

However, Mark has doubts as to whether or not they will succeed and has serious reservations about the merits of a career away from engineering. He stated that if, after the allotted six months, his band does not succeed, he will start re-applying for engineering jobs:

> I must admit that ... anything away from a regular form of employment I'm a bit unsure about. Other peoples' impressions of what you're doing – they think 'oh, that's not a proper job'.

In contrast, Andy (23) has no doubts about the merits of his musical interest. He has been unemployed for three-and-a-half years and for the last six years has been continuously involved in various rock bands as a vocalist. Unlike Mark, Andy's faith in his current band, and his commitment to its success, is total:

> We're good and we really mean what we're doing ... We want not extreme financial success, but just being able to earn a living wage. I mean the dole is alright but you've got to work hard to make it what it is.

Such commitment requires a considerable amount of personal investment and Andy acknowledges that unemployment gives him this necessary freedom:

> The commitment towards the band for me is getting higher and higher and it seems that way for the rest of them. Everybody seems to be having to give up more, and more, and more time to devote to it ... It (unemployment) allows me more time with the band. It allows me more time with my obsessions. It allows me to be myself whereas, if I had a job, I'd be financially better off, but I'd probably be a little more artistically restrained.

Andy is prepared to work for the band's success over the next 18 months, and if after this it still eludes them, he then has plans to take his band to America and try there. His life-style illustrates how even more leisure-based activities can be approached in a work-like manner.

Thus whilst differences exist between Mark and Andy in the precise nature of their musical involvements, both have developed life-styles during unemployment which are centred upon their interest in music. Note however, that important differences exist in the way they perceive their own respective involvements, with Mark's reservations and Andy's faith, having implications in terms of both their feelings towards their interests, and, more generally, to being unemployed.

Two final points need to be stressed in relation to main activities. Firstly, whilst Mark and Andy had aspirations to twin their leisure interests with financial gain, other people engaged in activities without such aspirations. One such example was David (19) who spent a lot of time making and flying radio-controlled model aircraft, but he did not personally envisage this developing into anything more than a hobby. Secondly, main activities need not necessarily be linked to a particular pursuit. For example, social interaction may constitute a main preoccupation for some unemployed people and they may develop a sense of commitment to this in a way similar to those who are devoted to more activity-based concerns.

For instance, Stephanie (28), who had been unemployed for over two years, stated that she spent at least three days a week visiting friends who lived locally and also visited more distant friends by coach every other weekend. She also did casual work on a market stall, which provided yet another source of friends. She would even go to the market to see these friends when she was not working on the stall. The fact that many of her friends were also unemployed has important implications in terms of the social networks she developed whilst unemployed. For example, she notes that amongst her circle of friends:

> There is a real sort of community spirit for going 'round junk shops, jumble sales and markets, and there's always something going on nearly every day ... it got to the stage where I was busier unemployed than I was while I was at work ... People keep saying 'When are you in, for God's sake? Every time I ring up, you're out, and when I come round, you're out!'

Amongst such a supportive network of people in comparable situations, it is not surprising to find unconventional attitudes to employment emerging:

> I think if I was on my own, it would be totally different: I'd be out there working no matter what it was. But the fact that there is safety in numbers and the fact that people are in the same boat as you, it can put you off applying for jobs.

Such was Stephanie's commitment to her social interests that when she was offered employment she could only accept it on the basis of financial expediency and because of its short-term nature:

> When I got offered this job the other day, it frightened me to death. Because I thought 'What am I going to do? I won't have time to go there, I won't have time to see so and so. I don't want a job!' It means I'm going to be unavailable for eight hours of the day and I'm not at the moment. I can drop whatever I'm doing and go. Because the nature of my work at the market means that I can say 'No, I'm not coming in ... I'll come tomorrow' ... It got to the point where I could manage my time so well that it was like being employed ... I've got so many things going on at one time that I get very jealous of my time and the thought of anything impinging on that, money aside, you start to get a bit annoyed about it ... I don't want a job to take over my life, which is why I take temporary jobs or short-term jobs.

Inactive life-styles

Graham and Tony
Other people, however, reported very low levels of personal activity and tended to describe symptoms indicative of a maladaptive response to unemployment. For example Graham, a 23-year-old ex-RAF driver, had been unemployed for six months and described how most of his day was spent at home with his mother. During the day he would either read or watch television. Occasionally, he would visit a friend who was also unemployed and together they would either chat or watch a video. He also described how he would go out drinking with friends on some evenings and perhaps watch the local football team play home fixtures. However, the lack of any predominant interest, together with spending most of the day at home, is a fairly typical life-style of unemployed people who report having problems with unemployment. In Graham's case, he remarked how the lack of doing anything substantial with his day affected such things as his memory for events and has resulted in a steady decline into apathy:

> You just don't do much, so there's nothing much to remember ... If you asked me what I did last month ... I don't think I could even remember an individual day ... I'm starting to be a bit lazy now, it just creeps in after a bit ... If my Mum gives me a job to do now, I must admit that it'll take me about a week to get around to do it, even though I've got loads of spare time ... I just sit about all day doing nothing.

Tony (27) was another person who, like Graham, was rated as being generally inactive and without a predominant main activity. When interviewed, he had been unemployed for one and a half years and graphically described the boredom and isolation he occasionally felt:

> Just occasionally I get desperately bored, and lean on the window-box, looking out the window and thinking, 'I wish to God somebody would walk down this road and knock on my door because I'm so bored' ... probably a couple of times in a fortnight I'll get like that. It's basically because those nights I would normally go out; to a show, or to the pub and I haven't got the bread [i.e. money] to do that, and I'm generally bored with the radio and bored with reading and feeling like my mates have seen enough of me this week.

Tony however is not without interests. He is, in fact, a keen photographer, but feels constrained by having limited financial resources:

> If I had another £20 per week to play with, I'd be fairly content to stay on the dole ... because £20 per week would be enough for me to play with to make a bit more money. Like, I could invest some of it in photography and perhaps make another ten, fifteen quid a week now and then ... There's lots of things that I'd like to be doing.

Consequently he tends to engage in photography only sparingly; only doing it when he really needs something to do:

> I try and save till I'm desperate ... When it gets really bad, out comes the photo gear ... Just now and then I'll take it out (photo gear) and do three or four frames. It just gives me something to do really ... It's like a pressure valve, a safety valve. When things get really desperate and I'm feeling crazily depressed, then I can grab my camera and go out and just wander about and perhaps meet somebody and talk to them.

This final case raises the issue of the importance of money for engaging in activities whilst unemployed. Clearly, the lack of money can be a constraining factor, acting as a barrier to certain activity engagements. However, whilst this may constrain or restrict what people do during unemployment, also of importance is the ability to overcome such obstacles. Personal resources (e.g. knowledge of cheap facilities, friends in right places, useful skills, persistence in the face of adversity) can also be valuable to an unemployed young person, as are, obviously, financial resources.

Summary of study

It can be seen from this selective report of the study conducted by Evans (1986b) that unemployed people in the 18–30 age group manifest a variety of life-styles and engagement in activity, some of which correlated with aspects of psychological well-being comparable to employed people. While some individuals show the 'in and out of work' life-style described by Roberts *et al.* (1982), others show that a range of activities can be pursued during employment and that these activities can develop over time. Some individuals show positive 'approach' behaviour in engaging in activities, but for others, engagement in activity appears to arise more as a consequence of the avoidance of negative experiences. For a number of individuals activity is characterised by 'purposiveness' and in this sense may be similar to work. Yet for others, activity is of a more generalised nature encompassing both social relationships and leisure activities, showing the importance of considering an individual's perceptions of activity. A not insubstantial proportion of the sample, however, found difficulty in engaging in personally meaningful activity and showed the negative symptoms associated with unemployment now documented in many studies.

Conclusions

The focus of this chapter has been on the role and nature of personally meaningful activity in moderating the negative consequences of unemployment. At the current stage of development of society in Britain, and many other Western countries, perhaps the best encapsulating statement regarding activity is that by Warr (1984a) when he notes that

> the large majority of people out of work today are clearly employable and clearly want a job

However, to paraphrase Warr and Payne (1983)

> sustaining activity levels ... for unemployed people has a great deal to recommend it.

We would also add that the way in which activity levels can be sustained requires a recognition of the importance of differences in individual requirements which may change over time, as well as the provision of the necessary financial resources to sustain activity. The research literature on non-employment and our studies show that an individual's perception of the meaning of an activity is an important factor in the effect of that activity on a person's quality of life, rather than this being solely a function of activity *per se*. Similarly, an individual's ascription of enjoyment to engagement in activity can be an important correlate of well-being (Haworth and Millar 1986). It is also apparent that the desirable level of activity varies for different individuals. Research into early retirement also indicates that the experience of flexible work-leisure life-styles can be beneficial in facilitating adaptation to non-employment and that long-standing leisure interests can be expanded.

Earlier in this chapter a series of questions were formulated which are important for research into the experience of unemployment and the nature of personally meaningful activity. It is now pertinent to note that many of these questions relate to factors and processes which are important in the organisation of behaviour and response to change, such as individual agency, situational factors (formal and informal institutional support), personally meaningful activity and life experience. Future research into the experience of unemployment and the variables which may moderate negative consequences will also need to include an examination of the role and interaction of these factors and processes in enhancing the quality of life in individuals.

One further important dimension to investigate in this connection is the part played by 'life themes' in both engendering and maintaining engagement in activity and in enhancing life satisfaction. Csikszentmihalyi and Larson (1984) argue that possession of a 'life theme' by an individual is an important organising force in behaviour. They consider that

> the ability to enjoy everyday experience is necessary but not sufficient to avoid psychic entropy in the long run

They propose that long term 'dissipative structures' are also required to produce order in consciousness and that this includes the 'meaningful interpretation of existence'. The ultimate achievement in this, they consider, is perhaps

> the development of a personal life theme ... a meaningful arrangement of goals and means

They also note that enjoyment and life themes are not the only hedges against psychic disorder, but that political institutions, religious beliefs, feelings of solidarity and love are also extremely important. This perhaps parallels both the stress by Jahoda (1984) on the importance of formal and informal institutional support in relation to human needs and the emphasis by Fryer and Payne (1984) on personal agency.

In their research in America into adolescents, Csikszentmihalyi and Larson (1984) report that only a few individuals actually develop fully authentic life goals, most being satisfied to pursue the goals society prescribes: a college education, a job, marriage, children and life within conventional standards of morality. While the 'authenticity' of life goals may be a particularly American concern, the question of life goals may be important, especially in situations where the prescribed goals of society are withheld from some sections of society.

Equally important is the process by which life goals are adopted. While Csikszentmihalyi and Larson (1984) and Csikszentmihalyi and Beattie (1979) emphasise the importance of conscious thought, they also recognise the importance of unconscious factors. Although the nature of these unconscious factors is not specified, a case can be made for examining the role of engagement in activity in subconsciously shaping attitudes, values and goals (Haworth 1986).

Obviously, further research into unemployment requires the use of both longitudinal studies and qualitative methods. Such research will give us a more sophisticated appraisal of the relative importance of 'work' and 'leisure' and varied life-styles in psychological well-being, including life satisfaction. It will also be useful in illuminating the processes used by individuals in responding to change. As we move into a post-industrial society, research of this kind will have important practical value, as well as theoretical relevance for models of adaptation, development and transition through life.

References

BECKER, H. S. (1960). 'Notes on the Concept of Commitment'. *American Journal of Sociology*, *66*, 32–40.

BRADBURN, N. M. (1969). *The Structure of Psychological Well-being*. Chicago: Aldine Publishing Company.

BRENNER, S. -O. and BARTELL, R. (1983). 'The Psychological Impact of Unemployment: a structural analysis of cross-sectional data.' *Journal of Occupational Psychology*, *55*, 129–136.

BUCHANAN, T. (1985). 'Commitment and Leisure Behaviour: a theoretical perspective.' *Leisure Sciences, 7*, 401–420.

CSIKSZENTMIHALYI, M. (1981). 'Leisure and Socialisation.' *Social Forces, 60*, 332–340.

CSIKSZENTMIHALYI, M. and BEATTIE, O. V. (1979). 'Life themes: a theoretical and empirical exploration of their origin and effects'. *Journal of Humanistic Psychology, 19*, 45–63.

CSIKSZENTMIHALYI, M. and LARSON, R. (1984). *Being Adolescent: Conflict and Growth in the Teenage Years*. New York: Basic Books.

EVANS, S. (1986a). 'Out of the Trap.' *New Society*, 10 January, 49–51.

EVANS, S. (1986b). *Variations in Activity and Psychological Well-being in Unemployed Young Adults* (Unpublished PhD thesis). Manchester: University of Manchester.

EVANS, S. (1986c). *Personal Activity During Unemployment: An Approach to its Study in Terms of its Effect on Psychological Well-being*. Paper presented to the British Psychological Society Northern Branch and Occupational Section conference on 'The Psychology of Unemployment', Manchester.

FEATHER, N. T. and BOND, M. J. (1983). 'Time Structure and Purposeful Activity Among Employed and Unemployed University Graduates.' *Journal of Occupational Psychology, 56*, 241–254.

FRYER, D. and PAYNE, R. (1984). 'Proactive Behaviour in Unemployment: findings and implications'. *Leisure Studies, 3*, 273–295.

GLYPTIS, S. (1983) 'Business as usual? Leisure Provision for the Unemployed.' *Leisure Studies, 2*, 287–300.

GRAEF, R., CSIKSZENTMIHALYI, M. and GIANNINO, S. (1983). 'Measuring Intrinsic Motivation in Everyday Life.' *Leisure Studies, 2*, 155–168.

GROSSIN, W. (1986). 'The Relationship Between Work Time, Free Time and the Meaning of Retirement.' *Leisure Studies, 5*, 91–102.

HARTLEY, J. and FRYER, D. (1984). 'The Psychology of Unemployment: a critical appraisal'. In G. M. Stephenson and J. H. Davis (eds), *Progress in Applied Social Psychology* Vol. 2. Chichester: John Wiley & Sons Ltd.

HAWORTH, J. T. (1984). 'The Perceived Nature of Meaningful Pursuits and the Social Psychology of Commitment.' *Society and Leisure, 7*, 197–216.

HAWORTH, J. T. (1985). *The Perceived Nature of Meaningful Activity and the Social Psychology of Commitment*. Paper presented at the BPS Annual Conference: Symposium on 'The Psychology of Unemployment: Activity and Situational Factors', Swansea.

HAWORTH, J. T. (1986) 'Meaningful Activity and Psychological Models of Non-employment'. *Leisure Studies, 5*, 282–297.

HAWORTH, J. T. and MILLAR, T. (1986). 'Time Diary Sampling of Daily Activity and Intrinsic Motivation in Unemployed Young Adults'. *Leisure Studies, 5*, 354–359.

HEPWORTH, S. J. (1980). 'Moderating Factors of the Psychological Impact of Unemployment'. *Journal of Occupational Psychology, 53*, 139–145.

JAHODA, M. (1979). 'The Impact of Unemployment in the 1930s and the 1970s.' *Bulletin of the British Psychological Society, 32*, 309–314.

JAHODA, M. (1981) 'Work, Employment and Unemployment: Values, theories and approaches in social research.' *American Psychologist, 36*, 184–191.

JAHODA, M. (1982). *Employment and Unemployment: A Social-Psychological Analysis.* Cambridge: Cambridge University Press.

JAHODA, M. (1984). 'Social Institutions and Human Needs: A Comment on Fryer and Payne'. *Leisure Studies, 3,* 297–299.

KELVIN, P., DEWBERRY, C. and BUNKER, N. (1984). *Unemployment and Leisure* (Report for the ESRC/Sports Council panel on leisure research). London: Dept of Psychology, University College.

KELVIN, P., DEWBERRY, C. and BUNKER, N. (1985). *Unemployment and the Use of Time.* Paper presented at the BPS Annual Conference: Symposium on 'The Psychology of Unemployment: Activity and Situational Factors', Swansea.

KILPATRICK, R. and TREW, K. (1985). 'Life-styles and Psychological Well-being among Unemployed Men in Northern Ireland'. *Journal of Occupational Psychology, 58,* 207–216.

LONG, J. and WIMBUSH, E. (1985). *Continuity and Change: Leisure around Retirement* (Sports Council/ESRC Report). London: Sports Council.

McGOLDRICK, A. E. (1983). 'Company Early Retirement Schemes and Private Pension Scheme Options: scope for leisure and new life-styles.' *Leisure Studies, 2,* 187–202.

MILES, I. (1983). *Adaptation to Unemployment?* (SPRU Occasional paper No. 20). Falmer, Brighton: University of Sussex.

ROBERTS, K. (1981). *Leisure, Work and Education.* Bletchley, England: Open University Press.

ROBERTS, K. (1986). *E.S.R.C. Young People in Society/16–19 Initiative: A Sociological View of the Issues.* London: Economic and Social Research Council.

ROBERTS, K., NOBLE, M. and DUGGAN, J. (1982). 'Out-of-school Youth in High Unemployment Areas: an empirical investigation'. *British Journal of Guidance and Counselling, 10,* 1–11.

STEBBINS, R. A. (1981). 'Science Amateurs? Rewards and costs in amateur astronomy and archaeology.' *Journal of Leisure Research, 13,* 289–304.

STEBBINS, R. A. (1982). 'Serious Leisure: a conceptual statement.' *Pacific Sociological Review, 25,* 251–272.

STOKES, G. (1983). 'Work, Unemployment and Leisure.' *Leisure Studies, 2,* 269–286.

SWINBURNE, P. (1981). 'The Psychological Impact of Unemployment on Managers and Professional Staff.' *Journal of Occupational Psychology, 54,* 47–64.

TREW, K. and KILPATRICK, R. (1984). *Daily Life of the Unemployed: Social and Psychological Dimensions.* Belfast: Psychology Department, Queen's University of Belfast.

WARR, P. (1982). 'A National Study of Non-financial Employment Commitment'. *Journal of Occupational Psychology, 55,* 297–312.

WARR, P. (1984a). 'Economic Recession and Mental Health: a review of research'. *Tijdschrift voor Sociale Gezondheidzorg, 62,* 298-308.

WARR, P. (1984b). 'Work and Unemployment'. In P. J. D. Drenth, H. Thierry, P. J. Willems and C. J. de Wolff (eds), *Handbook of Work and Organisation Psychology.* London: Wiley.

WARR, P. (1984c). 'Job Loss, Unemployment and Psychological Well-being.' In V. L. Allen and E. van der Vliert (eds), *Role Transitions.* New York: Plenum.

WARR, P. (1984d). 'Reported Behaviour Changes after Job Loss.' *British Journal of Social Psychology, 23*, 271–275.

WARR, P., BARTER, J. and BROWNBRIDGE, G. (1983). 'On the Independence of Positive and Negative Affect.' *Journal of Personality and Social Psychology, 44*, 644–651.

WARR, P. and PAYNE, R. (1983). 'Social Class and Reported Changes in Behaviour after Job Loss.' *Journal of Applied Social Psychology, 13*, 206–222.

WARR, P. B. and JACKSON, P. (1983). 'Self-esteem and Unemployment Among Young Workers.' *Le Travail Humain, 46*, 355–366.

10

Stephen Fineman

Back to employment: wounds and wisdoms

Findings from studies on the unemployed suggest the following form of argument.

Without a job people are rootless. They become confused as to who they are and where they belong. They become disenfranchised citizens, poor, disoriented in time and generally psychologically disturbed (e.g. Cobb and Kasl 1977, Kelvin and Jarrett 1985, Jahoda 1982, Warr 1983, Feather and Bond 1983, Kaufman 1982, Fineman 1987a). Given this unsatisfactory state of affairs we must get people back into employment. It is only in employment, within a job, that distress will be alleviated and a state of normality resumed.

Such logic is consistent with schemes which aim to help the unemployed back to employment and it also fits comfortably with a political and economic language which defines the unemployed as potential workers awaiting their opportunity to become active again. Yet this form of thinking raises a number of important questions.

Firstly, is it a simple matter of re-employment resetting the psychological equation? While the 'psychological well-being' in a population may improve, as is indicated by the few nomothetic studies of the re-employed that have been conducted (e.g. Warr 1983, Shamir 1985), we have little indication of the more individual dimensions and contingencies underlying this apparent improvement. There is a hint of a more complex state of affairs from Shamir's analysis, which draws attention to the organisational circumstances surrounding the individual's entry into the new job, the security attached to that position, whether the new job requires a change in residence and how well the new job compares with the old. On this last point he found that, amongst a population of recently re-employed Israeli professional workers, improvement in psychological well-being occurs only in cases where the new job is seen to be at least as favourable as the previous one. A study of a similar group in the United Kingdom (Fineman 1983) revealed that those re-employed in jobs which they felt to be inadequate were experiencing more stress, and even poorer self-esteem, than they had during their period of unemployment.

Secondly, if unemployment is a distressing, even traumatising, event are there lasting psychological injuries or scars? If we consider that the route from job to unemployment, and back into employment, is a dynamic *process* characterised by the interactions of emotions and cognitions, can the individual ever be 'the same again', as mechanistic theory suggests? Moreover, thoughts and feelings are contextually based: they involve an individual's life position, family or community. A concern about the personal effects of re-employment surely should reflect how the unemployed experience these structures.

For example, approximately half those re-employed in the Fineman (1983) study revealed clear legacy effects from their unemployment, regardless of the quality of their new jobs. Some talked of a lasting blemish – the stigma was a permanent part of their 'record'. Feelings of personal failure at their previous jobs remained; they felt continuing doubts about their abilities. Others described behavioural changes due to their unemployment experiences, such as giving far less of themselves, of their commitment, to their new organisation, and taking great care not to make themselves too 'visible' by criticising others or 'rocking the boat'. Security and survival dominated their concerns; achievement and status were now luxuries they felt they could no longer afford. They would feel even greater responsibility for dependants who had suffered with them and would try to ensure that they were protected. These individuals are clear exceptions to the reported general 'improvements' on re-employment, as are the findings by Estes (1973) on re-employed professionals and also Fagin's (1979) suggestion of permanent personality changes.

Thirdly, if re-employment is to heal the wounds of unemployment, unemployment must be a wounding experience. If it is not, then what is its legacy? On reading the works of those who have made a close examination of the studies on the psychological impact of unemployment (e.g. Hyman 1979, Fryer and Payne 1986, Sinfield 1981, Kelvin and Jarrett 1985, Fineman 1983) it is hard to resist the conclusion that investigators have been very keen to characterise the trauma and shock of unemployment, while ignoring minority trends or exceptions to this 'rule'. For example, within classic studies such as those of Hall (1933), Wedderburn (1962) and even Eisenberg and Lazarsfeld (1938), there are unexplained subgroups, or individual differences, which contradict the uniformity-of-response thesis. Studies such as those of Swinburne (1981), Little (1976), Schlozman and Verba (1979), Hartley (1980) and Fineman (1979; 1983) are much firmer in their conclusions that unemployment *can* give rise to positive, if not euphoric feelings. This, of course, is no remarkable revelation for anyone just freed from a stressful or entrapping job. But it does alert us to be cautious of a psychology of 'statistical trend'; and it also confronts us with another possible dimension to the re-employment legacy. What, precisely, might this look like?

One-third of the group of 100 middle-class unemployed in the Fineman (1983) study, saw their unemployment as a delightful opportunity to escape from boring or stressful jobs and find employment which could meet long-frustrated needs. Those who did obtain such re-employment talked of the liberating experience and the renewed energy they had for their new job. Unemployment had opened up exciting horizons for them and any stigma that they felt (which most did) was now more than counterbalanced by the feelings of a 're-birth' in career. They felt that they had learned something valuable about themselves from the experience and were all the wiser for it. The legacy was a positive one.

For a proportion of this group, though, their dream had turned into a nightmare. High expectations about a new and different career rapidly turned to disillusionment as the rejections mounted. Some panicked and grabbed the first solid job offer that came along. They then realised that they had not made the change that they really wanted. In effect, this produced an enormous feeling of let-down and self-reproach. The new job was in no way 'normalising'. It had left them feeling inadequate and threatened in ways they had not experienced before: a pervasive sense of lost opportunity.

A final point from this study concerned the interpersonal, rather than individual, legacy of unemployment. Here views were polarised. Some of those re-employed would reflect on the family costs of getting back to work. They were left with fractured marriages and strained relationships which had not simply 'come to rights' with the new job. They also noted how certain old friends had drifted away — it seemed permanently. Yet others were proud of the new cohesion within their family: they had all worked together on the problem and the new job felt all the better for it. Independently, wives reported feeling less of appendages to their husbands' careers: they had had an active role in managing things during unemployment.

Legacies and time

The qualitative, individualistic, examination of the re-employed suggests a markedly more complex state of affairs than is revealed through more traditional forms of study. But the extent to which legacy matters — for psychological health, employment behaviour, family life — is partly a question of its nature and consequences in *time*. After re-employment an individual may move in and out of several new jobs, so unemployment, re-employment and legacies can be expected to operate interactively. We do not know whether those who experience pain and damage in the early period of re-employment will find their wounds healing as time passes. Or, to express it rather differently, under what circumstances, and over what period of time, their wounds will continue to fester, and in what form. Most people will eventually move into retirement, which raises questions about 'ultimate' legacies.

So legacy effects can be viewed as time-bound phenonema and it is arguable that we may learn different things about them according to the time-frame used. In my 1983 study there was a six-month follow-up of people, who, on average, had already been out of work some seven months. Legacy was in terms of what those who were re-employed felt they had inherited from their unemployment. This was inferred from their free-descriptions of their new circumstances and also structured measures which tracked changes in their psychological stress, symptoms of physical strain and self-esteem. In this chapter the time-span is considerably extended to gain insight into the phenomenology of legacy amongst a small group of the original population, now an average of six years (and a range of five to seven years) after the first meeting with them. It is a subgroup which provides a micro-longitudinal perspective and a little sense of the detail of individual experiences.

Some real lives

The home address of all 100 managers and professionals in the original study had been retained. Most of them were obtained during field interviews in the years 1979–1980, so many were out of date by the time of the second follow-up in June 1985. It was hoped, however, that it would be possible to capture the detailed views of around a 20% cross-section, to represent the fortunes of those who were made initially unemployed at different stages of their career. It would seem that the stage at which a career is broken can be an important influence on the choices and expectations of the middle-class unemployed (see Fineman 1987b, Kaufman 1982).

Responses were obtained from 18 people. In the original research, two of them were near the beginning of their careers, ten were in mid-career and six in late career. The majority were managers or professionals who had been associated with manufacturing industries, although there were two school teachers. The original average age of the group was 43: they were now approximately six years older.

Following the format used for the six-month follow-up, each person was mailed an open-ended, two-part, questionnaire, together with a personal letter. The first part asked them to describe, in as much detail as they could, their career moves to date, their present job, and their current thoughts about their period or periods of unemployment. They were also asked to reflect on what they thought the future held for them and for the country. In the second part, legacy was addressed more directly. They were asked to consider, from their present position, if they felt that unemployment had left them feeling permanently different about things. What changes, if any, were there in their views about their work, themselves or other people? Did they see themselves behaving differently because of their previous unemployment experiences? They were provided with two sides of blank paper to comment as they wished.

The content of their scripts were analysed for indications of legacy effects. For some this amounted to the odd word or two; for others it comprised detailed introspections and retrospections. Most perceptions were rooted in around six years of their career history, which is hard to do 'whole-person' justice to in the limited space of one chapter. Here, therefore, are a selected eight 'nodal' summary accounts, which, between them, focus the different themes expressed by individuals across the total group. Each account portrays three points in time. The first is from the years 1978–1980, during which time individuals participated in counselling by myself (described fully in Fineman 1983). The second is from a questionnaire follow-up six months after the counselling (also described in the 1983 publication). The third is from the findings from the most recent, 1985, follow-up.

The protraits are organised according to the respondent's stage of career at the first meeting. Those who were then between the ages of 35–45 inclusive are designated 'mid-career', while those who were below or above this band are respectively 'early' or 'late' career.

Early career

Jim: honours graduate in maths and physics

In March 1980 Jim, age 27, recounted the difficult start he had had to his career. Three years previously he had responded to the shortage of maths and physics teachers as a second-best choice to a research job — which he had found unobtainable. He soon hit problems: 'It was the disciplining. My teaching was ideal for the way *I* would learn but not ideal for 11–13 year olds.' He was dismissed after only six weeks work. He then spent a short period in 'soul destroying' supply teaching, to be followed by 18 months unemployment.

The unemployment period was punctuated by spells in various short-term jobs: librarianship, clerical posts. 'It gets quite depressing with refusal letters, but you just throw them away and start again'. At about this time he had a crisis of image:

> I learned that if I am going to get a job again it must be with people I consider social equals. It's no good trying to forget I've got a degree. I'm not 'chief' material, but I'm certainly not one of the 'indians'.

From thereon Jim went through the motions of job-search, including applying for training courses, '... but I hadn't the motivation to really concentrate on what I was doing; I failed. The carrot of employment was going a bit mouldy around the edges.' Then a combination of cynicism and inertia enveloped him. The university degree no longer automatically secured interviews; but he also had a sense of impending failure before he started any new application. Unemployment had become a way of life for him, and he talked wistfully, even romantically, of the 'ideal path' that teaching might have been. He tersely summarised his position:

> Whatever job I get now must be considered against the personal freedom, and independence I have in unemployment. I have no fixed hours. The only thing I miss is money. I don't want companionship. So the job I require must have money *plus* the benefits of unemployment.

Six months later Jim had little to report. He was seemingly entrenched in unemployment. He took pains to justify his position:

> I've done absolutely nothing about finding work. Since unemployment my life has been much more pleasant. My status has now shifted from unemployed to retired.

Despite his 'retirement', five years on finds Jim, now age 32, having been in and out of work. He has had a seductive taste of research — but the post was for a fixed term of one-year only. He has improved his qualifications to teach by gaining a certificate in education, but '... after 54 applications and two interviews, no job offer.' The few potentially-satisfying jobs which have come his way have been impermanent and insecure — which has added to a cumulative sense of injury and despair. Thus the legacy of cynicism from his chronic unemployment has in no way been mollified by the taste of work. If anything we encounter a reversal — where unemployment is the dominant 'occupation' interspersed by distressing periods of work.

Mike: mechanical engineer

In June 1979 Mike, at 33, had been jobless for three months. There had been 10 months of rumour about redundancies in his organisation, but he had felt safe because he was the only specialist in his sort of work. Consequently he had been alarmed by the sudden 24-hours notice to quit:

> In one way it was the greatest thing since sliced bread — a new start! In another way I was rather frightened and concerned because I bought a house a year ago and I'm overcommitted on it. So if I don't get a job before this Christmas I'll be in trouble. It's a challenge to find new work and I had expected this to happen one day, but not now!

Six months later, and after 35 interviews, Mike had found himself a job as a supervisor with a car manufacturer: 'It was bloody hard work being unemployed and this job is worse than my previous one in terms of what I do and job title. But unemployment has left me thinking more about security than the prospects in my job — something that never used to bother me.'

After a further six years, and now approaching 40, Mike is in the same job and feeling bored and edgy. He has become particularly nervous about the effects of the recession on his company, something, he claims, that has '... always been not far below the surface of my mind since I lost that job.' He has grown progressively more cynical about any employer providing him with the job challenge and security that he desires and he talks now of being prepared to '... milk the system for all the grants and support to start my own business. It's the only way I can achieve long-term financial independence.' Clearly, the ghost of insecurity has haunted Mike thoughout his re-employment.

Mid-career

Bob: car-sales manager

The first meeting with Bob was in October 1978. He was then 36 and had been unemployed one month, having been dismissed from his job.

He had had a public school education in South Africa which he 'didn't make enough of.' His career had gradually moved towards selling in the late 1960s which '... I got to hate. Furthermore, I married a very able, successful woman, and I tend to compare myself unfavourably to her.' His penultimate job was in South Africa as a sales representative for a national oil company. He had to 'ensure' sales targets in the company's petrol stations:

> I knew my territory and knew the company's percentage *couldn't* be reached. Some colleagues would fight. I also fought a bit — but got screwed for being 'negative' in my approach. I was asked to resign because of poor performance.

He said he was overjoyed and relieved to leave that job and looked forward to a new challenge in England. He soon got a job in car sales — and was soon overwhelmed:

> I think I tried to cope with too many changes at the same time. Change of country, change of job, change of home, trying to start-up a new office. I do wonder what I am capable of.

Six months later Bob described himself as finally 'coming down to earth'. He was employed as an instructor to salesmen, which he found 'enjoyable'. The only way he could come to terms with his last 'debacle' was treat it as a sabbatical period in which to 'sort himself out'.

We meet him again in his mid-40s, six years on. He has now moved, without a career-break, to a more senior position in another company. He reflects on his unemployment periods as times which have helped him to assess himself — his attitudes, his performance and his abilities. Yet the legacy he portrays is a sharply divided one:

> When you are in employment, reviews are seldom objective. You often hear of your shortcomings, not your strengths. Unemployment has helped give me a sense of perspective. But having been told that I was 'redundant' has certainly left some scar tissue as well. I sometimes find myself looking over my shoulder. There's the ever-present feeling that it could happen again. It leaves me feeling that my destiny is not in my own hands.
>
> I'm nervous now of how I'm judged. Senior management may feel I'm unnecessary and make me redundant. Deep down I lack confidence after my previous blows. I'm reluctant to commit myself to things in case I find myself unemployed again. I hold back, following the line of least resistance.

Helen: graduate in English; qualified teacher

Helen spoke frankly and passionately about herself during her counselling in April 1979. Four years previously her teaching had come to an abrupt halt because of a bout of mental illness. She had now been declared fit and had been longing to get back to work — but she found herself stigmatised:

> I started applying very enthusiastically. The job hunt had a challenge to it. Now my money is running out and I'm getting more and more depressed. My expectations keep dropping. I'm looking for *any* job. But everywhere I turn this medical record catches me out. And to make matters worse my fiancé is also unemployed.

At the six month follow-up Helen talked of 'still nothing to show'. She was feeling desperate to find an escape from the constant rejections. She had started a job as a trainee market researcher, but found it so dissatisfying and poorly paid that she gave it up. She was now married, and her husband was employed. Nevertheless, she was very worried that his job might not last.

Time confirmed her anxieties for, six years later, her husband was unemployed and had been so for some time. For herself, after several years of 'odd jobs' (one as a taxi driver which she loved but her husband did not and forced her to quit), she is now holding a part-time job as an escort to handicapped children, a job she has had for three years. 'I've been reduced to being thankful for what I've got. I've never been able to get a job which remotely matches up to my qualifications. This job leaves me enormously under-utilised'.

Helen is explicit about the contradictory feelings that stay with her following unemployment:

> Joblessness has left me feeling permanently imprisoned by my past and tied to a mediocre future in an unfulfilling, poorly-paid job. It remains a totally wretched experience. On the other hand it has made me much more

resourceful at grabbing virtually any chance to bring in extra cash. I've even been doing a child's paper round! It has also made me appreciate the fringe benefits of my existing job — companionship, the respect and affection of the children, gossip and regular hours.

Martin: director with a multinational car manufacturer
In April 1980, aged 41, Martin had just been made redundant after a 'remarkably successful' career with his company. The business, based in the Philippines, had been sold-up because of the increasing political tension in the region. He and his wife had returned permanently to the United Kingdom, but he was experiencing certain privations:

> The only crisis I've had since I've returned is one of loneliness. It was almost like running a permanent club where I worked. Big, beautiful house, lots of guests and parties. Apart from that there are no regrets. I want to be a normal person for a while. It got to a stage where, because of our chronic problems delivering vehicles, I was the centre of hatred — always the villain.

Although Martin had no financial difficulties, he described himself as facing a watershed in his life. He was looking for something different: a new identity, away 'from feeling like a refugee': 'I guess I do miss the big "I am" side of things and I keep finding my experiences are only credible in the automobile field. But that's the one area I want to get away from!'.

Martin had made the big change when he responded to the follow-up six months later. He had a job as an administrator with a social work charity and was very happy: 'I found unemployment a very good time to reassess everything — and also engage in physical activity I sadly needed! I would say that my life was enriched as a result of unemployment.'

At 46, five years on, Martin is in the same job and enjoying it. He hankers a little for the cut and thrust of his industry years, though he is delighted to have more time to spend with his family. He now talks of retiring in his early 50s. Unemployment, he says, has left him constantly more aware of 'self-preservation' at work. He now curtails expressing views which might jeopardise his position, something he 'would not have dreamt about doing before'. Politically, he has become more intolerant of left-wing politics and trade unions 'whose main aim seems to be to achieve glory by putting everyone on the dole'.

Late career

Ian: electrical engineer

> I really feel I've made such a cock-up of the last 4–5 years that I've got pretty panicky at times. It was grimmest when I was demoted and then dismissed. If a Ford Granada wasn't a very stable car I'd have killed my

wife and myself. I was driving at 60 miles an hour when she said something to me which hit a very sore nerve. I braked hard and turned the steering wheel and hoped something would happen. But it didn't.

So, in April 1978, Ian portrayed his feelings at getting fired a year previously. He was 52 years old when it happened. He fought, and won, a case of unfair dismissal '... but the financial compensation didn't compensate me, in my 50s, for not having a job'. He had sought consultancy assignments and had taken one very short job abroad. All in all, though, he felt very confused: 'I need a much clearer view of what I should do'.

Six months later he had a job as a computer consultant with 'excellent terms and conditions'. He was happy but apprehensive about the technical demands of the job — which he felt were moving beyond his competence and control. He saw his family looking much more relaxed, however.

After six more years he is working with the same company having moved through three different departments. He sees his work a mixture of rewards and disappointments, the latter because of failings he observes in top management. Unemployment, he says, has given him little to be thankful for: 'My experiences have only made me even more cynical about the stupidity of people higher up the pyramid'. He speaks of a legacy of caution: of having to guard his security by steering clear of trouble:

> I have to keep a low profile now, which I hate. To avoid issues even when I know, from experience, that the policies are faulty. I move cautiously with an eye on retirement within five years. I constantly think about the vulnerability of my job, at my age, in this recession.

He keeps these anxieties to himself, cultivating 'normal appearances'. In this way people treat him normally. He is wistful, though, about this survival strategy:

> Unemployment *does* give you a chance to switch to a job where you can try that new personality you wish you had. The trick is to avoid relapsing into the old one before you have reaped the benefits of the new one!

Dick: engineering consultant

When Dick initially described his career, in February 1980, he was 57 years old. He portrayed a life of contrasts, developing from engineering to management, and from consultancy to a Managing Directorship in a major engineering corporation:

> It was success stories and high politics — enormous fun. In 1970 I was on £14,000, plus Jaguar, plus chauffeur — which was a lot for then. But success bred jealousy. I got sacked by the Chairman. It also bred complacency. I had turned down a job offer in another company shortly before I got the chop — because they wouldn't pay me £17,000.

Dick then moved into consultancy, which failed disastrously. 'I now drink more, scan newspapers, spin-out the day. Unemployment has been bloody hell.'

Six months later he was despondent and depressed. He had continued to seek consultancy work, but to no avail. He had stopped applying for jobs.

After a further five years Dick has been retired for a year. He had followed an archetypal riches-to-rags path: from a top job, to selling insurance, door-to-door — which he did for three-and-a-half years:

> I hated it. I had a mental hang-up about being an insurance salesman, having been brought up to regard it as the lowest form of job.

He never really felt 'employed' during this period and continued to drink. He felt the job to be demeaning, which created so much domestic stress that his wife left him. This is something for which he cannot forgive himself. Unemployment has left him with nagging uncertainties about the way that he has conducted his life:

> My mistake has been in concentrating on avoiding financial catastrophe at the expense of emotional stability — love. I see myself as a failure.

His unemployed time, 'in the shallows', has heightened his awareness of spiritual values compared to material ones and he earnestly desires to rectify the balance a little '... by serving the community, without financial gain, in my remaining years.'

Eric: manufacturing manager

> Fifty-seven is a bit of a difficult age. I've replied to 150 advertisements and written to 50 local companies. I've got four on the go and have reached a couple of short-lists. I have been offered a temporary job, which wasn't suitable. Not too bad for 57 I suppose!

This was in August 1979. The company where Eric was employed had contracted and made him redundant four months before. He talked about his wife as a major source of pressure — she was very worried about being no longer 'a senior executive's wife.' Otherwise he felt financially reasonably secure because of a good redundancy payment and a car. Nevertheless, he yearned to work again — perhaps in self-employment.

Six months later Eric was about to launch his own manufacturing business. He was apprehensive. He had had little success from job applications because, he concluded, of his age. He now felt much poorer, financially, and his wife had started a part-time job — which proved a difficult decision for both of them.

At the age of 63, six years on, Eric's small business is now established. He is finding it strenuous physically and the early years were particularly arduous. His wife still has to work — which he feels very guilty about.

Their new, enforced, style of life has shattered their late-career dreams. Instead of enjoying easier living, with the children independent and away from home, unemployment has pushed them into a frugal and somewhat relentless existence. Both of them experience sleepless nights, worrying about their future. Friends, notes Eric, now avoid asking how they are doing.

Eric is driven-on for financial reasons, being concerned about his poor pension prospects. Although people view him as 'someone who has achieved something under difficult conditions' it does not feel quite like that to him. He feels he has been forced into something which he would have preferred to be without at his stage of life. His re-employment leaves him with a certain weariness about his predicament, '... but, on balance this is better than my unemployment — that has really bad memories for me'.

Looking at legacies

The portraits, and the group from which they are drawn, reveal a number of themes concerning the long-term legacies of unemployment:

There is clear evidence of long-term legacies in the accounts of people now in employment, some six years after a major bout of unemployment. Generally, such legacies have been reinforced and sharpened by any interim periods of unemployment. It seems that the seeds of long-term legacies can be well established by the sixth month following a job loss, although it may be that, for some people, 'permanent' impressions are set even earlier-on.

The act of becoming re-employed does not, in itself, mean that negative consequences of unemployment are automatically reversed. There is a likelihood of increased anxiety, and susceptibility to stress, in circumstances where financial and emotional security are threatened. Self-doubts about occupational competence remain as the image of the pain and stigma of unemployment lingers. Responses, in terms of individual work behaviour, are characteristically defensive. New jobs are regarded more for their security than as opportunities to take risks and stretch one's abilities. There is a sense of caution and wariness about commitment to an employer. No longer is the protection of an employing organisation taken for granted.

At the outset, job loss need not be a traumatic or distressing affair for the individual. It can be experienced as a time to reflect on one's life; to escape from weary routines; to find new and rewarding employment. If an individual succeeds in achieving expectations of these sort — especially in obtaining a 'better' job — then long-term reflections are mainly positive ones. Unemployment has, on balance, turned out fine in the end. Yet, such people also find themselves less certain about the security of their jobs, mindful of the unpleasant, stigmatising experiences of unemployment which they have suffered and markedly less tolerant of political arguments about the 'necessity' to tolerate unemployment for the eventual good of the economy.

If, however, job-market experiences prove to be full of immediate disappointments — rejections and blockages to desired directions — then early euphoria can rapidly turn to dejection. Six years on, some individuals talk of having had to make unacceptable compromises to obtain employment — *any* employment. The aftermath of unemployment has left them feeling depressed and cynical. Their new jobs have in no way met their fantasies about a changed life and an exciting new career.

Legacies in context

The overall picture, as presented above, disguises a range of individual differences in feelings, attitudes and behaviour. These differences have something to do with the manner in which people attempt to create meaning and purpose in their lives through the socially constructed institution of employment. Societal myths about 'the career', 'progress', 'achievement', and 'reward-for-effort' are challenged by unemployment. In particular, the notion of an orderly progression, or maturation, in occupational career is rendered invalid. Societal pressures conspire against those who need to re-start, or re-formulate, their lives. And then, any eventual new start may carry with it some form of legacy which can taint intentions and create problems of personal adjustment. The extent of such difficulties depends, in part, on when in the life/career stage job loss has occurred. This is an area illuminated by the present study.

In early career, chronic unemployment amongst the well-qualified can lead to them feeling progressively more jaundiced in their view of the world and themselves. Temporary work, regardless of its intrinsic attractions, can be experienced as more unsettling than settling. This is a disturbing picture when viewed against continuing unemployment amongst new graduates from higher education (HMSO 1985). Job prospects are poor for those who have recently graduated in less-fashionable, 'low-tech', or 'non-productive' subjects, and for those who simply have not a good enough qualification to succeed in the fierce competition for jobs. For these people unemployment may soon appear as the only relevant way of life. They join a highly-qualified, expensively educated, population who become socialised towards seeing themselves as occupational casualties, even before they get a reliable taste of employment. They are offered no alternative, remunerative, 'work' structures through which to build their lives in a way commensurate with their qualifications and skills (see Fineman 1987b).

Early career is also a time of financial precariousness, when income is relatively low, but expenditure and debts can be high. A forced expulsion from work can result in panic and grabbing the first job that comes along. In later years an impetuous decision can be regretted, while a vague sense of insecurity remains.

By mid-career, the jaws of the 'trap' of an unsuitable, or stressful, job are beginning to close — so, for some, unemployment can come as a welcome release. A profitable process of self-examination and adjustment of expectations can occur, the results of which may form a significant part of the positive long-term legacy of unemployment in a 'good' new job. While a number of people emphasise this feature, others reveal different, less-comfortable, experiences. Running alongside their 'new' selves they are aware of a heightened sense of possible failure and vulnerability to unemployment, years after job-loss. They handle this by performing more cautiously and defensively, avoiding commitment and controversy. They talk of survival and self-preservation.

There are those who have not welcomed their mid-career unemployment and the only jobs they can secure leave them feeling grossly underemployed. They can then face years of anguish and depression. For them, the essential damage of job loss remains: they have been robbed of years of personal investment, something that cannot simply be recaptured. The income and social contacts from re-employment offer but modest compensation for their original loss. They work with disgruntlement or resignation.

By late career we can see an entrenchment of some of the mid-career tendencies. If a person is less employable by mid career, in late career the options are even slimmer. Many are faced with a crisis of security. The realisation of pensions, retirement plans, and for some the purpose of a lifetime of work, can be thrown into disarray by unemployment. In a very short space of time (sometimes literally overnight), a senior manager or professional can be permanently separated from the results of many years of effort, from status and colleagues and from a sizeable income. Not surprisingly, those who become re-employed are unlikely to easily redeem their status and security: to employers the old look poorer 'investments' than the young. This can leave the re-employed with lasting feelings of inadequacy and underemployment. Some will closet themselves in their jobs, privately nursing their grievances. They become super-cautious and calculating about their behaviour, taking care, as far as possible, not to create situations which might result in negative judgements on themselves. But, in minimising risks they also blunt their creativity at work. All such activity is defensive, to offer protection against the awesome prospect of yet another job loss.

One route to employment for the late-career unemployed, and sometimes the only viable route, is self-employment. This can effectively retrieve an individual's sense of control over his or her destiny. But, in older age, the physical and mental effort entailed in starting a business can be considerable. Apart from the unfamiliar 'red-tape' to negotiate, there is the anxiety of using personal savings, or undertaking a loan, at a time of life when, normally, financial pressures would be easing. The pace of life can be strenuous and unwelcome. Also, as pressures increase, the business can begin to encroach upon familiar domestic routines. There is then the risk of significant difficulties in family relationships. Generally, those who took the self-employment path felt ambivalent about it. On the one hand they were free from the 'unemployed' label, and there was a sense of direction for their energies. But on the other hand it did not provide the stability and security they had once enjoyed and it pushed them to do things which they would much rather not have had to undertake at their time of life.

Eventual retirement, it might be thought, is a time to wipe the slate clean, free from the lingering bur of unemployment. There were two retired people in the long-term follow-up and neither of them fitted this image. One, already mentioned, cited his painful unemployment and re-employment experiences as absolutely fundamental in determining the direction of his retirement activity. It had forced him to review the validity of his life values, and find 'redeeming' ways of spending his retirement time. A second man expressed similar sentiments, but following a very satisfying period of re-employment:

> Unemployment destroyed the picture I had been taught — having a responsible position so that one could be someone in society. Friends and neighbours judge one's standing on the basis of progress up the organisational ladder. I learned, during unemployment, that it's not the be all and end all that it appeared to be. I could appreciate a job for reasons other than seniority — and I did! Now work is behind me, but what I experienced during this period — the bad times and the good — will always be with me.

Conclusion

The basic contention of this chapter has been that the social and psychological difficulties of unemployment do not necessarily right themselves at re-employment. The evidence presented here indicates that job loss can take on a range of personal meanings, according to when and how it occured and what follows it. It is often a major life event, which, like other major life events, can colour subsequent perceptions — especially the meaning and significance of a new job. The so-called re-balancing effect of re-employment presumes a fairly mechanistic, 'hydraulic', model of social psychological functioning. This appears an altogether inadequate conceptualisation of what can happen to people's feelings, attitudes and behaviours when they return to employment.

It might be expected that a job loss which has been especially injurious to self and/or immediate family will inevitably leave scars as a permanent reminder, regardless of the post-unemployment circumstances (e.g. see Iacocca 1986, for a powerful example of this point). While this might be so, the present study suggests that the social definition, or stigma, of unemployment, may well be the 'bottom-line' legacy, for *all* those who look back on their unemployment. It is something that is remembered years after the event and it is something which makes them 'different' employees: more cautious, more wary.

The personal adjustments required in the face of any major change can also leave people feeling wiser after the event. Unemployment, and subsequent re-employment, seems no exception to this. A legacy of new learnings about self, employment, and society can emerge from job-loss, learnings which coalesce into wisdoms which assist individuals to manage the present and the future.

References

COBB, S. and KASL, S. V. (1977). *Termination: The Consequences of Job Loss.* Cincinnati, Ohio: National Institute for Occupational Safety and Health.

EISENBERG, P. and LAZARSFELD, P. F. (1938). 'The Psychological Effects of Unemployment.' *Psychological Bulletin, 35,* 358–389.

ESTES, R. J. (1973) 'The Unemployed Professional: the social, emotional and political consequences of job loss among education workers.' Unpublished doctoral dissertation. Berkeley, California: University of California.

FAGIN, L. H. (1979). 'The Experience of Unemployment II. Unemployment and Family Crisis.' *New Universities Quarterly,* Winter, 66–74.

FEATHER, N. T. and BOND, M. J. (1983). 'Time Structure and Purposeful Activity among Employed and Unemployed University Graduates.' *Journal of Occupational Psychology, 92,* 241–254.

FINEMAN, S. (1979). 'A Psychosocial Model of Stress and its Application to Managerial Unemployment.' *Human Relations, 32,* 323–345.

FINÉMAN, S. (1983). *White Collar Unemployment: Impact and Stress.* Chichester: Wiley.

FINEMAN, S. (ed.) (1987a). *Unemployment: Personal and Social Consequences.* London: Tavistock.

FINEMAN, S. (1987b). 'The Middle Class: unemployed and underemployed.' In S. Fineman (ed.) *Unemployment: Personal and Social Consequences.* London: Tavistock.

FRYER, D. M. and PAYNE, R. L. (1986). 'Being Unemployed: a review of the literature on the psychological experience of unemployment.' In C. L. Cooper and I. Robertson (eds) *Review of Industrial and Organisational Psychology 1986.* Chichester: Wiley.

HALL, O. M. (1933). 'Attitudes of Unemployed Engineers.' *Personnel Journal, 12,* 222–228.

HARTLEY, J. (1980). 'The Impact of Unemployment upon the Self Esteem of Managers.' *Journal of Occupational Psychology, 53,* 147–155.

HMSO (1985). *The Development of Higher Education into the 1990s.* London.

HYMAN, M. M. (1979). 'The Effects of Unemployment: a neglected problem in modern social research.' In R. K. Merton, J. S. Coleman and P. H. Rossi (eds) *Qualitative and Quantitative Social Research.* New York: Free Press.

IACOCCA, L. (1986). *Iacocca.* London: Bantam.

JAHODA, M. (1982). *Employment and Unemployment. A Social-Psychological Analysis.* Cambridge: Cambridge University Press.

KAUFMAN, H. G. (1982). *Professionals in Search of Work: Coping with the Stress of Job Loss and Underemployment.* New York: Wiley.

KELVIN, P. and JARRETT, J. A. (1985). *Unemployment: Its Social Psychological Effects.* Cambridge: Cambridge University Press.

LITTLE, C. B. (1976). 'Technical-Professional Unemployment: middle class adaptability to personal crisis.' *Sociological Quarterly, 17,* 262–274.

SCHLOZMAN, K. L. and VERBA, S. (1979). *Injury to Insult.* Cambridge, Mass.: Harvard University Press.

SHAMIR, B. (1985). 'The Psychological Consequences of Re-employment.' Jerusalem: Department of Sociology and Social Anthropology, The Hebrew University of Jerusalem.

SINFIELD, A. (1981). *What Unemployment Means.* Oxford: Martin Robertson.

SWINBURNE, P. (1981). 'The Psychological Impact of Unemployment on Managers and Professional Staff.' *Journal of Occupational Psychology, 54,* 47–64.

WARR, P. (1983). 'Work, Jobs and Unemployment.' *Bulletin of the British Psychological Society, 36,* 305–311.

WEDDERBURN, D. (1964). *White Collar Redundancy.* Cambridge: Cambridge University Press.

Name Index

Abrams, M., 95, 102, 108
Adamson, L., 95, 108
Allin, P., 95, 108
Argyle, M., 176, 191
ASTMS, 191

Bakke, E.W., x, xiii, 90, 92, 197, 201, 214
Balloch, S., 196, 214
Banks, M.H., 102, 109, 111, 128, 145, 147
Bartell, R., 242, 264
Barter, J., 267
Beales, H.L., x, xiii, 91, 92
Beattie, O.V., 264, 265
Becker, G.S., 217, 239
Becker, H.S., 246, 264
Bell, C., 238, 239
Beral, V., 191
Berk, R.A., 217, 237, 239
Berk, S.F., 217, 237, 239
Berry, J.E., 215
Binns, D., 196, 204, 214
Blackburn Borough Council Planning Department, 219, 239
Bond, M.J., 243, 265, 268, 283
Booth, M., 191
Bradburn, N.M., 105, 106, 253, 264
Bradshaw, J., 105, 106, 148, 156, 164, 171, 172, 202, 214
Brake, M., 142, 145
Breakwell, G., 124, 145
Brenner, S.O., 242, 264
Brown, G.W., 99, 109, 197, 214

Brownbridge, G., 267
Buchanan, T., 247, 265
Buehler, C., 31, 63, 73, 75
Buehler, K., 75
Bunker, N., 266
Burghes, L., 149, 172
Burr, W., 201, 214

Cameron, D., 188, 192
Cantril, H., 91, 92
Cashmore, E.E., 126, 128, 131, 132, 135, 139, 140, 141, 145, 146
Chamberlain, G., 191
Chappell, H., 207, 214
Chester, R., 195, 214
Clark, M., 149, 172
Clayton, Y.M., 192
Clegg, C.W., 109
Cobb, S., 93, 268, 283
Coleman, D., 191
Cook, D.G., 197, 214
Cook, J.P., 110
Cooke, K., xii, 171, 172, 202, 214
Cooper, C.L., 182, 183, 191
Courtney, G., 219, 220, 239
Coverdale, A.G., 154, 173
Cowan, J.R., xiii
Coyle, A., 95, 109, 197, 210, 214
Csikszentmihalyi, M., 247, 263, 264, 265
Cummins, R.O., 214

Daniel, W.W., 149, 172
Danziger, L., 82

Subject Index